AMERICAN EMPIRE

American
EMPIRE

THE REALITIES AND CONSEQUENCES
OF U.S. DIPLOMACY

ANDREW J. BACEVICH

HARVARD UNIVERSITY PRESS

CAMBRIDGE, MASSACHUSETTS / LONDON, ENGLAND / 2002

Library of Congress Cataloging-in-Publication Data

Bacevich, A. J.
    American empire : the realities and consequences of U.S. diplomacy /
Andrew J. Bacevich.
        p. cm.
    Includes bibliographical references and index.
    ISBN 0-674-00940-1 (alk. paper)
    1. United States—Foreign relations.   2. United States—Foreign relations—
Philosophy.   I. Title.

E183.7 .B284 2002   2002068740
327.73—dc21

CONTENTS

*To my mother
and
to the memory
of my father*

DESPITE THE PASSING of a decade since its end, few Americans who lived through the Cold War view it as mere history. Especially for those born in the late 1940s and early 1950s, reaching maturity in the 1960s and 1970s, the controversies roiling those decades—McCarthyism and communist subversion, the nuclear arms race and the rise of the military-industrial complex, the Cuban missile crisis and Vietnam, the assassination of one president and the toppling of another—remain indelibly part of "our times."

Those events not only shaped the consciousness of successive generations but also divided members of those generations into opposing camps: right and left, hawks and doves, anticommunists and anti-anticommunists, the uptight and the hip, the credulous and the skeptical. Underlying this split was a fundamental disagreement regarding the Cold War itself. One group accepted the orthodox interpretation that U.S. policies were necessary to defend the free world from communist aggression, actual or potential. The other group saw the American preoccupation with communism, at home and abroad, as unhealthy and probably unnecessary.

By upbringing, education, and youthful occupation, I identify with the former group. As a serving military officer, I accepted the view that American power provided the essential check upon those who conspired against freedom. Compared to the comprehensive horrors perpetrated by the regimes it opposed, the sins attributed to the United States during the Cold War—Washington's complicity with unsavory dictators, the conspiracies to overthrow unfriendly regimes, the mindless invasion at the Bay of Pigs, and the assassination of South Vietnamese president Ngo Dinh Diem—seemed venial. I never saw Fidel or Che, Mao or Ho as agents of liberation and human fulfillment. Nor do I see reason to modify my view on these matters today.

And yet: in the years after the dismantling of the Berlin Wall—the event that validated U.S. exertions across the previous half-century—American statecraft seemingly jumped its traces. Whereas before

1989 U.S. foreign policy appeared in the main realistic, with the stated objectives of diplomacy quite limited—to protect our homeland, to preserve our values, to defend our closest allies—in the 1990s those objectives aimed at nothing short of a full-scale transformation of the international order. Whereas during the Cold War Americans had justified the maintenance of a great military establishment as a necessary (but presumably temporary) departure from the Founders' republican vision, they now flaunted their nation's status as the world's only superpower.

I was by no means alone in being troubled by these developments; others of the conservative and "realist" persuasion expressed dismay at the policies pursued by the administrations of George H. W. Bush and Bill Clinton. The explanations fashioned by these critics differed in their particulars. Yet tacitly at least, they tended to share two assumptions. First, they took for granted that the events of 1989—when the Soviet Union effectively called off the Cold War—marked a culmination: at that moment, the United States had fulfilled its strategic purpose. In this reading, the breaching of the Berlin Wall rendered obsolete the policies that had guided American statesmen for decades. By extension, the overriding imperative facing the current generation of statesmen was to devise a new policy, one as coherent in design and as prudent in conception as the strategy that in achieving success had outlived its usefulness. The 1990s, therefore, challenged the architects of American statecraft to think anew and offered an opportunity for creativity not seen since the immediate aftermath of World War II.

Second, these observers generally agreed that first Bush and then Clinton muffed that opportunity. American activity in the international arena during the 1990s—as measured by summits convened, agreements signed, interventions undertaken—was ceaseless, but critics interpreted that activity as aimless flailing about, as evidence of a strategic void.

At first glance plausible, this interpretation struck me as increasingly unpersuasive as the events of the decade unfolded. Examining more closely the clichés to which political leaders reflexively resorted when explaining foreign policy, I began to see them for what they were: coded messages deeply rooted in American history and as such freighted with meaning. When describing America's role in the world, leaders like George H. W. Bush and Bill Clinton believed that they spoke great truths.

The difficulty lay in extracting from the ritualistic allusions to freedom, world peace, and global leadership the hard reality embedded within. For that I needed a key. Once I found it—and viewed the events of the 1990s through the interpretive framework that it offered—the conventional notion that American statecraft in the 1990s amounted to little more than confused and capricious improvisation collapsed. Linking American words to American actions, the key revealed a pattern and offered evidence of a coherent grand strategy conceived many decades earlier and now adapted to the circumstances of the post–Cold War era.

The strategy is a problematic one, and the scope of the project is nothing short of stupendous. Related to that project are large prudential questions (about feasibility and cost) and even larger moral ones (about justification and consequences) that remain unanswered, indeed, all but unexamined. (Pretending that the United States really doesn't have a strategy offers one way of dodging those questions.)

This book offers a critical interpretation of American statecraft in the 1990s. It invites readers to reexamine what they "know" regarding the guiding principles and underlying purposes of U.S. foreign policy—because what they think they know is becoming increasingly irrelevant. It advances the proposition that the partisan debate over U.S. policy—for the past decade little more than a pseudodebate—has reached a dead end. It proposes a reconciliation with a couple of patriot-heretics whose long-discredited ideas anticipated the snares and pitfalls awaiting a democracy playing the role of sole superpower. To Americans frightened or bewildered by the events of September 11 and their aftermath, it posits at least one answer to the question "How did we get here?"

. . .

We did not of deliberate choice undertake these new tasks which shall transform us . . . All the world knows the surprising circumstances which thrust
them upon us came . . . as if part of a great preconceived plan . . . The whole
world had already become a single vicinage; each part had become neighbor
to all the rest. No nation could live any longer to itself . . . [It has become] the
duty of the United States to play a part, and a leading part at that, in the
opening and transformation of the East . . . The East is to be opened and
transformed whether we will or no; the standards of the West are to be
imposed upon it; nations and peoples which have stood still the centuries
through . . . [will be] made part of the universal world of commerce and of
ideas . . . It is our peculiar duty . . . to moderate the process in the interests of
liberty . . . This we shall do . . . by giving them, in the spirit of service, a government and rule which shall moralize them by being itself moral.

Woodrow Wilson, October 1900

. . .

If we have to use force, it is because we are America.
We are the indispensable nation.

Madeleine Albright, February 1998

INTRODUCTION

THIS BOOK IS a venture in contemporary history, an effort to place in perspective developments that in some respects are not yet fully resolved. Its subject is U.S. foreign policy during the administrations of George H. W. Bush and Bill Clinton, with a coda encompassing George W. Bush's first year as president.

During this period, members of the foreign policy elite, breathing deeply the intoxicating vapors released during the *annus mirabilis* of 1989, concluded that history stood poised at a turning point. Bill Clinton interpreted the end of the Cold War as signifying "the fullness of time"—a scriptural allusion to the moment when God chose to transform history.[1] The collapse of communism and the triumph of liberal democratic capitalism offered similar prospects for transformation, this time through human rather than divine agency.

As the bloody twentieth century drew to a close, God's promise of peace on earth remained unfulfilled; it was now incumbent upon the United States, having ascended to the status of sole superpower, to complete God's work—or, as members of a largely secularized elite preferred it, to guide history toward its intended destination.

President Clinton and his secretary of state Madeleine Albright were explicit on this point: the United States had emerged at the dawn of the new millennium as the "indispensable nation" endowed by providence with unique responsibilities and obligations.[2] Republican leaders employed different language but endorsed the sentiment. Average citizens, though attending only fitfully to the world beyond America's borders, tacitly agreed. In their eyes, the advantages accruing to the world's only superpower promised to be substantial. The costs of sustaining that position appeared minimal. Except among a crabbed minority on the far right and far left, a concept of the United States shaping a new global order in its own image evoked more satisfaction than complaint.

Existing alongside this broad acceptance of America's transcendent mission and transcendent status was a second and paradoxical asser-

1

tion: that once the Cold War ended actual U.S. policy languished in permanent disarray. That the United States found itself after 1989 bereft of strategy became part of the next decade's conventional wisdom. What passed for policy amounted, it was said, to little more than improvisation and crisis management. "There is an absence of any grand design," lamented the diplomatic historian John Lewis Gaddis. Gaddis and other observers could discern no overarching conception that explained U.S. behavior. There was no Big Idea. The only consistent pattern Gaddis could detect was "one of responding to crises. There's a kind of incrementalism and ad-hocism to things."[3] Pundits, talking heads, editorial writers, politicians, and mere interested citizens without number echoed this view.

As early as April 1992, a Democratic aspirant to the White House, a southerner with only the flimsiest foreign policy credentials, took the incumbent president to task for failing "to articulate clear goals for American foreign policy." Governor Bill Clinton complained that "George Bush has invoked a new world order without enunciating a new American purpose."[4] Eight years later the partisan tables had turned, but the critique remained unaltered. During his two terms as president, Bill Clinton had "pursued a feckless, photo-op foreign policy," charged John McCain, the influential Republican senator from Arizona. The Democrats had made "little or no effort to define a coherent plan for United States engagement in the world."[5] Clinton had failed to establish an "overarching intellectual framework" for policy, wrote Richard Haass, who had served in the Bush White House.[6] The result, according to Robert Zoellick, another veteran of the elder Bush's foreign policy team, had been "ad hockery and case-by-case actions lacking in strategy."[7]

In short, according to the conventional wisdom at least, the record of American statecraft in the 1990s was one of opportunity wasted. At the very moment when the United States should have acted with purpose and resolve, policymakers dawdled and diddled.

This book takes issue with that view. Since the end of the Cold War the United States has in fact adhered to a well-defined grand strategy. To be sure, given the exigencies of politics in the real world, that adherence has been less than perfect. From time to time, considerations unrelated to strategy—the influence of domestic politics prominent among them—caused the ship of state to tack to port, then to starboard, and then back again. Yet to interpret this zigzag pattern as indicative of confusion is to sell short those charged with the ship's navigation. Those who chart America's course do so with a clearly defined purpose in mind.

That purpose is to preserve and, where both feasible and conducive to U.S. interests, to expand an American imperium. Central to this strategy is a commitment to global openness—removing barriers that inhibit the movement of goods, capital, ideas, and people. Its ultimate objective is the creation of an open and integrated international order based on the principles of democratic capitalism, with the United States as the ultimate guarantor of order and enforcer of norms.

In the eyes of American policymakers, an open world that adheres to the principles of free enterprise is a precondition for continued American prosperity. An open world that is friendly to liberal values seemingly assures American security. The operative "signs of the times"—both technological and cultural—fuel expectations that the world is indeed moving, inexorably and irreversibly, toward greater openness. Should events belie either of those expectations, the United States will employ its dominant military power to thwart any conceivable challenge to its preeminence.

From the perspective of its architects, this "strategy of openness" is benign in its intent and enlightened in its impact. On this point, the views of those subjected to the Pax Americana vary. Many accept it, with greater or lesser degrees of enthusiasm, as preferable to any plausible alternative. Some accept it grudgingly; for the moment at least, they have little choice but to do so. Others denounce U.S. hegemony as a variant of imperialism, distinctive in form but nonetheless relying on repression and exploitation. Whether through direct or indirect action, they resist. Quelling that resistance mandates the use of force. As a result, not only the nurturing of military power but also its expenditure become integral to U.S. strategy.

This book argues that the strategy of openness derives directly from U.S. principles and practices elaborated and implemented during and even before the Cold War. Rather than marking the culmination of U.S. strategy, the collapse of the Berlin Wall simply inaugurated its latest phase.

In short, this book finds continuity where others see discontinuity and identifies purpose and structure where others see incoherence.

➤ This book also explains why most Americans remain oblivious to this strategy—why the notion that throughout the 1990s Republicans and Democrats alike were making things up as they went along received ready acceptance, with observers dismissing as mere rhetoric official explanations of the principles guiding American policy. The culprit, in this instance, is an abiding preference for averting our eyes from the unflagging self-interest and large ambitions underlying all U.S. policy.

Thus, for example, do we enshrine the Cold War as a crusade against the evil of communism. The Cold War was that, but it was never only that. To conceive of U.S. grand strategy from the late 1940s through the 1980s as "containment"—with no purpose apart from resisting the spread of Soviet power—is not wrong, but it is incomplete. More to the point, such a cramped conception of Cold War strategy actively impedes our understanding of current U.S. policy.

No strategy worthy of the name is exclusively passive or defensive in orientation. Evidence that from the outset of the Cold War the United States sought something more than simply to check the spread of evil was available all along, recognized by a few, largely ignored by the majority. Lord Ismay's famous description of the North Atlantic Treaty Organization's several founding purposes captures the point: the alliance was formed in 1949 to keep the Russians *out*, the Americans *in*, and the Germans *down*. Of course, Ismay's was a British perspective; an American might have inserted after the preposition "in" the phrase "and on top." For the United States viewed NATO not only as a bulwark against Soviet aggression but as an instrument to promote Europe's political and economic transformation while cementing the advantageous position that America had secured in Europe as a result of victory in World War II. A politically integrated Europe open to American enterprise and dependent upon the United States for its security suited Washington just fine.

In short, U.S. grand strategy during the Cold War required not only containing communism but also taking active measures to open up the world politically, culturally, and, above all, economically—which is precisely what policymakers said they intended to do. Consider a speech made at Monticello on July 4, 1947, by President Harry S Truman. Addressing a crowd gathered around the east portico of Thomas Jefferson's home, Truman described America's purpose as world peace, "not peace in our time—but peace for all time." The balance of his presentation constituted a blueprint for fostering that peace.

That blueprint contained no reference to containing communism. Indeed, although his administration was even then putting the finishing touches on its strategy of containment—Mr. X's essay unveiling "The Sources of Soviet Conduct" had just appeared on the nation's newsstands—the president never mentioned the Soviet Union by name. Only twice did he refer even obliquely to the Kremlin, chiding Soviet leaders for opposing U.S.-sponsored reconstruction efforts on the "fallacious" grounds that "this would mean interference by some nations in the internal affairs of others."

Looking beyond the essentially negative objective of restraining communism, the strategy sketched out at Monticello outlined a comprehensive vision for constructing a new international order. That vision had two main features. The first Truman described as the great lesson of the recently concluded world war, namely, that "nations are interdependent and that recognition of our dependence upon one another is essential for life, liberty, and the pursuit of happiness of all mankind." The second was that peace is indivisible. "So long as the basic rights of men are denied in any substantial portion of the earth," the president declared, "men everywhere must live in fear of their own rights and their own security."

Recognition of the interdependence of nations and the indivisibility of peace demanded the removal of barriers between nations. Truman called for the "full exchange of knowledge, ideas, and information among the peoples of the earth, and maximum freedom in international travel and communication." He expressed support for "economic and financial policies to support a world economy rather than separate nationalistic economies." Crucial to this end were ongoing efforts to reduce tariffs and to create what Truman referred to as an International Trade Organization.

The responsibility of the United States was to take the lead in removing such barriers. In this effort, technologies in which the United States enjoyed a pronounced advantage would play a key role, eliminating obstacles that traditionally separated nations. "We have the mechanical facilities—the radio, television, airplanes—for the creation of a worldwide culture," a prospect that the president clearly welcomed.[8]

As Truman's Independence Day oratory suggests, from the earliest days of the Cold War the United States entertained a strategic vision that looked well beyond the imperative of defending the free world against communist aggression. More was required to fulfill that vision than the defeat of the Soviet Union and the demise of Marxism-Leninism.

The collapse of communism at the end of the 1980s offered an unprecedented opportunity to fulfill Truman's vision. In the ensuing decade the architects of U.S. policy consciously set out to make the most of that opportunity. Seeking to perpetuate American preeminence and to foster an international order conducive to U.S. interests, the administrations of George H. W. Bush and Bill Clinton revived the project that Truman had sketched in July 1947. Whereas the orientation of U.S. policy had been primarily defensive, it now became largely offensive. This shift in emphasis did not imply that Americans had developed a sudden hankering for conquest or old-fashioned empire. In fact the overall objective remained unchanged from Truman's day.

Though garnished with neologistic flourishes intended to convey a sense of freshness or originality, the politicoeconomic concept to which the United States adheres today has not changed in a century: the familiar quest for an "open world," the overriding imperative of commercial integration, confidence that technology endows the United States with a privileged position in that order, and the expectation that American military might will preserve order and enforce the rules.

Those policies reflect a single-minded determination to extend and perpetuate American political, economic, and cultural hegemony— usually referred to as "leadership"—on a global scale. The chapters that follow describe the strategy of openness whereby the United States since the Cold War has pursued that purpose.

Our point of departure, however, lies earlier, in the writings of two long-deceased and largely discredited scholars, one now regarded as a proponent of so-called isolationism, the other as an ardent critic of U.S. foreign policy from what purported to be the radical left. Each in his own day got the very biggest question dead wrong. But together they developed a distinctive angle of vision that exposed the underpinnings of American statecraft. That perspective is their legacy, one that is today more valuable than ever.

CHAPTER 1

THE MYTH OF THE RELUCTANT SUPERPOWER

Of course, our whole national history has been one of expansion.
Theodore Roosevelt, December 1899

"SOME NATIONS ACHIEVE GREATNESS," observed the historian Ernest May; "the United States had greatness thrust upon it."[1] Rendered forty years ago at the very acme of the Cold War, May's judgment referred specifically to the events culminating in the great outward thrust of 1898 and America's dramatic emergence on the world stage. Yet it also encapsulates the story of America's rise to power the way Americans themselves prefer to tell it.

Above all, May's pithy remark directs attention not to purpose but to posture: greatness was not sought; it just happened. In this view, American policy is a response to external factors. The United States does not act in accordance with some predetermined logic; it reacts to circumstances. Although the events of 1898 accelerated its ascent to world power, the United States—unlike other nations—achieved preeminence not by consciously seeking it but simply as an unintended consequence of actions taken either in self-defense or on behalf of others.

Thus, in 1898 Americans chose war only when the continuing depredations of Spain's General Valeriano ("Butcher") Weyler in Cuba had become intolerable. When in 1914 the "Great War" began, the United States remained neutral, intervening only in response to Germany's violation of U.S. neutral rights. Even then, in contrast to every other belligerent, the United States fought for altruistic purposes, seeking to end war itself and to make the world safe for democracy. Similarly, when a new European war began in 1939, Americans

7

again stayed on the sidelines until provoked by Japan's surprise attack at Pearl Harbor to enter the conflict and to embark on another crusade for democracy.

This pattern of evil spurring the United States into action persisted into the postwar era. Hence American engagement in the Cold War marked, in Arthur Schlesinger's classic formulation, "the brave and essential response of free men to Communist aggression."[2] Even after the Cold War, distant events continued to compel the United States to exert—and perforce to expand—its power. In 1990, Iraqi aggression threatening the West's access to Persian Gulf oil obliged the United States once again to respond. As the century drew to a close, events came full circle: Americans found themselves going to war on behalf of a tiny province in Serbia, the brutality of Slobodan Milošević in Kosovo having become as intolerable as that of General Weyler in Cuba a century before.

Few scholars specializing in American diplomatic history today accept such an outline of twentieth century U.S. foreign policy. But in practice, the myth of the "reluctant superpower"—Americans asserting themselves only under duress and then always for the noblest purposes—reigns today as the master narrative explaining (and justifying) the nation's exercise of global power.

The myth survives in the post–Cold War era less because it is true than because it is useful. Its utility stems in large part from the fact that it comes complete with its own cast of stock characters. Its heroes are "internationalists," wise, responsible, and broad-minded in outlook. Opposing the internationalist project is a motley crew of narrow-minded, provincial, and frequently bigoted cranks, known collectively as "isolationists." For leading politicians and members of the foreign policy establishment, endlessly recounting the internationalist struggle offers the preferred method of inoculating successive generations of citizens ostensibly susceptible to the isolationist virus.

The myth of the reluctant superpower serves other purposes as well. Aspirants to the inner circle of national politics testify to the narrative as a means of signaling their trustworthiness and reliability. Here, for example, is a thumbnail sketch of postwar history offered by presidential hopeful Bill Clinton in December 1991:

> I was born nearly a half century ago, at the dawn of the Cold War, a time of great change, enormous opportunity, and uncertain peril. At a

time when Americans wanted nothing more than to come home and resume their lives of peace and quiet, our country had to summon the will for a new kind of war—containing an expansionist and hostile Soviet Union which vowed to bury us. We had to find ways to rebuild the economies of Europe and Asia, encourage a worldwide movement toward independence, and vindicate our nation's principles in the world against yet another totalitarian challenge to liberal democracy. Thanks to the unstinting courage and sacrifice of the American people, we were able to win that Cold War.[3]

In such a rendering of the tale, "we" acted as one; doubts, divisions, disappointments disappear. By reciting this sanitized version of the postwar era, Clinton not only affirmed its essential truth but also situated himself among those who fought the good fight against totalitarianism on behalf of democracy.

The myth of the reluctant superpower also curbs any inclination to consider anew the purposes served by America's now unquestioned global dominance. In a post–Cold War world, does the paradigm of America having "greatness thrust upon it" retain its explanatory power? If so, with the United States now clearly on the top of the heap, who or what is doing the thrusting? These questions go unasked. Foreign policy "debate," such as it is, confines itself to matters of tactics: Are the sanctions working? Will bombing alone suffice? How could we have been surprised? As if by default, the hallowed precepts of liberal internationalism perdure.

That those precepts imply a conception for marrying instruments of national power to broad policy objectives serving concrete American interests goes unmentioned and all but unnoticed. Instead politicians, abetted by the media, offer political theater: Republicans berate a Democratic president for failing to articulate a foreign policy "vision"; given the chance, Democrats return the favor. Lost amidst the posturing is the extent to which both parties and virtually the entire foreign policy elite tacitly share a common vision and conform in practice to a strategic consensus of long standing.

➤ On two occasions during the century of America's rise to global preeminence, critics mounted a vigorous challenge to that consensus. First during the decade leading up to World War II and subsequently during the protracted crisis centered on the Vietnam War, dissenters subjected the myth of the reluctant superpower to sustained assault. They began by rejecting the premise that America's foreign policies were a function of developments beyond its borders. They argued instead that those policies—commercial relationships, decisions for war and peace, the designation of others as "friends" or "enemies"— derived from influences closer to home. Underlying those specific decisions and actions and endowing them with an overall unity was a particular worldview rooted in calculations of political and economic self-interest.

These dissenters viewed those policies as wrongheaded, undemocratic, unnecessary, even dangerous. They formulated their own alternative to the myth of the reluctant superpower and campaigned energetically to convert the American people to that alternative.

In each instance, events discredited that alternative, an outcome for which Americans should be grateful. For the critique mounted in the 1930s discounted the threat posed by Adolf Hitler. Had it prevailed, Nazi Germany might well have escaped destruction. For their part, the dissenters who appeared during the Cold War, while acutely sensitive to America's flaws, were seemingly oblivious to the defects of communism and to the danger posed by Soviet power. Had they succeeded, the Cold War might have had a different and less satisfactory outcome.

The failing to which these critics were prone was astigmatism.[4] They were blind to inconvenient facts (usually pertaining to American adversaries) to which others attributed paramount importance. Meanwhile, they assigned great significance to matters (typically pertaining to America's own behavior) that others viewed as inconsequential or benign. Obsessed with unearthing the inner logic of U.S. policy, they called attention to a different set of inconvenient facts that the defenders of liberal internationalism preferred to overlook. In short, their efforts yielded hitherto undiscovered insights into the origins, motives, and actual conduct of U.S. foreign policy, insights that discomfited those dedicated to preserving the mythic rendition of America's ascent to global power.

Neither the course of World War II nor the outcome of the Cold War has invalidated those insights. Indeed, as a point of departure for examining U.S. policy in the post–Cold War era—notable for the absence of any adversary remotely comparable to Hitler's Reich or Stalin's Soviet Union—views deriving from the premise that external factors have *never* adequately explained American behavior deserve respectful consideration.

The chief proponents of these heresies—rejected in their own day, relevant to our own—were the American historians Charles A. Beard and William Appleman Williams.

► Through the first half of the twentieth century, Charles A. Beard (1874–1948) was by common agreement the most influential historian in America.[5] Widely ranging in his interests, boldly original in interpretation, politically progressive, personally courageous, and astonishingly prolific, Beard could wield his pen as "either shillelagh or stiletto" and was equally adept at writing for academics, policy professionals, or the general public.[6] From the publication of his controversial *Economic Interpretation of the Constitution of the United States* before World War I until his death, he remained a towering figure in American intellectual life, frequently the source and subject of controversy and seldom outside of the public eye.

Raised in Knightstown, Indiana, in middle-class comfort, Beard attended a Quaker school and then DePauw University, graduating in 1898. Over the next four years he studied at Oxford, where he was instrumental in the founding of Ruskin College, a school to provide educational opportunities for members of the British working class. In 1902 Beard returned to the United States and enrolled at Columbia University, earning his doctorate two years later. He immediately accepted an offer to join Columbia's history department, then among the country's most distinguished.

Beard taught at Columbia until 1917, resigning in protest against the firing of a colleague who opposed U.S. entry into the European war. Retreating to his dairy farm in Connecticut, he remained thereafter an independent scholar and commentator on events of the day.[7] Over the course of his career, Beard published forty-two volumes of history and political science and coauthored another thirty-five. His masterful overview of U.S. history, *The Rise of American Civilization*, written with his wife, Mary R. Beard, became a bestseller and a Book-of-the-Month Club selection. His histories alone sold 11.3 million copies during his lifetime.[8] Beard's articles and reviews—numbering in the hundreds—appeared in virtually all the leading scholarly and general-circulation journals of his day.

Yet by the time of his death Beard's reputation stood, in the words of another prominent scholar, as "an imposing ruin in the landscape of American historiography." His views on foreign policy—the subject that preoccupied Beard beginning in the 1930s—amounted to a "tattered shambles," of interest only to crackpots and conspiracy theorists.[9] Long an outspoken advocate of reform, Beard found himself in the last decade of his life denounced as an apologist for fascism, in the words of Lewis Mumford "a passive—no, active—abettor of tyranny, sadism, and human defilement."[10]

If by the end of Beard's life his reputation lay in ruins, it was because Beard himself put a torch to the edifice. In an extraordinary act of professional self-immolation, he closed out his career by denouncing as fraudulent the text most crucial to sustaining the myth of the reluctant superpower: the orthodox account of U.S. entry into World War II.

In two scathing volumes—*American Foreign Policy in the Making* (1946) and *President Roosevelt and the Coming of the War, 1941* (1948)—Beard accused Franklin Roosevelt of outright deception in his conduct of foreign affairs. Running in 1940 for an unprecedented third term, FDR had famously declared, "I have said this before, but I shall say it again and again and again: Your boys are not going to be sent into any foreign wars." In doing so, Roosevelt, in Beard's view, had made a solemn covenant with the American people.[11] Without missing a beat, the president then proceeded to violate that covenant. Indeed, according to Beard, even as he was promising to keep the country out of the war, Roosevelt was conniving to maneuver the United States into it.

Historians today admit to a modicum of truth in Beard's charge.[12] Roosevelt's lack of candor, notably in misrepresenting U.S. naval involvement in Great Britain's battle against the U-boat threat, is well documented. But in the war's immediate aftermath—and with internationalists rousing Americans to support another great crusade, this time against communism—Beard's attack was not just impolitic; it was impermissible. By indicting the recently deceased Roosevelt, he forfeited whatever authority and credibility he had accrued over several decades of research and writing. Refusing to recant the isolationist creed, Beard consigned himself to the status of miscreant, guilty not only of scholarly malpractice but of having committed an unforgivable act of civic blasphemy.

Beginning his career in the camp of left-leaning heterodoxy, reaching in midlife the heights of respectability and influence, Beard in his dotage had seemingly fallen into the embrace of the disreputable right. However, Beard's intellectual journey proceeded from the center out—from the inner workings of the republic at its founding to America's external relations as it approached maturity. Coming to maturity himself in the heyday of Progressivism, Beard was stirred by the social ills afflicting that era, by-products of the laissez-faire attitudes that had with brutal efficiency propelled the United States into the forefront of industrialized nations. As a result, he initially devoted his attention to domestic concerns: How had such a society come into existence? What explained the distribution of wealth and power within it?

Beard approached his task by examining the past through the lens of political economy. His first major book, *Economic Origins of the Constitution*, scandalized patriotic-minded defenders of historical orthodoxy by arguing that the Framers had pursued their task less under the spell of the high ideals of 1776 than with their eyes trained on the main chance.[13] Encouraging commerce and manufactures, protecting private property, establishing financial instruments essential for economic development—these were the issues that preoccupied those participating in the secret deliberations in Philadelphia—issues in which they themselves had a large personal stake. The product of their labors preserved that stake. "The Constitution," Beard concluded, "was essentially an economic document based upon the concept that the fundamental rights of property are anterior to government and morally beyond the reach of popular majorities."[14]

Beard's characterization of politics as a bargaining process aimed at satisfying the disparate interests of economic elites informed much of his subsequent writing. Thus, the metanarrative of *The Rise of American Civilization* portrays U.S. history as a dialectic between the agrarian ideal of Thomas Jefferson and the capitalist vision of Alexander Hamilton. For Beard, the Civil War became the pivotal event in the history of the republic, resolving that competition and thus opening the way for the next stage in the nation's development. At root, this "second American Revolution" was not a dispute over slavery, Union, or states' rights, but a contest between two irreconcilable economic systems, each pushing to expand and facing inevitable decline if denied the opportunity to do so. On the one side was the burgeoning "industrial vortex" of the North, on the other a plantation economy confined to "a limited territory with incompetent labor on soil of diminishing fertility."[15] Appomattox settled the issue once and for all. Although in destroying slavery the North's victory brought some modest benefit to those freed from bondage, the real winners were rapacious captains of industry in the North and, to a lesser extent, the South. The result was the Gilded Age, a paroxysm of creativity, plunder, and excess that gave rise to the nation into which Beard was born.

Preoccupied until the 1930s with recasting U.S. history in terms of class conflict, Beard relegated foreign policy to the status of afterthought. Foreign policy derived from domestic policy. Its primary purpose was to advance commercial interests. Writing before U.S. entry into World War I, Beard acknowledged the American tradition of "splendid isolation," only to dismiss it as fiction. Whatever its pretensions to distancing itself from the rest of the world, he noted, "at no time has the United States refused to defend American commercial enterprise in any part of the globe." From the very outset, the United States had "been a world power, as far as has been necessary."[16]

American participation in World War I alerted Beard to the hazards implicit in commercial diplomacy. Although Beard supported U.S. entry into the war as necessary to check German militarism, his enlistment in Wilson's internationalist crusade proved short-lived.[17] No sooner had the guns fallen silent than the debacle of the Paris peace conference and the release of documents from German and Russian archives began raising doubts that the war had been, as advertised, a war of German aggression that threatened the survival of democracy. In short order, skeptical journalists and historians were advancing arguments that undercut the official interpretation of America's own role in the war. Specifically, these revisionists challenged the notion that the United States had remained genuinely neutral during 1914–1917 and that in entering the war it fought to advance democratic ideals.[18] Discounting Wilson's high-sounding rhetoric, revisionists characterized U.S. wartime policies as self-serving, reflecting an eagerness to cash in on Europe's misfortune. A phony neutrality permitted a massive trade in arms with the Allies, propped up by American loans. The result at home was large profits for bankers and arms merchants and a general economic boom, sustainable only so long as the slaughter on the western front continued. By 1917 those policies culminated in intervention at the behest of Wall Street tycoons who would face ruin if Great Britain and France lost the war. Once in the war, Wilson's idealistic posturing notwithstanding, the U.S. government turned a blind eye to secret deals and became complicit in Allied schemes of imperial aggrandizement.

Throughout the 1920s the revisionists piled up evidence and argued their case. Like many other scholars, Beard eventually found that case persuasive. With perhaps the majority of Americans, he concluded by 1930 that U.S. entry into the war had been a mistake and that Wilson's peddling of the elixir of internationalism had been tantamount to fraud. This conclusion transformed his thinking about American statecraft.

Looking back from the 1920s at U.S. foreign policies well before 1914, Beard now discerned the outlines of a more complex and sinister dynamic. In the decades following the Civil War, he wrote, "as the domestic market was saturated and capital heaped up for investment, the pressure for the expansion of the American commercial empire rose with corresponding speed."[19] Henceforth, sustaining American prosperity under existing political arrangements would require the unimpeded growth of trade and investment abroad. Here for Beard was the master key that unlocked the inner secrets of American statecraft. It not only explained why the United States had gone to war in 1898 and in 1917, but also revealed more fully the nexus between politics and diplomacy: American leaders chose intervention abroad in order to dodge politically difficult decisions at home—decisions that might call into question the constitutional framework that guaranteed the privileges of the propertied classes.

Asked once to describe his own ideal for America, Beard responded: "It is a workers' republic."[20] For Beard and other progressives, World War I had quashed their hopes for creating that republic—a society more genuinely democratic, more equitable, and more humane. The onset of the Great Depression barely a decade later only highlighted the consequences of that earlier failure. But economic crisis also suggested the possibility of reviving that effort. Thus, when Franklin Roosevelt, wrapping himself in the mantle of progressivism, won the presidency in 1932, Beard enthusiastically endorsed FDR's promise of a New Deal.

Yet wariness tempered that enthusiasm. Disillusionment at Wilson's hands heightened Beard's concern that Roosevelt might lack the courage to make good on his bold promises. He feared that, in the manner of past administrations, FDR might opt for adventurism abroad to evade the imperative of change at home. That way, in Beard's view, pointed toward a repetition of the error of imperialism as in 1898 and, worse, the disaster of all-out war as in 1917. Ominous developments overseas in the early 1930s—Japan's incursion into Manchuria and Hitler's coming to power in Germany—suggested that a president seeking to dodge the need for structural change at home could easily find a pretext for finding solutions to the country's ills elsewhere.

Throughout the 1930s Beard devoted his formidable talents to averting such an eventuality. In a torrent of books, pamphlets, and articles, he warned against being dragged into problems that were Asia's or Europe's, but not America's. He labored furiously to alert his fellow citizens to the folly—and the danger—of reviving Woodrow Wilson's project. He insisted that if the United States *did* go to war, it should at least do so democratically, not as a result of backroom machinations by a handful of politicians.

In advancing these arguments, Beard was fully alive to current trends toward interdependence. "Nations are no longer isolated entities represented by rulers who may make or break official intercourse at will," he acknowledged in 1930. "Underlying the whole fabric of modern civilization is a network of physical, economic, social, and cultural connections. Railways, steamships, telegraphs, cables, and wireless communications unite homes, offices, industries, and farms in a universal web."[21]

Beard had flirted briefly with the notion that this universal web might spell the obsolescence of war. But the depression convinced him otherwise. Despite "growing interdependence," he concluded in 1934, "the tendency of nations to engage in armed conflicts has not disappeared."[22]

By 1934 the possibility of renewed war on a large scale, whether in Asia or Europe or both, was becoming self-evident. Beard's reading of American history over the preceding half-century convinced him that, barring a major recasting of its foreign policy, the United States would almost inevitably find itself drawn into such a war, with dire consequences. But reorienting U.S. policy was unlikely unless Americans confronted the underlying assumptions and principles that for decades had determined U.S. behavior toward the world beyond its borders. Beard took it upon himself to instruct his fellow citizens accordingly.

His own interpretation of American statecraft derived from his belief in two controlling maxims: that foreign and domestic policy "were parts of the same thing" and that "nations are governed by their interests as their statesmen conceive these interests."[23] In the case of the United States—whose chief business, after all, was business—economic considerations ranked foremost among the factors determining how policymakers defined those interests.

Industrialists, bankers, and farmers—and their advocates in Washington—had long since concluded that the domestic market alone would not satisfy their own or the nation's requirements. They believed, wrote Beard, that "American industry, under the regime of technology, is producing more commodities than the American people can use or consume, and the 'surplus' must be exported." The same applied to capital and the products of American agriculture. Influential members of these constituencies believed that failure to secure outlets for these surpluses would have (and in the 1930s was having) ruinous consequences, not only obliterating individual fortunes and causing widespread economic hardship but also threatening the social order.[24]

For these "adepts at the center of things," therefore, the essence of statecraft was not the once-in-a-generation crisis that obliged a McKinley or a Wilson to choose between war and peace. What really mattered were the long stretches between wars, when the attention of the press and public lay elsewhere. That was when the adepts, left alone, addressed the issues that really counted. Reduced to its essentials, U.S. foreign policy was an either/or proposition: "a question of commercial expansion or stagnation and decay; world power or economic decline."[25]

Viewed in this light, exporting economic surpluses—the "industrialist way of escape"—constituted *the* overriding national interest. It was not simply a matter of making money—although it included that, of course—but of preserving long-standing arrangements for allocating power and privilege within American society. According to Beard, efforts to protect that interest ran like "a powerful motif through state papers from the inauguration of President McKinley to the retirement of President Hoover."[26] For all the peculiarities in style and temper distinguishing McKinley from Theodore Roosevelt, William Howard Taft from Wilson, or Warren G. Harding from Calvin Coolidge, each of those presidents had adhered to a common strategy. Though cloaked in professions of America's aversion to old-fashioned imperialism and its hopes for world peace, the centerpiece of that strategy was economic expansionism. Implementing that strategy involved "pushing and holding open doors in all parts of the world with all the engines of government ranging from polite coercion to the use of arms."[27] Only by opening the world to American trade and investment could the United States flourish and ensure the permanence of its existing domestic order.

Beard faulted this strategy on five separate counts. First, he ridiculed dreams of endless economic expansion as illusory. There simply was "no way of securing ever-expanding outlets abroad for the ever-expanding potentials of great technology by any system of foreign exchange and trade promotion."[28]

Second, the more insistently the United States pressed in its determination to open the world, Beard believed, the greater the opposition it was likely to encounter. He cautioned against the American tendency to see the world as "something mechanical, on a plane surface." Such an oversimplified view led to "the exclusion of the national cultures—ideas, loyalties, passions, political traditions, the development and clash of races and nations" that were the very stuff of history. The contrary claims of internationalists notwithstanding, the world was not completely malleable. Others would not obligingly conform to American preferences. To insist otherwise was to court perpetual conflict.[29]

Third, in provoking resistance, the effort to open doors for American trade and investment abroad also opened the door, Beard feared, to militarism at home. To overcome that resistance the United States would find itself increasingly resorting to force. Indeed, the officer corps stood ready with arguments explaining the need to expand U.S. military capabilities. But any nation "compelled to devote immense energies and a large part of its annual wealth production to wars, to preparation for wars, and to paying for past wars" risked becoming Sparta, its civil and cultural institutions transformed into "the servants of military purposes and the military mind."[30]

Fourth, by Beard's estimate, American political culture and the composition of American society were ill suited to such an expansionist strategy. Divided ethnically and religiously, celebrating individual liberty and self-gratification, and "without the cement of a long-established monarchy, State Church, or fixed landed aristocracy," Americans lacked the cohesion, the habits of self-abnegation, and reflexive deference to authority. That is, they possessed few of the qualities suggesting an aptitude for arduous and protracted campaigns to rearrange the international order. America's inherent virtues were not those of imperial Rome or imperial Britain.[31]

Fifth, and above all, Beard insisted that the preoccupation with opening doors misconstrued the nation's true interests. To be sure, "the supreme interest of the United States" properly included a commitment to providing all Americans with a decent standard of living. But the desideratum of economic growth did not trump all other considerations. The nation's true interests required statesmen to pursue economic objectives in a way "conducive to the promotion of individual and social virtues *within the frame of national security.*"[32] In Beard's view, the importance of this final point was paramount. To pursue the nation's material well-being by venturing *beyond* the frame of national security—by engaging in frequent interventions abroad or in wars not involving national survival—was to court overextension, exhaustion, and collapse. Furthermore, the "frame" of American security, in Beard's view, was not difficult to identify. Defined by the two great oceans that set the New World apart, it coincided with the limits of the Western Hemisphere.

To those who believed that the United States could not prosper without access to European and Asian markets, Beard pointed to the underdeveloped condition of America's own vast internal market. The periodic economic woes besetting the United States stemmed not from a lack of aggregate wealth, resources, productive capacity, or population. The problem, he believed, was that an insufficient proportion of that population functioned as effective consumers. But for that problem, a by-product of an inequitable distribution of wealth, there existed a simple remedy: redistribution.

Beard generally viewed moral and humanitarian arguments on behalf of internationalism as mere camouflage. But to those given to the "theological assertion" that God had anointed "American law, order, civilization, and flag" to serve as his agents, he replied by calling attention to the country's callous neglect of its *own* poor. America's own boundaries contained more than enough human tragedy and misfortune to absorb the energies of citizens eager to uplift the downtrodden. Citing the plight of several million African Americans, Beard suggested that "Those who are deeply moved in the virtuous sense implied by 'the White Man's burden' can . . . find extensive outlets for their moral urges at home," thus postponing any requirement "for acquiring by force additional congeries of 'brown brothers.'"[33] To the extent that the United States did have obligations to the rest of humankind, it would be more likely to fulfill those obligations by setting an example than by imposing its values on others.

As an alternative to opening doors abroad, Beard proposed that the United States "substitute an intensive cultivation of its own garden for a wasteful, quixotic, and ineffectual extension of interests beyond the reach of competent military and naval defense."[34] Such an undertaking did not imply severing all connections with the world at large. However, it would emphasize self-reliance and economic self-sufficiency, thereby maximizing American freedom of action.

In 1935 Beard laid out this argument in *The Open Door at Home,* his most comprehensive foreign policy statement to date. But if Beard hoped to win over government policymakers, he was sadly disappointed.[35] By the end of Roosevelt's first term, Beard realized that the New Deal was essentially a salvage operation. Once he understood that FDR was intent on preserving democratic capitalism, Beard concluded that the president was unlikely to break with the open-door strategy of his predecessors, like them looking abroad for solutions to America's problems at home.[36]

At no time during the decade leading up to World War II did Beard portray the looming crises in Europe and Asia primarily in moral terms. In his view, no great power was innocent. No victim was completely without fault. No disgruntled nation was without some legitimate grievance—usually dusted off whenever it became expedient to challenge the status quo. Surveying the worsening political situation in 1936, with Hitler denouncing the Versailles Treaty and reoccupying the Rhineland, Beard refused to see a composition in black-and-white: "greed, lust and ambition in Europe and Asia do not seem to be confined to Italy, Germany and Japan," he cautioned; "nor does good seem to be monopolized by Great Britain, France and Russia."[37]

Ambiguity shrouded the motives and actions of states—including those of the United States.

In a series of essays published in 1936, Beard warned Americans against seeing international politics as the handiwork of nefarious individuals. "War is not the work of a demon," he insisted. "It is our very own work, for which we prepare, wittingly or not,"—meaning that statesmen responded to the demands or expectations of the populations they governed.[38] Americans possessed the power—if they would recognize it—to prevent the nation from sliding toward another Armageddon.

By early 1937, with German rearmament well under way and Spain's civil war fixing the attention of American elites, Beard sensed that FDR himself was showing signs of becoming "intoxicated by moral exuberance."[39] By summer's end—with Japan now fully engaged in a war to conquer China—he concluded that Roosevelt had "made it manifest that he still follows the creed that the United States must do good all around the world. That creed will plunge him into war," Beard predicted.[40] Roosevelt's call that autumn for an international effort to "quarantine" aggressors confirmed those fears.

With mounting urgency, Beard both denied that foreign quarrels had a moral basis or that involvement in those quarrels would produce anything but disaster for America. In professing their devotion to peace, Britain and France sought primarily to guarantee their "possession of all that they have gathered up in the way of empire by methods not entirely different from those recently employed, let us say, by Italy in Ethiopia." Beard mocked those calling for "another preposterous crusade for democracy on the battle-fields of Europe." To Americans who believed that in failing to stem aggression abroad the United States was "shirking" its responsibilities, he again invited attention to problems festering in their own backyard. "[A]nybody who feels hot with morals and is affected with delicate sensibilities can find enough to do at home," he wrote on the eve of the *Anschluss*, "considering the misery of the 10,000,000 unemployed, the tramps, the beggars, the sharecroppers, tenants and field hands right here at our door." How could a nation that had manifestly failed to get its own house in order "have the effrontery to assume that we can solve the problems of Asia and Europe, encrusted in the blood-rust of fifty centuries?"[41] "The very essence of statecraft, at home and abroad,"

Beard warned as Hitler dismembered Czechoslovakia in the spring of 1939, "is a sense for the limitations of power and for the consequences that may flow from the exercise of power . . . As a matter of cold fact—men, guns, ships, and equipment—the United States cannot 'whip creation' and police it."[42]

Beard had placed himself at the forefront of a grassroots movement opposing U.S. intervention in the war that now loomed on the immediate horizon. For their efforts, Beard and his allies were savaged as "isolationists," a caricature that has ever since proven of incalculable value to proponents of American globalism. But the isolationists gave as good as they got.

Even the Wehrmacht's invasion of Poland in September 1939 did not shake Beard's conviction that this was not America's war. If anything, the reverse was true. As Roosevelt responded to German military successes by edging ever closer to direct American involvement, Beard continued to insist that flaws within the American system of political economy, not distant security threats, determined U.S. policy.

In a last-ditch effort to make the case for restraint and self-sufficiency, Beard in 1940 reiterated his arguments in *A Foreign Policy for America*, emphasizing that "foreign and domestic policies are inseparable parts of the same thing."[43] Reviving Wilsonian arguments about America's grandiose obligations to the rest of the world, FDR was taking the United States into the war to compensate for the inadequacies of his own New Deal. Thus, when Roosevelt vowed in the fall of 1940 that American boys would not be fighting in another foreign war, Beard *knew*—at least to his own satisfaction—that the president's promise was a cynical political gesture that he had no intention of honoring.[44]

Thirteen months later—a period that saw the passage of Lend-Lease, the tightening of sanctions against Tokyo, offers of military support to China and the Soviet Union, and the launching of an undeclared naval war in the Atlantic—Japan bombed Pearl Harbor. The argument about whether or not the United States would avoid involvement in another world war abruptly ended. Brooding and embittered, disregarding his expressed belief that war is not the work of demons, Beard proceeded to construct his own "devil theory" to explain American intervention, with Franklin Roosevelt standing in for

Satan. After the war, at precisely the moment—the onset of the Cold War—when the myth of Roosevelt as heroic "soldier of freedom" stood at its zenith, he charged FDR with dishonesty and deception and with hijacking the Constitution. Critics rightly lambasted Beard's two books on U.S. entry into World War II as tendentious and mean-spirited. On Hitler, Roosevelt had been right, and Beard's 1940 prescription for U.S. foreign policy would have been a disaster.

Yet six decades later, with the United States now a globe-straddling colossus—but with peace nowhere to be seen—it becomes apparent that although he had missed one large truth, Beard had hit upon others. Resurrecting those other truths provides an essential point of departure for understanding American statecraft today.

▶ Like Beard, William Appleman Williams (1921–1990) was a midwesterner; but there any similarity in upbringing ends.[45] Williams was born and raised in Atlantic, a small town in rural Iowa. After his father was killed when the boy was eight, his mother left him temporarily in her parents' care, enrolled in college, earned a degree, and eventually returned home to reclaim care of her only child and to work as a schoolteacher. Williams later portrayed his mother as an exemplar of self-reliance and strong-willed individualism and his hometown as the embodiment of "community."[46] After high school, Williams spent a year at Kemper Military Academy on a basketball scholarship and won an appointment to the U.S. Naval Academy. Commissioned in 1944, Williams served until the war's end in the Pacific.

In 1947 Williams left the Navy to study history at the University of Wisconsin, an institution famous, among other things, for its "notorious loyalty" to the teachings of Charles Beard.[47] An assignment in Corpus Christi, Texas, just after the war, exposing him to racial segregation and the embryonic civil rights movement, had begun his political awakening. In short order, the heady progressivism of Madison completed his transformation into a self-described radical.

At Wisconsin, Williams earned a doctorate in U.S. diplomatic history. His first book, *American-Russian Relations, 1781–1947*, published in 1952, implicitly questioned orthodox views of the Cold War's origins, much as Beard had questioned the conventional wisdom about American entry into World War II. After a series of short teaching appointments elsewhere, Williams returned to Wisconsin in 1957 and quickly established himself in the front rank of American historians. Politically, he was also among the most controversial. Williams became the founding father and abiding inspiration of the "Wisconsin School" of revisionist history that examined the underside of U.S. foreign policy and found there an American variant of imperialism. With events in Cuba and then Vietnam lending added salience to his views, he gained access to noted journals of opinion such as *Commentary, The Nation,* and the *New York Review of Books.* On campus, he was a wildly popular teacher. During this period he published his two most influential works, *The Tragedy of American Diplomacy* (1959) and *The Contours of American History* (1961).

Though an avowed man of the left, by the mid-1960s Williams found himself increasingly out of sympathy with the political views of the Vietnam-era student radicals, among whom he had achieved the status of icon. He considered the antics of the counterculture to be childish and self-indulgent. He found the sexual revolution to be repugnant. In 1968, exhausted and with his personal life careening out of control, he fled Madison for the Pacific coast, where he remained until his death. Although he continued to write, he had little to offer except self-parody. Aside from a one-year term as president of the Organization of American Historians in 1980, his final years were largely reclusive.

In his writings, Williams freely acknowledged his debt to Beard at a time when Beard's professional reputation was hitting rock bottom. Insights taken from Beard—that foreign policy "is intimately connected with domestic affairs," that "empires are not built in fits of absent-mindedness," and that expansion "complicates and deepens" rather than resolves problems—provided the foundation of his own critique of U.S. history.[48]

Williams endorsed Beard's view that expansionism was integral to the American story. Rather than tracing the expansionist impulse to the rival visions of Jefferson and Hamilton, however, Williams saw it as an expression of a struggle for America's very soul. The crucial question was not whether American society would be predominantly rural or urban, or whether citizens would earn their livelihood as virtuous agrarians or as merchants, craftsmen, and factory workers. Rather, the central question was whether Americans would descend into shallow, grasping materialism or keep faith with the intentions of the Founders to create a "Christian commonwealth."[49] As Williams saw it, Americans faced a choice. They could either give themselves over to the pursuit of hedonistic and ultimately dehumanizing individualism, or they could accept "the demands and the self-discipline of living with other human beings in a truly responsible, humane fashion."[50] An expanding frontier and an expanding economy deferred the day of reckoning. Thus, the weltanschauung guiding American politics was a simple one: "problems are solved by growth or further expansion." As a result, according to Williams, a "charming but ruthless faith in infinite progress fueled by endless growth" became central to the American way of life. But the closing of the frontier by the 1890s and the onset of severe economic crisis in the same decade obliged Americans to look farther afield. Henceforth, expansion abroad "provided the *sine qua non* of domestic prosperity and social peace."[51]

But the United States pursued expansion abroad in a way that reflected particular American interests and values. After a brief, unsatisfactory experiment with old-fashioned empire in the wake of the Spanish-American War, American leaders abandoned efforts to assemble an array of distant possessions as the preferred means of sustaining economic growth. Given the costs of pacification, administration, and defense, colonies offered a poor return on the dollar. In addition, the nation's own revolutionary heritage and its traditional anti-imperial sympathies were at odds with the notion of U.S. soldiers subduing alien populations. The challenge confronting American leaders was to formulate policies that provided the benefits of empire without its burdens. In that regard, what mattered was not ownership or even administrative control but commercial access.

To secure that access, American leaders devised a supple and highly innovative strategy that Williams dubbed "Open Door imperialism." The famous Open Door Notes issued by Secretary of State John Hay in 1899 and 1900 both inaugurated this shift in strategy and provided its definitive expression. The Open Door Notes declared America's interest in preserving China's territorial integrity and in claiming for the United States the same privileges enjoyed in China by the European powers and Japan. Nominally, Hay's diplomatic initiative amounted to a brief on behalf of fairness. Williams saw it as much more. Underlying Hay's appeal to permit U.S. access to China's market were expectations that, given half a chance, Americans would reap more than their fair share of the benefits. An ostensibly level playing field actually tilted in favor of American enterprise.[52] In short, the policy of the open door was "a classic strategy of non-colonial imperial expansion." Moreover, the policy devised for China applied equally well to other regions of the world. Hence, concluded Williams, for decades to follow "the history of the Open Door Notes became the history of American foreign relations."[53]

In Williams' view, the architects of the open-door policy did not foist it on the masses. They had no need to: Americans embraced the policy as their own, because it encompassed aspirations that extended well beyond the economic realm. Bundled into the concept of openness were several other values. A world open to American enterprise and influence was a world conducive not only to economic opportunity but also to political liberty. In the eyes of most Americans, according to Williams, the two were linked inextricably. "Expanding the marketplace enlarged the area of freedom. Expanding the area of freedom enlarged the marketplace."[54] Openness became a precondition of freedom and democracy. It implied stability and security. (Resistance to openness evidenced untrustworthiness if not outright antagonism.)

America's own commitment to openness testified to its own benign intentions—and therefore justified American exertions on behalf of an open world. Openness was not simply a cover for exploitation. "Most imperialists believed that an American empire would be humanitarian, and most humanitarians believed that doing good would be good for business."[55]

The dogma of openness became a component of American ideology, the principle upon which the world should be organized, the basis for a broad national consensus on foreign policy, and a rationale for mustering and employing American power. In essence, wrote Williams, the open-door policy legitimated "the endless expansion of the American frontier in the name of self-determination, progress, and peace."[56]

Williams laid the template of the open door upon the major events of the twentieth century and pronounced the fit to be precise. In doing so he turned the myth of the reluctant superpower on its head. In taking the United States into World War I, Woodrow Wilson had revealed "the Imperialism of Idealism," a crusade to graft American values onto the entire world and to thwart all others—such as Lenin—who fancied themselves engaged in an analogous undertaking. The isolationism reputed to characterize American diplomacy during the interwar period was, according to Williams, little more than "legend." World War II—commonly viewed as a conflict thrust upon the United States and fought against aggression—became, in Williams' view, "the War for the American Frontier." But it was in interpreting the war's aftermath in light of the open door that Williams showed himself at his most audacious.

The war's end, wrote Williams, left Americans "casually confident that their earlier visions of Manifest Destiny were materializing as the reality of the present." Viewing the atomic bomb as a "self-starting magic lamp," they looked forward to the arrival of "their long-sought City on the Hill in the form of a *de facto* American Century embracing the globe." The officials who directed U.S. foreign policy took it for granted that "such benevolent Americanization of the world would bring peace and plenty without the moral embarrassment and administrative distractions of old-fashioned empires."[57]

Josef Stalin, however, entertained aspirations of his own. Refusing to open the devastated Soviet nation to the outside world, suspicious of Western eagerness to rebuild Germany, and determined to establish a protective buffer of compliant satellites, the Soviet dictator marked himself in the eyes of American policymakers as not only supremely ungrateful but also dangerous. His acquisition of the atomic bomb in 1949 confirmed his hostile intentions. Soviet military power now posed a threat without precedent. When other political movements, armed insurgents, and revolutionaries in Europe, Asia, and even the Western Hemisphere proclaimed fealty to socialism and looked to the Kremlin for support, officials in Washington concluded that the United States was facing a global conspiracy.

Williams rejected the orthodox view that fastened blame for starting the Cold War squarely on Moscow. Soviet behavior, he believed, could plausibly be explained as defensive in nature. It was the United States more than the Soviet Union that was bent on exploiting victory in 1945 to expand its influence, an effort consistent with America's long-term strategy of shaping a world order receptive to its own values and conducive to its own prosperity.

This version of the Cold War's origins all but ignored the character of the Soviet regime. The abuse of human rights, denial of freedom, and absence of democracy in the communist world did not figure prominently in Williams' narrative. Purges, mass starvation, the wholesale displacement of populations, and the system of prison camps that Aleksandr Solzhenitsyn labeled the Gulag Archipelago likewise received short shrift. Though careful not to defend communism as such, Williams could find no useful moral distinction between one side of the Iron Curtain and the other. "There is, and always has been," he observed in 1962, "good *and* evil in the United States, in the Soviet Union, in Nigeria, in Cuba, and on down the list."[58]

Williams' iconoclasm and polemical style were tailor-made for the 1960s. Discovering that the age of Eisenhower had been an era of repressive conformity, the products of Middle America who filled his classroom and the readers who devoured his books delighted in the zest with which Williams skewered sacred cows. Ostentatiously contrarian, he presented Abraham Lincoln not as the Great Emancipator martyred for the nation's sins but as the dark prince of capitalism. At a time when most Americans held Herbert Hoover personally responsible for the Great Depression, Williams celebrated the thirty-first president as a courageous visionary.[59] Favorable allusions to Karl Marx and Fidel Castro conveyed a frisson of bravura and insolence.

The decade's unfolding events—with the body count from assassination climbing, domestic turmoil on the rise, and Vietnam becoming the war without apparent end—transformed Williams, in the eyes of his admirers, from gadfly to seer. His critique seemed not only provocative but true; open-door imperialism made sense of developments that otherwise seemed senseless. Above all, Williams' insistence that America's never-ending quest for new frontiers invited the ultimate disaster—"the frontier was now the rim of hell, and the inferno was radioactive"—lent urgency to the efforts of those promoting radical change.[60]

Beard's attempt to legitimize a revisionist perspective on the origins of World War II had destroyed his reputation. In contrast, Williams' challenge to Cold War orthodoxy became both fashionable and immensely influential. The Wisconsin school did for all of U.S. diplomatic history what the revisionists of the interwar period had done for American entry into World War I. The new revisionists threatened the internationalist consensus undergirding postwar U.S. policy, and with it popular support for the ongoing crusade against communism. That prospect outraged and dismayed defenders of orthodoxy, both inside and outside the academy, among them the historian Arthur Schlesinger Jr., who was determined to "blow the whistle before the current outburst of revisionism regarding the origins of the cold war goes much further."[61] As in Beard's day, politics and scholarship had become inextricable.

What alternative did Williams offer to a strategy of continuous expansionism? With the rest of the world "clearly moving toward" a "true human community based far more on social property than upon private property," he wanted the United States to hop onto the bandwagon. The only real challenge left to Americans was "to create the first democratic socialism in the world."[62] But for all his apparent radicalism, the specific remedy he offered reflected a deep-seated conservatism—and was even more improbable than Beard's plea for Americans to tend their own garden while Nazi Germany was overrunning most of Europe.

For Williams, democratic socialism was indistinguishable from Atlantic, Iowa, in the 1930s. Above all, socialism meant community. Williams yearned to recover the remembered—or idealized—life of a small boy growing up in the American heartland, watched over by hardworking plain folk, who were neither corrupted by great wealth nor afflicted with extreme poverty. To revive that world, he believed, required an experiment in radical decentralization.[63] The radical historian's alternative to empire was to dismantle the Union of fifty states, "breaking the Leviathan into community-sized elements."[64]

Williams' advocacy of national dismemberment generated no discernible interest. By the end of the 1970s, his own growing disillusionment with the left had displaced nostalgia.[65] Apart from its opposition to the Vietnam War, the New Left had failed to develop a coherent program and had sunk into irrelevance.

In the last years of Williams' life, his grim warnings of Armageddon sounded increasingly preposterous.[66] The Cold War did reach a denouement, but it did so quietly. The Soviet empire rather than the American-led free world cracked up, and the United States reached a new apogee of power and self-confidence. By the time of his death, although Williams still commanded a following in faculty lounges, most Americans probably credited Ronald Reagan with possessing a surer—or at least more accurate—instinct for history.

Yet if the quiet passing of the Cold War demolished Williams' credibility as prophet and polemicist, it also made it easier to assess his scholarly legacy with dispassion. As with the master, so, too, with the disciple: lodged within the ruin of the enterprise Williams inspired lies much to inform our understanding of the present.

When Williams insisted in 1971 that "The issue is the nature and dynamic of the American empire, *not* the validity of Lenin's thesis," he was wrong.[67] If in 1971 Lenin's thesis did not qualify as the only issue, it certainly ranked as a very important one. Three decades later, with events having resoundingly exposed communism's failings, "the nature and dynamic" of American power has indeed become *the* question.

From Williams' efforts to understand American power, four noteworthy points survive. The first is that during the twentieth century the United States came to play a role that cannot be understood except as a variant of empire. That notion, employed in the midst of the Cold War more as an epithet than as an explanation, became by the 1990s almost a statement of the obvious. In the aftermath of the Cold War, references to an American empire or to American hegemony, which formerly came with barbs attached, were no longer fighting words. Though still avoided by government officials, such terms infiltrated the lexicon of everyday discourse about U.S. foreign policy. As even Schlesinger, Williams' particular nemesis, conceded, "who can doubt that there is an American empire?—an 'informal' empire, not colonial in polity, but still richly equipped with imperial paraphernalia: troops, ships, planes, bases, proconsuls, local collaborators, all spread around the luckless planet."[68]

A second element of Williams' legacy was to render untenable claims that this informal empire "just grew like Topsy," coming into existence as an accident of nature or an unintended consequence of events beyond American control.[69] Williams showed that the American empire emerged out of a particular worldview and reflected a coherent strategy to which the American people gave their support.

Third, Williams identified key elements of that American strategy. Building on insights first developed by Beard, he unearthed the assumptions underlying the doctrine of liberal internationalism, explained its logic, identified its purposes, and divined its implications. He showed that the essential aim of liberal internationalism was to open the world to American enterprise. He revealed the conviction, widely shared among successive generations of American statesmen, that only an open world could permit the American system of political economy to function effectively while also assuring U.S. national security.

Finally, Williams understood that in practice, the only sure way to guarantee openness was through the exercise of dominant power. Openness adapted the logic of empire to suit the needs of democratic capitalism.

Whereas Beard first identified the underlying logic of American expansionism, Williams went a step further, urging Americans to contemplate the implications of their imperium. "Assume empire is necessary," he wrote; "what is the optimum size of the empire; and what are the proper—meaning moral as well as pragmatic—means of structuring, controlling, and defending the empire so that it will in practice produce welfare and democracy for the largest number of the imperial population?"[70]

As the United States embarked upon a new century, those questions returned to the fore.

CHAPTER 2

GLOBALIZATION AND ITS CONCEITS

[H]ow near one to the other is every part of the world. Modern inventions have brought into close relation widely separated peoples and made them better acquainted . . . distances have been effaced . . . The world's products are being exchanged as never before . . . Isolation is no longer possible or desirable.

William McKinley, September 1901

WHEN PRESIDENT BILL CLINTON, speaking in the presence of President Jiang Zemin at a 1997 White House press conference, chastised the Chinese government for being on the "wrong side of history," he treated his listeners to a quintessentially American moment.[1] Standing at the epicenter of American power and authority, the president surveyed the vast panorama of the past and rendered judgment. In doing so, he was exercising a prerogative unique to this nation at this time.

Set aside the fact that the politician offering this sweeping pronouncement embodied a generation whose historical horizon barely extended to Chuck Berry and black-and-white television. Overlook the fact that few such presidential declarations are spontaneous, that Clinton's rebuke—ostensibly on behalf of democracy and human rights—was quite likely a calculated attempt to deflect criticism for wining and dining a bona fide despot in the White House. Whatever the messenger's motives, Mr. Clinton's utterance captured—and seemed to validate—the grand political postulate of the age.

The president's point, of course, was not simply that Jiang and his misguided collaborators were fighting a battle that they were destined to lose. Rather, it was that the United States had planted itself squarely on the right side of the historical divide. Indeed, as Clinton later explained with all the certainty and fervor of an old Marxist-Leninist ideologue, America itself had come to define "the right side of history."[2] It had blazed the trail that others followed. Progressive, forward-looking, divining the spirit of the age, America epitomized the destination toward which all humanity is inevitably traveling.

For proof, one need look no further than the outcome of the twentieth century's epic political struggles. In the end, war, revolution, insurgency, and international conspiracies pursued with totalitarian ruthlessness never really came close to displacing the American system, with its blend of individual freedom, popular government, and market economics. Rivals who once advanced counterclaims to having unlocked the secrets of history all fell by the wayside, their pretensions exposed as empty. Having vanquished all challengers, the juggernaut of liberalism rolled triumphantly on. No real alternative to that system existed: that, indeed, was Clinton's message to Jiang Zemin—and is contemporary America's message to the world.

The mission of the United States at the beginning of the new millennium was to coax others into acknowledging the direction in which historical forces pointed, to commend nations moving in concert with those forces, to chide those slow to get with the program. As Clinton told reporters a year later, explaining the rationale for his own trip to China, "one of the things I have to do is . . . to create for them a new and different historical reality." Reshaping China's view of the past would enable the government in Beijing to "feel more confident in doing what I believe is the morally right thing to do."[3]

As Americans, Secretary of State Madeleine Albright once remarked, "we have our own duty to be authors of history."[4] But this confidence that the United States at the dawn of a new millennium possessed the capacity not simply to discern but to direct history was not unique to President Clinton and members of his administration. Democrats and Republicans may cross swords about the feasibility of ballistic missile defense. They may differ on the wisdom of intervening in ethnic conflicts and may disagree about the danger posed by global warming. But these amount to little more than quibbles over operational details. When it comes to fundamentals undergirding U.S. foreign policy, consensus reigns on all but the extreme left and right. That consensus is so deep-seated that its terms have become all but self-evident, its premises asserted rather than demonstrated.

In 1999, for example, Condoleezza Rice, a Republican national security specialist, echoed President Clinton's judgment about America's role, employing precisely the same rhetorical formulation. The collapse of the Soviet Union and triumph of capitalism, in her view, demonstrated incontrovertibly that the United States had deciphered history's intent. Outlining the foreign policy challenges of the twenty-first century, Rice suggested that the essential question was whether or not the United States was "going to accept responsibility for being on the right side of history." If the nation failed to do so, missed opportunities would result and new threats to U.S. security emerge. In that event, she predicted that Americans two or three decades hence would be asking "why we were on the right side of history, and did not take care of this."[5]

In an essay published early in the run-up to the 2000 presidential campaign, Rice offered a purportedly Republican perspective on the post–Cold War world. "Dramatic changes in information technology and the growth of 'knowledge-based' industries [have] altered the very basis of economic dynamism," she wrote, "accelerating already noticeable trends in economic interaction that often circumvented and ignored state boundaries." The United States had "emerged as both the principal benefactor of these simultaneous revolutions and their beneficiary." She detected "powerful secular trends" that were "moving the world toward economic openness and—more unevenly—democracy and individual liberty. Some states have one foot on the train and one foot off." Yet this much was clear: "the United States and its allies are on the right side of history."[6]

The assumptions, the reasoning, the expectations all could have come from any Democratic or, for that matter, almost any of the ostensibly nonpartisan pundits, scholars, and analysts who make up the foreign policy establishment. Rice's "dramatic changes" referred to the information revolution. The accelerating economic interaction she cited was a reference to globalization. That the United States was principal instigator and leading beneficiary of these twin phenomena and that together they heralded a more open world had become the conventional wisdom of the 1990s. In an essay intended to explain how Republicans and Democrats differed on foreign policy, Rice demonstrated how much they had in common.

The information revolution and globalization did not constitute the substance of the foreign policy consensus, which predated by several decades the invention of the personal computer and the Internet. But together they enabled the keepers of that consensus to adapt it to an era in which the traditional rationale for American globalism—the existence of an overriding threat to the nation's very existence—no longer pertained. In the aftermath of the Cold War, the clichés of the information age imparted a gloss of novelty to what was in fact a time-honored approach to policy.

➤ Lending those clichés added weight was the widely accepted view that the events of 1989 marked a sharp break in world history. For decades, the Soviet-American competition had dominated and defined international politics. The resolution of that competition was said to have changed everything. "With the collapse of the Soviet Union, a new era in world history began."[7] When a centrist like Senator Richard Lugar, a stalwart Indiana Republican, expresses such sentiments, we know that they have become uncontroversial.

By implication, endgame in the Cold War signified the fulfillment of the strategy devised by Harry Truman, George Marshall, and Dean Acheson and refined by their successors. Containment had achieved its purpose and, having done so, had become obsolete. For specialists in international relations, 1989 became "Year Zero." When Madeleine Albright dismissed works of scholarship written prior to that year—"They are about as useful now as archeology; they are ancient history"—she endorsed this notion.[8] Such a perspective suited Albright's claim of participating in the Clinton administration's ostensibly grand reconceptualization of American foreign policy.[9]

But it did more than that: sealing the Cold War in amber struck preemptively against potential revisionism. For policymakers, the postwar decades retained utility chiefly as a vehicle for reminding Americans that statesmanship required boldness, courage, and perseverance—and deference to those in positions of authority. To interpret the Cold War as anything other than a heroic struggle on behalf of liberty—for example, to view it through the optic of U.S. policies *since* 1989—could jeopardize that freedom. Depicting 1989 as an unbridgeable divide—with a new era on one side and "ancient history" on the other—minimized that danger.

Yet the new era was not new simply because the Soviet threat had vanished. The defining characteristics of the era just begun were daunting complexity and profound change proceeding at a dizzying pace. By the 1990s it turned out that, at least by comparison, the Cold War had been a period of remarkable clarity and predictability.

"It was easy when we could simply point to the Soviet Union and say that what we had to do was to contain Soviet expansion," Secretary of State Warren Christopher reflected early in President Clinton's first term.[10] Clinton himself reportedly expressed nostalgia for the Cold War's comparative simplicity. General Henry Shelton, chairman of the Joint Chiefs of Staff during Clinton's second term, concurred. Reminiscing about the Cold War, he recalled: "Life was simpler back then. We lived in a black-and-white world. We knew who the good guys were and who the bad guys were. 'Us' and 'them' were easy concepts."[11]

Not so during the era following the Cold War. Surveying the world from the vantage of the 1990s, Christopher's successor, Madeleine Albright, remarked, "what we have out there is basically a much more complicated world." In that new world, Albright continued, "protecting our territory is a more complex issue than before. Protecting our citizens is more complicated . . . And then our way of life. Our way of life is extremely complicated and depends on a global economy, depends on not having drugs, depends on not having more refugees than this country can handle, disease coming in." As a result of such concerns, statecraft had become "a much more complex issue than it was at the beginning of the century."[12]

This complexity stemmed in part from the tempo of events, which by common assent was quickening. "The pulse of the planet has accelerated dramatically and with it the pace of change in human events."[13] Anthony Lake, national security adviser in Clinton's first term, spoke those words in 1993. But the conviction that change was occurring more rapidly was not peculiar to Democrats or liberals or members of a particular administration. It was one of those things that observers of world affairs simply knew to be true.

By common assent, the leading agent of change was the information revolution. According to Secretary of Defense William Cohen, a Republican serving a Democratic president, "a worldwide transition from military industrial economies reliant upon government capital to information-based economies reliant on intellectual capital" had commenced. "It's a trend, of course, that's now transforming virtually every aspect of our life the world over."[14] The "of course" was Cohen's way of acknowledging that he was merely expressing views self-evident to anyone claiming to be in the know.

As a result of the information revolution, distance had collapsed. According to President Clinton, "the world is growing smaller and smaller." Distance was losing its traditional significance. In the information age, remarked Madeleine Albright, "the idea of an ocean as protection is as obsolete as a castle moat." Everything was connected and everything was near at hand. "Technology is actually miniaturizing the globe," said Secretary Cohen. "I like to say that the globe is not much bigger than that ball that is spinning on the finger of science. If you think about it, the vast oceans have been reduced to ponds." Lands across the sea "are now almost as close as neighboring countries today. And it only takes a nanosecond for someone's voice or image to be transported to another country, so nothing is done in isolation today."[15]

The capacity to transmit and receive information in nanoseconds fostered the process of integration called globalization. But more than mere information was moving. Technological innovation and political principles, tastes and fashions all rode the electronic rails of the information age. More and more people were crossing borders in pursuit of opportunity, education, and pleasure (or mischief). The volume of goods being exchanged internationally continued to swell, as did the transnational flow of capital. As a result, declared Samuel R. Berger, Lake's successor as national security adviser, "we have experienced the emergence of a global economy and a cultural and intellectual global village."[16] As depicted by its proponents, globalization was not an emerging reality. It had *become* reality.

With its connotations of technological triumphalism, unprecedented affluence, and the implacable advance of democratic capitalism, globalization supplanted "Power to the People" as the preferred maxim of the baby boomers who set the agenda of American society. As depicted by its many boosters in and out of government, globalization was a force of nature, transforming politics and economics alike. No one made the point more succinctly than Thomas L. Friedman, foreign affairs columnist of the *New York Times*. "Globalization," he wrote, "is not just a trend, not just a phenomenon, not just an economic fad. It is the international system that has replaced the cold-war system."[17]

Friedman's views received a ringing endorsement from the Oval Office. Globalization, Bill Clinton declared, was "the central reality of our time," a revolution "that is tearing down barriers and building new networks among nations and among individuals."[18] The imagery of globalization and information technology demolishing barriers was one to which White House speechwriters during the Clinton era returned time and again. Describing globalization on another occasion, President Clinton waxed eloquent about the "worldwide changes in how people work, live, and relate to each other," characterizing them as "the fastest, and perhaps, the most profound in history." As a result of those changes, "The blocks, the barriers, the borders that defined the world for our parents and grandparents are giving way, with the help of a new generation of extraordinary technology. Every day millions of people use laptops, modems, CD ROMS and satellites to send ideas, products, and money all across the planet in seconds."[19]

The post–Cold War era thus acquired a distinctive identity: it was the Age of Globalization. For any nation or group to imagine that it could impede or deflect this transformation was the height of folly. According to Berger, "you can't stop globalization and you can't stop global integration." Or, more emphatically still: "we cannot turn back the tides of globalization any more than King Knute [sic] could turn back the tides."[20] Emphasizing that "the train of globalization cannot be reversed," President Clinton went on to explain the implications of what he called globalization's "inexorable logic": henceforth "everything, from the strength of our economy to the safety of our cities, to the health of our people, depends on events not only within our borders, but half a world away."[21] Again, the idea was not unique to a particular administration or party. Brent Scowcroft, the elder President Bush's national security adviser, agreed: "America has never been more dependent on the outside world for its well-being and that dependency is steadily growing."[22]

As such remarks suggest, American enthusiasm for globalization stemmed in part from the conviction in Washington that removing blocks, barriers, and borders served urgent American interests. "You know, we're going to do very, very well, as the world becomes more interdependent," President Clinton assured a student audience at the end of his second term.[23]

But if globalization, in the first instance, was an economic phenomenon, it was not only that. Its political, social, and cultural implications were no less profound. Though in an immediate sense about profit, globalization ultimately was about power. On the surface it promised a new economic order that would benefit all. Beneath the surface it implied a reconfiguring of the international political order as well. Globalization established the rules for the latest heat in the long-standing contest to decide which nation—and whose values—would predominate.[24] Writing in 1995, Speaker of the House Newt Gingrich depicted the stakes in precisely this way. If Americans seized the opportunity offered by globalization, they would bequeath to their children "a country unmatched in wealth, power, and opportunity." If they squandered that opportunity, they would "at best have a lower standard of living and at worst find that another country has moved into the new era so decisively that it can dominate us."[25]

Given the zero-sum basis of that competition, U.S. officials were understandably chary about discussing it too openly. But they did concede that globalization had a political dimension. According to President Clinton, "Globalization is empowering people with information, everywhere." The inevitable result was political liberalization: "The more people know, the more opinions they're going to have; the more democracy spreads."[26] "In the new century," Clinton suggested, "liberty will spread by cell phone and cable modem." This connection between the information revolution, globalization, and political liberalization figured frequently in discussions of China, widely viewed as the most likely challenger to American preeminence. Why were China's party leaders reluctant to conform to "the right side of history"? President Clinton offered a ready answer: "They realize that if they open China's market to global competition, they risk unleashing forces beyond their control," including a "greater demand for freedom."[27] But the new technology had doomed Beijing's old guard. If the fall of the Berlin Wall had not marked the official "end of history," then the creation of the Internet certainly had, at least in the estimate of enthusiasts. As Thomas Friedman gushed, "Globalization means the spread of free-market capitalism to virtually every country in the world."[28]

American policymakers were likewise reticent about discussing another facet of globalization: their confidence that the United States "owned" it. A central feature of the new era is that "Knowledge, more than ever before, is power," wrote Joseph S. Nye and William A. Owens, former high-ranking Pentagon officials. "The one country that can best lead the information revolution will be more powerful than any other. For the foreseeable future, that country is the United States."[29] On that score, reasoned Samuel Berger, the United States was the nation "best placed to benefit from globalization."[30]

But the meaning of "power" in the age of globalization was becoming increasingly diffuse. Nearly twenty years ago, Theodore Levitt, an early prophet of globalization, wrote that the emergence of a global market foretold "a general drift toward the homogenization of the world." According to Levitt, "nothing confirms this as much as the success of McDonald's from the Champs Elysées to the Ginza, of Coca-Cola in Bahrain and Pepsi-Cola in Moscow, and of rock music, Greek salad, Hollywood movies, Revlon cosmetics, Sony televisions, and Levi's jeans everywhere." "Different cultural preferences, national tastes and standards, and business institutions," Levitt concluded, "are vestiges of the past."[31]

In practice, as Levitt's list of brand names suggests, homogenization meant Americanization. As Friedman observed, "Globalization-is-U.S."[32] In a sense, the wonders of the digital age offered to the 1990s what the atomic bomb seemingly provided to the late 1940s: the technological means of ordering the world while fostering the spread of American values and assuring continuing U.S. preeminence.

To proponents of globalization, it was evident that the United States created the technology, provided the medium of exchange—in a global economy, American dollars and American English reign supreme—and prescribed the lifestyle to which the universal consumer aspired. The "global theme park" that Benjamin R. Barber labeled McWorld took its cues from American pop culture and showcased the latest handiwork of Hollywood, Madison Avenue, and Silicon Valley. According to Bill Gates, chairman of Microsoft, U.S.-based companies held positions of leadership "in almost every technology that will be a part of building the broadband infrastructure: microprocessors, software, entertainment, personal computers, set-top boxes, and network-switching equipment." When President Clinton announced that "We clearly have it within our means . . . to lift billions and billions of people around the world into the global middle class," the barely disguised subtext was one that most Americans find reassuring: globalization meant that "they" would become more and more like "us."[33]

As Clinton's remark suggests, globalization promised the creation of wealth on a scale hitherto unimaginable. Tapping this potential for a continuously expanding economic pie—benefiting all nations, but the United States most of all—became for American officials an abiding preoccupation. As Clinton phrased it, "we must never lose sight of what the fundamental problem is—we need . . . more growth in this world today."[34]

This preoccupation with growth—never absent from U.S. foreign policy, and by the 1990s even more explicit—meant that political economy took its place alongside (and in some respects supplanted) security as the paramount national interest. Traditional distinctions between the nation's physical security and its economic well-being were among the barriers that globalization swept aside. According to the emerging conventional wisdom, in the post–Cold War era "national economic interests should not be considered 'secondary' or subordinated to traditional security interests." "Broadly construed," national security henceforth included "both economic and geopolitical concerns."[35]

Even before Bill Clinton's inauguration in January 1993 and prior to his own confirmation as secretary of state, Warren Christopher was telling the Senate Foreign Relations Committee that among the three pillars of the new administration's approach to foreign policy, economic growth ranked first.[36] Clinton's creation of a National Economic Council (NEC) as a counterpart to the National Security Council at the outset of his first term testified to this reordering of priorities. According to Robert Rubin, who chaired the NEC before becoming treasury secretary, "the big change" introduced by Clinton's approach was that "the economic component of any problem gets on the table at the same time as other issues." In practice, the economic component meant expanding trade, gaining access for capital, and protecting property rights. As Mickey Kantor, chief trade negotiator during the first Clinton administration, proclaimed, "Trade and international economics have joined the foreign-policy table." Kantor described Clinton as "the first president to really make trade the bridge between foreign and domestic policy."[37]

In terms of historical accuracy, Kantor's claim of a Clinton administration "first" was bogus. Economic and commercial considerations had loomed large in American statecraft since the colonial era.[38] But as an indication of how policymakers viewed foreign policy after the Cold War his remark was revealing and important.

As depicted by those policymakers, a world transformed by the forces of globalization would allow little room for power politics and coercion. In a globalized world, concepts such as spheres of influence and balance of power—always viewed by most Americans as suspect—would lose their validity. War itself would face obsolescence. Instead, a web of efficient and well-regulated networks would bind nations together in a common pursuit of prosperity. Trade and investment would flourish, to the benefit of all. Economic development, in turn, would foster liberal ideals and a thirst for freedom. Popular government would spread, and, as Albright stated, "we know that democracy is a parent to peace." Democracies behaved themselves. They were, wrote Deputy Secretary of State Strobe Talbott, "demonstrably more likely to maintain their international commitments, less likely to engage in terrorism or wreak environmental damage, and less likely to make war on each other."[39] Peace-loving democracies, in turn, were ideally suited to collaborate in pursuit of sustained economic growth. The ultimate promise of globalization was of peace, prosperity, and democracy, all reinforcing one another in a self-perpetuating cycle.

This vision of a globalized world was replete with irony. On the one hand, those charged with responsibility for U.S. foreign policy portrayed a world in flux. The world that they depicted was experiencing changes unprecedented in speed and scope. The world in which they themselves had come to adulthood—defining wealth in terms of heavy industry, dependent on fossil fuels, preoccupied with power politics, and drenched in blood—was fast disappearing. A radically different order was emerging, indeed, was already at hand. That new order promised to be immensely complex, stemming in part from the fact that rapid, technology-driven change had now become a defining feature of life.

On the other hand, members of the foreign policy elite and high-ranking U.S. officials expressed confidence that they had divined the inner dynamic of this new order. They had discerned the means to tame it, to guide it, and to make it work for Americans and all others. On that score, they professed to have no doubts. They offered no ca- veats or qualifications. In this increasingly complex world, the for- mula for utopia turned out to be surprisingly straightforward. Thus, for example, Secretary Cohen identified just "two axioms" that the United States needed to impress on others. The first was that "democ- racy means stability." The second—and here Cohen cited a recent book that "reminded us that democracies do not fight one another"— was that "stability grounded in democracy is a precondition for en- during success in the global economy."[40] Q.E.D.

➤ Thus, globalization presented the United States with a combina- tion of imperative and opportunity. Framing—and in some respects complicating—the American response to this phenomenon were the "Three Nos" of contemporary U.S. foreign policy.

Belief in the uniqueness of the American experiment is deeply em- bedded in the nation's psyche. The United States is not only different. It possesses special responsibilities. "We Americans are the peculiar chosen people—the Israel of our time," wrote Herman Melville in 1850. "We bear the ark of the liberties of the world."[41] A century and a half later, this insistence that the United States, a great power unlike any other, retains a special mission to the world survived undimin- ished.

The three nos—no to power politics, to war, and to limits—sus- tained the myth of American exceptionalism into the post–Cold War era. At the same time, they imbued public discourse related to Amer- ica's role in the world and U.S. policies abroad with an element of surrealism. Certain obvious truths remained unuttered. Other dubi- ous propositions got repeated endlessly and went unchallenged.

The first of the three nos—to power politics—might also be known as the Wolfowitz Indiscretion. During the administration of George H. W. Bush, Paul Wolfowitz, a highly regarded national security spe- cialist, served as undersecretary of defense for policy, the third-rank- ing civilian official in the Department of Defense. Among his other duties, Wolfowitz was responsible for coordinating the annual review of the Defense Planning Guidance (DPG), one of the documents forming the basis of the Pentagon's system of planning, programming, and budgeting. In "normal" times, interest in the DPG did not extend much beyond the Pentagon. Changes from one year to the next tended to be incremental. Although it might redistribute service budget shares ever so slightly or determine the fate of some controversial new weapon system, the latest DPG could be counted on to leave overall strategy largely intact.

Wolfowitz understood that the early 1990s were not normal times. The Cold War had ended, and the apparent success of Operation Desert Storm had elevated American power and prestige to unparalleled heights. Believing the moment ripe for a full-fledged overhaul of national security strategy, Wolfowitz seized the opportunity. As he saw it, the annual review of the DPG, usually a matter of intramural concern, offered an ideal means of prodding not just the military but the entire national security establishment into reassessing American strategy.

For Wolfowitz, rethinking strategy required a frank acknowledgment of actually existing power relationships combined with an unsentimental appraisal of long-term U.S. interests. The draft DPG prepared under his supervision offered both. The central reality of the new era was American preeminence. At the moment, plausible challenges to that preeminence did not exist. The paramount interest of the United States was to perpetuate that situation.

Accordingly, the document that Wolfowitz drafted in the wake of the Persian Gulf War called for U.S. strategy to focus henceforth on "convincing potential competitors that they need not aspire to a greater role or pursue a more aggressive posture to protect their legitimate interests." Properly conceived, American policies would "sufficiently account for the interests of the advanced industrial nations to discourage them from challenging our leadership or seeking to overturn the established political and economic order." Beyond such efforts to co-opt the willing, however, it was also incumbent upon the United States to "maintain the mechanisms for deterring potential competitors from even aspiring to a larger regional or global role."[42] Though couched in measured language—"mechanisms" was a euphemism for superior military power, for example—the draft DPG was in effect a blueprint for permanent American global hegemony.

Which was precisely the problem. Wolfowitz's DPG abandoned

any pretence of reluctance about being a superpower. Worse, it implied a radical departure from the conception of international politics embedded in Woodrow Wilson's Fourteen Points, Franklin Roosevelt's Four Freedoms, or John F. Kennedy's unconditional promise "to assure the survival and success of liberty." *That* was the language of American statecraft. The draft DPG's candor—with the interaction of power and interests eclipsing universal ideals as the grammar of statecraft—had a decidedly alien ring. That such an approach might have found favor in nineteenth-century Paris or Berlin was perhaps to be expected, but it would not in twentieth-century Washington, D.C.

Predictably, in March 1992 Wolfowitz's draft, then circulating for comment within the executive branch, leaked to the press. Once public, it encountered furious criticism, fueled in part by the fact that it was an election year. Critics professed shock that U.S. officials would conceive of America's role in such terms. Though more colorful than most, the comments of Senator Alan Cranston captured the essential point. The Democrat from California derided the Bush administration for proposing to make the United States "the one, the only main honcho on the world block, the global Big Enchilada."[43] Such a goal was arrogant, foolhardy, and, most of all, un-American.

Embarrassed, the Bush administration quickly disowned Wolfowitz's handiwork, depicting it as the musings of an insignificant lower-tier appointee acting without official sanction. When an approved Defense Planning Guidance did eventually emerge, it had been purged of all offending references suggesting big enchilada–like aspirations. The resulting document, published in the very month that Bush left office, contented itself with vague references to preserving the "strategic depth won at such great pains" during the Cold War but emphasizing the U.S. preference for acting in concert with its allies.[44]

Wolfowitz had been indiscreet. He had openly suggested that calculations of power and self-interest rather than altruism and high ideals provided the proper basis for framing strategy. For his candor, Wolfowitz himself was roundly denounced. But an important lesson had been learned. No other responsible official in the Bush administration—or in the successive administrations of Bill Clinton and the younger Bush—repeated his mistake. The calculus of power that is inherent in the very nature of politics did not disappear, but it remained hidden from public view. In the new unipolar moment, the function of foreign policy discourse was not to inform Americans or to promote a serious dialogue about the implications of global preeminence. Rather, its purpose was to reassure the public that the promotion of peace, democracy, and human rights and the punishment of evil-doers—*not* the pursuit of self-interest—defined the essence of American diplomacy. To the extent that interests figured at all, policymakers typically insisted that American interests and American ideals were congruent. Opening markets abroad might serve U.S. economic interests—but the real aim was to promote liberalization and democracy. Military intervention in the Balkans might be necessary to sustain American claims to leadership in Europe—but it was advancing the cause of human rights that really explained U.S. actions.

The second of the three nos—the no to war—found expression in Albright's Rule. A prominent player in American diplomacy throughout most of the 1990s, first as U.S. ambassador to the United Nations and then as secretary of state, Madeleine Albright may in the end be best remembered for her vigorous advocacy of the expansive use of American military power.

If the American-led success in the Persian Gulf War of 1990–91 made U.S. military superiority manifest to all, it also left the impression that the United States would, as a matter of course, use its military power selectively and with restraint. Certainly, that was the clear preference of the military itself, led by a generation of officers whose views on the appropriate use of force stemmed directly from their searing Vietnam experiences twenty or more years earlier. Foremost among those officers was General Colin Powell, the telegenic, politically savvy, and immensely influential officer who from 1989 to 1993 served as chairman of the Joint Chiefs of Staff. Powell believed passionately in the Weinberger Doctrine—criteria governing the use of force enunciated by Secretary of Defense Caspar Weinberger in 1984.[45]

The purpose of the Weinberger Doctrine was not to facilitate but to inhibit. It established a set of demanding preconditions for committing U.S. forces abroad. Intervention should occur only when vital national interests were at stake. When the United States did intervene, it should do so "wholeheartedly, and with the clear intention of winning." Clearly defined political and military objectives should guide any campaign. No administration should order U.S. troops into harm's way without "some reasonable assurance" of popular and congressional support. Last but not least, the United States should never use force except as a last resort.[46]

In effect, Weinberger codified the military's own lessons of Vietnam. As the Defense Department's senior civilian official, he fixed his personal seal of approval to a set of propositions that his soldiers viewed as immutable truths. Indeed, the purpose of the Weinberger Doctrine was less to promote the efficacious employment of American power than to preclude any possible repetition of the disaster that had befallen the military in Southeast Asia.

Several years later, when the Bush administration responded to Saddam Hussein's invasion of Kuwait by dispatching U.S. troops to the Arabian Peninsula, key officials went out of their way to show that there would be no repetition of the errors that had led to disaster in Vietnam. There would be no micromanagement, no political meddling, no half-measures, and no quagmire.[47] In that sense, the Gulf crisis of 1990–91 became a test case for the Weinberger Doctrine. Senior civilians, beginning with President Bush, and senior military officers, led by Powell, made a concerted effort to portray Desert Shield and Desert Storm as military campaigns designed and conducted with Weinberger's admonitions in mind.

That the war ended in military victory, cheaply and quickly won, seemingly validated Weinberger's approach. As principal steward of that approach and chief military architect of victory, Powell himself acquired enormous additional standing with the public and the press, so much so that in the media the Weinberger Doctrine was promptly eclipsed by a nearly identical Powell Doctrine. That Powell's own frequently expressed convictions—above all a belief in overwhelming force employed decisively on behalf of vital interests—would henceforth constitute "the American way of war" seemed all but self-evident. Indeed, the Bush administration's subsequent reluctance to intervene in the horrific civil war in Bosnia testified to the authority of the Powell Doctrine and of Powell himself.

Madeleine Albright would have none of that. At the outset of the Clinton administration, she chided Powell for his reluctance to employ American military prowess to sort out the problems besetting various hot spots in the Balkans, the Horn of Africa, and the Caribbean. "What's the point of having this superb military that you're always talking about," she wanted to know, "if we can't use it?"[48]

Such a seemingly cavalier willingness to put G.I.'s in harm's way infuriated Powell. But the view that Albright expressed was not merely her own. As others have noted, the end of the Cold War and victory in the Gulf triggered a remarkable ornithological reversal in which old hawks became dovish and doves of impeccable pedigree suddenly evinced fiercely hawkish inclinations.[49] Albright exemplified this transformation: in the heady aftermath of Operation Desert Storm there was abroad in the land a growing inclination to employ American military power as a swift sword to set things right.

But eagerness to "use" the military did not imply eagerness for war. On the contrary, in professing their devotion to peace, Albright and her colleagues in the Clinton administration were no less sincere than their Cold War–era predecessors. Yet in seeking to establish the *basis* for that peace, the temptation to capitalize on America's strong suit—military striking power—became well-nigh irresistible.

For Albright, an appetite for coercion was not to be confused with being bellicose or with courting full-scale armed conflict. Attempting (without success) to drum up popular support for punishing Iraq during one of the periodic U.S. showdowns with Saddam Hussein, she made the point explicitly. Critics who worried that then-pending air attacks might plunge the United States into a messy, protracted struggle just didn't get it. "We're talking about using military force, but we are not talking about a war," Albright snapped during a presentation to university students in February 1998. "I think that is an important distinction." Throughout the sundry military enterprises of the 1990s —some as modest as single salvo of cruise missiles, others as extensive as bombing campaigns lasting weeks or even months—American officials clung resolutely to this distinction. The cause of peace and justice might from time to time impel the United States to use force; but peace-loving Americans did not make war on others: that was Albright's Rule.

Indeed, Albright's distinction between force and war became central to U.S. foreign policy in the age of globalization. War typically involves suffering, bloodshed, loss on a large scale. Waging war implies national sacrifice. War gives birth to unintended and unforeseen consequences. The horrific record of the preceding century suggested that war by its very nature was uncontrollable. Time and again, statesmen presuming to bend war to their own designs—most notably in 1914 and 1939, but also in 1965—instead cast their own nation and others into the abyss.

Force, as conceived by Albright's Rule, obviated such concerns. Henceforth, military power was not to be unleashed; it was doled out in precisely measured increments. The use of force against carefully selected targets—preferably inanimate objects—precluded the prospect of slaughter. By capitalizing upon advanced technology to deliver ordnance from afar, targeting opponents presumed to have little or no capacity to retaliate, the United States minimized the risk to its own forces. Expending American military power for limited and carefully (indeed, often publicly) delineated purposes while avoiding the prospect of anything resembling "combat" all but eliminated uncertainty.

Colin Powell retired from active military service before the end of 1993. In short order, the Clinton administration also eased into retirement the doctrine associated with the general's name. Albright's Rule prevailed and spurred innovative thinking about the proper relationship between diplomacy and military power. Powell's own successors found such thinking increasingly congenial to the Pentagon's interests. Shedding old inhibitions, Americans became more comfortable with the use of force. Hardly noted, U.S. foreign policy became increasingly militarized.

The last of the three nos—the no to limits—might also be known as Tarnoff's Taboo, in honor of Peter Tarnoff, who served Clinton as undersecretary of state for political affairs. In the spring of 1993, with the Clinton administration still getting its footing in foreign affairs, Tarnoff hosted a handful of reporters for breakfast at the State Department. The purpose of the event was to provide selected journalists with an appreciation of the new administration's evolving approach to foreign policy. Tarnoff intended that his remarks be not for attribution. To his considerable chagrin, and the administration's embarrassment, they became front-page news.

The newspaper reports that appeared—citing the remarks of an unnamed senior official—conveyed the impression that the George McGovern wing of the Democratic party circa 1972 had seized control of the State Department. The official—soon revealed to be Tarnoff—seemingly made a point of *lowering* expectations that U.S. diplomacy was likely to accomplish very much. "We simply don't have the leverage, we don't have the influence, we don't have the inclination to use military force, we certainly don't have the money to bring to bear the kind of pressure which will produce positive results anytime soon."[50] To dismayed critics, such sentiments suggested timidity and faint-heartedness.

Like Wolfowitz just a year earlier, Tarnoff seemed to cast doubt on America's claims to uniqueness. Wolfowitz had erred in basing his Defense Planning Guidance on the premise that when it came to foreign policy the United States, like any other nation, should take considerations of power and interest into prime account. Tarnoff made a similar error by implying that in assessing what it could realistically accomplish in the world the United States, like any other nation, needed to recognize the very real limits of its capabilities. Like Wolfowitz, Tarnoff had committed heresy and found himself roundly chastised as a result.

As quickly as the Bush White House had abandoned its undersecretary of defense for policy, the Clinton White House disowned its undersecretary of state for political affairs. Tarnoff's boss, Secretary of State Warren Christopher, took immediate action to correct the unfortunate impression left by his subordinate's remarks. Within twenty-four hours, he used the occasion of a previously scheduled speech to make the point that the foreign policy ambitions of the Clinton administration were anything but puny. In describing America's role, Christopher employed variants of the terms *lead* and *leadership* no less than twenty times.[51]

The controversy that Tarnoff unwittingly stirred up soon blew over. Yet, as had Wolfowitz, he taught an important lesson. America's claim to global leadership was sacrosanct. Never again would any high-ranking official express doubts on that score. Henceforth, Tarnoff's Taboo remained inviolate.

➤ Indeed, apart from Tarnoff's egregious misstep, in their appreciation of America's proper role in the world, Democrats and Republicans spoke with impressive unanimity: there existed no substitute for U.S. leadership. The one thing that could derail the prospects for creating peace and prosperity in the age of globalization would be for the American people to succumb to the temptations of isolationism, as they were reputedly wont to do.

According to Brent Scowcroft, who had served two Republican presidents as national security adviser, American leadership remained "the indispensable ingredient in fashioning a stable world order." No other nation, combination of nations, or international institution could do the job. They were all too inept, too weak, or too parochial. "Whether we like it or not," Scowcroft observed, "the U.S. alone can provide that leadership." For Americans to fail in their obligation to lead, in Scowcroft's view, was to court disaster. "Left to its own devices, history will sooner or later serve up another nasty surprise." Jack Kemp, Republican vice-presidential candidate in 1996, agreed. "Quite simply, America must lead," he remarked. Newt Gingrich went even further. "Unless we accept our role as world leader, our planet will eventually be a dark and bloody place," predicted the speaker of the U.S. House of Representatives. "No other nation is in a position to assume our mantle." President George H. W. Bush's view, expressed in the concluding paragraph of his foreign policy memoir, was that "If the United States does not lead, there will be no leadership."[52]

The opinions expressed by Scowcroft, Kemp, Gingrich, and the elder President Bush not only commanded support throughout their own party. They also corresponded with the Democratic conviction that "the United States has an absolutely inescapable obligation to lead."[53] Thus, according to Strobe Talbott, "If we do not provide international leadership, then there is no other country that can or will step in and lead in our place as a constructive, positive influence." Addressing an audience of cadets at West Point, Vice President Al Gore seconded that motion: "America's destiny is to lead, not retreat," he said. "We will not be daunted. We will not be deterred" until the "great worldwide march to democracy" reaches its goal. Cribbing a phrase favored by Madeleine Albright, Bill Clinton declared definitively that "America remains the indispensable nation."[54]

Others not only want the United States to lead; they are counting on it. As Gingrich wrote, "No country has ever had the potential to lead the entire human race the way America does today. No country has ever had as many people of as many different backgrounds call on it as we do today. No country has ever had as many neighbors who suspect, distrust, and, in some cases, hate one another call on it to help achieve peace and help transform conflict into community. No country has ever had as many former dictatorships call on it for advice about how to create free government, free markets, and a military that can operate within the rule of law and under civilian control."[55]

The nations of the world feared one thing only: that the American people might flinch from fulfilling their obligations and turn their backs on the world. According to Kemp, "if the people of the world could vote by secret ballot, they would reject the idea of giving their own representatives power at the expense of the United States. They are seriously looking up to us . . . for guidance in how to make the coming century one of harmony and prosperity . . . Mankind did not struggle over all these millennia to see America—the nation of nations—finally get to the top, only to find it pulling the ladder up and resolving to keep the rest of the world in its place, underfoot and outside our borders." As the last, best hope of mankind, the United States "cannot afford to let the future take care of itself."[56]

What precisely does "leadership" entail? As employed in contemporary discourse about U.S. foreign policy, this most important term came to be freighted with multiple meanings. Leadership imposed obligations, and it bestowed prerogatives. As the world's sole remaining superpower, the United States shouldered the former and enjoyed the latter. America was not simply one sovereign nation among many. Leadership connotes relationships based on deference and respect. It confers authority. It justifies the acquisition of immense power. Wielded by others, that power might appear threatening, but in the leader's hands it is by definition benign. The leader does not exploit or dominate but acts on behalf of purposes that look beyond mere self-interest. "Much of our energy at the State Department," explained Madeleine Albright, "is spent encouraging foreign governments to act for what we perceive to be the common good."[57] Leadership suggests an ability to rally others in a worthy cause. But the leader may—at times, must—act unilaterally when consensus proves elusive. Leadership implies influence—the ability to affect events without the necessity of actually expending power. But absent regular reminders of the leader's willingness and capacity to act, influence becomes a wasting asset. So reputation and credibility matter. As a result, leadership is never passive. Nor do the matters within its purview have fixed limits; indeed, they are infinitely expansible. "American leadership is not divisible," Samuel R. Berger avers.[58] If the United States fails to lead *here,* then its capacity to lead *there*—and eventually everywhere—may be called into question. The credibility of American leadership ranks among the greatest of the nation's assets and must continually be reaffirmed.

Ultimately, leadership requires vision and power. At the dawn of the Cold War, in perhaps the most famous essay on U.S. foreign policy ever written, the diplomat George Kennan expressed gratitude to providence for granting to Americans "the responsibilities of moral and political leadership that history plainly intended them to bear."[59] When Kennan wrote those words in 1947, the awesome power of the atomic bomb, possessed by the United States alone, seemed to offer proof positive that providence had singled out America to usher history toward its preordained destination.

Far sooner than many analysts expected, the United States lost its nuclear monopoly. Similarly, from time to time in the decades that followed events challenged Kennan's confident assertion regarding history's intentions. But in the 1990s, with the Cold War safely won and American power greater than ever, Kennan's successors in the foreign policy establishment embraced his conviction with a vengeance. Indeed, they asserted claims going beyond Kennan's own. The providential gift of leadership, they contended, endowed the United States with a unique capacity to decipher history and an inescapable responsibility to bring it to fruition.

Supporting that conviction was a belief that the international environment offered a moment of unprecedented opportunity. The transition from the Cold War to the age of globalization had created an environment peculiarly malleable—and therefore receptive as never before to America's universal message of liberty, democracy, and market economics. Globalization had become the new magic lamp. Now was the time, therefore, to make good on America's obligation to secure the adoption of those values everywhere, offering "our creative, entrepreneurial society with more and more personal freedom" as the model for the rest of the world to adopt.[60] That the continuing success of democratic capitalism at home depended upon the creation of an integrated world order conducive to private enterprise simply lent to the enterprise an acute urgency. For the world's well-being and its own, the United States had to seize that opportunity before it vanished. Charles Beard's trenchant observation, made with regard to an earlier era, applied precisely to Americans in the aftermath of the Cold War: "The structure of their ideas and the structure of their interests coincided with impressive exactness."[61]

Reinhold Niebuhr was right. Americans—at least those Americans charged with framing the nation's basic policies—do view themselves as "tutors of mankind in its pilgrimage to perfection."[62] In that sense, the advent of the age of globalization permitted the United States to return to its true vocation. Yet as Niebuhr fretted, that vocation is fraught with hazards, political, strategic, and, above all, moral. Niebuhr's contemporary George Kennan himself recognized those perils—or at least came to that recognition over time. But the available evidence indicates that Kennan's successors in the post–Cold War era remained oblivious to them.

CHAPTER 3

POLICY BY DEFAULT

Whether the United States shall actually acquire territorial possessions, shall set up captain generalships and garrisons, [or] whether they shall adopt the middle ground of protecting sovereignties nominally independent . . . is a matter of detail . . . [What matters] is that the United States shall assert their right to free markets in all the old countries which are being opened to the surplus resources of the capitalistic countries and thereby given the benefits of modern civilization.

Charles A. Conant, September 1898

IN ADAPTING U.S. FOREIGN POLICY to the end of the Cold War, the contribution of the first Bush administration was tentative and incomplete. A president demonstrably uncomfortable with what he called "the vision thing" was not well equipped to rearticulate the basis of U.S. strategy in the midst of seemingly unprecedented change.[1] Moreover, the president surrounded himself with advisers who mirrored his own strengths and limitations. Deeply imbued with the habits of the Cold War, they did not easily shed those habits, regardless of the developments that were all too obviously shattering a status quo with which they had grown comfortable. Yet in ways that Bush himself hardly recognized, his administration began the process of modifying (not abandoning) long-standing premises of U.S. policy to changing conditions, handing off this effort to his successor, who would complete it.

Having schooled himself over a period of decades in the arcane skills required to be a great Cold War president, George Bush had the luck to become chief executive just as those skills became obsolescent. Taking possession of the Oval Office in January 1989, Bush was the equivalent of an ace typewriter repairer issued his master mechanic certificate just as the age of personal computing was dawning.

The men forming the inner circle of Bush's foreign policy and na-

55

tional security counselors—Brent Scowcroft, Secretary of Defense Richard Cheney, and Secretary of State James Baker—came out of the same mold. Scowcroft, a retired Air Force general chosen by Bush to be national security adviser, had already completed one tour in that post during the administration of President Gerald Ford. Cheney, a former member of Congress, had served with Scowcroft during the Ford years as White House chief of staff. Baker—who of the three claimed the most intimate relationship with Bush—was likewise a veteran of the Ford administration. But Baker had come fully into his own during Ronald Reagan's two terms, achieving prominence first as White House chief of staff and then as secretary of the treasury.

The Bush team lacked the hard ideological edge of the administration it replaced. Whereas a viscerally anticommunist, archconservative temperament had suffused the Reagan White House, the quality shared by Bush's senior appointees was pragmatism. Scowcroft, Cheney, and Baker—like Bush himself—were proven commodities, respected for their prudence and judiciousness. As seasoned Cold Warriors, they were intimately familiar with a clearly defined problem set governed by well-established rules: superpower summitry and alliance management, credible deterrence coupled with arms control, constant probing for marginal advantage at the expense of the Soviet adversary—all undertaken with one eye fixed on the overriding imperative of avoiding any misstep that might destabilize East-West relations. On matters of high policy, Bush and his advisers were not given to risk-taking or to flights of fancy. They were stewards not visionaries, technocrats not philosophers. Touting his qualifications to serve as secretary of state, James Baker—describing himself with evident pride as "more a man of action than of reflection"—claimed simply that he brought to Foggy Bottom "the necessary political and negotiating skills to perform credibly."[2] What precisely was to be negotiated was, by implication, all but understood, requiring neither explanation nor consideration. Baker's long memoir of his tenure in the State Department reflects that assumption: it offers detailed accounts of innumerable trips and high-level meetings, laced with anecdotes but devoid of all but the most superficial reflection.

"Coming into office with a relatively open and flexible frame of mind," wrote Baker, "I think I was ready to roll with the changes better than others might have been."[3] This inclination in the midst of upheaval to "roll with the changes" defined the Bush approach to foreign policy. Rolling with change did not imply passivity. But it did suggest a preference for established routines. When President Bush soon after his inauguration directed the National Security Council to undertake a full-scale review of U.S. national security policies, he emphasized that "I do not expect this review to invent a new defense strategy for a new world." Existing fundamentals remained sound.[4]

When events rendered particular routines patently irrelevant, the Bush administration improvised, frequently demonstrating considerable skill in the process. But Bush and his advisers never found a way to repackage American strategy in a way that took into account the rapidly changing circumstances triggered by the events of 1989.

In short, Bush and his team could never quite bring themselves to let go of the Cold War paradigm that they had for so long viewed as sacrosanct. Even when so much was in flux, old habits proved almost impossible to break. Consider Brent Scowcroft's reaction to the breakup of the Soviet Union in December 1991. Contemplating the implications of this event, arguably the most portentous in the latter half of the twentieth century, Bush's national security adviser confined himself to calculating how it might "serve to dilute the size of [a nuclear] attack we might face."[5]

To be sure, facilitating the transition from one era to the next is a necessary and difficult task. In guiding the bitter Soviet-American competition to a quiet dénouement, Bush and his advisers could take justifiable pride. The administration's signature achievement—securing Germany's unification within NATO in 1990—erected safeguards against any possible recurrence of the "German problem" and paved the way for the United States to remain the dominant power in Europe. This was a triumph of statesmanship afterward too casually taken for granted.[6]

Yet veterans of the Bush team tried to claim credit for more than just ushering out a dying era. By their own account, they also acted as midwives to the new.

They staked that claim above all on the administration's handling of the Persian Gulf crisis of 1990–91, the episode of which Bush himself was clearly proudest. *A World Transformed*, the foreign policy memoir coauthored by Bush and Scowcroft, makes the point. All but ignoring other significant events—such as the U.S. invasion of Panama to overthrow Manuel Noriega and American policy toward China after the massacre in Tiananmen Square—the authors largely confined their attention to two topics: reaching endgame with the Soviets and responding to Iraq's invasion of Kuwait. As if to emphasize their belief that little else really mattered, their composite account ends abruptly in December 1991 with the collapse of the Soviet Union. Bush and Scowcroft thereby ignore altogether the administration's final fourteen months, a period including the Bosnian civil war, U.S. intervention in Somalia, negotiation of the North American Free Trade Agreement, and further jousting with Saddam Hussein.

Their focus on making the case that the Bush presidency produced a global transformation led Bush and Scowcroft to interpret the end of the Cold War and the liberation of Kuwait as events of comparable importance. Indeed, they depicted the two as melding into a single coherent whole. From the outset of the Gulf crisis, wrote Bush, "we had started self-consciously to view our actions as setting a precedent for the approaching post–Cold War world."[7] That precedent would, in the administration's view, imprint onto the era just dawning several grand truths extrapolated from the era coming to a close.

If properly handled, the Gulf crisis would first of all affirm that stability remained the international system's paramount value. Prompt and unerring punishment of Iraqi aggression would restore the admonitory relevance of Munich. Second, expeditious handling of the Gulf crisis would permit the United States to show that it had fully absorbed and digested the lessons of its own recent past, especially those stemming from the Vietnam War. As the United States embarked upon the post–Cold War era, it would leave behind the inhibitions induced by past failures. Third, ousting Saddam Hussein's army from Kuwait would showcase the capabilities and competence of the U.S. military. In addition to justifying the hugely expensive defense buildup of the preceding decade, such a campaign would demonstrate the utility of American military power, now outside the context of the Cold War. Among other things, such a demonstration would preempt anticipated calls for drastic cuts in defense spending, thereby making it possible to preserve the military primacy that the United States had sought to maintain throughout the postwar era. Finally, the Gulf crisis would validate America's continuing capacity to exercise global leadership—thereby giving the lie to forecasts, then much in fashion, that the United States faced imminent decline, its standing soon to be eclipsed by economic powerhouses like Japan or a just-reunified Germany.[8]

All these depended on a decisive victory at reasonable cost by the United States and its coalition partners. In the event, the success achieved by Operation Desert Storm met—and indeed surpassed—expectations for such a victory. In liberating Kuwait, the Bush administration seemingly made a clean sweep. Iraqi aggression *was* turned back. As the president himself proclaimed, the United States *had* "kicked the Vietnam syndrome." "The troops" performed splendidly, not only earning public adulation but also squelching any inclination to make the end of the Cold War an occasion for haphazard demobilization. Rather, after Desert Storm, the United States tacitly committed itself to maintaining its military dominance in perpetuity. Finally, Desert Storm put paid to vaporous predictions that Japan or Germany might soon overtake America. The United States emerged from the war as the acknowledged "sole superpower," with challengers to that title nowhere in sight.[9]

The war's dramatic outcome created a moment seemingly pregnant with possibilities. Addressing a joint session of Congress in the immediate aftermath, President Bush spoke of "a new world coming into view" and outlined the prospects for a "new world order."[10] Yet few of the Gulf War dividends anticipated by the president and most other observers actually materialized. In the end, the precedents ostensibly established by the triumph in the desert did not count for all that much.

Part of the problem stemmed from a misreading of the war's significance, both military and political. As a feat of arms, the American-led victory in Desert Storm just might qualify as the most overblown achievement since the U.S. Navy, nearly a century before, handily dispatched a rickety Spanish fleet in Manila Bay. Like Admiral Dewey's storied victory, Desert Storm appears in retrospect far less momentous than it seemed at first blush while giving rise to outcomes far different from and more problematic than those anticipated when the smoke of battle first cleared. Above all—and contrary to expectations—the liberation of Kuwait, like the naval action off Manila, ended up being decidedly peripheral to the era that it inaugurated.

Dewey's success confronted the administration of William McKinley with an unexpected question: what should the United States do about the Philippines? McKinley's answer—annexation and an effort to uplift "little brown brother"—led in short order to a protracted, costly, and at times ugly pacification campaign and handed the American military planners a strategic dilemma—how to defend this distant possession—with which they wrestled unsuccessfully for four decades. In short, Dewey's victory gave birth to more problems than benefits.[11]

Something of the same can be said of Desert Storm. This late-twentieth-century equivalent of a "splendid little war" was by no means without positive effects: the desert campaign broke Iraqi military power, dealt a setback to Saddam Hussein's efforts to acquire weapons of mass destruction, and secured Western access to Persian Gulf oil. But few of the expected second-order benefits actually accrued. Indeed, the war's legacy proved to be both less and more than advertised.

Among other things, the Gulf War itself was less novel than it first appeared. To dazzled onlookers the advanced weaponry employed conveyed the impression of revolutionary advances in military art. But Desert Storm was less a trial run for a new style of war—a harbinger of the so-called Revolution in Military Affairs—than a final demonstration of methods dating to World War I. The liberation of Kuwait provided the concluding reel in a long-running serial, a final, picture-perfect display of mechanized industrial-age warfare as it had evolved over the larger part of a century.

That the show was a spectacular one is beyond dispute. Whether Desert Storm possessed any salience beyond the particular setting of a fight in the Arabian desert against an unwieldy and poorly led Soviet-style army was not necessarily self-evident. On that score, however, Bush himself had no doubts. He expected that exhibiting American military might in the Gulf would have a broad salutary effect. "I would think because of what has happened," he remarked just after Desert Storm, "we won't have to use U.S. forces around the world. I think when we say something is objectively correct . . . people are going to listen."[12]

As events would prove, however, some people did not listen—or, in listening, drew different conclusions. The Somali warlord Mohamed Farah Aidid, the megalomaniacal Serb nationalist Slobodan

Milošević, and the radical Islamic terrorist Osama bin Laden, for example, evaluated the performance of American legions in the Gulf much as the Filipino nationalist Emilio Aguinaldo had assessed Admiral Dewey's squadron floating in Manila Bay: American military power was impressive, certainly, and hardly to be ignored; but its existence did not necessarily preclude effective resistance to U.S. policy.

In 1898 Aguinaldo was willing to bet that it did not. The result was the long and bloody Philippine Insurrection, to which American authorities responded with more repression than uplift. Although U.S. forces eventually put down the Filipino uprising, they quickly found that the majestic white warships embodying America's emergence as a great power were of little use in the effort. Establishing U.S. authority in the islands demanded methods that were primitive and brutal. "Civilize 'em with a Krag"—a reference to the Krag-Jorgenson rifle carried by American infantrymen—became the operative slogan for the bloody campaign that ensued.

In the 1990s, Aidid, Milošević, and bin Laden, each in his own way, made a bet similar to Aguinaldo's. And once again the ultramodern symbols of American power, so effective in the circumstances of Operation Desert Storm, proved to be of limited utility.

In terms of its political significance, too, the Persian Gulf War failed to live up to expectations. In truth, Bush's hoped-for "new world" wasn't really very new at all; it was pretty much like the old one, albeit with Cold War–induced tensions and dangers removed. But the easing of those tensions proved to be a mixed blessing. To an extent too little appreciated at the time, the Cold War had imposed a measure of discipline on the international system. The end of the Soviet-American rivalry—and especially the demise of the Soviet Union itself—released long-pent-up centrifugal forces. Rather than a new world order, the result was a world of increased disorder infecting areas of acute sensitivity. Although Saddam Hussein's reckless invasion of Kuwait was among the first manifestations of this disorder, it was by no means the last.

In short, although in some quarters the demonstration of American prowess in Operation Desert Storm inspired awe and deference, elsewhere it did not. For those unwilling to abide by the rules of George Bush's vaguely defined new order, the "lessons" of the Persian Gulf War suggested not overwhelming American strength but vulnerabilities they might be able to exploit. Among those potential vulnerabilities, three stood out: expectations that high technology would provide U.S. forces with a decisive edge, skittishness about engaging in intense combat in close quarters, and lack of ruthlessness.

As a result, contrary to Bush's expressed expectations, in the aftermath of the Gulf War the United States found itself employing its military forces more frequently rather than less. "The troops" shouldered a plethora of new missions in strange and distant places. Although critics associated this increased willingness to use force with Bush's successor, the phenomenon most emphatically began while Bush occupied the White House. It was President Bush who in 1991 committed the United States to protecting Iraqi Kurds and Shiites from the depredations of Saddam Hussein—a commitment leading to the creation of quasipermanent "no-fly zones" patrolled by U.S. aircraft over northern and southern Iraq. The following year it was Bush who sent American troops into Somalia, a humanitarian intervention of unprecedented scope and ambition. And it was Bush who in the waning days of his administration inaugurated the practice—soon to become routine—of using pinprick air attacks against Iraq to express displeasure with Saddam Hussein.[13]

So the war touted as setting powerful precedents ended up setting next to none. Even at his moment of supreme triumph, Bush himself seemingly had an inkling of what the future might hold. Recording in his diary on February 28, 1991, the congratulations of his subordinates as Operation Desert Storm wound down, Bush noted uneasily that he himself was experiencing "no feeling of euphoria." The president sensed that victory had left much unresolved. "It hasn't been a clean end," he wrote with evident disappointment; "there is no battleship *Missouri* surrender. This is what's missing to make this akin to WWII, to separate Kuwait from Korea and Vietnam . . ."[14]

Of course, the same could also be said of the end of the Cold War. In that regard, too, there had been no formal surrender and no final accounting. The collapse of the Soviet empire resolved some very large questions and left others dangling. It also created daunting new challenges. Rooted intellectually in a world created by the crises of the 1940s, Bush was simply not up to the task of explaining how those less than clean ends—eastern Europe throwing off the yoke of communism, followed by the disintegration of the Soviet Union— connected seamlessly to the next chapter in an unfolding narrative.

➤ To be fair, it is not clear that any of Bush's Cold War predecessors would have done any better had the Soviet empire collapsed on their watch. Yet when it came to articulating a new rationale for U.S. strategy, apart from the clumsily conceived and hastily disowned Wolfowitz Indiscretion, Bush and his team made little effort even to try. So the president was left to mouth platitudes. Given the troubling reality of post–Desert Storm developments in the Soviet Union, the Balkans, and the Horn of Africa—which belied expectations of a "new world coming into view" and to which the Bush administration responded with manifest reluctance or not at all—phrasemaking alone was not good enough. The "new world order" soon enough became a staple of jokes on late night talk shows.

The impression took hold that Bush possessed neither the historical imagination nor the moral sensibility to comprehend all that the fall of the Berlin Wall signified. Speaking from the "bully pulpit," he failed to convey any real sense of conviction. His administration's involvement in four highly controversial incidents only cemented this impression.

The first occurred during the run-up to Operation Desert Storm. In the months following Saddam Hussein's forcible absorption of Kuwait into Iraq in August 1990, as U.S. forces flowed into Saudi Arabia, Americans assessed the stakes in the Persian Gulf and debated whether those stakes were worth fighting for. Neither defending the Saudi monarchy nor restoring the emir of Kuwait to his throne—both regimes unsympathetic to Western notions of democracy and human rights—qualified as likely to advance the cause of freedom. With the Cold War now essentially over, Iraqi aggression, unlike other Middle East crises of recent memory, did not represent a continuation of the Soviet-American competition by other means. There was no evidence that the Kremlin was in any way complicit in Saddam's actions. Nor was the U.S. economy directly dependent on oil imported from Kuwait. Most Persian Gulf oil went to Western Europe, where eagerness to fight for the emir was muted at best, and to Japan, where it was nonexistent.

Bush's announcement in early November that he was ordering the deployment of additional troops to create an "offensive option" roused the skeptics even further. Admiral William J. Crowe, Colin Powell's predecessor as chairman of the Joint Chiefs of Staff, was among those warning that "the U.S. initiating hostilities could well exacerbate" Middle East tensions and calling on the Bush administration to "give sanctions a fair chance."[15] Zbigniew Brzezinski, the normally hawkish national security adviser to President Jimmy Carter, concurred. He testified that the interests at stake in the Gulf were neither vital nor urgent and that any war would be "highly counterproductive"—inflaming the Arab world, roiling Middle Eastern politics, and alienating America's European allies.[16] Opinion polls showed that public approval of the president's handling of the Persian Gulf crisis had plummeted some thirty points since the beginning of the crisis in August.[17] Was restoring the independence of Kuwait worth the bones of even a single American grenadier?

The following month Secretary of State James Baker inserted himself into the middle of this debate, taking it upon himself to bring things "down to the level of the average American citizen." Even if the gas that Americans pumped into their automobiles did not come from the Persian Gulf, Baker could explain why Kuwait was worth fighting for. "If you want to sum it up in one word," he remarked succinctly, "it's jobs."[18]

Whatever the accuracy of that assessment—and it was not entirely off the mark—Baker's formulation did not go down well with either the administration's supporters or its critics. "Blood for jobs" possessed none of the grandeur that Americans expected as a justification for sending U.S. troops into harm's way. Although Bush himself labored to invest the crusade to dislodge Saddam's forces from Kuwait with a sense of high purpose, the damage was done. His secretary of state had left the indelible impression that the calculations underlying administration policy in the Persian Gulf were merely crass.[19]

The second incident, occurring in the immediate aftermath of the infamous massacre in Beijing's Tiananmen Square, actually predated Baker's misstep regarding the Gulf conflict, but it did not become public knowledge until several months later. Beginning in mid-April 1989, Tiananmen had been the site of popular demonstrations, with ever-growing numbers of Chinese, many of them students, denouncing the regime and demanding freedom and democracy for the Chinese people. The events in Beijing inspired similar demonstrations in cities across China, posing a threat to the Communist party's hold on power. In May, in an effort to reassert its authority, the now thoroughly alarmed government declared martial law. When that action had no noticeable effect, the government upped the ante. On the night of June 3 heavily armed units of the People's Liberation Army—their actions broadcast live around the world—swept into the square and brutally suppressed the ongoing demonstration. Several hundred protesters—the exact number remains unknown—were killed outright. The crackdown in Tiananmen proper was followed by a wave of harassment, arrests, show trials, and imprisonment that crushed the prodemocracy movement.[20]

The Tiananmen incident created a furor in the United States. Influential voices in the media and Congress demanded that China be severely punished. Bush's own inclination was to condemn the crackdown publicly and to impose relatively mild sanctions on Beijing while working behind the scenes to limit damage to the Sino-American ties cultivated by every president since Richard Nixon. This was not any easy tightrope to walk. As Bush noted in his diary on June 20, "I'm sending signals to China that we want the relationship to stay intact, but it's hard when they're executing people, and we have to respond."[21] Chief among the signals that Bush sent was a personal letter to Deng Xiaoping in which the president all but apologized to the Chinese leader for the actions that the United States had taken.[22] Despite the fact that the administration had publicly declared a ban on "high level exchanges of government officials with the People's Republic of China," Bush proposed to send a secret emissary to Beijing.[23] Deng accepted Bush's offer, and before dawn on June 30 Scowcroft and Deputy Secretary of State Lawrence Eagleburger took off in an unmarked U.S. Air Force cargo plane bound for China.

In Beijing Scowcroft and Eagleburger conducted a series of cordial meetings with Deng and other senior Chinese officials. By his own account, Scowcroft told the Chinese that the sanctions being imposed on Beijing were intended for domestic consumption, describing them as part of an effort to "cope" with the uproar that Tiananmen had unleashed. "That is the crux of the problem President Bush now faces," he told Deng.[24] In essence, Scowcroft assured the Chinese leadership that that the events in Tiananmen Square need not jeopardize the underlying Sino-American relationship.

By July 3 the two American officials had returned home, convinced that their mission had succeeded on two counts: they had conveyed the president's reassurances to Beijing, and they had eluded discovery by the media. But even the best-kept secret has a limited life span. In this instance, it would not survive the year. In December 1989 Bush dispatched Scowcroft and Eagleburger on a second mission to Beijing. This one was not clandestine and became a public-relations calamity, famous for the photographs of a smiling Scowcroft exchanging toasts with the "Butchers of Beijing." Immediately after this second mission, word leaked of the earlier trip, undertaken less than a month after the Tiananmen massacre itself. The outcry was as loud as it was predictable.[25] Americans now knew what the government in Beijing had known since July: when it came to human rights, the Bush administration all along had not really meant what it had been saying; restoring Sino-American relations to business-as-usual took priority.

The perpetrator of the third gaffe was President Bush himself and occurred during his appearance before the Ukrainian Supreme Soviet in August 1991. Two years after Soviet satellites in eastern Europe had broken free of Kremlin control, non-Russian components of the Soviet Union itself—chief among them Ukraine and the three Baltic republics—were themselves now vying for independence. For decades American leaders had decried the fate of these "captive nations." Throughout the Cold War, calls for their liberation had been a staple of U.S. policy.

Just arrived in Kiev from his latest tête-à-tête with Soviet leader Mikhail Gorbachev, Bush used his visit to throw cold water on any such hopes. He cautioned his listeners—ardent nationalists—that "freedom is not the same as independence." In remarks seemingly designed to discredit Ukrainian politicians eager to break away from the Kremlin, the president warned that "Americans will not support those who seek independence in order to replace a far-off tyranny with a local despotism. They will not aid those who promote a suicidal nationalism based upon ethnic hatred."[26]

In the media, Bush's presentation became known as his "Chicken Kiev" speech. The label stuck. Whether intentionally or not, the president's remarks, which managed to be both strident and opaque, suggested an American preference for propping up the existing order even at the expense of denying the aspirations of peoples hitherto categorized as oppressed. From the administration's perspective, the status quo promised to be more lucrative. "Business is attracted to larger markets," Scowcroft explained to reporters accompanying Bush. "Therefore, a reversal of that in the Soviet Union would not enhance business."[27]

In the eyes of his critics, Bush's remarks seemed to indicate that the United States was abandoning principle, cynically tilting in favor of propping up an old, discredited, and bankrupt regime.[28] According to the conservative columnist William Safire, for example, the American president had "lectured Ukrainians against self-determination, foolishly placing Washington on the side of Moscow centralism and against the tide of history."[29] Expectations of profit had trumped the imperatives of freedom.

The final incident—and of the four the most damning—concerned Bosnia. During the Cold War, the vast majority of Americans had neither heard of nor cared about Bosnia-Herzegovina, one of the republics constituting the Yugoslav federation. But in June of 1991, with the secession of Slovenia and Croatia, that federation began to unravel. One consequence was a vicious civil war in Bosnia itself, pitting Bosnian Muslims, Croats, and Serbs against one another. Inspired by ethnic chauvinism and goaded by unscrupulous politicians, the combatants in this conflict perpetrated atrocities not seen in Europe since World War II. Bosnia's Muslims got the worst of it. In hopes of incorporating portions of Bosnia-Herzegovina into a Greater Serbia, Bosnian Serbs engaged in a conscious policy of "ethnic cleansing," killing or uprooting the Muslim population and laying siege to Sarajevo, site of a breakaway Bosnian government.[30]

Among American progressives Bosnia quickly achieved the status of a cause. Bosnia became to the early 1990s what Spain had been during the mid-1930s: a horrific war in its own right but one freighted with moral and political significance transcending the issue immediately at hand. Like Spain, Bosnia symbolized a much larger struggle. Whereas Spain had served as a proxy for the contest between communism and the dark forces of fascism, Bosnia pitted the hopes for humane, secular multiculturalism against the dark forces of ethnic intolerance infused with religious fervor. Through the artful selection and arrangement of facts, Bosnia, like Spain, became a compelling morality play.[31]

As Sarajevo rose to the status of Madrid or Guernica, Bush and his advisers were caught flat-footed. At least initially, Bush and his advisers saw Yugoslavia as a distraction, a problem to be contained and managed lest it divert attention from more important priorities such as Russia and the Persian Gulf. As a result, the administration's initial inclination was to define Bosnia as a European problem for the European Community to handle. A widely quoted remark by James Baker captured the essence of the administration's initial response to the breakup of Yugoslavia. With developments in Bosnia-Herzegovina recalling to some observers the events of the Holocaust, the secretary of state, speaking in the vernacular of his native Texas, insisted: "We don't have a dog in this fight."[32]

As to the proper U.S. role, the idea was to give the appearance of doing something while minimizing any actual commitment. In 1936 Franklin Roosevelt had with notable fanfare embargoed all arms shipments to Spain—an action that had the unintended consequence of working to the disadvantage of the Republican cause.[33] Similarly, in September 1991 Bush threw U.S. support behind a United Nations Security Council resolution prohibiting arms shipments to Bosnia— an action that had the unintended but predictable consequence of placing the Bosnian Muslims at a military disadvantage. As a practical matter, with Europe and the United Nations floundering in their efforts to restore peace to Yugoslavia, the effect of the embargo was to favor one of the "dogs" in the fight, namely, the Serbs, widely perceived to be the chief perpetrators of evil. On top of "blood for jobs" in the Persian Gulf, Scowcroft toasting the Butchers of Beijing, and Bush's Chicken Kiev blunder, the administration's Bosnia policy seemingly provided further proof that the reigning architects of U.S. foreign policy were morally obtuse.

➤ That impression stuck. Meanwhile, the impression that Bush and his team had demonstrated great skill in managing the Persian Gulf War—in the immediate aftermath of Desert Storm a sentiment all but universally held—did not. As year followed year with an unrepentant Saddam Hussein still in power, the war's outcome no longer appeared as decisive as it had in 1991. Expectations that the end of the Cold War, combined with victory in the Gulf, would give rise to a new world order likewise came to seem risible. With the passage of time, sustaining claims that the Bush administration had transformed the world became increasingly difficult.

Yet just as it would be a mistake to allow the elder Bush to dictate his own administration's foreign policy epitaph, it is foolhardy to assess the administration simply on the extent to which its own claims have or have not stood up. Giving George Bush his due requires looking beyond the handful of episodes that the former president himself claimed as the proper basis for evaluating his foreign policy legacy.

The actual theme of that legacy—revealed by words and actions that do not get highlighted in memoirs—is one of continuity, not of transformation. To an extent that neither he nor his saxophone-playing successor are wont to acknowledge, Bush sounded many of the notes that Bill Clinton subsequently wove into a finished composition and rehearsed endlessly through two terms as president.

The first hint that the end of the Cold War was unlikely to live up to its advance billing as opening up a new age requiring a completely new American strategy came even before Saddam Hussein invaded Kuwait. Indeed, it came within weeks of the fall of the Berlin Wall. George Bush inaugurated this ostensibly new era by doing precisely what American presidents had been doing regularly for the better part of a century—using U.S. military power to dictate political conditions in the Caribbean Basin.

In Bush's case, the target was Panama. More specifically, it was Manuel Noriega, an unsavory former Central Intelligence Agency asset who controlled Panama's security establishment and as Panama's de facto dictator had turned that country into a hub of drug trafficking and money laundering. More recently, Noriega had taken to harassing American soldiers and their family members stationed in Panama. Thugs in Noriega's employ had murdered one U.S. military officer and had assaulted the wife of another, outraging Bush. More oblique efforts to remove Noriega having failed, Bush and his advisers decided in December 1989 that it was time for direct action.

In the early hours of December 20, U.S. forces already stationed in Panama, reinforced by units flying in from bases in the United States—a total of 26,000 troops—launched an attack against the Panama Defense Forces and pro-Noriega paramilitary units. Within hours they destroyed or disarmed their opponents, deposed the Panamanian strongman, and installed as president Guillermo Endara, winner of an election that Noriega had annulled the previous May. Twenty-three American soldiers were killed along with several hundred Panamanians. Although Noriega himself eluded capture for an embarrassingly long time, the operation was a classic assertion of a great power's prerogative to police its sphere of influence.[34]

Throughout months of planning, the code name for this operation had been "Blue Spoon." Just prior to execution the Pentagon relabeled it "Operation Just Cause." No doubt Bush believed that his cause was just. But then so had every other president, from McKinley through Reagan, who had ordered comparable military operations throughout the Caribbean.

That tradition had originated in 1898, when, in the wake of Dewey's moment of glory, the United States forcibly ejected Spain from Cuba and seized Puerto Rico. It continued through the early decades of the twentieth century as the United States forced Colombia to relinquish Panama (thereby acquiring the right to build a canal through the isthmus) and sent U.S. forces—in some instances, on multiple occasions—into Cuba, Mexico, Nicaragua, Haiti, and the Dominican Republic. The stated rationale for these exercises in gunboat diplomacy, ordered by Republican and Democratic presidents alike, varied. But whether intended to protect American lives and property, to advance the prospects of democracy, or to foreclose the possibility of European meddling in the New World, the cause was, from a U.S. perspective, always just.

After a brief lapse during the period leading up to and during World War II, American interventionism in and around the Caribbean resumed. Whether using U.S. forces, covert means, or proxies, from the 1950s through the 1980s the United States intervened in Guatemala, Cuba, the Dominican Republic, Grenada, Nicaragua, and El Salvador. The announced rationale for military action changed, reflecting the ideological preoccupations of the Cold War. But whether it was Eisenhower destabilizing leftist regimes, Kennedy scheming to overthrow Fidel Castro, or Reagan sending U.S. soldiers and marines to rescue American medical students, presidential confidence in the righteousness of U.S. actions and in the American prerogative to intervene remained constant.

Operation Just Cause carried this tradition into the post–Cold War era. Bush's successor would build on that precedent, undertaking his own Caribbean intervention. More significantly, both Bush and Clinton expanded on the established practice of employing military power in the familiar confines of the "American Lake"; they now used U.S. forces to punish misbehavior and quell disorder in regions well beyond the Western Hemisphere.

In one of the first books to examine the events leading up to Operation Just Cause, the journalist Bob Woodward captured the essential point. Bush's actions in Panama showed that "The military was not going to play a smaller role in the new world, as some expected." Indeed, the scope of responsibilities assigned to American soldiers grew. In the years following Operation Just Cause, U.S. military power became not less important but more. As Woodward presciently observed, "It was moving to center stage."[35] Bush's own use of the military contributed mightily to that outcome.

➤ Bush's contribution to preserving the essential continuity of U.S. policy across the historical divide of 1989 extended beyond his use of force. In fact, all but buried in the dross of Bush's public papers are bits and pieces of the argument that Bill Clinton subsequently employed to justify American globalism, even after the original rationale for globalism—the existence of overriding threats to national security—had vanished. Adhering to the patterns of American statecraft first identified by Charles Beard and William Appleman Williams, Bush (the self-proclaimed conservative) cited and endorsed principles that Clinton (a supposed liberal) fashioned into a coherent description of the post–Cold War order and America's place in that order. Indeed, the basic ideas that Bush's successor would employ to recalibrate U.S. strategy were already in wide circulation during Bush's own presidency. All that was needed—and this was the one thing that Bush and his advisers were singularly ill equipped to provide—was packaging.

That Bush and Clinton spoke in the same terms highlights the perspective common to the two administrations—a fact that is frequently overlooked because of the tendency to confuse partisan posturing with genuine policy differences. Except in moments of extreme emergency (and even then, largely for tactical purposes), political opponents will seldom pass up the opportunity to score points at any president's expense. The belief that politics stops at the water's edge warms patriotic hearts, but throughout U.S. history it has been largely a fiction. Whatever slight restraining influence this hoary notion might once have exercised was swept away by Vietnam. Since the Nixon-Kissinger era, sharp, categorical, and unremitting criticism of each successive administration's foreign policy has become the norm, one unaffected by the end of the Cold War. Congressional opponents backed by like-minded ideologues castigate the president (whoever he happens to be) for being shortsighted, feckless, and timid—or of pandering to domestic interests. That was true of Democrats during the Bush presidency and of Republicans during Clinton's. For its part, the administration responds in kind, charging its critics with acting in bad faith and claiming that the occupant of the Oval Office alone acts for motives that rise above mere politics. Accepting this continuous volley of charge and countercharge at face value, journalists and historians frame the story of U.S. foreign policy accordingly, treating each administration as a discrete entity and emphasizing its claims to distinctiveness.

The result is to undervalue the evidence of continuity between administrations and, indeed, between historical eras. Yet when it comes to the fundamentals of U.S. policy, those continuities loom large. In foreign policy as elsewhere, the Clinton administration excelled not in creating something genuinely new but in gathering up ideas already in circulation and imparting to them a gloss of originality or freshness. In practice, Clinton and his advisers drew on basic ideas that Bush and his team had already put in play and that, indeed, formed the received wisdom of American statecraft accumulated across a century or more.

In that regard, five ideas stand out—each one embraced by Bush, each figuring in Clinton's rearticulation of U.S. strategy: the identification of interdependence as the dominant reality of international politics; a commitment to advancing the cause of global openness; an emphasis on free trade and investment as central to that strategy and a prerequisite for prosperity at home; a belief in the necessity of American hegemony—while avoiding any actual use of that term; and frequent reference to the bugbear of "isolationism" as a means of disciplining public opinion and maintaining deference to the executive branch in all matters pertaining to foreign relations.

To be sure, Bush was never the huckster for globalization that Clinton would become and indeed evinced little awareness of that concept. In Bush's public papers, for example, the term *globalization* appears only three times.[36] But Bush did promote the notion that the dramatic advances in information technology that were creating an increasingly connected world had significant implications for politics, both domestic and international. Addressing the United Nations General Assembly in the aftermath of the failed Soviet coup of August 1991, for example, Bush celebrated the fact that "In many parts of the world technology has overwhelmed tyranny, proving that the age of information can become the age of liberation."[37] Bush also anticipated Clinton (and echoed the views of American statesmen throughout the preceding century) in declaring that U.S. prosperity was dependent on economic conditions abroad. Reviewing what he called "some implications of the global economy" while campaigning for reelection in 1992, Bush declared: "When growth slows abroad . . . our own growth slows as well." Bush believed that "America will only grow in the next century if we can compete globally in every part of the world. So we must seize every opportunity to open new markets."[38]

Indeed, openness was the key quality that Bush intended U.S. policy to promulgate. "I see a world of open borders, open trade and, most importantly, open minds," he enthused to the General Assembly in 1990.[39] Always, when it came to openness, expanding U.S. access to markets abroad was the first order of business. Opening the world's markets would allow the United States to do well even as it did good. Leaving a meeting of the G-7 leading industrial powers in 1991, Bush proclaimed himself "more determined than ever to press for open markets, free and fair trade around the world, and open investment opportunities everywhere. This isn't to benefit solely the United States, and yes, we would benefit, but it is to benefit every single country that participates in achieving these goals."[40] Bush did more than just talk about openness. He pressed for it. In 1992 his administration successfully negotiated the North American Free Trade Agreement (NAFTA) with Canada and Mexico. The Bush administration also played a key role in founding the Asia Pacific Economic Cooperation (APEC) forum, which Clinton subsequently exploited in pursuit of U.S. commercial objectives in the Far East.

In Bush's view, the benefits of openness extended beyond the realm of economics. International commerce was as much about politics as about profit. Commerce, according to Bush, means "the exchange of goods and ideas that foster free markets, free governments, and ultimately freedom itself."[41] In an age of interdependence, domestic prosperity and world peace were becoming inextricably linked. Describing what he called his "Agenda for American Renewal" in 1992, the president told his listeners: "The most important thing that I've tried to say [is that], 'It's one global economy.' We are in this now together, linking international trade to opportunity for the American worker, linking international trade and global peace and security to prosperity for every American job holder."[42] By implication, in an open, interdependent world where peace, prosperity, and security were all intertwined, the scope of U.S. interests was limitless. There was nothing that did not matter.

Openness did not imply that no one was in charge. On that point, Bush entertained no doubts whatsoever: an open world was one over which the United States would necessarily preside. In their foreign policy memoir, the president and his national security adviser made that point explicitly. After the Persian Gulf War, Bush and Scowcroft had concluded that "It was important to reach out to the rest of the world," but, they noted candidly, it was "even more important to keep the strings of control tightly in our hands."[43]

Though not acknowledged with similar candor, control from time to time meant coercion, actual or implied. The key was to adapt the existing instruments of coercion to make them relevant to the tasks now at hand. Although the transition of the U.S. military from a warfighting establishment into a global constabulary occurred during the Clinton years, Bush gave impetus to that process. U.S. intervention in southeastern Turkey and northern Iraq to protect the Kurds and in Somalia in response to famine—ordered by Bush in 1991 and 1992 respectively—initiated the trend toward what the Pentagon was soon calling Operations Other Than War (OOTW). Neither bureaucratic euphemism nor a preference for benign-sounding operational code names like Provide Comfort and Provide Hope concealed the fact that in the wake of the Persian Gulf War the role of America's armed forces increasingly resembled that of a quasi-imperial police force.

Much the same could be said with reference to NATO, the U.S.-led alliance that was the jewel in the crown of Cold War security structures. The collapse of the Soviet empire might have suggested that

NATO had accomplished the purpose for which it had been created, permitting U.S. troops to come home and allowing Europe to attend to its defense without American assistance. Not so: the completion of one mission meant instead that NATO needed to find another. The actual conversion of NATO from a defensive alliance into a vehicle for projecting power "out of area" occurred during the Clinton presidency. But here, too, Bush put the wheels in motion. As the Soviet threat receded, it was Bush who discovered that "NATO is not simply a military pact joined only to face a common threat." Rather, he declared, the larger purpose of the North Atlantic partnership was actually to "enrich our peoples, create new opportunities, and fuel growth." Pursuing those expanded goals required the alliance to reinvent itself. "There is no question that NATO will change," Bush intoned. Central to that change was the creation of "highly mobile, multinational forces, greatly reduced in size but unmatched in human and technological quality," enabling the alliance to venture farther afield. That the United States would exercise a dominant voice in determining the use of those forces went without saying.[44] Bush's successor went far toward making that vision a reality.

What was the threat against which the U.S. military and allies would "defend"—with the meaning of that word now broadened to include elimination through offensive action? Bush also anticipated his successor in enumerating a laundry list of dangers, most of them having existed throughout the Cold War but after 1989 identified as increasingly acute. Among these dangers were narcotrafficking, terrorism, and the proliferation of weapons of mass destruction.[45]

But to judge by Bush's frequent remarks on national security, the most worrisome danger facing the United States lay not abroad but at home. As would be the case with Clinton, Bush professed to be mightily concerned that Americans after the Cold War would again succumb to the temptation to which he believed they were peculiarly susceptible: turning inward and ignoring the rest of the world.

No cause was more important than that of saving his fellow citizens from that error. Decrying the danger of isolationism became a frequent theme of the president's speeches. Bush denounced those who would "retreat into an isolationist cocoon." He railed against those "on the right and left [who] are working right now to breathe life into those old flat-Earth theories of protectionism, of isolationism." He even resorted to unvarnished demagoguery. At ceremonies marking the fiftieth anniversary of Pearl Harbor, the president declared that "isolationism flew escort for the very bombers that attacked our men 50 years ago," thereby finding the millions who before December 7, 1941, opposed U.S. entry into World War II guilty not simply of bad judgment but of treason.[46]

For Bush, the parallels between the end of the Cold War and the aftermath of the two world wars were self-evident. "As in 1919 and 1945, we face no enemy menacing our security," he remarked at Pearl Harbor. "And yet we stand here today on the site of a tragedy spawned by isolationism. And we must learn, and this time avoid, the dangers of today's isolationism and its economic accomplice, protectionism. To do otherwise, to believe that turning our backs on the world would improve our lot here at home, is to ignore the tragic lessons of the 20th century."[47]

There were in fact few indications that the American people after the Cold War were inclined to "turn their backs on the world"—few, indeed, that they had ever done so throughout their history.[48] But by reviving this shopworn refrain—and by portraying every foreign policy issue as a test of whether Americans would stay the course or shirk their duty to the world—Bush used isolationism as a calculated device for shoring up popular and congressional deference to the executive branch. Bill Clinton would do likewise.

➤ "The present international scene," George Bush reflected in retirement, "is about as much a blank slate as history ever provides."[49] That insight, at once plausible and wildly misleading, lies at the heart of Bush's shortcomings as a statesman.

To the extent that conditions beyond America's borders determined U.S. policy, events such as German unification, the collapse of the Soviet Union, and the liberation of Kuwait might have seemed to wipe clean the slate of history. But in attempting to fathom the implications of these developments, Bush and his advisers had little to go on. The resources that they drew on in approaching that world consisted of a handful of canonical lessons from World War II and the early Cold War: Munich, Pearl Harbor, Yalta, and Vietnam, with Truman's ill-fated decision to advance north of the 38th Parallel after Inchon and Kennedy's two Cuban crises as important addenda. Only when a particular event could be made to "fit" some part of Bush's modest repertoire—as when Saddam Hussein in the role of Adolf Hitler invaded Kuwait, standing in for Poland—could the administration fashion a reasonably sound response. When confronting events without obvious parallel during the 1940s, 1950s, and 1960s—the Balkans providing the most telling example—the president and his advisers found themselves at a loss. Hesitation and half-measures were the result. To the extent that the post–Cold War world did constitute a blank slate, Bush was singularly ill equipped to write upon it.

But to the extent that the true wellsprings of American statecraft lie within the United States itself, the events of 1989–1993 did not make an end to history. From this point of view, even to declare that a "new world order" was at hand was to sow confusion, making it difficult to recognize all that had *not* changed: first, that U.S. foreign policy remained above all an expression of domestically generated imperatives; second, that economic expansionism abroad, best achieved by opening the world to trade and foreign investment, was a precondition of America's own well-being and therefore the centerpiece of U.S. strategy; and third, that the cause of peace was best served by the United States' occupying a position of unquestioned global preeminence. The events of 1989 and thereafter had altered none of these firmly held convictions.

In short, the end of the Cold War left U.S. interests and the weltanschauung informing those interests intact. In some vague, inchoate sense, Bush understood that, as his rambling foreign policy speeches suggest. But Bush was not up to the task of transferring old wine into new bottles decorated with handsome new labels. It would be left to his successor to do that.

According to the oddsmakers, George Bush's victory in Desert Storm all but clinched his own election to a second term. When voters in November 1992 handed him instead a humiliating rejection, analysts attributed the outcome to Bush's mishandling of domestic issues and, above all, to a slack economy. In large part, no doubt, that analysis is correct. But Bush's defeat also reflected dissatisfaction with his handling of foreign policy. Defending his decision to send Scowcroft and Eagleburger to Beijing in the immediate aftermath of Tiananmen Square, the president had remarked in December 1989 that if the "American people don't like it, I expect they'll get somebody else to take my job."[50] Bush and his advisers did fail, egregiously so, to provide a satisfactory explanation for their China policy. But their failure was larger than that. It lay in their fumbling inability to articulate a plausible rationale for the exercise of U.S. power in a post–Cold War world. To provide that rationale the American people did indeed find somebody else to do Bush's job.

CHAPTER 4

STRATEGY OF OPENNESS

Fate has written our policy for us; the trade of the world must and shall be ours . . . And American law, American order, American civilization, and the American flag will plant themselves on shores hitherto bloody and be-nighted, but by those agencies of God henceforth to be made beautiful and bright.

Albert Beveridge, April 1898

AMERICA'S STRATEGY OF OPENNESS, in place for more than a century, derives from twin convictions widely held by members of the political elite and the foreign policy establishment. The first conviction is that robust and continuing economic growth is an imperative, absolute and unconditional. The aggregate wealth and sheer affluence of American society may be the greatest that the world has ever seen, but they do not suffice. In the aftermath of the Cold War, the famed slogan devised by James Carville during the 1992 Clinton-Gore campaign has enshrined itself as an inviolable rule of national politics: "It's the economy, stupid." According to Carville's Law, officeholders who allow the economy to stagnate get sent packing. Those who can plausibly claim credit for fostering prosperity, whatever their other misdeeds or indiscretions, win forgiveness—and re-election.

But the imperative of economic growth is not simply a matter of electoral politics. It also grows out of far-reaching changes in the nation's culture.

During the half-century following World War II, the bonds of American civic identity noticeably frayed. In his detailed and persuasive assessment of American community, Robert Putnam described the broad trend toward civic disengagement and the mounting sense of social isolation, both accelerating as the "long civic generation" that fought World War II began passing from the scene.[1] As one

79

consequence of the resulting "democratic malaise"—the term is Christopher Lasch's—the once robust plant of American citizenship withered.[2] Apart from a requirement to pay taxes, personal responsibilities demanded of the larger community during the 1990s were nil. Even in national elections, the majority of eligible voters could not motivate themselves to go to the polls.[3]

As for the ancient republican tradition that citizenship entailed a duty to contribute to the nation's defense, it got left behind on the near side of President Clinton's famous bridge to the twenty-first century. To the extent that some vestige of patriotism survived into the post–Cold War era, it did so as nostalgia, sentimentality, martial exhibitionism, and a readily exploitable source of entertainment. The moviegoers who thronged to *Saving Private Ryan* stood in awe of the "greatest generation," which had surmounted the Great Depression and won World War II. But they evinced little intention of modeling themselves after that generation and could not conceive of making comparable sacrifices on behalf of country.[4] The core values of the "bourgeois bohemians," constituting according to David Brooks the new establishment and defining the sensibility of the age, were individualism and freedom—chiefly their own personal freedom. Their missions were consumption and self-actualization. They exhibited little interest in enlisting in great crusades—especially if doing so threatened to crimp their lifestyle.[5]

In a society in which citizens were joined to one another by little except a fetish for shopping, professional sports, and celebrities along with a ravenous appetite for pop culture, prosperity became a precondition for preserving domestic harmony. Arguing on behalf of a populist vision of an engaged, independent, self-reliant citizenry, an acerbic critic like Lasch might rail against luxury as morally repugnant, insisting that "a democratic society cannot allow unlimited accumulation." But in reality the prospect of unlimited accumulation had long since become the lubricant that kept the system functioning. A booming economy alleviated, or at least kept at bay, social and political dysfunction. Any interruption in economic growth could induce friction, stoke discontent, and bring to the surface old resentments, confronting elected officials with problems for which they possessed no readily available solutions. Lasch may well have been correct in charging that "the reduction of the citizen to a consumer" produces a hollowed-out American democracy.[6] But by the 1990s no one knew how to undo the damage without risking a massive conflagration.

A second aspect of cultural change complicated the problem even further, namely, the growing confusion over whether and to what extent the United States qualified any longer as a "nation." Even before the Cold War had ended, in progressive quarters especially, a faint odor of disrepute had enveloped the very concept of nationhood. To the extent that nationalism implied a homogeneous outlook, values shared by the members of one group and distinguishing that group from all others, it was suspect. Among the enlightened, terms such as *nationalist* or *nationalistic* were understood as sinister code words suggesting suffocating conformity if not the threat of violence against those not qualifying for tribal membership or those violating its code.[7] By the end of the twentieth century, nationalism—still on display in places such as the former Yugoslavia and the Middle East—had become synonymous with bigotry and atavism.

Within recent memory, the proposition that the United States possessed its own distinctive national identity had been noncontroversial. That the project launched in 1776 had created a distinctively American "new man" was taken for granted. That as a result the United States differed from France or Japan as much as each differed from the other was all but self-evident. Indeed, documenting and celebrating those differences became a point of pride. Serious people— H. L. Mencken, Vernon L. Parrington, and, of course, the Beards— wrote thick, influential books limning the characteristics of "The American Language," exploring the "Main Currents of American Thought," and tracing "The Rise of American Civilization." Specialists surveyed the literature, art, music, and architecture produced on native grounds and saw there the outlines of a unique and vibrant American culture.[8]

The chief ornaments of that culture and their very distinctiveness offered cause for celebration: they testified to the peculiar genius of the American people. Indeed, a common American culture encompassed the character, ideals, and aspirations of all who lived in the United States, however recent and whatever the circumstances of their arrival. At least so the mythology of the melting pot prevailing through the first half of the twentieth century asserted.

In the second half of that century, serious people devoted them-

selves to debunking that notion and to demolishing the mythology
of a common culture. From its outset, the Cold War that began at
midcentury was a conflict fought on two fronts at once: a political and
military struggle abroad and a political and cultural struggle at home.
By the end of the twentieth century it was apparent that the side that
had won abroad had lost at home—and vice versa. In the external
conflict, the forces of democratic capitalism, led by the United States,
vanquished the forces of Marxism-Leninism, embodied by the Soviet
Union. But in the internal conflict, the cultural left prevailed, not by
destroying the right but by compromising it irredeemably. The counterculture of the 1960s had by the 1990s effectively become the dominant culture. As Eugene Genovese has explained, the débacle of
1989 may have "exposed the false premises on which the Left has
proceeded, but it has done so at a time in which the Right is embracing many of those premises, notably, personal liberation and radical
egalitarianism." Or, as Gertrude Himmelfarb, reflecting the chagrin of
many Cold Warriors, has observed: "Having been spared the class revolution that Marx predicted, we have succumbed to the cultural revolution."[9]

That cultural revolution invalidated the old notion of the American melting pot and replaced it with the creed of America as multicultural mosaic. As Michael Lind rightly noted, multiculturalism became
not simply a proposal or a possibility but "the de facto orthodoxy of
the present American regime."[10] According to the terms of that orthodoxy, the United States was called upon to become a country embracing no particular culture but one in which all cultures, values, and beliefs might enjoy equal standing. (In this context, President Clinton
professed to be troubled by the concept of "tolerance," since it seemed
to imply "that there's a dominant culture putting up with a subordinate one.")[11] No longer was the basis of society the individual created
in the image of God and possessed of inalienable rights. Rather it was
the group, its identity and interests determined by considerations of
race, class, ethnicity, gender, or sexual orientation.

In such a society anything smacking of enforced conformity was
bad; "diversity" by definition was good. Indeed, diversity bestowed legitimacy. Thus, in the workplace, the media, the arts, the university,
and throughout modern American politics, a commitment to "inclu-
siveness" became obligatory. Obeisance to diversity signaled that one

acknowledged (and repudiated) the error of viewing Americans as a people deriving a common identity from heterosexual white Protestant males whose forebears had arrived from northern and western Europe. To embrace multiculturalism was to renounce the old habit of "privileging" White Anglo-Saxon Protestant conventions (and hypocrisies). By default, the preeminent American value became recognizing the equal legitimacy of all values, all artistic traditions, all moral codes, all religions, and all "lifestyles." When Vice President Al Gore translated the motto *E pluribus unum* as "out of one, many," he committed a famous gaffe.[12] But his faulty translation captured quite nicely the emerging zeitgeist.

The terms of that zeitgeist complicated the crafting of U.S. foreign policy during the 1990s. In the midst of continuing cultural fragmentation, accurately discerning an overarching common interest became problematic. Mobilizing national power in pursuit of those interests posed a daunting challenge. The past practice of conceding such matters to the purview of the repressive "white patriarchy" whose authority cultural revolutionaries aimed to overthrow obviously would not do.

The notorious Whitney Museum Biennial of 1993 illustrated the point. To "absolve themselves" of cultural imperialism, visitors entering this exhibit of cutting-edge art were obliged to don buttons that read "I can't imagine wanting to be white."[13] But when it came to political, diplomatic, or military affairs, the traditional face of power *was* both white and male. A culture war seeking to discredit the white patriarchy found itself also compelled to discredit or transform the institutions that the patriarchy had created and over which it held sway.

The commissioning of female fighter pilots and black generals and the appointment of gay ambassadors and of Madeleine Albright and Colin Powell as successive secretaries of state were all touted as milestones in this effort to chip away at the dominance that straight white males enjoyed in the world of power. But however notable they may have been in a personal sense, these achievements were largely beside the point: in practice, the individuals involved proved to be far more likely to be transformed by their institutions than they were to become agents of fundamental institutional change.

Creating a policy elite that "looks like America" might appease some proponents of cultural change, but it would not remedy the underlying problem with which the culture war has confronted policy-makers: in practice, the abandonment of a common culture points toward the loss of collective purpose, especially if pursuing that purpose might entail sacrifice or loss.

To the curators who mounted the Whitney Biennial, their exhibit was a bracing expression of a larger enterprise to challenge limits, celebrate the marginalized, and settle scores with groups and institutions that had been the source of repression. To its critics, the show offered irrefutable evidence that that project was giving rise to a vulgar, debased, and narcissistic culture.[14] But the concern here is not with artistic merit. Rather, it is that in its disdain for national mythology, its rejection of the very concept of truth, and its embrace of "skeptical relativism," that project of which the Biennial is representative recasts America as an entity that no one in his right mind would view as worth dying for.[15]

In short, multiculturalism and value-free, nonjudgmental tolerance combined with an ever-widening definition of personal autonomy had produced indifference to the fate of the nation. In the wake of the cultural revolution, apart from providing an excuse for fireworks, quaint parades, and long holiday weekends, authentic patriotism had become absurd. By the 1990s Memorial Day was no more about revering those who had made the supreme sacrifice than Christmas was about recalling the birth of Jesus Christ. The common folk, bobbing along behind the tsunami of cultural change, may not have fully comprehended all that was transpiring. But the inhabitants of faculty clubs, board rooms, and editorial offices—that is, the privileged minority of citizens actually in the know—certainly did.[16]

For the would-be statesman, the implications were clear: an ever-expanding pie satisfying ever more expansive appetites was the only "crusade" likely to command widespread and durable popular enthusiasm. Political rhetoric might still swell with stirring Wilsonian allusions to democracy, peace, and freedom, but these amounted to little more than window dressing. They were not words entailing any obligation to act. Pressing for ever more material comforts and pleasures with ever fewer restraints on the sovereign self: this defined the closest thing to a national purpose. The condition might prove reversible, but by the 1990s at least the American people no longer held *in common* any higher purpose.

Old-line liberals and neoconservatives devoted to the spread of democracy worldwide or passionately committed to the protection of human rights and eager to expend serious national resources on behalf of those goals bridled at such an assertion. They insisted that American power had always served larger and grander purposes and that it must continue to do so. "Our mission is the advance of freedom," proclaimed Michael Ledeen, expressing sentiments common in this camp.[17]

In American political discourse today, such views are still accorded a place of honor, much as many a Bible remains prominently displayed even in households whose members have long since abandoned the church. The familiar language of idealism reassured Americans that they had not yet sold their souls. The homage regularly paid by senior officials to hallowed ideals was a way of asserting that self-interest alone did not explain U.S. policy and that in its willingness to take moral considerations into account the United States differed from every other great power in history. But homage should not be confused with influence. When it came to motivating the majority of Americans to throw their support behind a course of action, it was the rare policymaker who counted on Wilsonian ideals to carry the day.

➤ In addition to ever-increasing prosperity as the surviving residue of national purpose, a second conviction underlay the strategy of openness. The nation's political leaders and their economic advisers concluded that by itself the internal American market was insufficient to sustain the necessary level of economic growth.

Reiterating views that Beard and Williams attributed to prior generations, U.S. officials in the 1990s—especially members of the Clinton administration—concluded that American prosperity was unsustainable absent access to an ever-expanding array of lucrative new outlets for trade and investment. According to Warren Christopher, "We've passed the point where we can sustain prosperity on sales just within the United States."[18] Given the limitations of the internal market, expansion abroad became essential. Speaking with characteristic directness, Samuel R. Berger said that "we have to continue to open markets" for one very obvious reason: "because that's where the customers are . . . We have a mature market—we have to expand, we have to grow." Madeleine Albright agreed: "our own prosperity depends on having partners that are open to our exports, investments, and ideas." Or, most succinctly, "Growth at home depends upon growth abroad." Those particular words are Bill Clinton's, but the sentiment is one that both Democrats and Republicans have endorsed: if the United States is to expand economically, it has no choice but to look abroad.[19]

That said, the strategy of openness is not merely an avaricious scheme for increasing market share, of interest chiefly to entrepreneurs, plutocrats, and their tribunes in the Department of Commerce or the Office of the United States Trade Representative. In the age of globalization, economic considerations have become inseparable from those of national security. "Trade," according to Lawrence H. Summers, secretary of the treasury in Clinton's second term, "is the pursuit of peace by other means."[20] Both peace and prosperity require order. Both demand adherence to particular norms: respect for private property, financial transparency, and some semblance of checks on corruption. In that sense the strategy of openness encompasses and integrates a wide range of interests, both tangible and intangible. It is not simply the business of agencies concerned with economic or commercial policy. Architects of the strategy are just as likely to work in the State Department and the Pentagon. Indeed, they are as likely to work in Congress as in the executive branch and in the private sector as in government.

Although the strategy of openness implies expansion, it does not qualify as "imperialistic," at least in the conventional sense of the term. It is, for example, strongly averse to acquiring territory or colonies. But the strategy does seek to consolidate and even enlarge a particular conception of global order. More specifically, it seeks to make permanent the favored position that the United States enjoys as victor in two world wars and the Cold War, the furtive hegemony to which most Americans purport to be oblivious, but that others recognize as the dominant reality of contemporary international politics.

Thus, rather than a departure from past practice, the strategy of openness marks the fulfillment of that practice. Despite claims of novelty by its proponents, especially in the Clinton era, it is as much concerned with completing a project long under way as it is with striking out in some altogether new direction. Long before the Cold War ended, John Lukács noted with remarkable acuity that "If we judge events by their consequences, the great world revolutionary was Wilson rather than Lenin."[21] The strategy of openness returns to the revolutionary project that President Woodrow Wilson outlined during and immediately after World War I: bringing the world as a whole into conformity with American principles and American policies.[22]

The prevailing conception of America's role in world affairs does not easily admit to that of an engine of revolution. During the turbulent half-century from 1940 to 1990, the orthodox narrative characterized U.S. policy as an effort to *thwart* revolution, whether from the extreme right or the extreme left. Others attempted to overturn the existing international order; responding reluctantly to their provocations, the United States acted to preserve that order. Thus, during World War II the United States led a great effort to turn back German and Japanese aggression and restore peace. At the outset of the Cold War it rallied others to contain Soviet efforts to export Marxism-Leninism and to prevent the outbreak of a third world war. Conveying the impression that America's strategic orientation was defensive, the orthodox narrative served a useful purpose, endowing contemporary history with a powerful moral logic. Nor was the narrative wrong. It was, however, incomplete and therefore misleading.

To characterize any strategy as either defensive or offensive is to misconstrue the competitive nature of politics. Any strategy worthy of the name aims to protect important interests. But it does much more. It also aims to advance important goals. It attempts to limit efforts by competitors to increase their power. It also attempts to acquire power. It seeks to gain advantages, not only over adversaries but also at the expense of nominal allies. All these points apply to U.S. foreign policy throughout several decades of Cold War. As Ronald Steel has observed, it becomes clear in retrospect that containment *and* expansion formed the "twin anchors" of U.S. policy: "containment of Soviet territorial temptations through military and economic power; expansion through alliances, bases, investments, and bribes."[23] Yet until 1989 the anchor of expansionism remained largely hidden from view, concealed by incessant warnings about the omnipresent danger of communist aggression and the insistence of American political leaders that the imperative of defending freedom in the face of that danger provided the justification for U.S. policy.

By the end of the 1980s, with the Soviet empire now in a state of advanced decay, the ostensible threat posed by communism had become downright implausible. Containment—and seemingly, therefore, U.S. strategy itself—had outlived its usefulness. By the early 1990s, the irrelevance of guarding against communist aggression suggested the emergence of a policy vacuum, setting off a heated competition to devise a new strategic paradigm. Throughout the first decade following the end of the Cold War, the quest for the one Big Idea (or sound bite) to supersede containment continued unabated.

From the outset, that quest has been a phony one, as much an exercise in political theater as a genuine search for policy. Though seldom acknowledged as such, an operative strategic paradigm exists and claims broad bipartisan support.

The Big Idea guiding U.S. strategy is openness: the removal of barriers to the movement of goods, capital, people, and ideas, thereby fostering an integrated international order conducive to American interests, governed by American norms, regulated by American power, and, above all, satisfying the expectations of the American people for ever-greater abundance. The open world that describes the ultimate aim of U.S. strategy revives an approach to policy identified years ago by Beard and Williams and once subsumed within containment.

The strategy of openness may not be able to resolve all the anomalies or untangle all the contradictions of American policy since the fall of the Berlin Wall. Alone, it cannot explain why the United States in 1992 made a grand gesture on behalf of starving Somalis and then in 1994 callously ignored Rwandans suffering a far worse fate. Absent a larger context, it cannot explain why the United States began the 1990s insisting that the Balkans were a European not an American problem and ended the decade by exaggerating the plight of Kosovar Albanians to create a pretext for launching a war against Yugoslavia. At the end of the day, no single factor can account for every detail of U.S. policy abroad, in all its fits and starts. Certainly, one should never discount the extent to which pandering to a particular domestic constituency, the jockeying of opposing political parties or of rival government bureaucracies, or the yearning of a lame-duck president to leave a "legacy" may explain a particular initiative. But in the long view, and to a greater extent than any other factor, the pursuit of openness defines the essential azimuth of U.S. policy, a course set more than a century ago and followed ever since.

➤ As his résumé attests, George Bush fashioned a career out of being a Cold Warrior, a career culminating in 1988 with his election as president. The abrupt end of the Cold War a year into his presidency caught Bush by surprise. Rummaging through his own personal experience and his understanding of U.S. history for an explanation of what would come next, the president came up with useful if familiar odds and ends: the importance of American leadership backed by military strength, the efficacy of market principles, the value of free trade, and, of course, the evils of isolationism. But Bush failed to mold these elements into a fully realized explanation of where history was headed now that communism had failed and the Soviet Union had ceased to be America's archenemy.

As a candidate for president, Bill Clinton liked to play up his own connection with and appreciation for the long struggle against communism. "I am literally a child of the Cold War," he proclaimed on the stump.[24] In reality, Clinton's immediate, personal engagement with the Cold War was negligible. During the watershed decade that began in the mid-1960s, he had not gone to Vietnam, where he might have risked being killed. Nor had he taken the equally honorable path of actively resisting the war, which carried the risk of prison. Rather, Clinton artfully steered a course that enabled him to avoid military service while preserving his "viability" for a career in politics.[25]

In truth, the Cold War did not figure prominently in Clinton's worldview and possessed little relevance to his conception of politics. By 1992 this proved to be a real advantage. However dubious his credentials as a Cold Warrior, Clinton possessed one essential quality that George Bush lacked and that was more germane to the task at hand: he was a careful student of the forces transforming American society and the world at large.

In addition, of course, Clinton was a naturally gifted politician—glib, energetic, infinitely flexible in his principles, a man of outsized appetites for attention and power. Unencumbered by Cold War baggage and possessing a far surer grasp of how culture and technology were changing the United States, the nominally inexperienced Clinton arrived in the White House far better equipped than his predecessor to articulate a persuasive rationale for U.S. strategy. He scooped up Bush's odds and ends, appropriated a few ingredients picked up from the marketplace of fashionable ideas, and kneaded the result into something that—before his first term ended—he could proudly claim was very much his own creation. As an exercise in statesmanship, the result had more to do with style than with substance. Clinton imparted the appearance of freshness to notions that, coming from Bush, had seemed insipid or shopworn. But the accomplishment was a noteworthy one.

The process was by no means without misstep. Clinton and his lieutenants committed egregious errors in judgment—the most disastrous being the experiment with "nation-building" in Somalia that produced a war against Mohamed Farah Aidid and culminated by October 1993 in a costly defeat. They discarded ideas that either misfired or simply failed to catch fire—the ill-conceived concept of "assertive multilateralism" chief among them.[26] Over time the president's strategic vision both sharpened and became more expansive. But it ended up precisely where anyone familiar with the writings of Charles Beard and William Appleman Williams would have expected. In short, in his embrace of openness, Clinton did not invent something new to supplant a Cold War strategy that had outlived its usefulness; instead, he renovated and revived a strategy that predated the Cold War by several decades.

➤ Upon entering the White House, Clinton by all accounts was not especially well schooled in specific foreign policy issues.[27] But as a politician he had absorbed one great truth that had eluded George Bush, namely, that U.S. diplomacy is intimately and inextricably linked to domestic concerns. American statecraft is not, in the first instance, about "them"; it is about "us."

Indeed, Clinton fancied that he himself was the first to divine this truth, laying down the axiom early in his campaign for the presidency that "foreign and domestic policy are inseparable in today's world." Five years later, toward the end of his first term, Clinton still professed to be impressed by the significance of this discovery. "Something I need to take on even more," he told reporters, "is trying to figure out a way to make the American people believe . . . that there's no longer an easy dividing line between foreign policy and domestic policy, that the world we're living in doesn't permit that luxury any more."[28]

If Clinton had unearthed the taproot of U.S. policy, he was hardly the first to have done so. As early as 1935, Charles A. Beard had observed that for the United States "foreign policy and domestic policy are aspects of the same thing."[29] In 1957 William Appleman Williams endorsed that view, arguing that "domestic *and* foreign policy are two sides of the same coin."[30] Thus when candidate Clinton announced his discovery in 1991, it was not as original as he imagined it to be. But it was a crucial insight from which much else flowed.

Clinton defeated George Bush in 1992 by convincing a plurality of voting citizens that the country had stagnated economically and that Republicans were bereft of ideas about how to stimulate recovery. Once elected, Clinton vowed that he would "focus like a laser beam" on alleviating the nation's economic woes.[31]

That priority directly shaped the administration's initial diplomatic gambits. From the outset, foreign policy and economic policy became all but interchangeable. Secretary of State Warren Christopher bragged that the Clinton team had "placed economic policy at the heart of our foreign policy."[32] Indeed, in ticking off the administration's foreign policy priorities, Christopher ranked economic interests first. This was to be the administration's hallmark, setting its approach to diplomacy apart from its immediate predecessors'. To the extent that America's relations with the rest of the world could contribute to pulling the nation's economy out of the doldrums, they mattered. To the extent that a particular foreign policy issue did not promise near-term economic benefit, it was unlikely to attract more than lip service.[33]

This principle directly informed the administration's handling of those foreign policy issues—Bosnia and China—on which Clinton during the campaign had attacked George Bush. In both cases, candidate Clinton portrayed himself as someone who would put moral and humanitarian concerns first. Whereas Bush had resisted calls for the United States to intervene in the Balkans, Clinton insisted that he would act forcefully, using American air power if necessary to lift the siege of Sarajevo and put a stop to further ethnic cleansing.[34] While Bush in the aftermath of Tiananmen Square had labored to salvage relations with Beijing and in June 1992 renewed China's Most Favored Nation (MFN) trade status, Clinton ripped his opponent for "coddling dictators" and subordinating human rights and democratic values to trade.[35] This, Clinton vowed, he would never do.

Once in office, the new president jettisoned these views.

With regard to Bosnia, Clinton in the spring of 1993 flirted ever so briefly with an option known as "lift-and-strike." Acting in concert with its major European allies, the United States proposed to lift the arms embargo that had the practical effect of working to the disadvantage of the Bosnian Muslims, the principal victims of ethnic cleansing, and to the benefit of the Bosnian Serbs, the principal perpetrators. With the embargo removed, the Muslims could arm themselves and have at least a chance of putting up a meaningful defense. A more balanced military situation might eventually foster conditions conducive to a political settlement. At the same time, the United States and its allies would stand ready to launch air strikes to punish the Bosnian Serbs if they used the embargo's removal as a pretext for stepping up the level of violence. (Military involvement apart from air strikes was out of the question: the Pentagon adamantly opposed placing U.S. troops on the ground, and Clinton was not inclined to challenge the military on that score.)

In May 1993 Clinton sent Secretary of State Warren Christopher on a mission to European capitols to brief allied leaders on the American plan. As Christopher admits in his memoir, his instructions were to take a "conciliatory approach" with the allies, commending "lift-and-strike" to their consideration and "asking for their support."[36] The administration was unwilling to contemplate unilateral U.S. action. Nor was it willing to ride roughshod over European sensibilities, especially given the presence on the ground in Bosnia of lightly armed (and hence vulnerable) peacekeepers from several European nations.

But the Europeans had no stomach for involving themselves in a shooting war. Given the administration's tepid enthusiasm for its own proposal, withholding support seemed unlikely to entail real penalties. So Great Britain, France, Germany, and Russia all joined in categorically rejecting Christopher's proposal. "Lift-and-strike" was dead on arrival.

Humiliated, the secretary of state abandoned his mission. By the time he arrived back in Washington, he found that his boss, too, had lost whatever limited appetite he might have had for involving himself in the Balkan imbroglio. Thus, as Christopher delicately phrased it, for the next two years the Clinton administration's efforts to resolve the Bosnian crisis "proceeded fitfully."[37] More accurately,

Clinton bought into his predecessor's policy of inaction. With the administration focused on economic recovery at home, for the moment, at least, Bosnia did not qualify for serious attention.

Something of the same occurred regarding China. There, however, the additional influence of economic considerations made Clinton's turnabout seem more craven.

Clinton launched his China policy on an exalted note. In the United States, public discussion of U.S.-China relations centered on the question of trade. The annual renewal of China's MFN status provided an occasion for critics to vent their dissatisfaction with Beijing, especially on the matter of human rights. In May 1993 Clinton made it clear where he stood on this controversy when with considerable fanfare—Chinese dissidents attended the Oval Office ceremony—he issued an executive order that made the linkage between trade with China and human rights his administration's policy.

While extending China's trading privileges for another year, Clinton's executive order stipulated specific measures that Beijing needed to take to qualify for any subsequent extension. If a year hence Beijing failed to meet the standards that Washington had established—loosening emigration restrictions, curbing the use of prison labor, releasing dissidents, and permitting international radio and television broadcasts, for example—the United States would punish China by revoking its MFN status.[38]

Clinton's executive order enraged the government in Beijing, which refused to play along. Over the months that followed, China made no discernible effort to meet any of the standards that Clinton had set. As if to emphasize their defiance, when Secretary Christopher made his first official visit to Beijing in the spring of 1994, China's leaders made a point of launching a crackdown on pro-democracy dissidents. In meetings with the secretary of state, Premier Li Peng and Foreign Minister Qian Qichen laughed off his warning that China's behavior was placing MFN in jeopardy. They taunted Christopher—who had headed the panel formed to investigate the 1992 Los Angeles riots—by suggesting that the United States attend to its own human rights problems.[39]

At home Clinton's executive order also irked U.S. corporate executives whose firms had a growing stake in the China market. They, in turn, mobilized congressional support and dissenters within Clinton's own administration in a campaign to sever the link between commercial relations and human rights.[40]

Well before Clinton's June 1994 deadline, the failure of his get-tough policy had become evident. Whatever spotty improvements in China's human rights record optimists might detect, even Warren Christopher had to admit that progress was "not nearly enough to meet the standards we had announced."[41]

Faced with the prospect of forfeiting $40 billion in trade annually—an amount that was increasing rapidly—while getting nothing in return, Clinton caved. On May 26, 1994, he renewed China's MFN status without qualification and announced that U.S. policy toward China would henceforth "take a new path." The essential element of that path, as Christopher explained in a speech the following day, was "a comprehensive U.S. strategy of engagement" aiming "to integrate China into the global community."[42] In plain language, the United States would henceforth downplay human rights and emphasize commercial interests. Like his predecessor, Clinton had found it expedient, for the moment at least, to cozy up to the dictators in Beijing.

No one possessed a clearer understanding of where this new path pointed than did Clinton's enterprising secretary of commerce, Ronald H. Brown. Hardly had the shift in policy been announced than Brown was organizing a major trade mission to China. With U.S. executives in tow, the commerce secretary was soon off to Beijing, where he closed $5 billion in deals, thereby imparting substance to the concept of comprehensive engagement. Addressing a business audience in Beijing, Brown all but apologized for the temerity of his colleagues who had found fault with China's domestic policies. Declaring that "China's long history is deserving of respect and even deference that she has not always received," he emphasized that the United States was now sending "substantive signals that we regard China as a commercial ally and partner." "Once divided by ideology," he continued, eliminating in a phrase any differences between democratic capitalism and communism, "we are now drawn together by shared economic interests."[43]

In the eyes of his critics, Clinton's failure to make good on his campaign promises concerning Bosnia and China amounted to prima facie evidence that his administration was either weak, incompetent, or callow—or all three. It is more accurate to say that Clinton's turnabout on Bosnia and China manifested the shifting priorities of a team making the transition from campaigning to governing (while, inevitably, also continuing to campaign). As long as the U.S. economy was still limping along, ethnic cleansing in distant lands did not really matter. When faced with a choice between access to a market of particular promise and support for human rights, all other things being equal, human rights would have to give way. The inelegance with which the administration engineered these policy reversals may have caused it unnecessary embarrassment. But the outcome was in accord with a logic both hardheaded and realistic: foreign policy served domestic interests, and in 1993 the overriding domestic imperative was clearly to spur economic recovery.

➤ In a negative sense, the foreign policy priorities of the new administration had required an abandonment of campaign commitments regarding Bosnia and China. In a positive sense, those priorities required a full-court press to gain greater access to foreign markets for American goods and capital. What Christopher referred to as "the new centrality of economic policy in our foreign policy" manifested itself as an all-out effort to remove obstacles to foreign trade and investment.[44] This the administration proceeded to pursue with a globe-straddling gusto reminiscent of jingoes like Albert Beveridge nearly a century before.

President Clinton himself offered a preview of the administration's intentions in a speech delivered at American University barely a month after he took office. Shamelessly comparing his purpose to that of John F. Kennedy, who in a notable 1963 appearance at the same podium had described the quest for world peace as the foremost challenge of his day, Clinton announced that the paramount challenge of *his* day was asserting mastery over the emerging global economy. According to the president, it no longer made sense to talk about a domestic policy or a domestic economy. The United States was "woven inextricably into the fabric of a global economy," he said. "Capital clearly has become global . . . Products have clearly become more global . . . Services have become global . . . Most important of all, information has become global and has become king of the global economy." The implications were clear: American enterprise needed to operate on a global scale or it would stagnate and fail. "The truth of our age is this and must be this," Clinton declared: "Open and competitive commerce will enrich us as a nation." As a result, it had become "time for us to make trade a priority element of American security." The president promised a comprehensive trade policy that would "open other nations' markets" and "establish clear and enforceable rules on which to expand trade." Openness would benefit the entire world, economically and politically, but it would benefit the United States most of all.[45]

This was not simply idle talk. In his remarks at American University, the president singled out the North American Free Trade Agreement (NAFTA) as an example of the policies that promised to ignite growth. Creating a common market encompassing Canada, Mexico, and the United States, NAFTA was actually the handiwork of the Bush administration. But Bush's clock ran out before he gained the congressional approval needed to put the agreement into effect. Securing that approval became in Clinton's first year in office a major foreign policy priority.

Doing so obliged Clinton to ignore a clamor of opposition from organized labor and environmentalists, prominent among the constituencies that had elected him. When in November 1993 the president, relying largely on Republican votes, secured the necessary implementing legislation, he was more than justified in claiming that he had won a significant victory. Henry Kissinger touted NAFTA as "the first and crucial step" in the creation of a new architecture for U.S. foreign policy.[46] Clinton made it the cornerstone of his strategy.

The fact that NAFTA subsequently failed the job-creating expectations of its supporters is to a large extent beside the point. NAFTA was important as both signal and precedent. It showed that an administration of so-called New Democrats was no less friendly to corporate interests than its Republican predecessors had been. Furthermore, passage of NAFTA marked just the beginning of a campaign to remove barriers to trade and investment. In support of the administration's effort to open up the world, U.S. trade negotiators trolled the world in search of deals. By 1996, proud references to having signed "200-plus" trade agreements became a staple of administration rhetoric.[47] (By 2000 the number had jumped to over 300.)[48] Clinton's trade policy focused particularly on improving U.S. access to especially promising "emerging markets"—Mexico, Brazil, Turkey, China, and South

Africa, for example—projected to absorb within a decade $1.5 trillion in investments for airport expansion and telecommunications infrastructure alone.[49]

More important still was the creation of the World Trade Organization (WTO), promising worldwide reductions in trade barriers and guarantees of access and equitability. As with NAFTA, gaining congressional approval of the WTO found the White House making common cause with Republicans. But the role of the WTO's chief salesman was one in which Clinton enthusiastically cast himself. "It creates hundreds of thousands of high-paying American jobs," he proclaimed. "It slashes tariffs on manufactured and agricultural goods. It protects intellectual property. It's the largest international tax cut in history. Most importantly, this agreement requires all trading nations to play by the same rules. And since the United States has the most productive and competitive economy in the world, that is good news for our workers and our future." Removing barriers to trade and investment would benefit every participating economy, but the United States most of all. That became Clinton's constant refrain: "We are building prosperity at home by opening markets abroad."[50]

Not surprisingly, when the nation's economic performance improved dramatically, the administration was quick to credit its own policies as the chief cause. Americans found the claim to be at least plausible. In 1996 a country increasingly giddy with prosperity decisively elected Clinton to a second term. By 1998, with Clinton embroiled in sexual scandal, opinion surveys showed that the American public—whatever its reservations about the president's character—rated him the most successful foreign policy president of the entire postwar era.[51] But that success was measured almost entirely in economic terms. Beginning in 1998, a federal budget that had been in the red every year since 1969 was producing a substantial and growing surplus.[52] By the summer of 2000 the administration was claiming credit for having increased U.S. exports by 36 percent since the WTO's creation and for having created 22 million new jobs. The unemployment rate fell to 4.0 percent, the lowest the country had seen in three decades. During the Clinton presidency, average hourly earnings had jumped nearly 30 percent.[53] Politically, the administration's emphasis on economic expansionism abroad had been a thundering success.

➤ But did NAFTA, the WTO, and a passel of bilateral trade agreements really constitute a genuine basis for grand strategy? Any serious strategy must necessarily satisfy political and security needs as well as economic ones. Grand strategy implies a coherent vision for organizing and deploying power in pursuit of the state's larger purposes. In a democracy, it must give at least passing attention to moral considerations. Was not the Clinton administration—perpetrator of egregious flip-flops on Bosnia and China, suspected of being soft on defense and uncomfortable with the use of force—guilty of giving short shrift to noneconomic concerns in its headlong effort to restore a popular sense of well-being? Was the Clinton "strategy" not little more than a crass scheme to guarantee the president's reelection?

From the outset, senior administration officials invested considerable energy in attempting to show that such was not the case—that seizing a dominant position in the globalizing economy translated directly into political preeminence and offered the best guarantee of U.S. national security. Especially noteworthy in that regard was a much-publicized speech by Anthony Lake, the president's national security adviser, at Johns Hopkins University on September 21, 1993. If Clinton at American University had offered a blueprint for mastering the global economy, Lake at Johns Hopkins provided the most comprehensive explanation to date of how the administration's economic priorities formed one component of a subtle and sophisticated grand strategy.

The title of Lake's remarks conveyed his thesis: "From Containment to Enlargement."[54] Though couched in caveats and carefully avoiding the Wolfowitz Indiscretion, Lake's speech outlined a startlingly ambitious project. It was, in essence, a proclamation that the defensive phase of U.S. strategy, never intended to be more than temporary, had now officially ended. Changing circumstances dictated a more proactive, enterprising approach. Expressed in military terms, the United States in defeating communism had won a great battle. The moment was now at hand to exploit that success to achieve the final victory.

Lake began his presentation by identifying several large "facts" shaping the Clinton administration's worldview. First, freedom had prevailed. As a consequence, democracy and "market economics" (Lake resolutely avoided the term *capitalism*) were on the march. Second, the United States had emerged without question as the world's dominant power, economically and militarily and as the model of a "dynamic, multiethnic society." Third, the information revolution was accelerating the pace of global change. One notable result of that revolution was to create "new and diverse ways for us to exert our influence."

For the United States, these conditions were ripe with opportunity. The final triumph of democratic capitalism had become a reasonable prospect. Completing the process of aligning other nations with the United States ideologically—or, as Lake phrased it, securing the "enlargement of the world's community of free nations"—had become the proper goal of U.S. policy. Success would make for a world that was "more humane and peaceful." Not incidentally, it would also make the United States "more secure, prosperous, and influential." It would—although Lake did not state this outright—preserve and reinforce American preeminence.

On the one hand, the spread of democratic capitalism loomed as all but inevitable. On the other hand, the process was likely to be frustrated unless the United States exercised leadership commensurate with the position to which it had ascended. But leadership did not, in Lake's understanding, imply a futile and exhausting crusade in pursuit of grandiose ideals. The national security adviser emphasized that the fundamental purpose of pursuing a strategy of enlargement was to serve concrete U.S. interests. The Clinton administration was not proposing a full-throated Wilsonian revival.[55] The United States was not to become a global relief agency. Humanitarianism for its own sake would be the exception not the rule. Referring specifically to Somalia and Bosnia, Lake insisted that "they do not by themselves define our broader strategy in the world." Nor did enlargement imply that the administration was automatically reclassifying every non-democratic country as an enemy; Lake went out of his way to emphasize that the United States would "befriend and even defend non-democratic states" when doing so served American interests. A handful of holdouts—Lake called them "backlash" states—resisted the inevitable tide of history. As long as such nations remained recalcitrant—by way of example, Lake cited Iran and Iraq—it was incumbent upon the United States "to isolate them diplomatically, militarily, economically, and technologically." Sooner or later they would see the light—or be swept into the dustbin of history.

With regard to the feasibility of this scheme, Lake professed to be less concerned about any tricks the backlash states might have up their sleeves than about the capacity of the American people to see the project through. Raising the old hobgoblin of isolationism, he worried about the growing influence of "those in both parties who would have us retreat within the isolated shell we occupied in the 1920s and 1930s." He therefore enjoined internationalists of all stripes to set aside their differences over specific policies long enough to thwart this internal threat to American engagement with the outside world.

Lake's was a masterly performance incorporating and updating a variety of familiar themes. But the speech was as instructive for what it left out as for what it included. For starters, it left little room for politics, at least as that term is conventionally understood. Implicit in Lake's strategy of enlargement was a conception of international politics that was nothing if not revolutionary. At the end of a century in which various causes, most of them bad, had inspired men to slaughter one another with unprecedented ferocity, Lake seemed to imply that there was really nothing left to fight about. History had decided the big questions. Given the necessary U.S. leadership, globalization would combine with the widening community of democratic capitalist nations to supersede power politics and create what Lake described as "virtuous circles of international economic action." Cooperative economic interaction was now replacing antagonistic political competition.

And should that cooperation on occasion break down, the United States would retain the prerogative of setting things right. Absent from Lake's presentation was any reference to two goals that had long been at the center of the liberal internationalist agenda: worldwide disarmament and the creation of an effective global collective security organization. Both had figured prominently among Wilson's famous Fourteen Points. Both had regularly received lip service from U.S. administrations ever since. Neither figured in Lake's strategy of enlargement. It was not difficult to see why: to pursue disarmament would forfeit the ultimate expression of American authority. Similarly, to revert to the original conception of the United Nations would necessarily diminish American freedom of action. Lake could not say so directly, but his strategy of enlargement required that the United States retain its position of unquestioned military superiority and its ability to act unilaterally. They were essential to expanding and perpetuating the Pax Americana, which was the strategy's unspoken purpose.

➤ For all its brilliance, Lake's exposition of the Clinton administration's strategy of enlargement was incomplete. Apart from reciting a handful of clichés, he had not spelled out *how* the United States would bring others into conformity with the principles he described as "both American and universal." What was the operative mechanism? Nor had he provided a clear picture of precisely how the progressively enlarging community of democratic capitalist nations would function. How would it be organized and regulated?

In the months that followed, Lake's colleagues—and the president himself—expanded on and embroidered the themes that he had enunciated (although the term *enlargement* was soon dropped). As the U.S. economic recovery took hold, those representations became more forceful and direct. Once Clinton won reelection in 1996 and replaced his national security team—the lawyerly Christopher, the unassuming Lake, and William Perry, the technocratic secretary of defense—administration officials became positively buoyant in expressing their conviction that they had crafted a strategy ideally suited to the age of globalization.

Senior administration officials returned time and again to the same point: the means to the end that Lake had described—the key to exploiting the potential of globalization, ensuring the spread of democratic capitalism, and perpetuating American dominance—was "openness."

The *New York Times* might characterize the program as "peace through trade," but it was much more than that.[56] The key opportunity created by the end of the Cold War, Christopher explained, was "to shape a more secure world of open societies and open markets."[57] Christopher's successor, Madeleine Albright, was even more emphatic: "the driving force behind economic growth," she declared, "is openness—open markets, open investment, open communications and open trade." Indeed, without openness, growth would cease. According to Albright, "the health of the global economy will depend on maintaining and expanding the commitment to open trade, open markets, and open books." Without openness, the revival of old conflicts became possible. Therefore, "across the globe," U.S. policy was "emphasizing the value of open markets, open investments, open communications and open trade."[58] The drive for openness, declared Samuel R. Berger, who had served as Lake's deputy and then succeeded him as national security adviser, was "the President's strategy for harnessing the forces of globalization for the benefit of the people of the United States and the world." By the end of his second term Clinton had made himself, in the words of an admiring editorial in the *Boston Globe,* "the pied piper of capitalism," traveling the world to extol the virtues of openness as the means to achieve global prosperity.[59]

But the creation of an open world was not in the first instance a program of global uplift. Globalization is not social work. The pursuit of openness is first of all about Americans' doing well; that an open world might also benefit others qualifies at best as incidental. An open global order in which American enterprise enjoys free rein and in which American values, tastes, and lifestyle enjoy pride of place is a world in which the United States remains preeminent. Clinton and his advisers understood this.

▶ Pursuing the goal of openness in the 1990s did not oblige the United States to exert itself on all fronts with equal energy. Priorities were necessary. To maintain a semblance of balance between means and ends, the Clinton administration sought, as Lake himself indicated, to "focus our efforts where we have the most leverage." The idea was to attend first to regions "that affect our strategic interests."[60] In a rough if imprecise way, U.S. policy priorities in the first decade after the Cold War reflected this determination to match the level of commitment to the interests at stake and the prospects of achieving success.

Where significant interests coincided with substantial American leverage, the United States could be counted on to make a major effort. Europe offers a prime example. There the strategy of openness demanded that the United States promote continuing progress toward European integration and prevent any erosion in the credibility of Washington's claims that despite its location on the opposite side of the Atlantic Ocean the United States was Europe's leading power. The foremost Cold War–era expression of those claims—NATO—offered the most readily available vehicle for enhancing both the depth and breadth of European openness. But with the fall of the Berlin Wall and the collapse of communism, NATO had achieved the purpose for which it had been created: deterring or, if need be, defending against Soviet aggression. NATO's obsolescence prompted the United States to launch a major effort to "reinvent" the alliance—an effort that George Bush first conceived but that the Clinton administration adopted as its own. By 1997 that effort had produced a precedent-setting eastward expansion. NATO invited three former Warsaw Pact states—Poland, Hungary, and the Czech Republic—to join the alliance, with President Clinton vowing that "the first new members will not be the last."[61]

As if with a flick of the cartographer's pen, the cluster of nations that for decades had constituted "Eastern Europe"—and by implication had represented the antithesis of "Western Europe"—were redesignated. They now became "Central Europe," situated in the very heart of the continent, poised to be incorporated into "the West," in which it turned out they had always truly belonged. Short of Russia itself, there was to be no predetermined limit on how far NATO—and, by implication, American influence in Europe—might expand.

But NATO's reinvention implied more than simply adding new members. Having outlived its usefulness as a defensive alliance, NATO needed a new purpose, ideally one based on a broader definition of security and more proactive in its orientation. The problem to which a new NATO needed to respond, said Bill Clinton, was "creeping instability"—shadowy, hydra-headed, posing a threat as much political as military.[62] This problem obliged the alliance to develop new capabilities. In place of large, mechanized formations, long its mainstay, the alliance required smaller, lighter, more mobile units. Those units should be configured and trained for a wide variety of contingencies to include peacekeeping, peace enforcement, and humanitarian relief. Creeping instability also required that the alliance be willing to venture "out of area," exerting its influence beyond its territorial limits. But from an American perspective, all of this had to be accomplished in a way that preserved for the United States its leading role in the alliance. Thus, for example, American enthusiasm for reinventing NATO did not extend to such notions as appointing a European to the post of Supreme Allied Commander Europe (SACEUR). NATO's top-ranking military officer had always been and would remain a U.S. officer.

At the Washington Summit, convened in April 1999 on the fiftieth anniversary of NATO's founding, the alliance unveiled a "new strategic concept" responding to those requirements.[63] Whether coincidentally or not, as NATO's leaders convened their anniversary conclave the alliance itself was actively engaged in a major demonstration of the new concept—a war against Yugoslavia.

Operation Allied Force was actually NATO's second Balkan war of the 1990s. The first, Operation Deliberate Force, in August and September 1995, had been a brief bombing campaign—carried out largely by U.S. aircraft—directed against Bosnian Serb forces with the expressed intent of establishing some basis for a negotiated end to the Bosnian civil war. The same Bill Clinton who had flinched from using force in Bosnia in 1993 now embraced both an experiment in coercive diplomacy and the open-ended military occupation of Bosnia arranged during U.S.-sponsored peace talks in Dayton, Ohio. Clinton reversed course in 1995 not, as claimed, to put a stop to ethnic cleansing or in response to claims of conscience, but to preempt threats to the cohesion of NATO and the credibility of American power, each called into question by events in Bosnia.[64] In short, it was not Bosnia itself that counted, but Europe and U.S. leadership in Europe.

Much the same can be said with regard to the much larger military enterprise launched in connection with Kosovo in March 1999. Assertions that the United States and its allies acted in response to massive Serb repression of Kosovar Albanians simply cannot survive close scrutiny. Operation Allied Force was neither planned nor conducted to alleviate the plight of the Kosovars. When Slobodan Milošević used the start of the bombing as a pretext to intensify Serb persecution of the Kosovars, that point became abundantly clear: NATO persisted in a bombing campaign that neither stopped nor even retarded Serb efforts to empty the province of Muslims. To the extent that General Wesley Clark, the SACEUR, modified the script of his original campaign plan, he did so not by providing protection to the victims of Serb repression but by victimizing Serb civilians.[65]

Indeed, some members of the Clinton administration actively sought a showdown with Slobodan Milošević: Secretary of State Madeleine Albright designed the so-called Rambouillet peace conference in February and March 1999 so as to ensure that the Yugoslav president would reject any negotiated settlement of the Kosovo issue.[66] Effective diplomacy would have precluded NATO action. But military action was what the United States wanted: a demonstration of what a new, more muscular alliance under U.S. direction could accomplish in thwarting "creeping instability." The intent of Operation Allied Force was to provide an object lesson to any European state fancying that it was exempt from the rules of the post–Cold War era. It was not Kosovo that counted, but affirming the dominant position of the United States in a Europe that was unified, integrated, and open. As Clinton himself explained on March 23, 1999, just before the start of the bombing campaign, "if we're going to have a strong economic relationship that includes our ability to sell around the world, Europe has got to be a key . . . That's what this Kosovo thing is all about."[67]

When it came to measuring the success of the strategy of openness in Europe, NATO's two Balkan military interventions—each resulting in a semipermanent U.S. troop commitment—signified little. Military intervention was simply part of the inevitable price of doing business. The essence of that strategy *was* business and American political clout. Viewed within the frame of reference of U.S. policymakers, other indicators counted for much more than peacekeeping missions in Bosnia and Kosovo as evidence of what openness had wrought in Europe. For these policymakers, the real payoff lay in the fact that U.S. investment in Europe increased sevenfold between 1994 and 1998 and that trade between the United States and the European Union also rose handsomely, to $450 billion per year.[68] There was also the knowledge, vividly demonstrated in the skies over Kosovo, that Europe in the first decade after the Cold War had become more not less dependent upon the United States for its security. As European nations after 1989 cut their defense budgets, they forfeited all but the most modest military capabilities; as NATO ventured out of area, U.S. domination of the alliance became all the greater—to American policymakers a welcome development.

Europe was by no means the only region where interests combined with leverage to create the conditions guaranteeing sustained U.S. attention. Japan and South Korea, Russia and China, the "emerging markets" of Latin America and Southeast Asia, and, of course, the North American continent: each in its own way offered fertile ground in which the United States could plant the seeds of greater openness. The specific approach—particularly the emphasis placed on U.S. military power—varied from case to case, specific policies being tailored to local circumstances. But in each of these cases, U.S. policymakers nursed expectations that opening countries through trade, investment, and technology transfers would result in immediate benefits to the United States while in the longer term—thanks to globalization and the information revolution—fostering political liberalization. When it came to China, President Clinton even specified the threshold of interaction that would cause the dam to burst. "When over 100 million people in China can get on the Net," he announced in May 2000, "it will be impossible to maintain a closed political and economic system."[69]

In regions where U.S. interests were substantial but not matched by comparable leverage, policymakers opted for a less direct and more patient approach. American policy in the oil-rich Middle East illustrates the point. In 1991 Operation Desert Storm boosted the United States in the Persian Gulf to a position of unrivaled influence. But that influence rarely extended beyond matters related to military security. Any heavy-handed attempt to "break down barriers," especially if infringing upon culture and the political authority of entrenched elites, was too likely to backfire. The economic consequences of a bungled effort—a possible cutoff in the flow of oil—were unacceptable. Thus Washington—prior to September 11, 2001, at least—concluded that opening the Arab world was something that could wait for another day. In the torrent of high-sounding rhetoric churned out by the White House and the State Department, "Arab democracy" was seldom mentioned.

Diffidence did not imply a hands-off approach. Instead, through arms sales, advisory programs, frequent exercises, military-to-military contacts, and the continuing presence of U.S. forces—signified most prominently by the enforcement of the no-fly zones over Iraq—the United States sought to preserve the favored position it had won by liberating Kuwait. After 1991, U.S. troops garrisoned the Persian Gulf not to pry the region open to American enterprise and American values but to prop up the status quo. But only temporarily: in due course, the opportunity to open the Arab world would present itself.[70] For if, as members of the American policy elite insisted with near unanimity, democracy, market principles, and globalization were indeed sweeping the world, then existing regimes in key states like

Egypt and Saudi Arabia were living on borrowed time. When it became expedient to do so, senior U.S. officials could be expected to unveil all the truths that the White House and the State Department had for many years chosen to soft-pedal or ignore: that these regimes were deeply corrupt, denied civil liberties, engaged in wholesale violations of human rights, and resolutely opposed anything even remotely resembling popular rule. When they went, few members of the American foreign policy establishment would lament their demise. Virtually all would applaud the "opening" of the region to democratic capitalism that would presumably ensue. In the meantime, with the West as a whole maintaining its access to (relatively) cheap oil while the United States enjoyed the (sometimes lucrative) advantages that accrued from being chief guarantor of the developed world's energy lifeline, it was considered impolitic to speak openly of such things.[71]

Finally, where interests were slight, the United States seldom bothered even to make the effort to assert any substantial leverage. American policy toward Africa illustrates the point. Offering only the most modest near-term prospects for trade and investment, sub-Saharan Africa consistently ranks dead last in U.S. strategic priorities. The Bush's administration seemingly quixotic intervention in Somalia in 1992 suggested a departure from that pattern. But the Clinton administration, bruised by its defeat in Mogadishu the following year, soon turned its back on Africa. As evinced most vividly by the administration's studied inaction during the Rwandan genocide of 1994, the usual order of things had been restored.

In the wake of Rwanda, Africa qualified for presidential apologies and symbolic gestures but little effective action. In March 1998 Clinton made a highly publicized six-nation, eleven-day tour of the continent during which he expressed regret for "the sin of neglect and ignorance" that the United States had committed in its treatment of Africa, particularly during the Cold War. The president announced that it was "time for Americans to put a new Africa on our map" and for the United States to forge a new beginning in its relations with the peoples of that continent.[72]

The centerpiece of that new beginning, according to Susan E. Rice, assistant secretary of state for African affairs during the Clinton years, was a promise "to accelerate Africa's integration into the global economy." Expropriating the standard imagery of American economic expansionism, Rice portrayed Africa as the "last frontier for U.S. exporters and investors." The frontier that beckoned had in fact already been staked out by others. With the continent "still largely the province of our European and Asian competitors," taming it required that American business find ways to displace the competition, thereby gaining access to an indigenous population that commercial-minded U.S. officials referred to as "Africa's 700 million consumers." Increased U.S. economic penetration of Africa would benefit both Americans and Africans. For the United States, it meant the promise of jobs. For Africa, it meant development. "As economic growth spreads, as entrepreneurial talent is unleashed, and basic needs are satisfied," Rice promised, "democracy and respect for human rights will also lay down deep roots in Africa."[73]

In May 2000 the Clinton administration's Africa initiative assumed material form as the Africa Growth and Opportunity Act, designed to promote trade and investment. In President Clinton's view, this legislation cemented a "genuine partnership" between the United States and the nations of sub-Saharan Africa, "based on not what we can do for them, not what we can do about them, but on what we can do with them to build democracy together."[74] Taken at face value, such expansive language might suggest that in U.S. efforts to create an open, integrated world, Africa had achieved a standing comparable to that traditionally enjoyed by other parts of the world that commanded American attention.

Such was by no means the case. To be sure, the Africa Growth and Opportunity Act held out the prospect of Africa's someday taking its place in the global system that the United States aspires to organize. But with Africa currently accounting for a minuscule 1 percent of total U.S. trade, that moment is not now. The legislation was at best a promissory note, to be redeemed at Washington's convenience.[75] It did not imply any immediate commitment or obligation to eradicate the problems impeding African development. To put it bluntly, conditions that in the Balkans or the Persian Gulf the United States found intolerable were in Africa merely unfortunate.

Hence, when it came to specific cases, action did not match rhetoric. In domestic American politics, to find out who and what really counts, you follow the money. When it comes to U.S. strategy, the applicable rule is to follow the military. The presence of American troops and the willingness to employ U.S. military muscle offer the best measure of what policymakers actually value.

As a practical matter, even in the White House the old map of Africa remained in place—a map depicting a slough of ethnic violence, extreme poverty, and daunting social problems, all presided over by brutal and venal kleptocrats. Expectations that the continent might make significant progress toward peace and prosperity at any time in the foreseeable future were simply unrealistic. Actual U.S. policy reflected that sober assessment. Consider, for example, how the Clinton administration—ostensibly chastened by its moral failure in Rwanda and vowing never again to avert its gaze from massive suffering and injustice—responded to a large, yet not atypical, African catastrophe: the civil war in Sudan.

Sudan's internal crisis predated the end of the Cold War.[76] At the time of the president's heralded visit to Africa in 1998, the civil war was entering its sixteenth year. During that period, according to the State Department's own estimates, fighting between the secessionist South—mostly African and either Christian or animist—and the government-controlled North—mostly Arab and Muslim—had killed two million Sudanese and created another four million internal refugees. In its efforts to suppress the Sudan People's Liberation Movement, the Islamist government in Khartoum as a matter of policy engaged in widespread torture, routinely bombed civilian villages, forcibly conscripted children into the army, and coerced non-Muslims to convert to Islam. In the words of the State Department human rights report, Sudanese security forces "beat refugees, raped women, and reportedly harassed and detained persons on the basis of their religion."[77] Christians, in particular, were singled out for abuse, with government forces desecrating churches and destroying Christian schools. Slavery and other trafficking in human beings flourished. In the scale of humanitarian catastrophes, Sudan in the 1990s ranked as high as Somalia and Bosnia and well ahead of Panama, "Kurdistan," and Haiti, where conditions had compelled Presidents Bush and Clinton to intervene.

In the eyes of the Bush and Clinton administrations, Sudan never qualified for even remotely comparable attention. In Bush's foreign policy memoir the entire continent of Africa receives not a single mention. Before Clinton's Africa trip the U.S. response to the Sudanese civil war consisted of little more than conscience-salving gestures. State Department officials regularly condemned the behavior of the Sudanese government, affirmed U.S. support for international efforts to isolate Khartoum, and funneled money through the United Nations and other nongovernmental organizations to support Operation Lifeline Sudan, a program aimed at alleviating the suffering of the war's innocent victims. During the 1990s the United States contributed more than a billion dollars to that effort.[78] But U.S. support for Lifeline Sudan did nothing to address the cause of that suffering and may have actually prolonged the conflict. To draw an analogy with the 1940s, it was the moral equivalent of mailing relief supplies to those imprisoned in ghettos and concentration camps while refraining from entering the war against Germany.

To be sure, on November 4, 1997, President Clinton issued an executive order finding that the Sudanese government posed "an unusual and extraordinary threat to the national security and foreign policy of the United States." The president then proceeded to declare "a national emergency" to deal with that threat. But the sum total of the government's response to that emergency was to impose economic sanctions on Sudan.[79] Advertised as stringent and comprehensive, the sanctions did not live up to their billing. The fine print permitted most of the few existing American activities in Sudan to continue unimpeded. In a veiled reference to Sudan's oil reserves, the new policy even left the door open to continued commercial relations, promising that trade in a select "few cases" would be considered on "a case-by-case basis."[80] Although senior American officials insisted that it was U.S. policy "to isolate the Government of Sudan and to pressure it to change fundamentally its behavior," the pressure actually applied seldom rose above expressions of moral outrage.[81]

Only once in the 1990s—and then very briefly—did military power figure in the relationship between the United States and Sudan. On August 20, 1998, a handful of cruise missiles launched by U.S. Navy warships demolished the Al Shifa pharmaceutical factory in Khartoum. Yet this surprise American military action was completely unrelated to developments inside Sudan. Rather, the action came in response to the bombing earlier that month of U.S. diplomatic missions in Kenya and Tanzania that had left twelve Americans and several hundred Africans dead and many more injured. "Our target was terror," President Clinton told the American people in announcing the attack.[82]

In fact neither the Sudanese government nor the privately owned pharmaceutical factory was directly implicated in the embassy bombings. U.S. officials attributed responsibility for those attacks to the Islamic radical Osama bin Laden, thought to be hiding in Afghanistan. But Washington had long accused Sudan of offering safe haven to other terrorists (although in 1996 it had expelled bin Laden),[83] and U.S. intelligence agencies suspected that the Al Shifa plant was being used surreptitiously to produce Empta, a compound necessary for the production of nerve gas. The real purpose of leveling Al Shifa was less retaliatory than preemptive, the first shot in a campaign to deny would-be terrorists access to weapons of mass destruction.[84]

The fact that the Clinton administration chose Sudan as the place to make a statement about terrorism did not mean that it had reevaluated that nation's importance. On the contrary, no sooner did the United States complete its attack on Al Shifa than it forgot Sudan, once again averting its gaze from the ongoing civil war. But the story did not end there. Subsequent investigation by highly reputable American scientists provided compelling evidence that Al Shifa had never been used to produce Empta.[85] The factory had in fact been what it had appeared to be: a facility producing desperately needed pharmaceuticals for an impoverished Third World population. That the United States had used armed force not on behalf of the long-suffering Sudanese but to destroy the country's sole producer of pharmaceuticals said more about Africa's actual standing in American eyes than did the assurances of friendship and sympathy cascading out of the White House and the State Department.

Two years after President Clinton's trip to Africa, Richard Holbrooke, the U.S. permanent representative to the United Nations, was hard at work trying "to put to rest the canard that Africa doesn't matter."[86] But the canard keeps coming back. It does so not because U.S. policymakers are racists who value the lives of white Europeans above those of black Africans, but because Africa doesn't pay, at least not in comparison with other regions of the world. Even a major commitment to opening Africa would be unlikely to contribute much to U.S. economic well-being or American political clout—and such an effort would necessarily come at the expense of other areas possessing greater immediate promise. Viewed strictly in accordance with the logic of the strategy of openness—and despite earnest professions by U.S. officials to the contrary—American indifference to Africa makes sense.

In the global age, Bill Clinton liked to observe, "we can no longer choose not to know. We can only choose not to act, or to act."[87] As the Clinton era drew to a close, Assistant Secretary of State Susan Rice made a brief visit to Sudan. Having listened to the firsthand testimony of Sudanese just freed from bondage, she declared: "The U.S. will never tolerate slavery and will never rest until the suffering you and many others have experienced is ended." Rice then pledged $150,000 [sic] in U.S. aid to "provide southern Sudan with access to information technology" and departed.[88] When it came to Sudan—and much of the rest of sub-Saharan Africa—the United States, adhering to its strategic priorities, chose not to act.[89]

➤ Perhaps confusing hope with reality, Madeleine Albright in 1998 proclaimed that the strategy of openness had succeeded: "what we've done is kind of opened the whole system up."[90] But to Albright and other architects of U.S. policy an open system did not imply one in which anarchy prevailed. The rewards of openness rightly belonged to the most innovative, energetic, and competitive, not to those most adept at deception and fraud. "Experience tells us," Albright explained, "that there will always be some who will seek to take advantage by denying access to our products, pirating our copyrighted goods, or underpricing us through sweatshop labor." According to the secretary of state, "maintaining the equity of the system" required continuous vigilance against such intolerable practices.[91]

In short, an open system still had to *be* a system. It required order, stability, predictability. As President Clinton remarked in the wake of the Asian economic collapse of 1998, "The global economy simply cannot live with the kinds of vast and systematic disruptions that have occurred over the past year."[92]

Even as it worked to open up the global system, the United States claimed for itself the prerogative of detailing the rules governing that system. Citing the United States as the model that others should emulate, the president instructed the annual meeting of the International

Monetary Fund and the World Bank: "No nation can avoid the necessity of an open, transparent, properly regulated financial system; an honest, effective tax system; and laws that protect investment."[93] In ticking off the prerequisites for economic soundness, Clinton stressed that "this is not an American agenda. These are the imperatives of the global marketplace."[94] As always, American policies and principles were universal in application. The imperatives of the marketplace were just that: mandatory and inescapable. As the president explained to an audience of Russian students in 1998, "There is no way out of playing by the rules of the international economy if you wish to be a part of it."[95]

To the extent that these rules prevailed, globalization would foster what Albright termed a "process of constructive integration."[96] Out of that process a new international order would emerge. Consistent with the fashion of the 1990s, the preferred metaphor for describing that order was a web or network—fluid, without formal hierarchy, lacking a fixed structure, yet all the more supple and resilient as a result.

At the very center of that network, situated so as to play a commanding role, would be the United States. Describing her vision of the emerging global network, Albright declared that "America's place is at the center of this system." The United States is the "dynamic hub of the global economy."[97] Clinton himself insisted that "We have to be at the center of every vital global network." Such a central position, according to the president, "dramatically increases our leverage to work with people for peace, for human rights and for stability."[98]

The smooth functioning of the global network would, in the eyes of American statesmen, serve the interests of all. It followed, therefore, that most states would willingly submit to its discipline. In the event that the occasional dissenter might flout the rules and pose a hazard to the system, the United States with the assistance of likeminded allies would mete out the appropriate punishment and bring that violator back into conformity with the prescribed norms.

According to Secretary Albright, "however one states it, at this stage the United States is kind of the organizing principal of the international system."[99] It is not a misreading of Albright's intent to amend her statement just slightly: she and other senior officials were convinced that having shouldered the responsibilities of the world's organizing principal, it was incumbent upon the United States to play that role in perpetuity.

Just as George H. W. Bush had warned against a rising tide of isolationism, just as Anthony Lake in sounding the trumpet for enlargement singled out would-be isolationists for censure, so, too, other representatives of the Clinton administration preemptively fastened to critics of its policies this most damning of labels. Characterizing the United States as "a large country that has traditionally looked inward," Secretary of the Treasury Lawrence H. Summers lamented the ostensible American tendency to oscillate disastrously "between isolationism and global engagement." According to Vice President Al Gore, those who opposed the drive for openness spoke with "the shrill voices of isolation." When it came to entertaining dissent, proponents of American indispensability during the 1990s—Republicans and Democrats alike—were an intolerant lot. To question the strategy of openness invited charges of provincialism, expediency, and a level of partisanship bordering on treason. "These new isolationists," Gore charged, "seek nothing less than to impede President Clinton's ability to defend American interests and values."[100]

➤ "We want 'enlargement' of both our values and our Pizza Huts," Thomas Friedman has written. "We want the world to follow our lead and become democratic and capitalistic, with a Web site in every pot, a Pepsi on every lip, Microsoft Windows on every computer and with everyone, everywhere, pumping their own gas."[101] And, Friedman might have added, we want all of that on the cheap and with a clear conscience.

Across a century or more, an underlying consistency has informed the fundamentals of U.S. policy. Among other things, how the United States views itself in relation to the rest of the world has not changed. The end of the Cold War did not constitute a great discontinuity. The new era reputed to have commenced in 1989 does not necessarily differ as markedly from what had gone before as American policymakers profess to believe. It is all a matter of what story one wishes to tell. For those who conceive of the twentieth century as an epic political and moral drama in which liberalism (or freedom or democracy) succeeded at staggering cost in beating back challengers from the totalitarian left and right, the century ended in 1989. For those who conceive of that century as the epic geopolitical drama in which the rising colossus of the New World eliminated or eclipsed all other competitors for global dominance, the events of 1989 are a mere historical blip, and the "American century" continues. The first narrative is true but retains little direct relevance for the world we now inhabit. The second narrative is also true—and it offers the additional advantage of possessing enormous relevance. It is all a matter of perspective.

Proclaiming to the United States Senate in January 1917 that American principles and policies were those of all mankind, Woodrow Wilson went on to propose that the nations of the world should "with one accord adopt the doctrine of President Monroe as the doctrine of the world." Universalizing this quintessentially American policy, he continued, meant that henceforth "no nation should seek to extend its polity over any other nation or people." The result of making the Monroe Doctrine the doctrine of all humankind would be "that every people should be left free to determine its own polity, its own way of development, unhindered, unthreatened, unafraid, the little along with the great and powerful."[102]

Who could doubt that in uttering these words, Wilson, a man of high ideals whose devotion to the cause of peace was unwavering, spoke with conviction and from the heart? But outside the Senate chamber, at least in some quarters, a different perspective prevailed. According to that perspective, even within the Western Hemisphere the impact of the Monroe Doctrine was other than benign. Even during Wilson's own presidency, it served not as a guarantee that all nations would be permitted to determine their destiny unhindered, unthreatened, and unafraid, but as a mechanism for ordering relations between the strong and the weak according to terms dictated by the strong. By the time of Wilson's presidency, the Monroe Doctrine had evolved into a rationale for U.S. military intervention and the expansion of American power. Eager to see democracy prevail in the Caribbean (and unwilling to tolerate anything that smacked of radicalism or instability), Wilson sent U.S. troops into Haiti in 1915. Just weeks before his January 1917 speech, U.S. troops occupied the Dominican Republic. In each instance, the American stay proved to be a protracted one; in neither country did democracy flower as a result. Confident that he could shape the course of the Mexican Revolution and eager to teach others to "elect good men," Wilson had also meddled incessantly in Mexican internal affairs and dispatched military expeditions into Mexico in 1914 and 1916.[103] His quest to make the revolution more democratic and more humane failed utterly. Wilson succeeded only in poisoning U.S.-Mexican relations for decades to come. Yet in the president's own view, all these actions were well intentioned, and none was inconsistent with the doctrine of President Monroe.

In their urge to implement American principles and policies on a global scale, today's advocates of an open world are Wilson's heirs. Like Wilson, they categorically reject the notion that others might construe U.S. aspirations as imperialistic. They insist that the United States, uniquely among the great powers of history, employs its power to act on behalf of the common good. They profess to believe that the cause of openness is the cause of peace and development, democracy and human rights.

To compare the sincerity of those professions and Wilson's would be presumptuous. But it is neither presumptuous nor unfair to note the consequences that followed from Wilson's own convictions. It is precisely when those who tout American indispensability mean what they say that the danger of hubris looms large.

CHAPTER 5

FULL SPECTRUM DOMINANCE

There is a homely adage which runs, "Speak softly and carry a big stick; you will go far." If the American nation will speak softly and yet build and keep at a pitch of the highest training a thoroughly efficient navy, the Monroe Doctrine will go far.

Theodore Roosevelt, April 1903

IN THE AGE OF GLOBALIZATION, world peace—if by that term we mean international harmony and an end to war and violence—remains elusive. From the 1930s through the 1980s Americans were instructed that first fascists and then communists denied the peoples of the world the peace to which they aspired. Yet no sooner had the United States prevailed in the twentieth century's great ideological competition than a whole new set of obstacles to peace materialized. No one in the public arena—no president or secretary of state, no aspirant for national leadership, none of the journalists in their self-assigned role as the nation's truth tellers—ventured to explain why such an epic victory should have advanced the cause of peace minimally, if at all. Certainly no one dared to suggest that the very notion of world peace might all along have been a chimera. On the contrary, throughout the 1990s professions of America's commitment to peace issued with regularity from the mouths of U.S. officials. Peace lies just ahead, over the horizon. If we only persist, it will be ours. But for the moment, alas, the world remains a dangerous place.

Indeed, at the very heart of the strategy of openness lay a paradox: to the extent that the United States was succeeding in creating an open world, one consequence was to make Americans less rather than more secure. "The very openness of our borders and technology," explained Bill Clinton, "also makes us vulnerable in new

117

ways."[1] Dismantling barriers and easing the movement of people, capital, and commodities were making the United States more susceptible to attack by those not yet persuaded of the inevitability of the world's being remade in America's image. Nor was there any surefire way of insulating Americans from harm: "Twenty-first-century threats know no boundaries."[2] Coined by Madeleine Albright but echoed by others, this aphorism neatly captures the downside of globalization, even for its erstwhile beneficiaries.

In the global age, Americans were more vulnerable because the threats menacing the nation assumed more varied and more lethal forms. Henceforth, according to Albright, "we must plot our defense not against a single powerful threat, as during the Cold War, but against a viper's nest of perils."[3] The potency of those threats derived not from any ideological appeal—all alternatives to democratic capitalism having by common assent been exhausted—but from the same technological forces imbuing the new era with such promise. Thus, "the central reality of our time is that the advent of globalization and the revolution in information technology have magnified both the creative and the destructive potential of every individual, tribe, and nation on our planet." In combination with the openness that the United States sought to foster, this destructive potential was "making us more vulnerable to problems that arise half a world away: to terror, to ethnic, racial, and religious conflicts; to weapons of mass destruction, drug trafficking, and other organized crime."[4] Those particular remarks are President Clinton's but in the age of globalization such sentiments had long since become conventional wisdom. Technology was in the saddle and drove mankind. But in propelling Americans toward utopia, it hurtled down a path strewn with hazards of its own devising.

Not only were the threats of the post–Cold War era more numerous. They were also more dire. Consider, for example, terrorism, which Bill Clinton designated "the enemy of our generation."[5] Terrorism, of course, long predated the 1990s. Furthermore, as measured by the State Department's annual report on global terrorism, international terrorist activity declined substantially after the end of the Cold War. After reaching a peak of 665 incidents worldwide in 1987, the number of attacks per year dropped sharply. During the 1990s, in comparison with the previous decade, the average number of terrorist attacks dropped by 29 percent.[6] In 2000, 423 incidents occurred. Of those, fewer than half were directed at Americans or U.S. facilities, and the preponderance of those actions targeted property and caused no casualties. Of attacks during 2000 that the State Department classified as anti-American, well over 80 percent were attributable to Colombian guerrillas periodically cutting an oil pipeline owned by a California-based multinational corporation. During the eight years of the Clinton presidency, the number of Americans killed each year as a result of international terrorism averaged fewer than fourteen.[7] In the 1990s terror did pose a danger to Americans and their interests; but then so, too, did lightning and food poisoning.

Yet senior U.S. officials conveyed a quite different impression, discounting the trends suggested by their own data. Numbers didn't tell the real story. Indeed, the State Department coordinator for counterterrorism insisted that when it came to measuring terrorism "we shouldn't place too much emphasis on statistics."[8] Rather than data, officials pointed to a small number of incidents—the World Trade Center (1993), Oklahoma City (1995), Khobar Towers (1996), U.S. embassies in Kenya and Tanzania (1998), the USS *Cole* (2000)—as evidence that terrorism was on the rise and becoming ever more deadly. An incident hardly less significant than attacks occurring on American soil or targeting Americans abroad, in this view, was the Aum Shin Rikyo cult's release of sarin gas in the Tokyo subway system in March 1995, apparently signaling a willingness by terrorists worldwide to employ weapons of mass destruction.

Extrapolating from these incidents, senior officials in the Clinton administration conjured up a diabolical new terrorism. In the age of globalization, the face of terrorism was that of deranged but calculating primitives like the Unabomber or of maniacal, well-heeled extremists like Osama bin Laden—the two sharing little apart from their determination to derail the American project to refashion the world. Exploiting the openness of the emerging global order both as a source for increasingly lethal weapons and as a medium in which to perfect sophisticated techniques of attack and evasion, these so-called ultimate terrorists could, according to the official view, acquire the capability to wreak havoc on a scale hitherto unimaginable.

If armed with biological weapons, such terrorists could bring the world's only superpower to its knees. Appearing on national television, Secretary of Defense William Cohen warned of anthrax-wielding fanatics who in a single stroke kill half the residents of the nation's capital and paralyze the federal government. Depicting the "grave New World of terrorism" in an op-ed published in the *Washington Post,* Cohen painted a lurid picture of a surprise biological attack in which a lethal pathogen carried "across hemispheres in hours" infected "unsuspecting thousands," with devastating results. "Hospitals would become warehouses for the dead and dying. A plague more monstrous than anything we have experienced could spread with all the irrevocability of ink on tissue paper. Ancient scourges would quickly become modern nightmares." The question confronting Americans, insisted Cohen, was not if such an incident would occur, but when.[9] This belief that Americans faced the near-certain prospect of a devastating biological assault was not unique to Cohen. Reportedly influenced by his reading of *The Cobra Event,* a thriller about terrorists unleashing a deadly toxin in New York City, Bill Clinton himself confessed that worrying about a possible biological attack against the United States "keeps me awake at night."[10]

But biological attack was not the only concern. A veteran of Clinton's National Security Council warned of the prospect of a small nuclear device vaporizing the Empire State Building, contaminating the eastern seaboard with radiation, and leaving as many as 200,000 people dead.[11] Meanwhile Richard A. Clarke, White House terrorism czar during the Clinton years, pointed to the danger of an "electronic Pearl Harbor," a coordinated cyber attack on the nation's critical computer networks. Such an attack could well succeed in "shutting down 911 systems, shutting down telephone networks, and transportation systems. You black out a city, people die. Black out lots of cities, lots of people die. It's as bad as being attacked by bombs."[12]

As Clarke's remarks suggested, compounding the danger of terrorist attack was that America's wholehearted embrace of the information revolution seemingly rendered its critical infrastructure more fragile and more exposed. To cripple an information-centered society, an adversary need not destroy its army, demolish its factories, or level its cities. All that was required was disabling the crucial bit of circuitry or corrupting the right software program, something that even bright Filipino schoolboys could apparently do as a lark. In a world of interlocking, mutually dependent networks, the points of potential vulnerability became infinite. President Clinton speculated on the ease with which "terrorists, criminals, and hostile regimes could invade and paralyze these vital systems, disrupting commerce, threatening health, weakening our capacity to function in a crisis."[13] According to John Deutch, then serving as director of central intelligence, "Virtually any 'bad actor' can acquire the hardware and software to attack information-based infrastructures."[14] The challenge of mounting an effective defense increased accordingly.

By stipulating that American well-being depended not simply on developments at home but on the functioning of a global economy and on global adherence to certain norms, the architects of U.S. policy expanded the scope of concerns falling under the rubric of security. At the outset of the Cold War, concluding that the traditional term *national defense* no longer sufficed to describe the full range and purpose of American politico-military activities, policymakers opted for the term *national security* as a replacement. Over time the chief attribute of that expression would prove to be its elasticity. Even in the heyday of the anticommunist crusade, American officials would have been hard pressed to make the case that preserving the existence of the Republic of Vietnam was essential to this nation's "defense." But when leaders of the Kennedy and Johnson administrations argued with a straight face that South Vietnam was a vital U.S. "national security" interest, most Americans went obligingly along.

With the end of the Cold War, that elasticity once again proved invaluable. In the age of globalization, the definition of national security became ever more capacious. Trade became a full-fledged national security issue. So, too, did offshore money laundering and the price of oil, along with refugees, environmental degradation, large-scale violations of human rights, drug cartels, and computer hackers. By the close of Bill Clinton's second term, with his administration classifying climate change and the spread of AIDS as imminent threats to American well-being, it had become apparent that the range of security concerns to which the United States must attend in a global era was virtually without limit.[15]

Clearly, openness was the chief culprit exacerbating these various threats. But the option of curbing the threats by curbing openness itself—reinstituting controls on the movement of goods, capital, people, and ideas—never received consideration. For all of the dire predictions coming out of Washington, Americans—conditioned to see disaster as something that happened "there," not "here"—didn't really believe that the homeland was vulnerable to attack.[16] In the 1990s it was self-evident that, for the moment at least, the benefits of openness outweighed the risks. Besides, what was the alternative?

➤ With the United States vulnerable as never before, with globalization breeding nefarious new threats, with security taking on added dimensions, it was perhaps unsurprising that American attitudes regarding the role of military power also changed profoundly. In the decade after the Soviet Union imploded, the military component of U.S. policy became more not less important. As one respected analyst noted approvingly, "The bedrock of America's global leadership is military might."[17] But it was more than that: almost without anyone's noticing, military power became a central element in what little remained of an American national identity.

Recalling the outward thrust of 1898 to Cuba and the Philippines, George Kennan observed that "the American people of that day . . . simply liked the smell of empire." A century later it could be said that Americans had come to savor their possession of armed might.[18] Among a people who had once disdained military pomp and who kept a watchful eye on soldiers as potential instruments of oppression, the idea of being the world's only superpower found great favor.[19] That the United States ought to retain that status permanently was taken for granted across the spectrum of respectable opinion.

This represented a sea change in traditional American attitudes. Indeed, even as the United States rose to great-power status, Americans were of two minds about military matters. Antimilitarism informed the nation's founding. In American eyes, one of the factors distinguishing the New World from the Old was an aversion to war and to the wasteful and bloody military competition that was a by-product of Europe's preoccupation with power politics. Among the Founders, the belief that standing armies were antithetical to liberty was an article of faith. In the nineteenth century, Americans associated military professionalism with an elitism that did not sit well with a self-consciously democratic populace. When it came to national defense, Americans placed their trust not in the long-service regular but in Ralph Waldo Emerson's celebrated "embattled farmer"—the citizen-soldier.[20]

None of this meant that Americans, in practice, were given to pacifism. If anything, the reverse was true. Only through the sustained application of violence did they win their independence from Great Britain. In the decades following, Americans showed little reluctance to employ force.[21] They ruthlessly removed and pacified the indigenous peoples of North America, forced open markets abroad, conquered vast expanses of the West and Southwest, crushed an effort by several states to secede from the Union, and seized a far-flung maritime empire stretching to the western Pacific. Waiving the ostensible prohibition against mixing soldiers and politics, they routinely rewarded war heroes by elevating them to the presidency.

Out of this mix of antimilitarism punctuated by recurring outbursts of bellicosity there emerged a distinctive approach to military policy. From the Revolution through World War II, the United States adhered to that approach—finally abandoning it with the end of the Cold War.

In "normal" times, it became standard American practice to rely on standing forces of modest size and capabilities. Immune from immediate attack by a rival great power, the United States configured its minuscule regular army less as a "warfighting" force than as an adjunct to national development. Similarly, the Navy made itself useful less by preparing to fight large-scale fleet engagements than by supporting the nation's burgeoning commercial interests. Americans in general consigned both services to the margins of national life, both physically and psychologically. Throughout the nineteenth century, during the long intervals between real wars, the U.S. Army and U.S. Navy proved themselves to be eminently useful without the officer corps of either service being especially influential beyond the narrow confines of its assigned tasks.[22]

With the onset of emergency, whether real or contrived, all this instantly changed. Whether pursuing its "manifest destiny," responding to the crisis of secession, freeing Cubans from the yoke of colonial oppression, or setting out to make the world safe for democracy, the United States spared no effort to raise on a crash basis a mighty host of citizen-soldiers. Sheer mass rather than tactical finesse tended to be the distinguishing characteristic of the resulting force, but against Mexico, the Confederacy, Spain, and a Germany nearing the end of its rope in 1918, that force sufficed to get the job done.

Yet as soon as the crisis ended, with citizen-soldiers clamoring to go home, the military establishment reverted almost overnight to its pre-war configuration. Thus, during the Civil War the U.S. Army went from 17,000 regulars in 1861 to a force of over a million (mostly volunteers) by 1865. Just one year after Appomattox, only 57,000 soldiers remained, with that number soon reduced to an anemic standing force of 25,000 until the next emergency arose in 1898. The experience of World War II was similar. From a peacetime establishment of 334,000 long-service regulars in 1939, the U.S. armed services mushroomed into a force of 12 million by V-J Day. Within a year the services had been slashed by 75 percent and rendered combat ineffective.[23] Victorious American armies did not demobilize; they disintegrated.

The practice was enormously wasteful, not only fiscally but even more so in terms of losses sustained when the battlefield rather than the training ground became the medium where soldiers learned to fight, officers to lead, and political leaders to distinguish competent generals from the incompetent. But the American preference for extemporizing citizen armies offered compensating advantages. By keeping peacetime military expenditures low, it minimized the burden imposed on citizens and freed resources for other national priorities. By keeping the officer corps on a short leash, it served as a check against incipient militarism. Above all, by sustaining the view that in a republic military power, like political authority, derived from the people, it kept faith with the ideological legacy of the Revolution. Disdainful of European reliance on large conscript armies, deference to a quasi-aristocratic officer elite, and the surrender of control over military policy to cultlike general staffs, the United States affirmed the mythology of American exceptionalism: as in all other respects, when it came to military affairs America was a power unlike any other.[24]

A residue of these sentiments persisted well into the Cold War. Although the protracted standoff against communism obliged the United States to maintain a force of unprecedented size (sustained through the 1960s by a peacetime draft), doing so did not necessarily signify the conscious abandonment of traditional practice. At least in theory, the Cold War constituted an emergency, not a permanent condition. In the interim, wise heads kept a watchful eye out for signs that the United States might inadvertently assume the attributes of a "garrison state." In his Farewell Address of January 1961, President

Dwight D. Eisenhower, himself a five-star general, testified eloquently to his conviction that cultivating military power was at odds with the nation's true ideals. Perilous times might compel the United States to erect a vast "military-industrial complex," yet the necessity of doing so did not negate the risk to American democracy. By implication, Eisenhower seemed to suggest that if and when the Cold War ended, the United States would do well to revert to military normalcy.[25]

Forty years after Eisenhower spoke, his fears would have struck most Americans as quaint and his wariness about excessive military influence as verging on paranoia. In truth, when the Cold War finally did end, few even paused to contemplate Ike's concerns. After the Berlin Wall fell, there occurred no national debate about the proper role of military power as a component of U.S. policy and as an element in American life. To the extent that any inclination to entertain such a debate existed, the euphoria generated by Operation Desert Storm smothered it.

➤ "Today," announced National Security Adviser Samuel R. Berger at the much ballyhooed dawn of a new millennium, "just about everybody believes we need a strong military to protect our interests in a world of continuing if shifting dangers."[26] In a speech largely devoted to unrelated matters it was a throwaway line. But Berger's remark about U.S. military power was a revealing one. It was, for the most part, true. To the extent that it was not true, Berger erred on the side of understatement, which made it more remarkable still.

On at least three counts Berger's evaluation was too modest. First, his "just about everybody" included *literally* everybody—at least within the circle of those whose opinions counted in the world of national politics and policy. In the aftermath of the Cold War, the principle that the United States required great military strength commanded universal assent in Washington. To dissent from that position was to place oneself beyond the bounds of respectable opinion. By the 1990s the dovish McGovernite wing of the Democratic party was dead; and the so-called Republican Revolution of 1994 did little or nothing to revive right-wing skepticism of military spending associated with the defunct Taft wing of the G.O.P. Only a self-professed maverick like Patrick J. Buchanan dared to question the necessity of continuing to maintain the panoply of military commitments forged during the Cold War. But Buchanan's temerity in even raising the issue provided ammunition to critics eager to prove that he had taken leave of his senses.[27]

Second, the prevailing consensus regarding American military power is not simply that the United States needs a "strong military." Rather, it is that the United States must possess military capabilities enabling it to prevail over any conceivable combination of adversaries. In the early part of the last century, Great Britain as the world's dominant naval power adhered to a two-power rule—as a matter of policy maintaining a fleet large enough to defeat the next two largest navies combined. In support of its strategy of openness, the United States implicitly adheres to an $N + 1$ rule, where N equals the sum of the military capabilities of all nations who may make common cause against the United States. In a moment of exuberance, Berger declared in 1999 that U.S. "military expenditures now are larger than [those of] all other countries combined."[28] Although the claim was not precisely accurate, it captured the reigning spirit of the 1990s: Americans took it for granted that if annual U.S. defense expenditures might not literally exceed those of all other nations they would surpass those of all the other major military powers combined.[29] After the Cold War, the measure of adequacy was no longer simply military strength; it had become military supremacy, a position endorsed by liberals as well as conservatives, Democrats as well as Republicans.

Third, the purpose of using the U.S. military in support of the strategy of openness is not simply to "protect our interests," but to promote those interests actively and to do so on a global scale. In the aftermath of World War II the cabinet-level War and Navy Departments were subsumed in a new unified Department of Defense. Half a century later that department's blandly reassuring name—suggesting a strictly tutelary function—had long since become anachronistic. Although terms like *protect* and *defend* remained part of the lexicon that U.S. officials employed to describe the activities of American soldiers, they were at best inadequate and at worst misleading.

"For more than 50 years we were constrained by a bipolar rivalry with a superpower adversary," observed General John M. Shalikashvili, chairman of the Joint Chiefs of Staff, in 1997. "To deal with such a world, we relied on a strategy of containment and designed our military forces to react in case the strategy failed."[30] Shalikashvili was not alone in understanding that the end of the Cold War removed those constraints. The thrust of the programs in which the U.S. military engaged in the decade following the fall of the Berlin Wall was no longer passive or reactive. The "strategy of engagement" to which the Pentagon committed itself aimed explicitly to "shape the international environment" in ways that accommodated U.S. interests.[31] The United States employed military power not merely in response to a crisis or to signs that a crisis was brewing. It did so to reassure, anticipate, intimidate, preempt, influence, guide, and control. And it did so routinely and continuously. In the age of globalization, the Department of Defense completed its transformation into a Department of Power Projection.

In regions that figure as critical to the strategy of openness, the projection of power manifested itself in the form of permanent presence. Thus, a decade after the end of the Cold War rendered Europe whole, the United States maintained a garrison of 100,000 troops there. A force of similar size, stationed chiefly in Korea and Japan, outposted the Asia-Pacific region. In both instances the Pentagon showed every inclination of maintaining these forward-deployed garrisons regardless of any change in the local situation, political or otherwise. When Secretary of Defense Cohen, discussing the imperative of modernizing the armed services, declared that "everything's on the table for discussion," he pointedly made an exception for forward-deployed forces: "we're going to keep 100,000 people in the Asia Pacific region so that's off the table; and we're going to keep 100,000 people in Europe so that's off the table."[32] One legacy of the Persian Gulf War was to add yet a third standing requirement. A decade after the war concluded, approximately 23,000 American troops remained in that region as well, a commitment showing every likelihood of being of indefinite duration.

Elsewhere, that is to say in regions of emerging or lesser immediate importance, the United States projected military power in pulses of limited duration. These took the form of training exercises, ship visits, officer exchanges, and the deployment of "mobile training teams." The reach and diversity of activities sponsored by the Department of Defense became those of an empire on which the sun never sets. "We have people on the seas, people in foreign countries, all over the world, on every continent," President Bill Clinton enthused in 1999. "We are everywhere."[33] Paratroopers from the 82d Airborne Division jumping into Kazakhstan in multilateral peacekeeping exercises; U.S. Marines splashing ashore to "practice interoperability" with Croatian amphibious forces; American warships calling at Aden; Green Berets putting Colombian and Nigerian recruits through their paces or training Uzbeks in the steppes of the former Soviet Union; Warsaw Pact veterans studying at the George C. Marshall Center in Garmisch, Germany; the transfer of Abrams tanks to Egypt, Apache attack helicopters to Turkey, and F-16 fighter jets to Thailand: all these comprised elements of a comprehensive program designed, in the words of Secretary of Defense William Perry, to "build openness and trust between nations."[34] But in this context, too, openness was indistinguishable from American leverage and influence.[35]

These, then, formed the three premises of U.S. military policy after the Cold War: a broad (if unratified) consensus regarding the inherent desirability of military power; a commitment to maintaining U.S. global military supremacy in perpetuity; and support for maximizing the utility of U.S. military might by pursuing an ambitious, activist agenda. But to those three can be added a fourth, which Berger did not touch upon: an appreciation of the ultimate purpose of U.S. military engagement. That purpose is to maintain international order, thereby enabling the processes of globalization to continue and the American people to reap its rewards. As Secretary of Defense William Cohen explained, "economists and soldiers share the same interests in stability." By tapping American military power, "we are able to shape the environment in ways that are advantageous to us and that are stabilizing to the areas where we are forward deployed, thereby helping to promote investment and prosperity." The logic was all but self-evident: "when you have stability, you have at least the opportunity to enjoy prosperity because investment flows . . . When they find a secure environment, they will invest." Or put simply, "business follows the flag."[36]

None of this implied an expectation that in shaping the environment the U.S. military would forcibly impose its will on others. Rather, American policymakers entertained the expectation that the indisputable fact of U.S. military dominance would speak for itself, without the necessity of actually resorting to out-and-out coercion.

By its very existence, American military power would deter adversaries and comfort friends and allies. The chief rationale for maintaining the forward deployment of U.S. forces long after the Soviet threat had evaporated was not to engage in combat operations, but "to shape people's opinions about us in ways that are favorable to us," Secretary of Defense Cohen explained; "when people see us, they see our power, they see our professionalism, they see our patriotism, and they say that's a country that we want to be with."[37]

In practice, a foreign military presence offended some even as it reassured others. Certainly, the United States had found this to be true throughout the postwar period. Long after they recovered from World War II, nations such as Germany and Japan continued to host large U.S. garrisons, thereby minimizing the defense burden imposed upon their own people. In return for guaranteeing the security of its allies, the United States assumed a privileged position politically—enjoying a preponderance of influence in what was ostensibly a partnership of "equals." To elites on both sides, the benefits of this bargain were self-evident. For those outside elite circles, the evidence was not always so clear. At critical junctures of the Cold War—notably the Vietnam War and the Reagan presidency—the presence of G.I.'s inspired not a desire to "be with" the United States but an active opposition, ranging from mass demonstrations to bombings, aimed at pressuring the Americans to go home.

The post–Cold War designation of American troops as agents of "engagement" produced a similarly mixed reaction. Some nations, such as Kuwait, did not even bother to disguise their eagerness to become, militarily at least, an American client. Elsewhere the U.S. military presence inspired a negative reaction that one critic has characterized as "imperial blowback."[38] In Japan, the misconduct of individual American service personnel (especially in preying on young Japanese women), aircraft noise, and complaints about the cumulative environmental impact of decades of military exercises provoked widespread protest, most passionately expressed by the residents of Okinawa, longtime home to a U.S. Marine division.[39]

In the Persian Gulf, an American military presence of more recent vintage produced a more lethal form of "blowback," manifested in a series of attacks directed against U.S. personnel in the region. Attributed by U.S. officials to the Saudi renegade Osama bin Laden, these attacks scored a series of impressive tactical successes. In November 1995 a car bomb near a U.S. facility in Riyadh killed five American advisers assigned to the Saudi Arabian National Guard. In June 1996 an even more devastating attack in Dhahran destroyed a high-rise being used as an American barracks. The Khobar Towers bombing left 19 airmen dead and over 270 wounded. In the waning days of the Clinton era, an attack on the USS *Cole* calling for fuel at Aden left a billion-dollar warship crippled and 17 American sailors dead. Shaping the environment was not without its costs.

➤ So the end of the Cold War did not see U.S. forces returning home to stand down. There was no return to normalcy. To the contrary: the security environment created as a by-product of globalization confronted soldiers with daunting new challenges. It saddled them with weighty new responsibilities that went well beyond standing in readiness to fight and win the nation's wars. Complicating efforts to fulfill those responsibilities were widespread expectations that soldiers would do so less through the actual use of force than by demonstrating such indubitable superiority that fighting itself would become largely unnecessary. As copywriters touting America's need for a "revolutionary" new jet fighter proclaimed, U.S. military dominance "will give potential adversaries a single option: Peace." American military superiority, gushed another ad, would not only destroy the enemy; it would prove "equally adept at destroying an enemy's desire to fight, long before there *is* a war."[40] What sort of military would be required to fulfill this very tall order?

The reality, however unwelcome in some quarters, was that the military establishment inherited from the Cold War was not especially well suited for this new era. That establishment had been designed to defend the free world against the vast mechanized legions of the Warsaw Pact. In the 1990s, with communism a dead letter, fears of World War III dissipating, and prospects of major conventional conflict after Operation Desert Storm remote, such a military looked increasingly like a magnificent but superannuated artifact. Indeed, with American troops being pressed into service as guarantors of international good behavior, some observers (though at first only a handful of soldiers) were concluding that post–Cold War conditions were rendering obsolete the military machine painstakingly rebuilt in the aftermath of Vietnam.

William Cohen dubbed it the "superpower paradox." U.S. supremacy in the realm of conventional warfare—the military's preferred style of combat—would not by itself keep would-be troublemakers in their place. Recognition of U.S. conventional superiority served only to redirect their efforts, prompting adversaries to avoid America's strong suit and "to increasingly pursue unconventional or asymmetric methods of warfare." As a result, a proven ability to close with and destroy an enemy force composed of tanks and planes—amply affirmed in the Persian Gulf—no longer sufficed. Henceforth, U.S. forces needed to be capable of much more. In a global age, Cohen declared, "our soldiers, sailors, airmen, and Marines, all our services, must be trained to do everything."[41]

This clearly asked a lot. But there was more: before training American military men and women to do everything, the Pentagon needed to ensure that soldiers had the equipment, force structure, and doctrine suited for a wider role. Above all, the Pentagon needed a conceptual template for converting the U.S. military into an instrument suited to the opportunities, challenges, and expectations of the age of globalization.

The Pentagon responded to this requirement by articulating what it called its "Joint Vision." This plan for restructuring the U.S. armed forces appeared first in 1996 as *Joint Vision 2010* and subsequently in revised form as *Joint Vision 2020*. Bearing the imprimatur of the chairman of the Joint Chiefs of Staff and warmly endorsed by successive secretaries of defense, both documents evoked a common theme, offering an authoritative blueprint for maintaining and expanding U.S. military supremacy. Toward that end, both promised the creation of a force "persuasive in peace, decisive in war, [and] preeminent in any form of conflict."[42]

At root, the expectation that the United States could sustain broad-gauged military preeminence rested on a specific understanding of the role that technology—in particular information technology—has come to play in modern warfare. That role was purported to be a decisive one. There was little in the Pentagon's Joint Vision to suggest that American soldiers were necessarily tougher than their adversaries. Nor were they braver or more eager to die for their cause. But they did possess a clear digital edge, and that, in the twenty-first century, was expected to make all the difference. Indeed, permeating both *Joint Vision 2010* and its successor was a confidence that information technology had endowed the United States with a unique capacity to alter the very nature of war.

Thus, according to *Joint Vision 2010*, information-age capabilities—stealth, precision strike, multispectral sensors, automated command and control—could be counted on to mitigate (if not quite eliminate) the fog and friction that throughout history have made combat the province of uncertainty and chance. As a consequence, warfare would become more "transparent." American commanders at all echelons would acquire a more comprehensive and accurate picture of the battlefield, enabling them to make better decisions and to act more quickly than the opposition. Massing forces in anticipation of launching an operation would become a thing of the past, technology making it possible to achieve the effects of mass—concentrated combat power—without the actual necessity of physically gathering forces in one place. Complex actions that had once unfolded sequentially would now occur simultaneously. Weapons effectiveness would increase by "an order of magnitude." Employing "fewer platforms and less ordnance," commanders would achieve their objectives "more rapidly and with reduced risk" to friendly forces and to noncombatants. The enemy's appreciation of superior U.S. capabilities might even obviate any need actually to employ the American arsenal, since "the presence or anticipated presence of a decisive force might well cause an enemy to surrender after minimal resistance." Alternatively, rather than relying on the threat of physical destruction, American commanders "in the arena of information operations" might employ "nonkinetic weapons" to disabuse the enemy of the least inclination to fight even before the contest had actually begun.[43]

"Seamless integration," "enhanced connectivity," "fused, all-source, real-time intelligence," "high fidelity target acquisition," "accelerated operational tempo," "asymmetric leverage," "total asset visibility," "dominant battlespace awareness," "near-simultaneous sensor-to-shooter data flow": the language employed to detail the Joint Vision testified to its full-throated technological romanticism.[44] At the heart of that vision lay this conviction: that exploiting the potential of the information revolution would enable U.S. forces, acting unilaterally or with allies, to overcome any conceivable adversary across the entire range of military operations, including conventional or unconventional wars and "those ambiguous situations residing between peace and war."⁴⁵ According to Secretary Cohen, "Technology now gives the United States an opportunity that no other military has ever had: the ability to see through the fog of war more clearly and to strike precisely over long distances. This is what we call the revolution in military affairs. It means fighting with more stealth and surprise. It means achieving greater effectiveness with less risk."⁴⁶

In short, having assessed the security implications of globalization—a process ostensibly making the world more complicated and more dangerous than ever before—the United States after the Cold War committed itself to establishing a level of military mastery without historical precedent. In magnitude and scope, the dominance to which the Pentagon aspired dwarfed that which American soldiers had imagined was in their grasp a half-century before when in sole possession of the atomic bomb. It far exceeded that achieved by imperial Rome or by France in the era of Bonaparte. The ambitions of the German General Staff in its heyday—launching the Schlieffen Plan in 1914 or Operation Barbarossa in 1941—appeared puny by comparison. Swift, unerring, implacable, and invincible, U.S. forces aimed to achieve something approaching omnipotence: "Full Spectrum Dominance."⁴⁷

➤ The Pentagon's extraordinarily ambitious Joint Vision tells one story of U.S. military policy in the wake of the Cold War. Actual progress made toward fulfilling those ambitions reveals quite another story—with the differences between the two defining the gap between the military capabilities that the strategy of openness ostensibly required and those that the services have been able (or willing) to mount.

The grandeur of America's post–Cold War military aspirations seemed to imply that the defense establishment as it existed in 1991 had to change, not in a small but in a large way. Not surprisingly, therefore, throughout the ensuing decade testimony by senior defense officials and documents issued by the Department of Defense alluded time and again to the imperative of "transforming" the armed services.⁴⁸

For soldiers and civilians responsible for national security policy, "transformation" in the 1990s became the equivalent of campaign finance reform in political quarters: endlessly discussed and effusively endorsed, yet at the end of the day producing results more cosmetic than substantive. The pattern first emerged during the administration of the elder President Bush with the unveiling of the "Base Force," the handiwork of General Colin Powell, then at the height of his influence as chairman of the Joint Chiefs of Staff. But the aim of the Base Force was less to get a head start on military reform than to pre-empt calls for a "peace dividend"—suggesting the possibility of draconian cuts in defense spending. To avert that threat, in a remarkable maneuver Powell arrogated to the Joint Staff the principal responsibility for determining the shape of armed services. "I was determined to have the Joint Chiefs drive the military strategy train," Powell later explained, "rather than having military reorganization schemes shoved down our throat."[49]

With this aim in mind, planners on Powell's Joint Staff stipulated that henceforth a cornerstone of U.S. national security posture should be to maintain the ability to fight two "nearly simultaneous" Desert Storm–size wars (now styled "major regional conflicts," or MRCs). That two-MRC requirement provided the basis for sizing the armed services and a rationale for setting clear limits on how far the existing military force structure could be reduced.

As a candidate for president, then-Governor Bill Clinton criticized the Bush administration's plans for military reform as timid. Claiming—not without reason—that the Base Force merely perpetuated a Cold War–era military, Clinton called for radical surgery. "We must restructure our military forces for a new era," he insisted in December 1991, promising that his administration would make defense reform a priority.[50] For Clinton's first secretary of defense, Les Aspin, redeeming that pledge became his first order of business. Less than a year after Clinton's inauguration, Aspin unveiled the administration's plan to do just that and proclaimed with evident satisfaction: "Well, consider it done."[51]

What was actually done amounted to precious little. On the basis of a much-hyped "Bottom-Up Review"—which began by affirming Powell's two-MRC standard—the Clinton administration insisted that expected technological "enhancements" would enable the Pentagon to do more with less. This finding provided the necessary justification for making additional cuts, amounting to 200,000 troops, beyond those exacted by the Base Force. Yet Aspin's claims notwithstanding, the defense establishment that emerged (and remained in place through the rest of the decade)—an Army of ten divisions, a Navy of twelve carrier battle groups, an Air Force of thirteen active fighter wings—was hardly distinguishable from the Cold War military, scaled down in size by roughly one-third.[52] It was, indeed, "Base Force lite."[53]

As it had during the Bush administration, the military itself managed to deflect Clinton from the issues that serious defense reform entailed. Despite its name, the Bottom-Up Review became in the end an exercise in forestalling large-scale change, an intramural fight between each of the services, backed by their respective political and corporate champions, over how to distribute cuts in force structure to achieve a predetermined reduction in overall defense spending. As such, more fundamental questions—what role those services ought to play and how, accordingly, they should be organized and equipped—largely escaped scrutiny.

No one was more determined to keep those questions off limits and to preserve the status quo than Powell himself. The Joint Chiefs chairman signaled as much during the press briefing at which he and Aspin detailed the results of the Bottom-Up Review. Powell prefaced his remarks by treating the reporters in attendance to "a little bit of a tutorial" about the American military's identity. "Notwithstanding all of the changes that have taken place in the world," he reminded them, "we have a value system and a culture system within the armed forces of the United States. We have this mission: to fight and win the nation's wars. That's what we do. . . . We're warriors."[54] Values, culture, and the traditional raison d'être of soldiering—these constituted the crown jewels of the military profession and remained nonnegotiable. The Bottom-Up Review might have cost Powell— who had risen to the top not as a warrior but as an unusually astute political general—an additional increment of troops. But that was a small price to pay in comparison to what he achieved: he successfully thwarted efforts to tamper with the things that really counted.

The evident limitations of the Bottom-Up Review—along with Powell's own impending departure from active duty—served only to goad those committed to serious defense reform into redoubling their efforts. As a result, the remainder of the decade saw sundry other high-profile, blue-ribbon efforts intended to provide a catalyst for

transformation: a Commission on Roles and Missions in 1994, a Quadrennial Defense Review in 1997, a National Defense Panel that same
year, and a Commission on National Security/21st Century, a three-
year effort headed by former Senators Gary Hart and Warren
Rudman that issued its preliminary findings in 1999. Each effort
highlighted the radically changed security environment produced by
the age of globalization. Each emphasized the limitations of the military establishment inherited from the Cold War when it came to dealing with that environment. With progressively greater enthusiasm,
each trumpeted the imperative of transforming that establishment by
marrying digital technology to military planning and operations to
bring about a full-fledged "revolution in military affairs" (RMA).

Whatever hopes inspired these efforts, the substantive results were
universally disappointing. Implicit in the calls for an information-
driven RMA was a willingness to entertain fundamental institutional
change—in Pentagon parlance, to break rice bowls. Revolutionizing
the military necessarily called into question long-standing and highly
cherished service conventions. It meant overturning hitherto sacrosanct agreements on roles, missions, and budget share that had for
decades provided a firebreak against destructive interservice rivalry. It
threw open for renegotiation the whole array of privileges, prerogatives, and responsibilities distinguishing military professionals from
their civilian counterparts. Not least of all, changing the military to
conform to the reigning imperatives of the digital age redefined combat and in doing so changed what it meant to be a "warrior."

Those whose status and self-image derived from the traditional tes-
tosterone-laced conception of soldiering could not be expected to
welcome this prospect. After all, everything that information-age institutions profess to be, a traditionally configured military is not. Information-age organizations are flat and fluid. Their culture is ostentatiously informal and individualistic. They neither acknowledge nor
covet a history. They are relentlessly result oriented. In contrast, traditional military organizations are rigidly hierarchical and highly bu-
reaucratized. Their culture centers on the twin concepts of deference
and paternalism, reflecting a highly stratified class system—an officer
elite on top, an enlisted "workforce" beneath—that predates the Industrial Revolution. Military institutions cherish history. They are
bound by the past and defer to its ostensible lessons. Among soldiers,

especially in peacetime, form and process count as much as substance.

The RMA posed a clear and present danger to the military as a way of life.[55] However much a global strategy in an era of globalization seemingly called for reorganizing the services according to the dictates of the information age, doing so came only at the cost of forfeiting much of what lent to a soldier's life its peculiar savor. Few senior officers, viewing themselves as stewards of their service and their profession, proved willing to pay that price.[56] In this regard, Powell, the protector of military culture and values, possessed a surer grasp of what soldiers cared about than did his successors, whose Joint Vision suggested a willingness to toss tradition overboard if the pursuit of Full Spectrum Dominance should require it.

Thus, during the first decade after the Cold War a gaping disparity emerged between the rhetoric and the reality of U.S. military policy. On the surface, the services proclaimed their fealty to the transformation project. Beneath the surface, meanwhile, each labored to stymie reform and to salvage as large a share of the existing force—an industrial-age military based on mechanized divisions, carrier battle groups, and manned jet aircraft—as it possibly could. To a very large extent—notwithstanding assurances by civilian officials nominally in charge that the Department of Defense fully embraced the RMA—this effort succeeded.[57] Thus, by decade's end a trenchant observer of U.S. national security affairs described the Pentagon as an institution mired in the past in which "inertia overwhelms the impulse to change." A decade after the fall of the Berlin Wall, wrote Eliot A. Cohen, American strategy still clung to "a Cold War–derived understanding of military power." The services persisted in purchasing hardware "suited for war in Europe with the defunct Soviet Union." The Pentagon continued to rely on command arrangements dating back to World War II and a personnel and recruitment system created during Vietnam.[58] Despite the lip service paid to jointness, senior military leaders refused even to consider eliminating the redundancies that had been the price of negotiating a truce in the interservice battles that had erupted as the Cold War was just beginning.

As a result, the military establishment of 2000—after a decade of so-called transformation—was organizationally all but indistinguishable from the military establishment of 1950. It continued, for example, to maintain four distinct "air forces," with the Army, the Navy, and the Marine Corps each maintaining fleets of aircraft on a par with the air arm of any other major power.[59] It also continued to field two distinct and formidable land armies, with the U.S. Marine Corps, 169,800 strong, larger than the entire army of Great Britain, France, or Italy. With its three potent and deployable combat divisions, the Marine Corps also offered considerably more muscle.[60]

Nor had the services themselves changed noticeably in the way they were internally organized and equipped. "What's wrong with this picture?" Cohen asked as the year 2000 came to a close.

> Last year, the U.S. military looked something like this: it had 1,380,000 troops, a budget of some $279 billion, and featured 10 active Army and three active Marine Corps divisions, about 20 active and reserve air wings, and 11 active aircraft carriers. Its forces drove M-1 tanks, flew F-15 and F-16 fighters and F-117 bombers, and sailed Nimitz-class carriers. They were organized into unified and specified commands, governed primarily by the Goldwater-Nichols Department of Defense Reorganization Act of 1986.
>
> Ten years earlier—with the Soviet Union still standing and the Gulf War soon to begin—the picture was strangely similar. The U.S. military had slightly over two million troops. With a budget of $382.5 billion (in today's dollars), it had 18 active Army and 3 active Marine Corps divisions, 36 active and reserve air wings, and 14 carriers. Its troops drove M-1 tanks, flew F-15 and F-16 fighters and F-117 bombers, and sailed Nimitz-class carriers. They too were organized into unified and specified commands, governed primarily by the Goldwater-Nichols Act.[61]

For all the windy talk of reform and restructuring, the defenders of the status quo had carried the day.

➤ But that victory proved to be a pyrrhic one. By the beginning of the third millennium, the United States was well on its way toward concocting a self-induced crisis in national security policy. On the one hand, members of the policy elite agreed that the age of globalization had given birth to dangerous new threats and had thrust upon the United States expanded responsibilities. These twin developments demanded a quantum leap in U.S. military capabilities, in both breadth and depth. American soldiers needed to expand their repertoire and to perform every routine within that repertoire all but flawlessly. For a society gripped with enthusiasm for the wonders of a digitized world, information technology offered a tantalizing prospect for effecting that quantum leap, revolutionizing military affairs just as it was ostensibly revolutionizing every other facet of human existence.

On the other hand, despite their own genuine infatuation with technology, few soldiers were willing to embrace that revolution if doing so required them to forfeit their autonomy, prerogatives, and cultural distinctiveness. In documents like *Joint Vision 2010,* the armed services embraced the "revolution in military affairs" and then did everything in their power to subvert, retard, or limit that revolution.

By the end of the 1990s this military schizophrenia had contributed to an ever-increasing deficit separating perceived national security requirements and the capabilities that U.S. forces could actually bring to bear. At a moment when to the rest of the world American military dominance was greater than ever, the notion took hold within the United States that the U.S. position was rapidly deteriorating. Respected scholars were publishing books lamenting American "military weakness" and warning that the situation in which the United States found itself bore striking similarities to that of Great Britain between the world wars, slumbering while Hitler rose to power.[62]

The brass and their supporters attributed the problem to a "strategy-force mismatch."[63] The most generously endowed military in the entire world concluded that it had been subsisting on half-rations and called for more money.[64] Meanwhile, as the campaign for the 2000 presidential elections heated up, Republican and Democratic contenders alike promised that if elected they would boost defense spending. In doing so they were merely following the polls. According to surveys conducted by the Gallup Organization, the percentage of Americans persuaded that the United States was spending *too little* on defense grew steadily in the decade following the end of the Cold War, from 9 percent in 1990 to 40 percent in August 2000.[65]

For his part, the Republican nominee and eventual victor, Governor George W. Bush, revived the plaintive call for reform that Bill Clinton had sounded nearly a decade before. "Our military is still organized more for cold war threats than for the challenges of the new century—for industrial-age operations, rather than information-age battles," Bush complained. "The last seven years have been wasted in inertia and idle talk." If elected, Bush pledged, he would "begin creating the military of the next century." Shortly before his inauguration he promised to initiate a "bottom-to-top review" of the military establishment.[66]

Thus did the debate over military reform come full circle. A decade after the end of the Cold War, efforts to reconfigure the U.S. military for the age of globalization remained unfulfilled. Within each of the individual services, opposition to those efforts by purists committed to the traditional warrior ideal and to the notion that the soldier's role was to fight and win the nation's wars, neither more nor less, showed no signs of diminishing. The Full Spectrum Dominance ostensibly required to achieve America's global vision remained a pipe dream.

CHAPTER 6

GUNBOATS AND GURKHAS

All that we desire is to see all neighboring countries stable, orderly, and prosperous. Any country whose people conduct themselves well can count upon our hearty friendliness . . . if it keeps order and pays its obligations, then it need fear no interference from the United States. Brutal wrongdoing, or an impotence which results in a general loosening of the ties of civilized society, may finally require intervention by some civilized nation, and . . . the United States cannot ignore this duty.

Theodore Roosevelt, May 1904

ON MARCH 28, 1999, the *New York Times Magazine* featured as its cover story an essay by the newspaper's star foreign affairs columnist, Thomas L. Friedman. The article offered a preview of Friedman's soon-to-be-published book, *The Lexus and the Olive Tree,* a treatise promoting globalization. Instead of featuring a computer or some other familiar symbol of the information age, the cover illustration presented a photograph of a clenched fist, brightly painted with the Stars and Stripes. The image captured the central point of Friedman's self-described "manifesto for the fast world": "the emerging global order needs an enforcer. That's America's new burden."[1]

Appearing the very week that the United States and its NATO allies had initiated hostilities against Yugoslavia, Friedman's message could hardly have been more timely. Touted as an effort to prevent the ethnic cleansing of Kosovo by Serb forces acting under the orders of Slobodan Milošević, Operation Allied Force seemingly testified to America's willingness to step up to its responsibilities. In the eyes of its architects, Allied Force was to be a brief, straightforward affair, more an exercise in muscle flexing than a war as such. A short, economical demonstration of allied (and especially American) air power

141

would end a hitherto intractable diplomatic standoff and produce a tidy outcome: the restoration of peace, the preservation of a multiethnic, multicultural Kosovo, and, ultimately, progress toward democracy.

Events soon exposed such expectations as naïve. By the time the pummeling of Yugoslavia ended eleven weeks later, giving way to an occupation of Kosovo during which allied forces tacitly presided over a process of reverse ethnic cleansing, Americans received an object lesson in just how daunting the role of global enforcer was likely to be. Viewed in retrospect, the manifestly fraudulent terms under which the campaign commenced, the constraints under which it proceeded, and the military, diplomatic, and moral complications encountered along the way all suggested that Operation Allied Force qualified as a true watershed.

Yet if Americans sensed vaguely that Kosovo had been a defining event, few placed it in its larger context. In fact U.S. involvement in a war for the Balkans marked the culmination of a decadelong process in which U.S. foreign policy became increasingly militarized. As Madeleine Albright noted, it was incumbent upon "the indispensable nation to see what we can do to make the world safer for our children and grandchildren, and for those people around the world who follow the rules."[2] Making a safe world required the use of force to ensure adherence to those rules. In pursuit of this requirement, actual U.S. military practice diverged ever further from published U.S. national security strategy and official U.S. military doctrine. Kosovo showed how wide the gap between policy and practice had become.

The contradictions that enabled tiny Yugoslavia to frustrate the world's only superpower and its allies for so many weeks are rooted in changing American views about the role of military power. Contrary to the expectations expressed by George Bush following the Persian Gulf War, Bush's successor hesitated only briefly before concluding that the mere possession of superior military power would not suffice to advance the cause of global openness. As a result, not force held in abeyance but force expended became a hallmark of U.S. policy in the 1990s. The two terms of President Bill Clinton produced an unprecedented level of military activism. A blue-ribbon commission appointed to assess future national security policy reported in 1999 that "since the end of the Cold War, the United States has embarked upon nearly four dozen military interventions . . . as opposed to only 16 during the entire period of the Cold War."[3]

➤ The road to Kosovo began in the Persian Gulf, where the seemingly easy triumph of 1991 fostered heightened expectations regarding the utility of military power, especially the high-tech capabilities on which the United States enjoyed a near monopoly. But the road to Kosovo also ran through Mogadishu, benighted capital of impoverished Somalia.

Somalia was the tar baby that George Bush bequeathed to his successor.[4] When Bush, already a lame duck, intervened in Somalia in December 1992, he promised that U.S. troops would complete their mission and withdraw by inauguration day. When January 20 arrived with 25,000 American soldiers and marines still in Somalia and the projected UN follow-on force nowhere to be seen, few informed observers were surprised. If there was any surprise, it was the alacrity with which Bill Clinton embraced George Bush's gift.

The Bush administration's declared purpose for going into Somalia had been to create a secure environment enabling humanitarian relief organizations to deliver food and other assistance to a stricken population.[5] Lulled by the apparent ease with which Operation Restore Hope began, Clinton expanded the mission.[6] Rather than simply feeding the starving, the United States sought to broker a solution to Somalia's long-running civil war—a proximate cause of the famine afflicting the country—and to rebuild Somali civic and political institutions. Albright described the undertaking as "an unprecedented enterprise aimed at nothing less than the restoration of an entire country as a proud, functioning and viable member of the community of nations."[7]

The United States turned to the United Nations as the vehicle through which to rehabilitate the failed state. When the official U.S. mission ended amid pomp, ceremony, and photo opportunities in May 1993, the follow-on entity, dubbed UNOSOM II, though ostensibly a UN enterprise, remained at its core a U.S. military undertaking, headed by Jonathan Howe, a retired four-star admiral. Though nominally reporting to UN Secretary General Boutros Boutros-Ghali, Howe had been handpicked for the job by the White House and took his orders from Washington. And although Lieutenant General Cevik

Bir, a Turk, exercised formal command of UNOSOM II's military contingent, the U.S. Army provided his deputy, Major General Thomas Montgomery. The peacekeeping force over which Bir presided was a motley one, drawn from two dozen armies, many of them indifferently trained and equipped. To the extent that UNOSOM II retained any serious fighting capabilities, they were concentrated in a so-called Quick Reaction Force (QRF), a brigade-sized reserve consisting entirely of U.S. troops. General Bir's authority did not extend to the QRF, which deployed only on the orders of Montgomery, his subordinate.

UNOSOM II's expanded mission put the United Nations and the United States at cross-purposes with tribal factions vying for control of Somalia's carcass. The warlords who controlled these factions were willing to acquiesce in a foreign military presence as long as the outsiders confined their activities to succoring the afflicted. But they viewed as unacceptable any effort to meddle in Somali politics. Chief among those warlords was Mohamed Farah Aidid, a wily former military officer, who was determined that he, not Admiral Howe, would dictate Somalia's fate.

In early June Aidid effectively declared war on UNOSOM II. On June 5 militiamen from Aidid's Somali National Alliance (SNA) backed by an angry stone-throwing crowd attacked a contingent of Pakistani peacekeepers, killing twenty-four. This was the opening shot in a protracted urban insurgency. Soon thereafter Howe placed a $25,000 bounty on Aidid and issued a warrant for his arrest.

Mogadishu became a battleground. When UNOSOM's peacekeepers ventured out from their compound at the defunct international airport on the city's outskirts, they encountered harassment, demonstrations, mob actions, and ambushes initiated by command-detonated mines. The burden of responding inevitably fell on the QRF. Through June and July Montgomery orchestrated multiple operations that sought to decapitate the insurgency by capturing or killing Aidid. This effort produced a series of clashes with escalating casualties on both sides but failed to net the Somali leader himself. In their frustration, the Americans became increasingly indiscriminate in their use of firepower—raking Somali crowds with automatic cannon fire from attack helicopters, for example.[8] Aidid skillfully exploited the rising Somali casualties—many of them women and children—to foment anger against UNOSOM II and especially the United States and to burnish his own image as a patriotic freedom fighter.[9] By midsummer control of Mogadishu teetered in the balance. Howe and Montgomery were clamoring for reinforcements.

Faced with a rapidly deteriorating situation, the Clinton administration upped the ante. Without fanfare and without consulting Congress, on August 22 the administration ordered a contingent of elite special operations forces designated Task Force Ranger to deploy to Somalia. In terms of training, equipment, and capabilities, these were the best of the best. But Task Force Ranger failed, spectacularly.

Reflecting its unique status (and confirming that the war against Aidid was Washington's, not the UN's), Task Force Ranger reported through U.S. channels, completely divorced from UNOSOM II. The reinforcements operated not only beyond Bir's purview but also beyond Montgomery's. Such casual disregard for the principle of unity of command provided a measure of the Pentagon's confidence that the rangers would make short work of their prey.[10]

But unity of command was only one of the principles of war that Task Force Ranger proceeded to violate. Two others were security and surprise. Once settled at Mogadishu International, the task force commander, Major General William Garrison, mounted the first in a series of daylight raids aimed at nabbing Aidid and his chief lieutenants. The raids followed a set pattern: responding to intelligence reports, a team of rangers would clamber aboard Blackhawk helicopters, fly to the target area in downtown Mogadishu, rappel to the ground, detain likely SNA suspects, and hustle them into an arriving convoy of trucks that whisked captives and captors alike back to the relative safety of the airfield. Garrison's first effort failed; the intelligence had been faulty. In the weeks that followed he tried five more times, adhering in each case to the same basic plan. Although rangers captured some lesser SNA leaders, Aidid eluded them.

At midafternoon on October 3 Garrison launched his seventh attempt. This time Aidid, now well schooled in the U.S. modus operandi, was waiting and turned the tables on his adversary.[11] The hunters became the hunted. Using short-range antitank weapons, SNA militiamen shot down three Blackhawks and damaged three other helicopters. The rangers' precisely synchronized plan collapsed. On the ground, a host of well-armed and angry Somalis surrounded the

rangers. Well-placed roadblocks and skillfully executed ambushes
boxed in the convoy, preventing an extraction.

A fierce firefight ensued, lasting well into the night.[12] While U.S.
helicopter gunships pounded the Somalis besieging the rangers, back
at the airfield Montgomery worked feverishly to cobble together a relief force. Only at midnight did the QRF arrive on the scene, riding in
Malaysian personnel carriers and escorted by a handful of aging Pakistani tanks. By the time the action ended, eighteen Americans were
dead and seventy-eight wounded. A badly injured American pilot
was being held captive. Television networks around the world broadcast videotape showing the mutilated remains of a dead G.I. being
dragged through the streets.

When news of the firefight detonated in Washington, poisonous
fallout blanketed the capital. The media played the story to the hilt,
second-guessing the entire ten-month Somalia intervention. Members of Congress professed outrage and demanded explanations. Public opinion, at first favorably disposed toward Operation Restore Hope
and then all but oblivious to its continuation, now seemed likely to
hold the Clinton administration accountable for what had become a
bloody mess. The search for scapegoats was on.

For the White House, a small war almost casually begun had become a first-class political crisis, all the more embarrassing when the
military, eager to divert attention from its own miscues, leaked word
that just weeks before the administration had denied Montgomery's
request for additional heavy armor. Critics were quick to suggest that
with American-crewed Abrams tanks and Bradley fighting vehicles,
Montgomery just might have been able to rescue the trapped rangers.[13] Having denied his generals the resources they needed to fight,
Bill Clinton stood accused of being complicit in recklessly sending
young Americans to their deaths.

Exhibiting a well-developed instinct for self-preservation, the administration shifted into full damage-control mode. Clinton's aides let
it be known that responsibility for hatching the war on Aidid lay not
with Washington but with the UN. It was really Boutros Boutros-
Ghali's war. To placate a Congress demanding someone's head, the
president offered that of his secretary of defense. Soon thereafter Les
Aspin resigned, his political career ended. Clinton also collaborated
with Pentagon efforts to portray the botched operation as actually a

victory. Above all, he cut his losses—terminating all efforts to get Aidid, withdrawing Task Force Ranger, confining the remaining American troops to the airfield, and declaring his attention to terminate the U.S. presence in Somalia altogether.

➤ The unhappy demise of Operation Restore Hope exerted a profound and lasting influence on subsequent U.S. military policy. For the rest of the 1990s and into the twenty-first century, whenever official Washington addressed questions pertaining to the use of force, the "lessons" of Mogadishu loomed in the background, shaping the options considered and the decisions made.

From its drubbing in Somalia the Clinton administration drew four related cautionary lessons. First, information age or no, ground combat, especially ground combat in cities, entailed a high degree of risk and uncertainty. To send U.S. troops into a sprawling, unfamiliar urban jungle teeming with noncombatants, where even distinguishing adversaries from mere bystanders offered a daunting challenge, was to forfeit the American technological edge that had made war in the skies or in the open deserts seemingly such a sure thing. A fight in close quarters against a well-armed foe willing to die in large numbers did not favor the United States.

Second, the events leading up to the firefight showed that the U.S. military's image of infallibility, which the Pentagon had so carefully nurtured since the Persian Gulf War, was illusory. When it came to proximate causes, defeat at the hands of General Aidid stemmed above all from faulty decisions made by military professionals— among them Howe, Montgomery, and Garrison—although it remained impolitic for an administration headed by a Vietnam-era draft dodger to say so publicly. The Bay of Pigs taught John F. Kennedy to take military claims of expertise with a grain of salt; Mogadishu provided Bill Clinton—who viewed JFK as his role model—with a comparable education.

The immediate aftermath of October 3 also taught Clinton that when things went wrong in the field, the first instinct of senior military officers was to unload responsibility onto someone else, preferably a civilian. At the very top, the tradition of officers as apolitical and obedient servants of the state had long since become something of a fiction. When the going got tough, the military's inclination was not to rally to a beleaguered commander-in-chief but to sell him down the river—as they believed themselves to have been sold out in Vietnam.[14]

Finally, Mogadishu showed that in situations in which something less than vital national interests were at stake, U.S. casualties had become all but unacceptable.[15] The loss of even a small number of American soldiers in action constituted prima facie evidence of an enterprise gone inexplicably awry and not worth pursuing further. To persist in a policy that required soldiers to die was to invite a dangerous political backlash.

Fight only in settings that play to American strengths. Keep a watchful eye on military leaders. Give the officer corps no cause to obstruct or complain. Above all, avoid casualties. These were the axioms that for the remainder of the 1990s guided policymakers as they attempted to extract a greater measure of political utility from American military might. Out of these lessons of Mogadishu there emerged a distinctive new approach to employing U.S. military power—a Clinton doctrine for the use of force.

➤ The essence of that doctrine, refined over the next several years, manifested itself in a reliance on gunboats and Gurkhas. The new doctrine did not quite amount to a new American "way of war"; after all, globalization had supposedly rendered war as such pointless and obsolete. But it created a basis for making a military establishment still wedded to the belief that it existed to "fight and win the nation's wars" relevant to actually existing grand strategy. The Clinton doctrine bent the military to the imperatives of maintaining the momentum toward greater openness, enforcing the rules to which a globalized world ought to adhere, and fending off doubts regarding the U.S. claim to world leadership. And it did so while taking into account the reigning cultural and domestic political sensibilities of postmodern America. The results were not always completely salutary. The mere effort generated formidable opposition from institutions and individuals resistant to change. But on balance civilian policymakers got most of what they wanted.

The Clinton administration found a modern equivalent of old-fashioned "gunboats" in cruise missiles and aircraft armed with precision-guided munitions. It employed these weapons routinely whenever it wished to coerce, cajole, or punish adversaries who violated the norms putatively governing the open world or to counter any impression that the United States lacked determination and resolve. Launched from surface ships or submarines operating "over the horizon" or from B-52 bombers flying beyond the range of enemy air defenses, cruise missiles offered the United States the ability to reach out and hit large fixed installations virtually anywhere. Better still, the use of cruise missiles effectively reduced the likelihood of U.S. casualties to zero. Piloted aircraft operating from carriers or fixed bases entailed slightly greater risk, but also offered greater flexibility. In practice, by giving respectful attention to an opponent's anti-air capabilities and through the judicious use of "stealth" and standoff capabilities for the most difficult missions, air commanders could get U.S. strike aircraft in and out of most environments safely. Together, the panoply of manned and unmanned weapons composing its air arsenal enabled the United States to customize the impact it wished to make—a big bang or a small one, a campaign or a onetime shot.

A hundred years before, when the United States first strode onto the world stage, the U.S. Navy had been the preeminent service. "It was at once imperially efficient and domestically clean," William Appleman Williams observed, "meaning it could deliver fire power abroad without threatening the domestic political process."[16] A century later, America's long-range striking forces ascended to that role, possessing a combination of imperial efficiency and domestic political acceptability that Admiral Dewey would have envied.

Even before the debacle of Mogadishu, Bill Clinton had begun experimenting with this approach. On June 26, 1993, in retaliation for an alleged plot to assassinate former President Bush and in order to affirm U.S. opposition to terrorism, he ordered an attack on an Iraqi intelligence headquarters. Twenty-three cruise missiles, each mounting a warhead with eight hundred pounds of explosives, winged their way to downtown Baghdad, twenty of them finding the target area.[17] The attack, which the president characterized as "a firm and commensurate response" to Iraq's provocation, was a milestone in Clinton's young presidency, marking the first time he had ordered U.S. forces into action.[18] The White House advertised it as a powerful indication of the president's intent to stand firm against Saddam Hussein. Despite some carping on the right that Clinton had let Saddam off too lightly and on the left that Washington had acted unilaterally, with stray missiles causing a handful of Iraqi civilian casualties, the operation met with general acclaim.[19] Congress offered more commendations than complaints, press reaction was largely favorable, and the military, which to that point had treated the new commander-in-chief with a dislike bordering on contempt, accommodated itself to Clinton's directives without complaint.

Similarly, in September 1996, after Saddam sent his troops against Kurdish dissidents in Irbil, their sanctuary in northern Iraq, President Clinton—not so incidentally in the midst of campaigning for reelection—felt the urge to "do something." Ever since George Bush had committed U.S. troops to Operation Provide Comfort in the immediate aftermath of Desert Storm, the United States had held itself responsible for shielding the Kurds from Saddam's wrath.[20] To deflect charges of inaction in the face of an egregious Iraqi misbehavior—but unwilling to risk a real showdown—Clinton again called out the gunboats. In Operation Desert Strike, B-52 bombers and U.S. Navy warships hurled a total of forty-four missiles that battered Iraqi air defense sites and command-and-control facilities in the desert to the north and south of Baghdad. The operation ended virtually as soon as it began, without loose ends or complications. As measured by U.S. losses, Desert Strike was flawlessly planned and executed. "Our missiles sent the following message to Saddam Hussein," the president announced. "When you abuse your own people or threaten your neighbors you must pay a price."[21] Critics derided the attack as militarily insignificant and devoid of value to the Kurds; but by this point any action aimed at the Iraqi dictator's hold on power commanded near-automatic public assent.[22] The administration touted Desert Strike as further evidence that those who flouted the international community's norms of behavior did so at their peril.

Iraqi diplomats and more than a few Western human rights organizations charged the United States itself with violating international norms, particularly in refusing to ease the crushing economic sanctions imposed on Iraq in 1990. Through the 1990s those sanctions exerted little discernible impact on Saddam or his Ba'athist regime. But evidence indicated that the Iraqi people were suffering grievously.[23] Senior Clinton administration officials denied any American responsibility for the impact of sanctions.[24] Any suggestions that U.S. efforts to isolate Saddam and contain Iraq were themselves of questionable legitimacy met with adamant rejection.

Perpetuating Saddam's status as an international pariah was essential for keeping the proximate (if no longer especially formidable) Iraqi military threat in check. But it was important for a second reason as well. Absent the continuing imperative of containing Iraq militarily, the immediate rationale for stationing U.S. forces in the Persian Gulf would evaporate. Without the flow of American troops rotating through Gulf nations for exercises or operations, without the presence of powerful naval forces in nearby waters, Washington's claim of having assumed the mantle of protector and arbiter for the entire region would lack authority.

Issuing periodic reminders that the outlaw regime was in Baghdad not Washington was a task made to order for gunboat diplomacy. Thus, in the fall of 1998, when Saddam, after years of jousting, expelled UN weapons inspectors charged with dismantling Iraq's nuclear, chemical, and biological weapons programs, Bill Clinton (facing impeachment) again resorted to force.

In duration and intensity, Operation Desert Fox, initiated on December 16, marked a significant escalation over previous attacks, rising almost to the level of a bona fide campaign. Yet Desert Fox, characterized by administration officials as "serious and sustained," was by no means intended to lay Iraq prostrate or remove Saddam from power. Senior officials indicated that the operation's objective was at most to "diminish" or "degrade" Iraqi capabilities, especially those related to developing weapons of mass destruction or ballistic missiles.[25] Over the course of four days, U.S. forces (with assistance from the Royal Air Force) blasted ninety-seven targets, among them weapons research facilities, barracks housing the Republican Guard, an oil refinery, and seven of Saddam's palaces. U.S. combat aircraft flew more than 600 sorties. American warships launched some 330 cruise missiles, with B-52s delivering another 90.[26] No American or British aircraft were lost. No allied personnel were killed or wounded. Press reaction was largely upbeat and supportive.[27] When the action ended, Secretary of Defense William S. Cohen declared it a success: Iraqi efforts to develop a new missile had been "set back by at least a year." The senior U.S. military commander in the Persian Gulf went so far as to claim that this latest bombing had left Saddam Hussein "shaken" and "desperate."[28]

Operation Desert Fox failed to persuade Saddam to permit the return of UN weapons inspectors, however. Indeed, this latest bombing seemingly left the Iraqi dictator all the more defiant. No sooner had the attack concluded than Baghdad announced that it no longer recognized the no-fly zones established as part of the post–Desert Storm effort to contain Saddam Hussein.[29] On December 28, 1998, surface-to-air missiles unleashed at coalition aircraft patrolling northern Iraq inaugurated a more aggressive Iraqi policy of contesting the no-fly zones. Three U.S. Air Force F-15Es responded immediately, attacking a radar unit and SAM-3 missile battery with precision-guided bombs. This encounter initiated what soon became an ongoing sequence of tit-for-tat actions in both the northern and southern zones. Iraqi air defenders began firing on intruding coalition aircraft or "painting" them with radar. From time to time Iraqi fighters dashed into forbidden airspace. U.S. (and sometimes British) aircraft responded by bombing some element of Iraq's air defense system—a radar, missile site, gun emplacement, or command-and-control facility.[30]

An inconclusive war of attrition resulted, likened by one commander to "a parole officer living in a house with a convicted criminal."[31] In a single twelve-month period, for example, crews supporting Operation Northern Watch out of Incirlik, Turkey, flew over 5,000 sorties during which they attacked some 225 targets. Operation Southern Watch, conducted from bases in Saudi Arabia and Kuwait and from carriers in the Persian Gulf, sustained an even greater level of effort; between December 1998 and the end of the Clinton presidency, Southern Watch aircraft reported coming under fire by Iraqi missiles or antiaircraft guns some 670 times.[32] This contest, unique in the annals of air combat, persisted through the remaining two years of the Clinton administration, with one air strike occurring in its final hours. In all during 1999 and 2000, U.S. forces expended some two thousand bombs and missiles against Iraqi targets.[33] Chiefly as a result of the fact that Iraqi gunners failed to down a single coalition aircraft, the entire campaign proceeded largely unreported by the media and all but completely ignored by the public.[34] Operationally, the results achieved were negligible. In the eyes of American clients in the Persian Gulf, however, the persistent sparring with Saddam affirmed the continuing need for a robust U.S. military presence in the region.[35]

Iraq was not the only adversary to feel the sting of U.S. air attack. When terrorist bombs in August 1998 devastated American embassies in Kenya and Tanzania, causing horrific casualties, early indications pointed to Osama bin Laden as the likely mastermind. Eager to show that he was taking terrorism seriously but leery of expending the level of effort needed actually to track down bin Laden himself, President Clinton stuck to his gunboats: on his orders, the U.S. Navy loosed missiles targeting reputed terrorist training camps in Afghanistan and the aforementioned pharmaceutical factory in Khartoum.

As portrayed by U.S. officials, the significance of this operation—to which the Pentagon assigned the grandiloquent codename Infinite Reach—was twofold. Previously the United States had classified terror as a criminal matter, falling under the jurisdiction of the police and courts. The attack on bin Laden's camps signaled a major shift in policy: fighting terror was now the Pentagon's responsibility as well. Furthermore, the attack on Khartoum indicated that in bringing its military power to bear on terror, the U.S. intended to take a proactive approach. The aim was not only to retaliate but, whenever possible, to preempt. Henceforth the United States would fight terror not defensively but offensively.[36] Although bin Laden escaped harm and continued thereafter to enjoy Afghan protection, the Clinton team rated Infinite Reach a resounding success, further evidence of its ability to use force effectively and yet judiciously.

As measured by the post-Mogadishu criteria of success, it had been. Like the administration's other ventures in gunboat diplomacy, the "fight," if it could be called that, occurred on American terms, with the U.S. military exploiting the high-tech long-range strike capabilities that were its strong suit. Unlike real war, in which interaction between adversaries is fraught with uncertainty, operations such as Infinite Reach all but eliminated the possibility of an opponent's pulling any surprises: from start to finish, the initiative remained with the United States. The attack illustrated one of gunboat diplomacy's central advantages: the president himself with his chief lieutenants could dictate minute adjustments in targets, timing, and weaponry, as if controlling events by rheostat from the Oval Office. Carefully circumscribed in time and space, the operation minimized the likelihood of American miscues. Infinite Reach amounted to little more than a targeting exercise. The responsibilities allotted to operational commanders did not extend beyond the technical task of putting ordnance on predesignated aim points. In contrast to the ill-fated cam-

paign to get General Aidid, such narrow terms of reference served as a
check against the possibility that some freelancing military subordinate might hand policymakers back in Washington more than they
had bargained for. Furthermore, because the strike posed little risk to
the forces conducting it, the Pentagon was happy to go along: there
were no leaks to newspapers signaling the military's unhappiness
with an upcoming operation and no inertia to overcome on the part
of commanders in the field. Finally and perhaps most importantly,
Infinite Reach came off without any U.S. losses. Press and public
evinced only passing interest. As a story, Infinite Reach had no "legs."

Like each of the other episodes in neo–gunboat diplomacy recounted above, Infinite Reach showed that when it came to using
force, presidential authority verged on the absolute.[37] Thanks to the
combined efforts of first George Bush and then Bill Clinton, prerogatives developed in earlier times under different circumstances trans-
ferred neatly to the post–Cold War era. The White House might,
according to its preferences, notify or "consult" select members of
Congress before acting. But the legislative branch played no meaningful role in deciding when and where U.S. forces went into action.
Thus did a chief executive with a free hand to wield American military might emerge as an essential adjunct to the larger strategy of
openness.

But the Clinton administration's preference for gunboat diplomacy
did more than affirm precedents regarding the freedom of action
claimed by the commander-in-chief. It gave birth to a new paradigm
in which the United States employed coercion in particular ways and
for particular purposes. During the 1990s Bill Clinton made long-
range precision air strikes an emblem of American statecraft.

Viewed individually, each of these operations might seem like
small beer. Collectively, however, Infinite Reach and the repetitive attacks on Iraq signified a radical departure from past practice. The
principles governing the conduct of Infinite Reach as a response to
the ostensibly deadly global contagion of international terrorism represented the inverse of those that had informed the combined
bomber offensive mounted to destroy Nazism. As evidence of U.S. determination to bring Saddam Hussein to heel, the endless policing of
the no-fly zones was the polar opposite of the sustained, unrelenting
air assault that had opened Desert Storm. If history offered a precur-

sor to the use of air power during the Clinton era, it was Lyndon Johnson's bombing of North Vietnam, informed by vintage-1960s strategic theories positing the calibrated application of force to punish, draw lines, signal, and negotiate. The abject failure of Operation Rolling Thunder had discredited those theories, seemingly forever. Now, for good or ill, they were back.

Above all, as a result of the Clinton administration's penchant for relying on missiles to spank and to scold, Americans became inured to the use of air power as an instrument of so-called coercive diplomacy. As bombing became routine, it also became noncontroversial. With the United States conferring upon itself wide latitude to wield its preferred military instrument, the American people and even American elites gave their tacit assent to a new Clinton doctrine governing the use of force. By the end of the decade the air weapon, as one senior military officer proclaimed, had "become the instrument of choice in America's foreign policy."[38] None questioned the truth of that assertion.

➤ But if air power was the preferred instrument, it was by no means the only one. As a practical matter, there were some things that gunboats couldn't do. Where air power didn't fit the bill, policymakers devised other techniques to enforce the rules. As a result, the military legacy of the Clinton era possessed more than a single strand.

Historically, empires have relied on colonial troops or mercenaries to ease the burden of imperial policing. This practice serves two purposes. First, it husbands national energies for more productive pursuits: generating the wealth on which the empire's long-term viability depends. Second, it reduces the sacrifices exacted of the home front, thereby propping up popular support for the imperial project. Similarly, in their efforts to advance the cause of global integration and to sustain U.S. preeminence, the architects of the strategy of openness sought to keep the yoke of empire as light as possible. By the end of the 1990s the United States was devoting less than 3 percent of its gross national product to defense, the lowest proportion since the eve of World War II.[39] In the distribution of total federal outlays, national security expenditures had for decades formed the largest single category. After the Cold War that was no longer the case; defense outlays lagged behind both social security and "non-defense discretionary" expenditures.[40] By the end of the 1990s Americans were spending more each year on liquor, tobacco, and dining out than they were on national defense.[41]

Equally significant, if seldom remarked upon, with fewer than one in every two hundred Americans in uniform, the proportion of the population in active military service had fallen to its lowest level since 1940.[42] Those who served did so strictly as a matter of personal choice, the state after Vietnam having forfeited its ability to compel citizens to participate in defending their country. For those making that choice, service in the armed forces also became appreciably less dangerous. During the 1990s fewer American military personnel lost their lives as a result of hostile action than in any decade since the 1930s.[43]

In 1961 Americans had thrilled to John Kennedy's charge to ask themselves what they could do for their country. Forty years later the implicit answer to Kennedy's question had become: as little as possible. Americans had acquired a taste for global leadership, but one that they wished to satisfy without blood, sweat, and tears and at a minimal cost in treasure.

Thus, when it seemed likely that the cause of openness might require real sacrifice, policymakers worked to ensure that someone other than an American soldier ventured into the line of fire. In 1900 the passionate promoter of empire Senator Albert J. Beveridge had beseeched his listeners to "Pray God the time may never come when mammon and the love of ease will so debase our blood that we will fear to shed it for the flag and its imperial destiny."[44] A century later something approaching that condition pertained. Postmodern Americans were not oblivious to the benefits of hegemony, but by the 1990s, for increasing numbers of citizens, military service had become an unacceptable imposition, and the prospect of laying down one's life for the flag and the cause that it represented had come to seem absurd.

As a result, when there was real fighting to be done or truly arduous tasks to be undertaken, the United States evinced a preference for having others shoulder the burden. The aftermath of the Cold War (and especially the aftermath of Mogadishu) found the United States relying increasingly on "Gurkhas"—foreign armies or other proxies—to perform missions entailing substantial risk of large-scale casualties.

This reliance on third parties did not mean that the United States ab-
dicated any involvement in situations likely to involve ground combat. Just as Queen Victoria's Gurkhas were raised, trained, equipped,
and paid by the Crown, so too the United States assisted, sometimes
quite generously, those acting on its behalf. But to the maximum extent possible, it came to expect that these surrogates would do the
dirty work.[45]

The assistance offered varied with the circumstances. At times the
United States provided specialized support to otherwise competent allied forces possessing only a limited capacity to deploy and sustain
themselves. Operation Stabilize in East Timor exemplified this approach. Ever since Indonesia had forcibly annexed East Timor in
1975, that region had seethed with violent resistance to the central
government in Jakarta. In a referendum conducted in August 1999,
an overwhelming majority of East Timorese voted against remaining
as part of Indonesia and in favor of complete independence. In retaliation, the Indonesian army, working hand in hand with nationalist
militias, mounted a campaign of terror in and around the East
Timorese capital of Dilhi. This action elicited sharp criticism abroad
and raised questions about Indonesia's already precarious political viability. But more than Indonesia's fate was at stake. In the estimate of
most American observers, its disintegration would directly threaten
prospects of a stable and economically open East Asia. Determined to
stem Indonesia's slide into chaos but wary of shouldering another potentially long-term peacekeeping commitment, Washington sought a
partner willing to take the lead in restoring order to East Timor, with
U.S. forces playing an essential backup role.[46] The government of
Australia dutifully volunteered.

The result was the International Force for East Timor (INTERFET),
which went into action in September 1999. Commanded by an Australian general officer, with Australia contributing the largest contingent of troops, INTERFET quickly deployed to East Timor, obliged
Indonesian regulars to withdraw, and restored order.[47] It was a handsome piece of work for which Canberra could rightly claim the lion's
share of credit. But Operation Stabilize would never have got off the
ground had Washington not provided communications, intelligence,
transportation, and logistics. Roughly 5,000 U.S. troops supported the
mission—though for the most part at some remove from the action

on the ground. Only 250 G.I.'s actually went ashore in East Timor. In February 2000, its mission complete, INTERFET handed over its responsibilities to the United Nations. By making available what the senior U.S. officer involved called America's "unique capabilities," the Clinton administration had subcontracted out a situation that might otherwise have obliged the United States to choose between remaining passive in the face of impending disaster and assuming unwanted new obligations.[48] For his part, Australian Prime Minister John Howard was so taken with the partnership that he proposed what came to be called the Howard Doctrine, under which Australia as a matter of policy would serve as America's "deputy sheriff" in maintaining East Asian stability.[49]

In other situations the Gurkha option involved the use of American expertise and material to upgrade otherwise substandard foreign armies, equipping those forces to handle tasks supportive of U.S. interests. The Africa Crisis Response Initiative, an effort to improve the peacemaking capabilities of select African militaries, illustrates this approach.

The lessons of Mogadishu had erected insurmountable barriers to the commitment of American combat troops to the sub-Sahara. At the same time, the United States found it increasingly awkward to ignore altogether the violence wracking that continent. The sad story of Sierra Leone offered a case in point. Throughout the Clinton era this small West African country was beset by a savage civil war, barbaric even by the breathtaking standards of the twentieth century. To cow the population, the rebel Revolutionary United Front (RUF) employed tactics that included raping young girls, forcing children to execute their own parents, and chopping off the limbs of anyone it viewed unfavorably.[50] Washington's initial response to these outrages was to seek a solution through traditional diplomacy. But although President Clinton's special envoy to Africa, the Reverend Jesse Jackson, helped broker the so-called Lome peace accord in March 2000, ending the civil war at the cost of legitimizing the RUF, that agreement collapsed within two months of being signed.[51] The RUF went back on the rampage. Only the arrival in Freetown of a British paratroop battalion acting in the best no-nonsense tradition of "the thin red line" restored a semblance of order.

Chagrined by its diplomatic failure, the Clinton administration went in search of Gurkhas to help maintain that order for the long term. The result was Operation Focus Relief, an initiative involving the deployment to Nigeria of several hundred Green Berets from the Third Special Forces Group to train and equip units from Nigeria, Ghana, and Senegal for subsequent deployment to Sierra Leone.[52] The United States outfitted the African troops with uniforms, helmets, and canteens and with weapons such as AK-47 assault rifles and mortars. U.S. trainers then put each battalion through a ten-week course of instruction encompassing everything from basic marksmanship to lectures on human rights.[53] The cost of the entire program to the United States was a modest $50 million. Whether the peacekeepers would actually succeed in ending the perpetual cycle of violence in Sierra Leone remained to be seen, but Focus Relief at least provided a partial response to charges that hypocritical Americans continued to turn a blind eye to Africa's plight.

In Colombia, a country wracked by civil war and the source of nearly all the cocaine and much of the heroin flooding into the United States, the State and Defense Departments collaborated on a train-and-equip program conceived on a still grander scale. They also flirted with more direct operational involvement, albeit through individuals not directly employed by the U.S. government. Drug trafficking, of course, ranked alongside terror among the threats that seemingly flourished as international borders gave way to openness. Secretary of State Madeleine Albright judged it a "global plague."[54] To maintain popular support for globalization, the U.S. government needed to demonstrate its capacity to cope with its downside; hence the imperative of stemming the tide of illegal drugs entering the United States from abroad. Earlier efforts, at times employing draconian measures, to eliminate cultivation of coca in Peru and Bolivia had enjoyed a measure of success. But the result was a proportional increase in the size of the coca crop in neighboring Colombia, which became the hemispheric leader in all aspects of cocaine production and export.[55] By the latter part of the 1990s Colombia had become the paramount test of whether the United States could shut down the drug trade at its source.

Colombia's drug trade was linked inextricably with Colombia's decades-old civil war. The rebels seeking to overthrow the government financed their operations by trafficking in cocaine and heroin.

So, too, did the right-wing paramilitaries that emerged as confidence in the government's ability to defeat the guerrillas waned. For this reason, drug trafficking had long since become more than a police problem. It was also a military one. In Colombia a war on drugs would involve a bona fide war. But according to the dictates of post-Mogadishu national security policy, someone other than American soldiers would wage that war. To crush this threat to openness, the United States much preferred to work through third parties.

Thus, when Colombia's President Andres Pastrana (with U.S. encouragement) conceived Plan Colombia, an ambitious effort to negotiate an end to the civil war, suppress the drug trade, revive Colombia's economy, and reconstitute its civic institutions, the Clinton administration promised wholehearted American support.[56] In reality, however, the United States confined its support to those aspects of the plan that responded to pressing American interests, namely, underwriting the creation of more effective instruments to cut off the northward flow of illegal drugs. President Pastrana calculated the total cost of implementing Plan Colombia at $7.5 billion, $3.5 billion of which he hoped to raise from foreign donors. In the summer of 2000 the Clinton administration, with congressional approval, came through with a $1.3 billion package of assistance, to be expended over two years.[57] Designed in large part by Barry McCaffrey, director of the Office of National Drug Control Policy and a retired U.S. Army general, that package earmarked American aid for specific purposes, with the vast preponderance going to improve the drug interdiction capabilities of Colombian security forces. In other words, although Washington paid lip service to President Pastrana's hopes of ending a debilitating civil war and salvaging Colombian democracy, when it came to action, 80 percent of U.S. aid went to countering the one aspect of the Colombian imbroglio that threatened openness.[58]

McCaffrey's plan had several facets. U.S. military advisers would assist Colombian officers in designing a comprehensive counterdrug campaign. They would outfit the Colombian army with several dozen helicopters to provide the mobility needed to penetrate the outback, especially the Department of Putumayo, the sprawling, rebel-controlled province in southern Colombia that had become to cocaine what Silicon Valley was to software. But mobility alone would not suffice. Attacking drug traffickers in Putumayo required military units to provide security so that the Colombian national police could dismantle the infrastructure of cocaine production and processing. Sending U.S. troops into guerrilla-infested Putumayo was, of course, out of the question. Instead the Clinton administration funded the creation within the Colombian army of a special counternarcotics combat force: these were McCaffrey's Gurkhas. In April 1999 troops from the U.S. Army Seventh Special Forces Group began training the first of several Colombian battalions to carry America's war on drugs into Putumayo.[59] To those anxious lest the United States somehow become slowly enmeshed in another endless jungle counterinsurgency, McCaffrey offered assurances that "the blood shed will be [that of] the Colombians."[60]

But the U.S. role in Colombia went beyond mere advising, equipping, and training. Under the terms of McCaffrey's plan, Washington also underwrote an aggressive program of using aerial-delivered herbicides to eradicate coca and opium poppy cultivation. In addition McCaffrey promised to improve the quality of intelligence available to Colombian security forces, crucial to operations in Putumayo but also to efforts by the Colombian air force to intercept the finished product in transit to its market. In these areas, too, American involvement was pronounced, with the terms of that involvement illustrating a variant of the Gurkha option—the reliance on government contractors in lieu of soldiers to perform select military functions.

As part of U.S. support for Plan Colombia, for example, civilian pilots employed by the Virginia-based firm DynCorp flew the crop-dusters spraying coca and opium poppy fields. They also piloted the helicopters ferrying Colombian troops into action. Other pilots from the Aviation Development Corporation, a company operating out of Maxwell Air Force Base in Montgomery, Alabama, and AirScan, based in Florida, crewed surveillance planes tracking airborne drug-runners. Another contractor with close ties to the Pentagon, Military Professional Resources Inc. (MPRI), assumed responsibility for training officers of the Colombian army and national police force.[61]

From the point of view of U.S. policymakers, contracting these functions out to profit-motivated private firms offered at least four benefits. First, it enabled the Department of Defense to comply with a congressionally mandated ceiling of 500 U.S. military personnel in Colombia. Second, with the existing U.S. force structure already taxed by other engagement-related requirements, the use of contractors kept the Colombia mission from becoming excessively burdensome. Third, because contractors do not submit to the sort of congressional oversight typical of a normal government agency, it allowed U.S. activities in Colombia to proceed with a minimum of outside scrutiny. Fourth, having contractors fill most of the risky aviation-related positions provided some insurance against politically sensitive military casualties. The loss of even a couple of U.S. soldiers could overturn an entire policy. The loss of a couple of civilians would hardly qualify as newsworthy.[62] A critic identified a possible fifth benefit: "Privatization is another way to reward the alumni"; most of the firms awarded federal contracts for military activities were run by retired senior U.S. officers.[63]

In another era, the former career professionals now cashing in on expertise acquired in service to nation would have been known as mercenaries or soldiers of fortune. In the decade following the Cold War, hiring out as a military trainer or operator lost the raffish or disreputable associations implied by those terms. For one thing, when ex-military pilots flew counterdrug missions in places like Colombia or Peru, they did so with the enthusiastic endorsement of U.S. authorities. These men viewed themselves not as swashbucklers but as business executives, delivering hard-to-find services and being compensated accordingly.

Nor was the use of contractors to outsource military functions confined to Andean drug wars. In the aftermath of the U.S. military intervention in Haiti, for example, the Clinton administration turned to DynCorp to create a new police force there. MPRI landed contracts to train armies in Angola and Liberia.[64] In Saudi Arabia, U.S. firms essentially enjoyed a virtual monopoly on military training. Saudi marines trained under the tutelage of Booz-Allen & Hamilton. Science Applications International Corporation (SAIC) trained the navy and Vinnell the Saudi national guard. All three are U.S.-based firms that prosper largely on the basis of government contracts.[65]

In the 1990s, for increasing numbers of former U.S. military officers, the privatization of war offered opportunities for a lucrative second career. For policymakers, meanwhile, privatizing war offered a way to tap a reservoir of American military expertise (purchased at considerable taxpayer expense) as a cost-effective, practical alternative to uniformed U.S. forces.[66] When it came to imperial policing, hired guns could do things that remained off-limits to soldiers.

➤ U.S. policymakers did not by any means view the gunboat and Gurkha options as mutually exclusive. On occasion they found it expedient to combine the two. When, for example, after great hesitation and with considerable trepidation, the Clinton administration in 1995 decided to intervene militarily in Bosnia, the United States (and its NATO allies) prevailed by synchronizing a modest air campaign with a ground offensive conducted by a contractor-supported foreign army. The result was a seemingly effortless victory.

The Bosnian crisis had frustrated and embarrassed both European and American statesmen since its beginnings in 1991. As a candidate for president, Bill Clinton had criticized George Bush's reluctance to act decisively in Bosnia. Once elected, he proved no more eager than his predecessor to embroil himself in the Balkans. But as the flow of refugees out of Bosnia continued, the death toll grew, and reports of atrocities, most attributed to the Bosnian Serbs, piled up, pressure mounted on Clinton to do more than just support high-minded UN resolutions.

For the United States, the interests at stake were not merely humanitarian. Bosnia called into question the relevance of NATO and, by extension, U.S. claims to leadership in Europe. It also called into question hopes for a world in which ethnic and religious tolerance was the rule rather than the exception—a corollary of openness. By 1995 the Clinton administration's standard line—that peace would come to Bosnia only when the warring parties chose peace, that a military solution did not exist—had worn thin.[67] With Richard Holbrooke, an influential Democrat, declaring in a widely noted article in *Foreign Affairs* that Bosnia was "the greatest collective security failure of the West since the 1930s," inaction was becoming untenable, both politically and diplomatically.[68]

Beginning in April 1993, U.S. and other NATO aircraft had enforced a no-fly zone over Bosnia. Operation Deny Flight—over 100,000 sorties by combat aircraft—had had minimal practical effect. In August of that year NATO began threatening air strikes to punish Bosnian Serbs (aided and abetted by the Serb government in Belgrade) for violating various UN directives, most notably by laying siege to Sarajevo. Starting in April 1994, NATO aircraft conducted occasional strikes against Serb targets. But these sporadic, small-scale attacks only temporarily blunted the Serb assault on the Bosnian Muslims. In July the Serbs gruesomely demonstrated their disregard for the international community, slaughtering thousands in an assault on Srebrenica, a supposed UN "safe haven."[69]

On August 28, 1995, a mortar round that ripped through Sarajevo's Mrkale marketplace proved to be the last straw. The killing of thirty-seven shoppers finally prodded the Clinton administration to act. The result was Operation Deliberate Force, a program of air strikes—more potent than anything seen thus far—intended to coerce the Bosnian Serb leadership into acceding to U.S. and European demands to negotiate an end to the civil war. NATO's bombing commenced on August 30 and continued until September 14. The operation involved 290 aircraft—most of them American—in more than 3,500 sorties delivering 1,026 pieces of ordnance against 48 targets. The entire operation amounted to approximately a single day's effort during Desert Storm.[70]

But it seemed to work. As subsequently portrayed by air power enthusiasts, Operation Deliberate Force created the conditions for the peace talks that began in November 1995 and soon yielded the Dayton peace accords.[71] Thus, at the public level, this first Balkan intervention seemed to offer an especially efficient (if, arguably, long-overdue) demonstration of what the well-conceived use of gunboat diplomacy could accomplish. But the real story was more complicated and more interesting.

For it was not air power alone that persuaded the Bosnian Serbs and their accomplices in Belgrade that the jig was up. Just weeks before Operation Deliberate Force began, the Croat army—the third party in the Bosnian civil war—launched Operation Storm, a powerful ground offensive aimed at freeing the Krajina region from Serb control. This operation—which proceeded with tacit U.S. approval—handed the Bosnian Serb army its first real setback since the struggle for Bosnia had begun.[72] Slobodan Milošević, president of what remained of Yugoslavia and self-professed patron of Serb nationalism, did not lift a hand to assist his Bosnian Serb brethren. In short, even before NATO launched its air campaign, the Krajina offensive tipped the military balance against the Bosnian Serbs. When the victorious Croats proceeded to implement their own program of ethnic cleansing against the Krajina Serbs, Washington turned a blind eye. A Croat failure to abide by the niceties of the laws of war was no cause to rein in their army, since, as one U.S. diplomat noted at the time, "We 'hired' these guys to be our junkyard dogs."[73]

Hired and trained, he might have said. For although the move was little noted at the time, in September 1994 the State and Defense Departments had approved arrangements under which the ubiquitous MPRI—headed by a cadre of recently retired U.S. military officers—undertook a crash program to modernize the Croat army. Operation Storm was widely seen as their handiwork. Observers of Operation Storm credited hitherto-unsophisticated Croat formations with using "typical American combined-arms tactics, including integrated air, artillery, and infantry movements, as well as maneuver warfare targeted against Serbian command, control, and communications systems."[74] The Serbs didn't stand a chance.

The next month, at the urging of Richard Holbrooke, now the chief U.S. envoy in Bosnia, the Croat offensive resumed, reinforced by units of the Bosnian Muslim army (soon to become another MPRI client).[75] The peace talks culminating in the Dayton accords followed.[76] From the perspective of a gratified Clinton administration, MPRI had "effectively acted as a mechanism of U.S. policy in the Balkans at less cost and lower political risk than that incurred if the U.S. military were directly involved"—the very essence of the Gurkha concept.[77] The bombs delivered by NATO aircrews had certainly helped bring the Bosnian Serbs to terms. But the effectiveness of Deliberate Force derived in large measure from the fact that it occurred in tandem with equally effective American-advised proxies on the ground—a combination of gunboats *and* Gurkhas to enforce the rules.

➤ Viewed in isolation, the U.S. military response to each of these wildly disparate situations suggested an administration flying by the seat of its pants, relying on improvisation rather than principle. That perception was not entirely without merit. If by its actions the Clinton administration showed that it had discarded the Weinberger-Powell guidelines for using force, neither the president nor any of his chief lieutenants made any apparent effort to articulate a replacement. There was no particular speech or authoritative document promulgating an official Clinton doctrine.

But over time, beginning with Mogadishu and proceeding through each of the episodes recounted above, unmistakable patterns emerged. When it came to employing its military power, the United States after the Cold War followed particular routines. There were lines beyond which American policymakers refused, except in extremis, to venture. Preferences repeatedly exercised became something like habits. By the end of the 1990s, habits hardened into a de facto doctrine for how the United States would fulfill its self-assigned responsibilities as star-spangled global enforcer.[78] Altogether, it qualified as an extraordinary achievement, the true centerpiece of Bill Clinton's legacy as commander-in-chief.

CHAPTER 7

RISE OF THE PROCONSULS

The American soldier is different from all other soldiers of all other countries since the world began . . . he is the advance guard of liberty and justice, of law and order, and of peace and happiness.

Elihu Root, October 1899

A GREATER RELIANCE ON COERCION as an instrument of policy offered only one manifestation of the increasing militarization of American statecraft after the Cold War. Equally striking was the tendency of serving officers to displace civilians in implementing foreign policy. At the very top, civilians might remain the architects of overall strategy, but just beneath them the military provided the engineers who converted design into reality. The emergence of a new class of uniformed proconsuls presiding over vast quasi-imperial domains was only one development among many making the 1990s arguably the most portentous and troubling period in the history of U.S. civil-military relations.

The note of apparent civil-military reconciliation on which the decade began proved ephemeral. Before the 1990s ended, evidence of civil-military dysfunction had become increasingly difficult to ignore. Meanwhile, events had exposed the limitations of the proconsular system—and of America's reliance on gunboats and Gurkhas to police the world.

➤ "Nearly a decade after its conclusion the Persian Gulf war is already looking like a footnote to American history." This appraisal of Operation Desert Storm, offered by Frank Rich of the *New York Times*, managed to be at once accurate and wildly off the mark.[1] To be sure, with the passage of time, the many millions who participated vicariously in the campaign to liberate Kuwait tended to remember it less as a serious armed conflict than as visually spectacular melodrama—almost a precursor to "reality TV." On this score certainly, Rich was correct.

Furthermore, few of the anticipated benefits of victory, seemingly so decisive as to be without precedent in the annals of military history, actually materialized. A decade after the war, a defiant Saddam remained firmly in power. Peace in the Middle East remained elusive. Evidence that this demonstration of U.S. military prowess had exerted a calming effect internationally was slight, further substantiating Rich's view that expectations raised by the triumph in the desert remained unfulfilled.

Nor was that all. Closer to home, Operation Desert Storm fostered hopes that U.S. civil-military relations, ruptured by the Vietnam War and never fully repaired, might at last be restored to health. Ever since Vietnam, American military leaders and their civilian masters had viewed each other at best warily and at worst with barely disguised suspicion and mistrust. More broadly, Vietnam had created a gulf separating the armed services from American society as a whole. While the Reagan administration, by disposition hypernationalistic and by choice munificent in its defense spending, made headway toward restoring civil-military comity, in the collective mindset of the officer corps the basic problem remained.[2]

For members of that officer corps, the Persian Gulf War in a single stroke healed psychic wounds that had festered for a generation. In the eyes of many military professionals, chief among them General Colin Powell, chairman of the Joint Chiefs of Staff, the manner in which the United States conducted and concluded the war and the way that Americans generally responded to the crisis exorcised the demons of Vietnam. Thanks to Operation Desert Storm, Powell believed, "the American people fell in love again with their armed forces."[3] Indeed, references to "the troops"—a term for which politicians, pundits, and network anchors all took a sudden liking—conveyed a not-so-subtle shift in attitude toward soldiers, suggesting a level of empathy, respect, and even affection absent and even unimaginable since the late 1960s. Buoyed by their sense of having achieved a remarkable battlefield victory, soldiers accepted these expressions of appreciation and regard as their due—indeed, as long overdue.[4]

Events soon revealed most of this to be illusory. Rather than point-ing toward a lasting relationship, America's love affair with the troops proved to be no more than a passing infatuation. Barely had the last parade celebrating the exploits of Gulf War veterans ended when ten-sions began to surface. When naval aviators, many of them fresh from flying combat missions over Iraq, gathered in Las Vegas in Sep-tember 1991 for the annual convention cum frat party of the Tailhook Association, their drunken antics—particularly their abusive treat-ment of women—touched off a full-scale war over American military culture.[5] A seemingly never-ending series of headline-grabbing scan-dals followed, each reinforcing impressions that on matters relating to gender the military was radically out of step with American society. In a prank at the U.S. Naval Academy, midshipmen chained a female classmate to a urinal, one among several incidents suggesting a perva-sive institutional hostility to women.[6] At Aberdeen Proving Ground, lubricious U.S. Army drill sergeants were found to have routinely granted preferential treatment to female trainees in return for sex—a story generating months of lurid media coverage.[7] The nation's first-ever female B-52 pilot achieved momentary fame by alleging that she was being run out of the Air Force for engaging in the sort of sexual exploits that in a male would have been winked at if not celebrated.[8] Faced with credible public allegations that its own senior enlisted sol-dier had repeatedly harassed female subordinates, a mortified Army leadership had little choice but to haul him before a court martial.[9]

The military's evident problem with sex was not confined to those for whom a youthful libido might offer some excuse, however lame. Parting the veil that in other times had shrouded flag officers from public scrutiny, an inquisitive press discovered that a penchant for sexual shenanigans extended into the upper reaches of the military hierarchy. One retired Army general found himself recalled to active duty to stand charges of misconduct that centered on sleeping with the wives of his own subordinates; he pleaded guilty.[10] The first woman ever to wear the three stars of a U.S. Army lieutenant general made the front pages by accusing a fellow general officer of pawing her in her own Pentagon office; his career ended forthwith.[11] The four-star admiral commanding all U.S. forces in the Pacific lost his job for remarks violating the canons of political correctness—with subse-quent investigations revealing that he was also misusing government resources to romance a female officer on his own staff.[12] Another four-star officer, nominated to become chairman of the Joint Chiefs, saw his candidacy collapse once it became publicly known that he had years before engaged in an extramarital affair.[13]

The gender bind—pressure from the outside to "get it" regarding women and from the inside to preserve the military's traditional culture—could be a vise.[14] Admiral Mike Boorda, who as chief of naval operations inherited the unhappy assignment of cleaning up the mess left by Tailhook, found those pressures unbearable. Assailed by critics for appeasing politicians at the expense of the service's core values, Boorda cracked. Standing in the backyard of his quarters at the Washington Navy Yard one sunny afternoon in May 1996, he put a pistol to his chest and killed himself.[15]

Whatever pummeling the services endured on matters regarding gender, when it came to the even more combustible issue of sexual orientation, they gave back as good as they got. Whether gays should be permitted to serve openly in the military emerged as the other hot-button issue in the civil-military culture war of the 1990s. In late 1992 President-elect Bill Clinton naively fired the first salvo in that battle when he let it be known that once inaugurated he intended to follow through on a promise he had made on the campaign trail: just as Harry Truman had issued an executive order ending racial segregation in the military, he would issue a similar order banning discrimination against gays and lesbians.

Clinton's remark unleashed a fusillade of protest from the officer corps—propelled in part by a visceral dislike for the "dope-smoking, skirt-chasing, draft-dodging" individual just elected to the post of commander-in-chief.[16] General Colin Powell spoke openly against the proposal. Press reports hinted that other members of the Joint Chiefs were prepared to resign in protest if Clinton went ahead with his plan.[17] Serving officers published irate op-eds, one in the *Washington Post* reviving Douglas MacArthur's contention that the officer corps "swears allegiance to the Constitution, not to the commander in chief." Any service chief failing to oppose the president on gays would undermine "his moral authority over his subordinates," Majors David S. Jonas and Hagen W. Frank warned, and would forfeit "the loyalty of his subordinates." Even more pointedly, the two marines warned that the president himself "should also be concerned about that loyalty," which evidently depended on his discharging his duties in ways the services themselves deemed appropriate.[18]

Only the brokering of the widely derided "don't ask, don't tell" policy averted an even greater crisis. But the awkward compromise that temporarily settled the controversy over gays did little to allay the sense—reinforced by subsequent events—that in the aftermath of the Gulf War civilian control of the military, the bedrock of civil-military relations in a democracy, was badly eroded. Since the end of the Vietnam War, the officer corps had become increasingly conservative in its outlook and Republican in its political sympathies.[19] Sensitive to this shift in sentiment, politicians took to treating the military like just another interest group, especially at election time. The Republican party encouraged this trend, wooing the military with as much care as Democrats devoted to courting African Americans or public school teachers.[20] The ideal of the soldier as self-effacing servant of the state guided by an austere military professional ethic no longer explained the actual behavior of increasingly partisan officers who did not consider themselves bound by the once-hallowed tradition of remaining aloof from politics.

In short, the officer corps of the 1990s not only possessed convictions; its members intended to act on them. The new military leadership embodied by Colin Powell—wise in the ways of Washington, cozy with the media, disdaining the provincialism of the typical just-in-from-the-hustings elected official—no longer acknowledged an obligation to restrict itself to proffering advice and then quietly following orders. Nor did it see any need to limit its attention to matters falling within the military sphere, the boundaries of which in any case were increasingly difficult to discern. On an ever-widening array of foreign policy issues—where the United States should engage, how, and for what purposes—the military functioned as an independent and powerful policy advocate that civilian officials ignored at their peril.[21] In the interagency policy coordination process, officers assigned to the Joint Staff represented the collective wisdom (and interests) of the uniformed military. Staffers from the Office of the Secretary of Defense represented the views of the secretary and his lieutenants. That the former would necessarily conform to the latter was not a foregone conclusion. When the outcome of the internal policy debate went contrary to the military's wishes, the generals found ways to make their unhappiness known.[22]

To be sure, as with some high-profile political marriages, the parties to the civil-military relationship adhered to the formal conventions of fealty and mutual regard. Outsiders found this reassuring. The cognoscenti understood the reality beneath the surface. Politicians pretended to issue orders, and soldiers pretended to accept them unquestioningly, but both were reciting lines scripted in advance through a delicate process of negotiation. Whether this meant that the military was careening "Out of Control," as one famous essay suggested, or whether the "American Military Coup of 2012" beckoned, as another speculated, comfortable assumptions that civilian control of the military was an absolute no longer held true (and perhaps never had).[23] In the post–Cold War era, the terrain where civilian interests, values, and fears intersected with those of the military became fiercely contested.

At the mass level, the problem was not so much one of Vietnam-era alienation—according to opinion polls, the military commanded widespread popular respect and admiration—but of growing public indifference.[24] Increasingly, the high regard that middle-class Americans accorded to those volunteering for military service was akin to that which American Catholics felt for fellow believers who embraced the celibacy of religious life: a choice worthy of the highest respect, it was also peculiar to the point of being unfathomable. For most people, that choice was one that they preferred to see someone *else's* son or daughter make.[25]

At the elite level, meanwhile, it was not indifference that prevailed but friction, frequently exacerbated by the sheer ignorance of civilian leaders. As the generation that had fought World War II and Korea passed from the scene, the number of political leaders possessing firsthand experience in soldiering dwindled. President Bill Clinton and his national security team exemplified this trend.[26] As this reservoir of firsthand experience dried up, the inclination of civilian elites to educate themselves in military matters did not experience a corresponding increase. In short, as one legacy of the Persian Gulf War, civil-military relations fell once again into disrepair, approaching if not quite attaining their post-Vietnam low.[27] Certainly in this regard, the war deserved recognition as more than a mere footnote.

➤ Never acknowledged officially, civil-military tension persisted throughout the Clinton era.[28] Official Washington seemingly took the view that the best way to treat the disease was to ignore the symptoms. In fact, continuing civil-military turmoil measurably loosened the bonds of civilian control. Seizing upon this opening, a select group of senior officers used it as an opportunity to accrue unprecedented additional authority in matters involving the formulation and implementation of U.S. foreign policy. These officers acted with the acquiescence if not the outright encouragement of their political masters. The emergence of a new class of military viceroys stemmed in part from the ineffectiveness of civilian agencies charged with making policy, above all the State Department, and from unintended and unforeseen consequences of defense reforms implemented in the latter part of the Cold War. But transcending these two factors was a third: the military's growing influence in matters relating to foreign policy reflected the underlying logic of American grand strategy and the role of military power in advancing the prospects of openness and integration.

The defense reform at issue was the Goldwater-Nichols Department of Defense Reorganization Act, a landmark measure passed with bipartisan support over Pentagon objections in 1986.[29] Among the several purposes of this legislation, two stand out. First, in an effort to sharpen the quality of professional military advice provided to the president and secretary of defense, Goldwater-Nichols designated the chairman of the Joint Chiefs of Staff as their sole military adviser and gave the chairman exclusive control of the Joint Staff. This had the effect of elevating the chairman's profile at the expense of the service chiefs. Heretofore the chairman had stood as first among equals; henceforth, if he chose to use the prerogatives of his office to the fullest, he was the boss. Second, the legislation sought to enhance the prerogatives of the commanders-in-chief of the various unified and specified commands—the "warfighting" CINCs. The intent here was to ensure that the priorities of those charged with implementing war plans received due attention back in Washington. Heretofore, the theater CINC charged with defending Korea or Western Europe had been beholden to the chiefs of the different services. Now the so-called warfighters wielded equal or even greater clout.

The full implications of this effort to reshuffle the locus of military authority did not become apparent for several years. In some respects, when the results did appear, they differed from what the framers of Goldwater-Nichols intended. Finding that a powerful JCS chairman could be as much an obstacle as an asset, civilian policy-makers consciously sought ways to reduce that obstacle—to make it a pebble instead of a roadblock. Meanwhile, at a time when policy-makers professed to believe that war as such was going out of fashion, while finding military power more useful than ever before, the CINCs began to define their role as something much more than warfighting.

Colin Powell was not the first post–Goldwater-Nichols chairman, but he was the first incumbent to exploit that legislation to its full potential. Credited (rightly or not) with having performed brilliantly during the successive interventions in Panama and the Persian Gulf, Powell by 1992 had become easily the most powerful JCS chairman in the history of that office. By the time Bill Clinton became president, the photogenic general was widely regarded as the second-most influential figure in Washington, held in high esteem by the public at large and considered prime timber for virtually any office to which he might aspire. In the early days of the Clinton administration, Powell used that clout to complicate the president's life appreciably, opposing the commander-in-chief on gays, attempting to "drive the military strategy train," and maneuvering to avert direct U.S. military involvement in the Balkans.[30]

For the Clinton administration, the expiration of Powell's term in the fall of 1993 came as a godsend. Powell's retirement from active duty offered a ready-made opportunity to relieve the president of having to accommodate a JCS chairman enjoying the status of semi-autonomous potentate. The solution: choose a successor possessing none of his qualities, thereby reducing the likelihood that he would exercise comparable influence. Thus, each of the two officers Clinton appointed to the post of JCS chairman—General John Shalikashvili (1993–1997) and General Henry Shelton (1997–2001)—represented a sort of anti-Powell. Each embodied the personal qualities of the good soldier—diligence, honesty, and devotion to duty. But neither manifested anything remotely like Powell's charisma, political savvy, and gift for manipulating the media. These decent but uncompelling men were made to order for a White House that had put up with about as much military obstructionism as it was willing to tolerate. The Clinton administration found Powell's two successors far more accommodating.[31]

The selection of a pliable JCS chairman removed impediments to the strategy of openness. But it did not necessarily ensure the vigorous implementation of that strategy. Implementation became the special niche of the regional CINCs. During the 1990s there were four of these officers who really counted, each presiding over vast swathes of earth, sky, and water. Headquartered in Pearl Harbor, Hawaii, the commander-in-chief of United States Pacific Command (CINCPAC) held sway over all of the Pacific Ocean and East Asia. In Stuttgart, Germany, the commander-in-chief of United States European Command (CINCEUR)—dual-hatted as supreme commander of all NATO forces, or SACEUR—was responsible for Europe, most of Africa, and portions of the Middle East, including Israel. The commander-in-chief of United States Central Command (CINCENT), headquartered in Tampa, Florida, kept watch over the remainder of the Middle East—including the strategically sensitive Persian Gulf, Central Asia, and the Horn of Africa. Finally, charged with responsibility for Central and South America and the Caribbean was the commander-in-chief of United States Southern Command (CINCSOUTH), recently decamped to Miami after decades in the now defunct Panama Canal Zone.

General Anthony C. Zinni, an outspoken marine who served as CINCENT in the late 1990s, likened the post–Cold War role of regional CINC to that of a proconsul of the Roman empire.[32] The comparison was an apt one. In the post–Cold War era—a time of permeable boundaries and blurred distinctions—political, diplomatic, and military concerns were becoming so mixed up together as to appear indistinguishable. When it came to advancing global U.S. interests in such a milieu, the first order of business was not campaign planning—preparing for the next Desert Storm—but governance. "I look longingly at the foreign affairs intelligentsia, but no one is addressing the cosmic issue; everyone's going tactical," complained CINCPAC Admiral Dennis C. Blair to a reporter. "What's the United States going to do with its superpowerhood? It drives me crazy."[33] To astute military officers like Zinni and Blair, it was readily apparent that no one was better positioned to fill this perceived void in cosmic thinking than the four-star regional commanders.

As Zinni himself acknowledged, his conception of soldiers crossing into the realm of statecraft was by no means novel. In the immediate aftermath of World War II, for example, the practice of assigning senior officers broad political-military responsibilities had for a time become commonplace. In Tokyo, Douglas MacArthur ruled as an American mikado, assigning to his own person something of the divine status previously reserved for the occupant of the Chrysanthemum Throne. In occupied Germany, General Lucius Clay's term as military governor elevated a heretofore faceless Army bureaucrat to national and even international prominence. Other senior officers served tours as ambassadors or filled important posts in the Department of State.[34] Rising above all the rest as the emblematic soldier-statesman of the day was General of the Army George C. Marshall. No sooner did Marshall step down as Army chief of staff than President Truman was pressing him into service, first as envoy to China and then as secretary of state during a crucial period of the early Cold War.

Aside from the record of the immediate postwar era, the American proconsular tradition had origins more immediately relevant to post–Cold War conditions. Nearly a century before Zinni became CIN-CENT, Leonard Wood, a military surgeon who emerged from the Spanish-American War as a general officer, had been among the first to shake free of soldierly inhibitions against straying beyond strictly military concerns. In 1898 the United States had won a great maritime empire. The task confronting the nation, Wood believed, in line with the most enlightened political thinking of his day, was not simply to sit on that empire but to transform it. Remade in America's image, the constituent parts of that empire would become stable, prosperous, and thus profitable. That the Army ought to play a leading role in this process meshed nicely with Wood's convictions and with his own very large ambitions. First as military governor of Cuba, then as governor of the Philippines' Moro Province, and ultimately as governor-general of all the Philippines, he threw himself into making good on that vision.[35] In so doing, Wood became the prototype of the senior commander as proconsul, inspiring a generation of protégés and acolytes.[36]

The new proconsuls of the post–Cold War era—including, along with the regional CINCs, Admiral Howe in Somalia and General McCaffrey waging America's "war on drugs"—approached their responsibilities very much in the spirit of Leonard Wood. They understood, as did Wood in his day, that the undertaking on which the United States had embarked was open-ended. At the beginning of the twentieth century, men like Wood, Theodore Roosevelt, and Elihu Root were convinced that Cubans were ill fitted for genuine independence; for decades if not generations to come, Cuba would require tutelage that the United States alone was fit to provide. A hundred years later their successors in the policy elite could not envision Europeans or Asians managing their own affairs absent the supervision of a watchful and benevolent United States.

Just as victory in 1898 transformed the Caribbean into an American lake, so too victory in 1989 brought the entire globe within the purview of the United States; henceforth American interests knew no bounds. To a marine like Zinni, familiar with the role that predecessors like Smedley Butler had played in policing the Caribbean during the interwar period, the historical parallel was all but inescapable.[37] "It's going to be back to the future," Zinni predicted, finding in the post–Cold War environment "some strong similarities to the Caribbean region of the 1920s and 1930s—unstable countries being driven by uncaring dictators to the point of collapse and total failure." Now, on a wider scale, instability and misbehavior were prompting "the Big Guy with the most formidable presence in the area" to intervene. When presidents did decide to act, they did as Theodore Roosevelt, Taft, Wilson, and Coolidge had done, turning to the present-day equivalents of Leonard Wood and Smedley Butler "to deal with each messy situation and pull everything together."[38]

In more traditional military precincts, the notion that the CINC's proper role was to sort out innumerable messy situations rather than to stand in readiness for a single major combat contingency met with considerable resistance. The officer corps contained many for whom "warfighting" remained the essence of their calling. In order to gain some doctrinal cover to justify shifting attention and resources elsewhere, the CINCs became enthusiastic proponents of what the Pentagon was calling "engagement," conducted regionally under their own auspices.

Among American officers, it had long been an article of faith that peacetime interaction with foreign military establishments—the panoply of visits, exercises, training missions, and educational exchanges lumped together under the tag "mil-to-mil contacts"—produced positive policy outcomes. With friends, mil-to-mil contacts enhanced mutual understanding, built trust, facilitated interoperability, and spread the gospel of American military professionalism. With potential adversaries, such contacts offered a way to divine enemy strengths and weaknesses. Within the services, these propositions were self-evident.[39] During the 1990s the CINCs parlayed the military's abiding faith in these truths with the administration's eagerness to pursue openness into making themselves the kingpins of regional strategy.

When it came to playing the role of foreign policy powerbrokers, the CINCs had three things going for them. First, as a matter of course, each approached matters from a regional rather than a bilateral perspective; in the management of empire, it is regions, not individual nations, that count. Second, each CINC could call upon a huge staff, filled with eager and industrious officers for whom planning and coordination were akin to breathing; all that was needed was to redirect those energies from combat contingencies to engagement.[40] Third, to translate ideas into action, the CINCs had resources vastly greater than those possessed by other government agencies such as the State Department. Those resources included not just military assets—carrier battle groups or fighter squadrons—but executive jets, instantly available secure communications, retinues of attentive aides, and lavish budgets for discretionary spending that no mere ambassador dared even to dream of.[41]

As engagement supplanted preparation for war as the focus of activity, the language employed to describe the purpose of these commands softened accordingly. CINCs' testimony before Congress began to sound increasingly like that of a progressive-minded assistant secretary of state. Here is how General Peter Pace of the U.S. Marine Corps described the five objectives—presumably listed in order of priority—constituting his "vision" for United States Southern Command:

Promote and support stable democracies.
Promote and support respect for human rights and adherence to the rule of law.
Assist Partner Nations to modernize and train their security forces.
Sustain and strengthen multilateral security cooperation.
Cooperate with regional forces to detect, monitor, and reduce the transit of illegal drugs.

For its part, U.S. Pacific Command's self-described aspiration was to be "an active player, partner, and beneficiary in pursuit of a secure, prosperous, and democratic Asia-Pacific community." U.S. European Command, meanwhile, committed itself to "two fundamental principles." The first aimed at "building strong relationships based on trust and cooperation" with nations throughout its area of responsibility while also "addressing the systematic problems facing much of the African continent." The second sought to capitalize on "a unique convergence of historical, economic, and diplomatic forces" in order to play a leading role "in guiding Europe, the Middle East, and Africa towards democracy, prosperity, and stability for the coming decades."[42]

Not every CINC's "vision" came across as quite so high-minded—the word *democracy* was notably absent from Central Command's strategy—but all conveyed a sense of having chucked old-fashioned concepts of power.[43] Such concepts were, after all, the very antithesis of the strategy of openness. Pondering the future, for example, Admiral Blair dismissed predictions of "a multi-polar world of emerging states vying with each other, building forces to threaten and bargain, shifting alliances and seeking to build their own power." This, he said, had been "the world of Bismarck and 19th Century Europe"—by implication, a world long gone and never to be revived. For his part, Blair favored an "alternative approach . . . where states are trying to build security communities, concentrating upon shared interests in peaceful development, and actively promoting diplomacy and negotiation to resolve disagreements."[44] The role of CINCPAC was to usher that happy world into existence.

Yet if their goals seemed effusive and fuzzy, the means used by regional commander-in-chiefs to pursue them were anything but. To achieve the objectives of his command, each CINC drew up a comprehensive and detailed theater engagement plan, a compendium of activities specifically tailored to achieve U.S. policy objectives throughout his area of responsibility. Taking as a given the efficacy of military activities as the means of influence, each plan described a program of ship visits, training assistance initiatives, multilateral exercises (usually with a humanitarian or peacekeeping motif), conferences, seminars, and officer exchanges.[45]

Complementing these activities was the nearly constant travel by the CINC himself to nurture personal relations with regional military counterparts but also, and perhaps more importantly, with kings, presidents, and foreign ministers. Nor did CINCs hesitate to speak over the heads of these officials to reach out to a wider audience. For example, during the nine months from the fall of 2000 to the summer of 2001, Blair pitched his vision for the Asia-Pacific region at press conferences or "media roundtables" in Russia, Singapore, Thailand, Japan, South Korea, Malaysia, New Zealand, Australia, India, and the Philippines.[46] Within their "CINC-doms," these four-star commanders became easily the most visible and arguably the most influential representatives of American power.

A CINC's take on his region was not necessarily congruent with views prevailing back in the State Department, the Pentagon, or even the White House. The willingness of a Zinni or Blair to express views at odds with those of their nominal superiors offered one measure of their growing autonomy. When the Clinton administration declared its support for efforts to overthrow Saddam Hussein, Zinni publicly dismissed the idea as a stupid one. According to Zinni, an angry Samuel R. Berger confronted him, demanding: "What gives you the right to say that?" "Well," the general replied, "the First Amendment."[47] When Blair found himself in disagreement with the State Department over demands that he sever all contacts with the Indonesian army in retaliation for its running rampant in East Timor in 1998, a nasty bureaucratic row ensued. In the end, the CINC's preferences—not those of the U.S. ambassador to Indonesia—prevailed.[48] To work around a foreign policy apparatus that the CINCs found to be unresponsive and overly cautious, the operative principle was to act first and seek permission later. General Wesley K. Clark, who served first as CINCSOUTH and subsequently as CINCEUR and SACEUR, described his approach this way: "Never ask 'Mother, may I,' unless you know the answer."[49] A decade after the Cold War, the four-star commanders who managed the far reaches of America's global imperium felt less and less inclined to ask.[50]

➤ In October 1998 Admiral Thomas J. Lopez, commander-in-chief of U.S. Naval Forces, Europe, arrived in Algiers for an official visit—one of countless such trips conducted annually by senior American commanders to various countries abroad. During Lopez's brief stay, units of the U.S. and Algerian navies collaborated in small-scale maneuvers, the first such maritime exercise since Algeria gained its independence in 1962. The Navy intended this initial contact to inaugurate an ongoing partnership between the military forces of the two nations, whose official relations had never been other than cool. A reporter covering this event for the *Washington Post* noted in passing that the Lopez mission fitted nicely within a larger trend. The Clinton administration was turning "increasingly to the U.S. military to initiate or lead its diplomacy in areas where the civilian foreign policy apparatus lacks access or resources." In seeking an opening with Algeria, the Navy was simply "repeating a role it has played in improving bilateral relations with China, Russia, Ukraine, Yemen, Mexico, Chile and Bulgaria, to name a few."[51]

In 1998, the passing mention of tiny Yemen as one nation among many that had drawn the attention of U.S. military diplomatists attracted scant notice. Less than two years later, with an American warship lying crippled by a terrorist bomb at the Port of Aden, Yemen became, however briefly, a hot topic. In the brouhaha that followed, it became evident that the USS *Cole* had not called for fuel at Aden because it had no other alternative; it had done so because such a visit supported General Anthony Zinni's ongoing attempts to "engage" Yemen, a state with a long record of harboring terrorists.[52] Yet in all the investigation, analysis, and second-guessing that ensued, virtually no one questioned either the propriety of having military commanders formulate regional policy under the guise of "engagement" or their qualifications for doing so. The absence of attention to these questions was telling: by the end of the 1990s a militarized foreign policy was something that most Americans took for granted.[53]

In fact a much larger episode more than a year before the *Cole* incident—the eleven-week war for Kosovo, followed by the U.S.-led occupation of that province—should have raised large doubts about the strategic competence of proconsuls. With Somalia, Kosovo marks a defining moment in the military history of the Clinton era. The two events bracket the evolution of military practice during the first post–Cold War presidency. In 1993 miscalculation had led to a humiliating policy failure. In 1999 the war for Kosovo also involved miscalculations. But in this case the end of the campaign approximated success, achieved by relentless bombing of the people of Serbia. The conduct of Operation Allied Force offered the fullest expression of how the United States had absorbed and codified the lessons learned at painful cost six years before. But Kosovo also offered the fullest illustration of the limitations and complications inherent in the system that the United States had evolved for employing its military might.

At the time, journalists dubbed Kosovo "Madeleine's War," and indeed in some respects it was. Particularly in her ham-handed management of the Rambouillet "peace talks," the U.S. secretary of state deserved credit for making the conflict unavoidable. But Kosovo qualifies in equal measure as a "proconsul's war," with the proconsul in this case being General Wesley K. Clark, then serving both as chief of United States European Command and as NATO's supreme allied commander.

Unlike Zinni, Clark did not use explicitly imperial language to characterize his role. Rather, he described himself as occupying "the cockpit of strategic command," uniquely situated at the nexus of political and military concerns and obliged to tend to both.[54] As events would show, it was a position whose responsibilities he was unable to fulfill.

Clark had been among the first after the Persian Gulf War to suspect that warfighting looked increasingly like a dead end.[55] In 1994, as a fresh-minted lieutenant general he was appointed Richard Holbrooke's chief military deputy and served in that capacity throughout the negotiations culminating in the Dayton peace accords. By Clark's account, the experience was akin to a religious conversion. Holbrooke's moral certainty and sense of purpose, his refusal to allow mere history to impede action, and his obsessive courtship of the media (and the benefits deriving therefrom) all left an indelible impression. Above all, there was Holbrooke's breezy confidence that "using military power to back diplomacy"—threatening air strikes to coerce political adversaries—would end a seemingly intractable conflict.

Holbrooke's success in bringing peace to Bosnia convinced Clark that the received wisdom about proper uses of American military power was obsolete. Henceforth, in the right circumstances and under the right leadership, U.S. military power could and should do much more than simply "fight and win the nation's wars."[56] From the moment Clark became SACEUR in July 1997, Kosovo beckoned as a comparable opportunity.

To Clark and to senior officials of the Clinton administration, the chief obstacle to peace in the Balkans was Slobodan Milošević, the ultranationalist Serb and president of what remained of Yugoslavia. During his service with Holbrooke, Clark had met with Milošević on many occasions. As a result, he was supremely confident that he knew what made the Serb president tick. Clark "had learned his fear"—the prospect of attack by American air power. In his capacity as a strategic commander, he intended to exploit that fear, maneuvering Milošević into ending his repression of the Kosovar Albanians while also coaxing him to embrace democracy—the only sure way to guarantee Balkan stability.[57]

Well before NATO initiated Operation Allied Force in March 1999, Clark was hard at work selling his "strategic vision" to Washington. Modeling his tactics after Holbrooke's in Bosnia, Clark favored what he called a "carrot and stick approach." The stick—the threat of bombing—would bring Milošević to the negotiating table. The carrot would come once serious talks were under way: Clark wanted "subtly to embed in the negotiations measures to promote the return of democracy to Serbia."[58]

Officials in Washington questioned some of the large assumptions underlying this thinking. Skeptical about the efficacy of threats alone to intimidate Milošević, General Joseph Ralston, an Air Force officer and vice-chairman of the Joint Chiefs of Staff, asked Clark: "What are we going to do if the air threat doesn't deter him?" As recorded in Clark's memoir, the following colloquy ensued:

> "Well, it will work," I said. "I know him as well as anyone. And it gives the diplomats the leverage they need."
> "OK, but let's just say it doesn't. What will we do?" he asked.
> "Well, then we'll bomb. We'll have to follow through," I said.
> "And what if the bombing doesn't work?"
> "I think that's unlikely, but in that event, I guess we'd have to do something on the ground, directed at Kosovo."
> "And if that doesn't work?" he persisted.
> "Well, then we keep going. But I think you have to work at the front end of the policy, on how to make it effective. Besides, I know Milošević; he doesn't want to get bombed."[59]

In the event, the threat of bombing failed either to cow Milošević or to persuade him of the benefits of liberal democracy. Yet at the beginning of March 1999, with the plight of the Kosovars worsening, patience with Milošević in Washington and Brussels wearing thin, and the Rambouillet talks deadlocked, Clark professed optimism. "I can't believe that Milošević won't sign, when the crunch comes," he told Deputy Secretary of State Strobe Talbott. "He always holds out. He has to be leaned on very hard. But he will come around."[60]

But Milošević did not come around. Not for the last time, the strategic commander underestimated his quarry. There remained no escape from the war that Clark had promised to avoid, a war now fought not on behalf of the suffering Kosovars, but to preserve NATO. "We've put NATO's credibility on the line," Clark reminded Albright. "We have to follow through and make it work. There's no real alternative now."[61] So on March 24, 1999, Operation Allied Force commenced.

Inexplicably, although NATO and U.S. staffs had spent months drafting, reviewing, and refining plans for an air campaign against Serbia, when hostilities began Clark seemingly had little conception of how the alliance would overcome its adversary. Granted, the operational problem was not a simple one. Concern for American public opinion and allied solidarity alike mandated that Clark adhere to President Clinton's announcement, at the outset of the campaign, explicitly ruling out the use of U.S. ground combat troops.[62] Clark would fight his war using gunboats (and perhaps Gurkhas), with the Clinton administration and allied governments hoping for a quick victory achieved with a minimum of carnage.[63]

Yet even given these constraints, Clark's approach defied logic. For public consumption, at a press conference packed with television cameras and journalists gathered from around the world, the supreme commander announced that NATO was going to "systematically attack, disrupt, degrade, devastate, and ultimately destroy" Yugoslavia's military and security forces, unless Milošević complied with the demands of the international community.[64] Clark's rhetoric reinforced public expectations that he would bring things rapidly to a conclusion.

Away from the glare of the cameras, Clark sounded a different and far more cautious note. In issuing instructions to his chief subordinates on the eve of hostilities, he specified three "measures of merit" that would guide Operation Allied Force. First: avoid the loss of allied aircraft. Second: "impact the Yugoslavian military and police activities on the ground as rapidly and effectively as possible." Third: "protect our ground forces"—meaning the peacekeepers, some of them Americans, already deployed elsewhere in the Balkans.[65]

Two of Clark's measures of merit focused not on achieving objectives but on preventing bad things from happening. The third was ambiguous: in operational terms what did it mean to "impact . . . activities on the ground"? And how would doing so achieve the political aims sought by Washington and Brussels?

Clark's measures of merit made sense only in the context of an additional key assumption, unspoken, unacknowledged, but widely held in the American camp: that Milošević was nothing but bluff; faced with the slightest demonstration of allied resolve, he would fold.[66] In short, as envisioned by Clark, the contest for Kosovo would involve only two moves, one by each side: NATO would bomb a few targets, and Yugoslavia would capitulate. "Get real, Mr. President," Clark had chided Milošević during a contentious meeting in Belgrade the previous fall. "You don't want to be bombed."[67] As the first NATO combat aircraft lifted off for Serbia months later, Clark still believed that he had his adversary pegged: Milošević didn't want to get bombed.

In short order it became clear that Clark—though not he alone—had miscalculated. A defiant Milošević did not fold. The first several days' bombing succeeded only in stoking the fires of Serb nationalism and in providing Belgrade with the excuse to accelerate its ethnic cleansing of Kosovo. Ethnic Albanian refugees poured out of Kosovo into neighboring Macedonia and Albania, a development that caught NATO flatfooted.[68] Despite this evidence of a full-fledged war, high officials in Washington continued to characterize the operation as a "humanitarian intervention," launched in response to Serb-perpetrated genocide.[69]

His own bluff called, Clark needed to make good on his threat to disrupt, degrade, devastate, and destroy Milošević's army. But the 366 aircraft assembled for Allied Force—the majority provided by the United States—proved inadequate to the task. Hampered by bad weather and difficult terrain, deprived of lucrative targets as Serb units dispersed or hid in Kosovar villages, allied aircrews proved unable even to impede Yugoslav operations on the ground, much less to destroy the forces conducting them. Given the overriding priority assigned to minimizing the risk to allied pilots—reinforced by the early loss of an F-117 stealth fighter to hostile fire—NATO pressed its attacks with less than all-out vigor or effectiveness. Clark's own senior air commanders, notably Lieutenant General Michael C. Short, believed that "the massive and laborious tank plinking effort in Kosovo was in many ways a waste of airpower."[70]

Speaking from the Oval Office on March 24, Bill Clinton had announced to the nation that NATO's goal was "to protect thousands of innocent people in Kosovo from a mounting military offensive." Within two days Clark was disowning the president's policy. In an interview he insisted: "It was always understood from the outset that there was no way we were going to stop these paramilitary forces who were going in there and murdering civilians in these villages."[71]

Having blundered into an open-ended conflict against an unpredictable, surprisingly defiant foe and with the future of NATO hanging in the balance, the United States found itself face to face with the limitations of the Clinton doctrine. Unlike the periodic post–Gulf War confrontations with Saddam Hussein or the retaliation for the terrorist attacks on the U.S. embassies in Africa, in this instance the United States could not lob a few pieces of ordnance, declare the operation a success, and call it quits. Nor, apart from the remnants of the Kosovo Liberation Army (KLA)—a battered and unsavory insurgent group known to be engaged in drug trafficking and terror—were there any readily available proxies to throw into the fray.[72] Simply trying harder was not an option: as the number of refugees streaming out of Kosovo mounted with each passing day, the inadequacy of the initial limited bombing became obvious.[73]

Clark's job was to find a way out of this predicament. In practice, only two alternatives existed. One course of action was to acknowledge that the war actually was a war and to prosecute it accordingly. Doing so implied bringing the full weight of allied military power to bear on Milošević to force him to submit—destroying his army, invading his territory, and, if need be, occupying his capital. In practice, of course, "allied power" meant for the most part American power.

Liberating Kosovo would entail serious fighting and held the almost certain prospect of U.S. casualties. But the Clinton administration—however misleadingly—had justified intervention primarily on humanitarian grounds, and Mogadishu had seemingly showed that Americans would not accept casualties incurred during humanitarian operations. Furthermore, organizing such a large-scale campaign would make it difficult to sustain the grand conceit of the global age, namely that war itself had become obsolete.

The second course of action called for NATO to forgo any goals of liberation while intensifying and recasting its bombing campaign. Even as it expressed continuing sympathy for the plight of the Kosovars and maintained a pretense of going after Yugoslav forces in the field, the alliance would shift the weight of its air effort to Serbia proper. Targeting government facilities, communications networks, the electrical grid, oil refineries, factories, and infrastructure, allied aircrews would wreak whatever level of havoc was required to convince Milošević that he had had enough. Put simply, instead of searching ineffectually for Serb forces scattered among the villages of Kosovo, NATO would go after downtown Belgrade. People might die as a result, but few if any of them would be wearing the uniform of a NATO nation. Furthermore, by averting the necessity of fighting on the ground, this approach would help sustain the tissue-thin fiction that this latest Balkan unpleasantness was not really a war, but simply an action by the "international community" to enforce the rules of a global age.

Yet Clark opted for the first alternative. By the beginning of April, the general who had long touted Milošević's susceptibility to a little bit of bombing was pressing Washington and Brussels to begin considering a possible invasion by ground forces. As a first step in that direction, he urged the immediate deployment of AH-64 Apache attack helicopters and rocket artillery—stationed in Germany and already assigned to his own U.S. European Command. In Clark's view, the firepower of these potent weapons would exact a heavy toll on Yugoslav formations operating in Kosovo.[74] If there was some risk involved, he was willing to take it.

Militarily, Clark's preferred course of action qualified as at least plausible. Morally, it was eminently defensible. But politically, it was a nonstarter. Having become a proponent of possible ground operations, America's proconsul in Europe revealed himself in Washington's eyes to be a naïf and a liability. With that, the jackals began to converge.

As SACEUR, Clark expected to be accorded the respect and deference due to a supranational military figure. As the successor to supreme commanders like Eisenhower, Alfred M. Gruenther, and Lauris Norstad, whose influence at least approached that implied by their magniloquent title, Clark expected, especially in the midst of hostilities, to exercise real command authority over the forces at his disposal. If nothing else, as a regional CINC in the midst of a sticky situation, he expected that the longstanding American tradition of backing field commanders to the hilt would guarantee him the full support of his fellow four-stars back in the Pentagon.

He was disappointed on all counts. To his political masters in Washington, Clark's support for a proposition so wildly at odds with the president's stated policy was unacceptable. Moreover, they were adamant that the White House and the Pentagon would make the key decisions. Nor were Clark's military peers in the Pentagon sympathetic: an advocate of using "military power to back diplomacy" had stumbled into a full-fledged shooting war—in their view an unnecessary one. Now Clark seemed determined to make things worse by enmeshing U.S. forces in a ground campaign of unknown cost and duration. They were determined to prevent him from doing so.

In essence, Washington opted for the lesser evil: a strategic bombing campaign to bring the Serb regime and, if need be, the Serb nation to its knees. Clark got more combat aircraft—as many as he could handle.[75] But the upper echelons of the Clinton administration and the uniformed military remained dead set against ground troops. Against this united front, Clark's dogged insistence that he needed attack helicopters assumed increased importance, symbolic as well as substantive. The Apaches became the expression of Washington's determination not to budge from the terms of the Clinton doctrine. At the same time, the argument over the Apaches was also an argument over who was running the war. It was a visible test of the SACEUR's authority, or lack thereof.

With a notable absence of enthusiasm, President Clinton on April 4 approved in principle Clark's request to commit an AH-64 battalion. But as is frequently the case with contentious issues in Washington, that "decision" actually decided nothing. Within the bureaucracy, intense guerrilla warfare ensued. The U.S. Army in particular did everything in its power to prevent the attack helicopters from actually going into action. In response to manufactured security concerns, the Army insisted on beefing up Task Force Hawk, as it came to be called, with a dozen seventy-ton Abrams tanks and forty-two Bradley fighting vehicles. To support the Apaches, the Army added thirty-seven other helicopters—Blackhawks and Chinooks. A larger, heavier force took longer to assemble, longer to deploy, and was more difficult to support. In all, protecting and sustaining a mere twenty-four attack helicopters ended up requiring 6,200 troops and 26,000 tons of equipment, to include 190 containers of ammunition and enough spare parts to support twice the number of aircraft actually deployed. Moving this mammoth task force to its designated staging area in Albania consumed 550 C-17 sorties. The cost to American taxpayers was an eye-popping $480 million.[76]

Even then, when Task Force Hawk finally arrived at its base in Rinas, Albania, the Army insisted that the Apache crews, nominally combat ready, undergo a lengthy period of training and rehearsals before being committed. Behind the scenes, Army Chief of Staff General Dennis Reimer was querying Clark's subordinates on whether the Apaches were *really* necessary—in effect, subverting the chain of command.[77] Meanwhile, two Apaches crashed in training accidents with the loss of two pilots—giving Task Force Hawk's opponents all the ammunition they needed to insure that it never engaged the enemy. The eleven-week war ended without a single Apache's firing a shot in anger. The episode shattered the supreme commander's pretensions to supremacy, even in his own realm.

Task Force Hawk was only one of many slights that Clark was obliged to endure. Apart from one phone call wishing him a happy Easter, he found himself walled off from direct contact with his commander-in-chief. Clark's performance during NATO press conferences irked Secretary of Defense William Cohen to the point that he ordered the SACEUR—using Shelton as his messenger boy—to "Get your f _ _ _ ing face off the TV. No more briefings, period."[78] Particularly galling to Clark were Washington's efforts to exclude him from any meeting of allied political leaders in which the war might figure as a topic.[79]

Similarly, as the air campaign both intensified and shifted its focus, Clark found even his control over ongoing operations eroding. Rather than a theater commander, he became hardly more than a kibitzer. Actual command authority fragmented, with General Short one of the beneficiaries. Convinced from the outset that the way to defeat Milošević was to turn out the lights of Belgrade, Short reoriented the air campaign accordingly. In effect, Short began taking his cues from other senior Air Force officers rather than from Clark.[80] Meanwhile, in a throwback to Vietnam days, senior political leaders began intruding into tactical minutiae: according to the *Washington Post*, "Generals raced across the Potomac River with satchels of targets to get the White House to approve the next night's work."[81]

By the first week of June, strategic bombing—that is, attacks designed to inflict maximum pain on the Serb economy and the Serb people—began to take its toll. Since mid-May 85 percent of Serbs had been without electric power.[82] Russia, the closest thing that Serbia could claim as a meaningful ally, signaled Belgrade that it was time to quit.[83] For its part, NATO quietly backed off from elements of the Rambouillet formula that Serbs had found most offensive.[84] A resurgent KLA, with indirect American encouragement and support, began operating out of base camps in Albania to harass Yugoslav units in Kosovo proper.[85] By no means least of all, British Prime Minister Tony Blair, most hawkish of NATO's European leaders, was on the verge of going public with plans to invade Kosovo, if need be without the Americans.[86] And the White House announced that Bill Clinton had invited the Joint Chiefs of Staff to consult—the president's first session with the JCS since the hostilities had begun. According to press reports, the purpose of the meeting was to provide cover for Clinton to announce that he, too, now accepted the necessity of preparing a ground option.[87]

At this juncture, Milošević indicated through intermediaries that Yugoslavia sought an end to the hostilities. Over a period of several days, after much wrangling, Yugoslav and NATO officers signed off on an agreement paving the way for the introduction "in Kosovo under UN auspices of effective international civil and security presences."[88] Implicit in this stilted phrasing was that the peacekeeping operation would not be exclusively a NATO one, a major concession to the Serbs. Prominent among the non-NATO nations scheduled to participate was Russia.

On June 9—after seventy-eight days, just over 38,000 sorties, and the expenditure of 28,236 weapons amounting to 12,000 tons of munitions—the bombing ceased.[89] In the days that followed, Serb forces, showing surprisingly little wear and tear, affected an orderly, at times almost impudent, withdrawal from Kosovo.[90] As the Serbs departed, the lead elements of KFOR, the NATO-led peacekeeping force, entered the province. The deployment became the occasion of Clark's final and most public humiliation.

Clark's plan for occupying Kosovo divided the province into five sectors, each assigned to a NATO member nation. Irked at the prospect of its own contingent's reporting to a subordinate NATO commander, Moscow took matters into its own hands: it would get its own troops into Kosovo first and carve out a distinctive Russian sector.[91] With that end in mind, the Russian peacekeeping brigade in Bosnia dispatched a small armored column toward Priština with orders to seize the main provincial airport there. If Russian troops could gain control of the airport, others could pile on to reinforce, presenting the allies with a fait accompli.

Viewing Moscow's move as a "strategic challenge" to NATO, Clark ordered the commander of KFOR, Lieutenant General Sir Michael Jackson, to beat the Russians to Priština by whatever means necessary.[92] When the Russians won the race anyway, Clark ordered Jackson to block the runways to prevent the arrival of reinforcements. Jackson bluntly refused. "I'm not starting World War III for you," the British general told Clark in an emotional outburst that captured the attention of the press.[93] More telling, however, is Clark's own account of the exchange. Jackson asked by what authority Clark was issuing his order.

"By my authority, as SACEUR."

"You don't have that authority."

That Jackson spoke the truth soon became evident even to Clark: wary of a confrontation that could derail the ongoing occupation, senior Pentagon officials, starting with Shelton, sided with the British three-star against the American four-star.[94] There would be no blocking of runways. As a gauge of Clark's impoverished standing as SACEUR, a more telling incident could scarcely be conceived. The proconsul had been hung out to dry.

➤ In its public assessment of Operation Allied Force, Washington chose not to dwell on such unseemly details. It preferred a simple, clean-scrubbed tale. NATO's bombing campaign had been an unmitigated triumph. The peacekeeping operation just commencing would be no less successful. "I can report to the American people that we have achieved a victory for a safer world, for our democratic values, and for a stronger America," proclaimed Bill Clinton; "in Kosovo we did the right thing. We did it the right way. And we will finish the job."[95] In fact, the outcome of the first proconsul's war was decidedly mixed.

On the one hand, for situations requiring the expenditure of U.S. military power in more than just penny packets, Operation Allied Force provided a model for how to fight. If in the post–Cold War era the ideal conflict is one in which no Americans get hurt and every American gets rich, then the war for Kosovo, in its own perverse way, approached perfection. In the end, the United States and its allies prevailed—albeit over a pint-sized nation whose entire gross national product amounted to one-sixteenth of the Pentagon's budget—without losing a single soldier killed in action.[96] During the air campaign, critics had lambasted the Clinton administration for its lackluster conduct of the war. But this amounted to just so much hot air. As long as there were no body bags coming home, the administration's actual control of policy was never seriously called into question.

No less noteworthy, the war came and went without causing Wall Street more than passing anxiety. Indeed, Operation Allied Force coincided with a stock rally of epic proportions. During the first week the Dow Jones industrial average closed above 10,000 points for the first time; barely a month later, with the bombs still falling, it surpassed 11,000. Never during U.S. involvement in a war had American stock portfolios fattened so generously and so quickly. President Clinton himself received scant credit for his Balkan victory—his standing in the polls actually dropped a bit—but he had seemingly stumbled onto a formula enabling the United States to fight wars without engaging the passions of the American people.[97] For a self-indulgent democracy in a postheroic age eager to maintain its global preeminence but disinclined to sacrifice, such a formula was likely to find future application.

The legal and political consequences of Operation Allied Force were more problematic.[98] With regard to international law, the intervention qualified in at least two respects as a precedent-setting event. In going to war over Belgrade's treatment of Kosovo, the United States and its allies demolished any lingering notion about the claims of sovereignty rendering internal matters off-limits to outsiders. Russia and China numbered among the nations viewing that precedent with alarm.[99]

In addition, although NATO had justified its resort to force as an action undertaken on behalf of the entire "international community," the body normally considered to represent that community had by no means given its approval. Indeed, given its inability to get the United Nations to authorize intervention—in the Security Council neither Russia nor China would concur—the alliance had in fact arrogated to itself the authority to act. That the world's only superpower could henceforth use a regional organization that it dominated to legitimate its own use of force did not find universal favor.

Politically, the war left relations between Washington and Moscow strained and between Washington and Beijing on the verge of a complete rupture—largely as a result of an errant U.S. bomb that pulverized the Chinese embassy in Belgrade on May 7, 1999. The successful conclusion of the war also did little to enhance NATO's own solidarity. Although nominally the alliance had demonstrated a hitherto-untapped capacity to venture "out of area" and even "out of charter," in the eyes of many observers, the war's chief lesson was never, ever to risk another such enterprise. A second such stressful event could well mean NATO's dissolution.

To make matters worse, with Operation Allied Force having demonstrated anew how far allied military capabilities lagged behind those of the United States, the European Union began talk of creating a separate defense identity, enabling it, if necessary, to act independently. Whether Europe possessed either the collective political will or the resources to reconfigure and modernize its forces remained to be seen, but the mere prospect did not bode well for American claims to leadership on that continent.

But all of this was as nothing in comparison with Kosovo's moral and ethical implications. Indeed, on these matters, the events during and after the conflict left a long skein of confusion trailing in their wake. Problems began at the moment of the war's conception. The United States and its allies publicly justified intervention as a necessary response to the horrors of ethnic cleansing. But once the shooting began, they took no meaningful action to protect the Kosovar Albanians, whose plight actually worsened as NATO proceeded with its attack. It was as if America actually had entered World War II to save the Jews and then still abandoned them to their fate.

Throughout the campaign, the American aversion to casualties remained acute. Combined with an unbridled infatuation with tech-

nology, this preoccupation yielded morally insidious effects. With airmen recycling old theories of strategic bombing, now larded with
expansive assurances that precision weapons released from afar could
achieve remarkable results at minimal risk to Americans, the principle of noncombatant immunity received short shrift.

The essence of war is a bloody interaction. Traditionally armies in-
teract with—that is, wage war against—other armies. But in Kosovo
the U.S. government was, for all practical purposes, unwilling to
countenance the loss of a single American soldier. Since making war
on the Serb army meant putting soldiers in harm's way—whether by
sending troops in on the ground or flying aircraft at lower operating
altitudes—every American in a position of authority (except Clark)
understood the necessity of recalibrating the terms of the interaction.
In essence, the United States needed to wage war in ways that deprived the enemy of any real opportunity to shoot back. The role assigned to military forces in Allied Force was not to fight battles but to
deliver ordnance.

Thus did it become expedient to target the Serb political and economic infrastructure, and inevitably Serb civilians. This shift in priorities showed in the results achieved. In contrast to their predecessors
during Operation Desert Storm, the aircrews who conducted Operation Allied Force showed themselves markedly less efficient in killing
enemy soldiers and more efficient in killing noncombatants.[100] To
some observers, such an outcome was anathema. Others—fired with
the conviction that the cause was just—disagreed. In any war, according to David Rieff, a journalist of progressive bent, regrettable incidents occurred: "you send your F-15 to help the Kosovars and what it
does is it blows up a bunch of children in a hospital. It is inevitable.
That's what war is. We've made a lot of claims for ourselves, for our
societies and for our moral aspirations. But without force or the
threat of force, they're hollow ideas."[101]

The disparity between professions of humanitarian concern and
the actual results achieved also pervaded the peacekeeping phase of
the operation. For KFOR, Clark laid down four new "measures of
merit," chief among them a requirement to "stop any crimes of revenge or Serb ethnic cleansing."[102] In the event, Kosovar refugees returned home thirsting for revenge and wasted little time slaking that
thirst. A savage process of reverse ethnic cleansing ensued, which
KFOR did little to impede.[103] Expectations that a Kosovo purged of its

ethnic Serb minority might become placid did not materialize. Despite having agreed to disarm, a resurgent KLA began agitating violently to unify all nearby ethnic Albanians into a "Greater Kosovo." Albanian insurgents infiltrated into Serbia and Macedonia, triggering border skirmishes that KFOR found itself attempting ever so gingerly to suppress.[104]

In the meantime, cautious American commanders in Kosovo kept their well-armed troops battened down in Camp Bondsteel, a sprawling, heavily defended base soon to be equipped with gymnasiums, recreation centers, and a shopping-mall-style food court.[105] Unlike in Bosnia, no one even pretended that the mission would end anytime soon: the troops settled in for a protracted stay. And whatever Clark's stated intent, the paramount concern for each U.S. unit that rotated through Kosovo, outweighing every other consideration, became "force protection," keeping the troops from harm.

Whatever the moral justifications for plunging Belgrade into darkness and for turning a blind eye as the persecuted turned on the persecutors in Kosovo, these developments left the very concept of a military professional ethic reeling. Even the most sympathetic observer was hard pressed to find in the allied assault on Serbia or in the peacekeeping efforts that followed evidence of gallantry or derring-do or fraternal self-sacrifice—any of the virtues that warring nations cite to imbue an otherwise squalid business with a modicum of dignity. Critics, viewing these events from afar rather than, say, from the cockpit of a fighter-bomber streaking across the night sky toward Belgrade, expressed concern that present-day soldiers appeared less eager to die for their country than earlier generations had been. Less than a decade after the high-water mark of Desert Storm, American military professionalism, they lamented, showed unmistakable signs of decay.[106]

➤ The debates provoked by these moral and ethical complications raised issues of profound importance to a democratic and, in many respects, God-fearing society. For those fancying that a star-spangled fist ought to enforce the rules of a globalized world, the moral complications lying in wait appeared formidable. Yet at the political center of things, these concerns barely registered. At the center, the war's architects understood that from the outset Operation Allied Force had never actually been about doing the right thing in the right way. Its purpose had been to sustain American primacy on a continent of vital importance to the United States, one that had advanced the furthest toward the openness and integration defining the ultimate goal of American grand strategy. The United States fought over Kosovo not to protect Kosovars but to forestall the intolerable prospect of Europe's backsliding.

Viewed from this perspective, the workmanlike demolition of Serbia might not qualify as a feat worthy of comparison with Gettysburg or the Normandy invasion, but it was what a great power did to fend off perceived threats to its preeminence. If Operation Allied Force did not rise to the level of a great moral victory, it was a necessary strategic one, an example of the work that goes along with running an empire.

Within the foreign policy elite, the relevant lessons of Kosovo concerned not issues of conscience but practical matters. By the end of the 1990s it became apparent to even the most enthusiastic booster of globalization and of American "leadership" that the enterprise to which the United States had committed itself was proving to be an arduous one. If the forces of globalization might one day perhaps render beggar-thy-neighbor politics obsolete, that day had certainly not yet arrived. Whatever the hopes that one day all the nations of the world would converge on the ideals of pluralistic democratic liberalism, for the moment at least, ethnic identity and cultural particularism remained ferociously and disconcertingly alive.

Furthermore, if the United States undoubtedly ranked as the greatest military power the world had ever seen, its capacity to overawe fell far short of being absolute. Keeping America's armed might in reserve would not suffice; using it necessarily entailed new obligations and commitments and in some quarters stoked greater opposition. With American citizens evincing little eagerness to shoulder the burdens of empire (while accepting its benefits as their due), innovative methods of imperial management were needed. The alternative—allowing the nation's own cultural maladies to circumscribe the exercise of American power—was simply unacceptable. If, in the particular case of Kosovo, the American proconsul had failed to fulfill his responsibilities, then the appointment of a more responsive and capable replacement was in order.

At the end of the 1990s, with the United States at the zenith of its influence, Kosovo served as a reminder that the obstacles to openness remained formidable. Overcoming those obstacles was proving less easy than Bill Clinton and Madeleine Albright had expected. Yet despite periodic posturing about America's imminent slide back into isolationism, virtually no member of the policy elite dissented from the proposition that the United States had little choice strategically but to press on. The anticipated consequences of doing otherwise—greater disorder abroad, diminished prosperity at home, and, inevitably, retribution at the ballot box—were simply too awful to contemplate. The consensus in favor of "global leadership" remained firm.

On June 2, with the outcome of Operation Allied Force still at issue, but with patience wearing thin and criticism of the administration's handling of the crisis approaching flood stage, President Clinton's national security adviser, Samuel R. Berger, summoned a group of "wise men" to the White House. To counter the perception that the president lacked the mettle to see things through, Berger outlined for his listeners "four irreducible facts": "One, we will win. Period. Full stop. There is no alternative. Second, winning means what we said it means. Third, the air campaign is having a serious impact. Four, the president has said he has not ruled out any option. So go back to one. We will win."[107]

The national security adviser did not speak idly. In Europe, NATO aircrews ratcheted up the punishment visited upon the Serbs. In Washington, the White House girded itself for the prospect of mounting an invasion. There would be no backing down. At the end of the day, the United States would do whatever was necessary to win.

Berger's crisp presentation serves as a fitting end point for an ostensibly humanitarian intervention that willy-nilly transformed itself into a full-fledged shooting war. But it serves just as well to capture the irreducible bottom line of U.S. grand strategy during the 1990s. Faced with opposition and under duress, the United States would do whatever was necessary to achieve its purposes. Period. Full stop.

CHAPTER 8

DIFFERENT DRUMMERS, SAME DRUM

The United States will hold the key, unlocking the gates of commerce of the world, closing them to war. If we have fighting to do, it will be fighting to keep the peace.

The editors, *Harper's Magazine*, 1893

IN THE AFTERMATH OF WORLD WAR II, the pivotal year for U.S. foreign policy was not 1947, the year of "Mr. X," the Truman Doctrine, and the Marshall Plan. Nor was it 1949, when the abrupt end of the American nuclear monopoly, followed just weeks later by the "loss" of China, left Washington reeling. Nor was it 1950, the year of National Security Council Resolution 68 and the Korean intervention, which together committed the United States to a massive program of rearmament. Rather, the defining moment occurred in 1953.

In January of that year, Republicans, after a long and frustrating absence from power, reclaimed the White House and in doing so reasserted control of U.S. foreign policy. For years the G.O.P. had been charging that on the paramount issue of the day—responding to the threat of communism—the Truman administration had been pusillanimous and inept. According to Republicans, the Democrats' strategy of containment amounted to acquiescence and accommodation—a "negative, futile, and immoral policy" that "abandons countless human beings to a despotism and godless terrorism."[1] Such a policy was altogether unworthy of a great nation such as the United States.

Throughout the 1952 presidential campaign, the Republican candidate, General Dwight D. Eisenhower, along with the party's chief foreign policy spokesman, John Foster Dulles, hinted at a radically different approach. An Eisenhower administration would seek ways to "roll back" communism. The United States would exert itself to liberate "captive nations." Referring to those countries on the far side of the Iron Curtain, candidate Eisenhower told cheering supporters: "The American conscience can never know peace until these people are restored again to being masters of their own fate." To enable that conscience to rest easy, Dulles spoke of finding ways to "split the satellite states away from the control of a few men in Moscow."[2]

That was what the electorate heard on the campaign trail. Privately, Eisenhower (if not Dulles) harbored somewhat different views. A pragmatic and prudent statesman, Ike did not seriously entertain a great crusade to dismantle the Soviet empire. He thought that the real danger facing the United States was the risk of exhausting itself through overextension. He favored lowering the U.S. profile abroad and reducing commitments. He even flirted with the idea of phasing American troops out of Europe.[3]

Once in office, Eisenhower neither followed through on his campaign rhetoric nor acted on his own inclinations. There would be no rollback or withdrawal. Instead, the new administration opted by and large for the status quo. There might be a modest course correction but no course change.

Once in power, Republicans embraced the fundamental logic of the strategy that the Democrats had devised. Eisenhower affirmed the commitments the Truman administration had made to defend Europe, Japan, South Korea, and Taiwan. In doing so he paid his predecessor a very large if backhanded compliment. More important, he invested U.S. national security strategy with a continuity that it would retain—except briefly following Vietnam—through a succession of administrations, Republican and Democratic.

In a similar sense, 2001 proved to be the pivotal moment that fixed the azimuth of U.S. policy in the emerging global era. The transfer of power from Bill Clinton to George W. Bush was the moment when Republicans, after a long and frustrating absence from power, after years of complaining about pusillanimity and ineptness, got their chance to reorient American foreign policy. Indeed, they came into office promising to do so. In the event, however, they ended up affirming the basic course set by Democrats—and in doing so reaffirmed the consensus underlying U.S. strategy.

➤ At least since the time of Woodrow Wilson's futile crusade for the League of Nations, public discourse about U.S. foreign policy has con-

tained strong elements of theater. In communicating to a wider public, the foreign policy elite prefers oversimplification, clichés, and caricature to candor, nuance, or complexity. The end of the Cold War has,
if anything, reinforced this tendency.

The quadrennial competition for the White House—and the role
foreign policy plays as a prop in that contest—offers a case in point.
Through tacit agreement, the two major parties approach the contest
for the presidency less as an opportunity for assessing U.S. policies
abroad than for striking poses—a hallowed and inviolable bit of political kabuki. The parts are prescribed, the players know their roles,
and everyone sticks to the script. The purpose of this ritual is not to
undertake any serious assessment or critique of American statecraft
but to sustain the fiction that in the forthcoming balloting the differences separating the candidates are large and the stakes high.

Thus as a factor determining the outcome of the presidential election of 2000, pitting Vice President Al Gore against Texas governor
George W. Bush, foreign policy barely registered. Whatever claims
may be made about that election, it was in no way a referendum on
the foreign policies of the Clinton era. Neither candidate made more
than passing mention of the subject.

But each ventured into the electoral arena armed with his own
prescribed set of sound bites. When, during the second of the three
presidential debates, the moderator charged the two candidates with
identifying the "guiding principles" of U.S. foreign policy, he was, in
effect, cueing them to perform. Governor Bush, coached to play the
role of hardheaded realist, duly recited: "The first question is what's
in the best interests of the United States." The vice president—don-
ning the mantle of the enlightened progressive—demurred: "I see it
as a question of values."[4]

Thus did the candidates pretend to differ. After the fact, partisans
in both camps pretended that those differences actually mattered.
Journalists chimed in with commentary pretending to spin out the
weighty implications.[5]

After the campaign ends, the posturing continues. But for the victor, the purpose changes: the intent is no longer to emphasize difference but to blur it. Once safely elected, but even before his inauguration, Bush was declaring his conviction that "American values always
are at the center of our foreign policy."[6]

In fact, comparing the actual views of Bush and Gore, or more generally comparing the views of Democratic foreign policy experts with those of their Republican counterparts during the campaign was akin to comparing the primetime programming of competing television networks. Some differences existed: after all, people actually make a living contrasting the finer points of the sitcoms on NBC with those broadcast on CBS. But enumerating those differences doesn't go very far toward identifying the true nature of the enterprise known as commercial television.

Similarly, some people actually make a living parsing the differences between where Democrats and Republicans stand on foreign policy—indeed, ideologues and those for whom the Washington Beltway defines the epicenter of the universe have an abiding interest in portraying those differences as acute. But whatever the satisfactions of that effort in terms of scoring partisan points or hyping "the news," it really doesn't get you very far toward understanding the essential nature of U.S. foreign policy. Indeed, it obscures more than it illuminates.

During the very long campaign, Governor Bush expounded on America's role in the world in only two speeches, one elucidating his vision for foreign policy and the other devoted specifically to national security. Afterward spokesmen for the Bush camp awarded their candidate the highest marks for depth, breadth, and originality. But with a handful of exceptions, the views expressed by candidate Bush differed little from those expressed by candidate Clinton in 1992 or by President Clinton in the years that followed.

Speaking on foreign policy at the Ronald Reagan Presidential Library, for example, Governor Bush explicitly, though without acknowledging the source, endorsed the Clintonesque teleology that "our nation is on the right side of history."[7] He also put his imprimatur on openness in statecraft, offering to his listeners "a vision in which people and capital and information can move freely, creating bonds of progress, ties of culture and momentum toward democracy." Like Clinton, Bush rejected the possibility that some might construe the role of the United States in presiding over such an open world as somehow imperial. "America has never been an empire," he declared with more fervor than accuracy. Indeed, "We may be the only great power in history that had the chance, and refused—preferring greatness to power, and justice to glory."

Like Clinton, Bush proudly identified himself as a free trader. Like

Clinton, he accepted as fact the correlation between free trade and political liberalization. "The case for trade is not just monetary, but moral," he enthused. "Economic freedom creates habits of liberty. And habits of liberty create expectations of democracy." Like Clinton and his lieutenants, Bush identified (or pretended to identify) the foremost threat to this vision of an open, prosperous, and democratic world as an American penchant for inattention: "America's first temptation is withdrawal—to build a proud tower of protectionism and isolation." Should the United States succumb to the temptation, the inevitable result would be "a stagnant America and a savage world." Bush shared Clinton's conviction regarding America's indispensability.

So what was it about Bush's version of internationalism that—as the title of his remarks promised—made it "distinctly American"? Certainly, Bush's enumeration of what he called the nation's "enduring national interests" did little to make any such distinctions apparent. The litany of interests that the governor recited could have been lifted directly from any stock foreign policy speech by Bill Clinton or Al Gore during the previous eight years: to work closely with allies, to promote democracy and trade, to prevent the spread of weapons of mass destruction, and to "defend America's interests in the Persian Gulf and advance peace in the Middle East, based upon a secure Israel."

To the extent that Bush held out expectations of anything novel, he promised a new tone, a new approach toward China, and a new emphasis on missile defense. The tone would be one of diffidence, backing off from the preachiness and bombast to which the Clinton administration had been prone. "We propose our principles," remarked Bush; "we must not impose our culture." The United States would exercise global leadership with "modesty" and "humility," meaning among other things that it would carefully consult with and cultivate its allies, who, Bush emphasized, were "partners, not satellites."

On China, Bush recycled the critique of administration policy that Clinton had used when attacking Bush's father in 1992. The Democrats had been too soft on China. Taking aim at Clinton's increasingly benign view of the People's Republic, Bush begged to differ: "China is a competitor, not a strategic partner."

On national and theater missile defenses, Bush pledged unambiguously: "If I am commander-in-chief, we will develop and deploy them." Bush assured his listeners that missile defenses would be directed not against Russia or China, but against "rogue nations," thereby adopting the Clinton administration's own formula for characterizing states such as Iran, Iraq, and North Korea.

In his speech on national security, Bush expanded on his commitment to missile defense while addressing additional themes. He began by affirming his belief in U.S. global leadership and his commitment to openness and integration. A world "shaped by American courage, power and wisdom now echoes with American ideals."[8] Through a century of struggle, the United States had secured the triumph of "a vision of freedom and individual dignity—nurtured by free markets, spread by information technology, [and] carried to the world by free trade." The challenge facing the United States now was to use its power—notably its military power—to consolidate that victory in the face of the "unconventional and invisible threats of new technologies and old hatreds." Chief among them were "car bombers and plutonium merchants and cyber terrorists and unbalanced dictators"—the same roster of threats that Clinton had so relentlessly promoted as America's new enemies. Indeed, most of the sentiments that Bush expressed could have been lifted directly from the Web site of the Clinton White House.

In addition to missile defenses, the national security program that Bush sketched had two components. The Texas governor promised to "renew the bond of trust between the American president and the American military"—an allusion to the rocky civil-military relations that had prevailed during the Clinton era. And he vowed to "begin creating the military of the next century,"—repeating the promise of Pentagon reform that Clinton had made in 1992 and that, eight years later, remained largely unfulfilled.

With regard to rebuilding trust, Bush promised soldiers a pay raise and made sympathetic if vague references to the services' being overstretched and underfunded.[9] Taking a swipe at the Clinton administration's penchant for peacekeeping, he vowed to put an end to "open-ended deployments and unclear military missions." Specifically, finding ways to "allow an orderly and timely withdrawal from places like Kosovo and Bosnia" would become a high priority for a Bush administration. This, of course, was not in any way to be confused with a step toward isolationism.

When it came to creating a new military, Bush signed onto the very same "revolution in military affairs" that Pentagon documents proclaimed to be at hand but that the services had energetically resisted. To judge by Bush's words, after years of "inertia and idle talk," he would make short work of that resistance. The time was long past to get on with transforming a military establishment still geared "for industrial age operations, rather than for information age battles." Once in office, Bush said,

> I will begin an immediate, comprehensive strategy review of our military—the structure of its forces, the state of its strategy, the priorities of its procurement—conducted by a leadership team under the Secretary of Defense. I will give the Secretary a broad mandate—to challenge the status quo and envision a new architecture of American defense for decades to come. . . . The real goal is to move beyond marginal improvements—to replace existing programs with new technologies and new strategies. To use this window of opportunity to skip a generation of technology.

Clearly, Bush expected that as commander-in-chief he would possess the authority to effect such broad institutional change. But then so had Bill Clinton.

A vow of humility, more careful nurturing of allied relationships, a tougher line on China, a restoration of civil-military harmony, another stab at reconfiguring the U.S. military: these few items—plus missile defense—were the best that the Bush team could come up with to distinguish its intended approach from that which had prevailed during the eight years of Clinton-Gore. For any observer not fired by partisan passions, the list, with the exception of missile defense, did not exactly rise to the level of a sweeping change. In short, the treatment of foreign policy during the 2000 presidential campaign testified not to division but to a fundamental similarity of outlook, at least as far as Republicans and Democrats were concerned.[10]

➤ On December 16, 2000, the curtain began to fall on the Clinton era of U.S. foreign policy. On that date George W. Bush, having prevailed in a bruising postelection battle that had left many still questioning the legitimacy of his claim to the presidency, announced that he was appointing General Colin L. Powell to be his secretary of state. Given Bush's own gossamer-thin foreign policy credentials, the announcement generated interest unusual even for such a senior post: it seemed clear that whoever headed the State Department would be the new administration's real foreign policy guru. Indeed, it was hard to imagine that Powell—former national security adviser, former chairman of the Joint Chiefs of Staff, bona fide national hero—would have accepted the offer without some assurance that he would indeed be the vicar of U.S. foreign policy. From the press and leaders of both political parties, the appointment elicited almost unanimous approval.

But Powell was only the first in a series of gilt-edged appointments as Bush assembled a national security team rich in experience and proven ability. Donald Rumsfeld, a brusque politician turned corporate executive who had served as secretary of defense under Gerald Ford, accepted Bush's invitation to serve a second tour in that post. Condoleezza Rice, widely respected for her service as a National Security Council staffer in the first Bush administration, now became national security adviser in the second. Paul Wolfowitz, perpetrator of the Wolfowitz Indiscretion, returned to Defense as Rumsfeld's deputy. Richard Armitage, another tough-minded veteran of the Defense Department under the elder Bush, became number two at State. For the post of U.S. trade representative, the new president chose Robert Zoellick, another key figure in his father's administration. And, of course, in the phlegmatic Dick Cheney, secretary of defense from 1989 to 1993, Bush had a vice president who was uniquely well equipped to assist him in navigating the thicket of international politics. If that wasn't enough, in a pinch the president could always consult his father.

During the eight years in the wilderness that began in January 1993, those now returning to power had numbered among the most vociferous critics of Clinton's foreign policy. In 1998 Rumsfeld, Wolfowitz, and Armitage, for example, sent President Clinton a letter denouncing the policy of containing Iraq as flaccid and insisting that removing Saddam Hussein from power was now "the only acceptable strategy."[11] Rumsfeld chaired a commission that made headlines by accusing the administration of underestimating the looming ballistic-missile threat and calling for the early deployment of missile defenses. During the campaign, several served as surrogates or advisers to the candidate. Rice, Wolfowitz, and Zoellick had been frequent visitors at the governor's mansion in Austin. At the invitation of *Foreign Affairs,* Rice and Zoellick contributed essays purporting to limn the distinctive principles of Republican statecraft. Armitage drafted Bush's address on national security policy. Whatever Bush's own limitations as a would-be statesman, he was at least surrounding himself with "adults"—comfortable with the exercise of power, guided by a clear purpose, and willing to make the tough calls. These were people who understood strategy and were adept at synchronizing the instruments of power to serve the national interest. Among those who had long since concluded that the policies of the Clinton era never rose beyond boosterism and improvisation, the character of the Bush team created expectations of major improvement.

Yet as Bush took office and his chief advisers made the transition from critics to policymakers, a remarkable thing occurred: the policies that in the Clinton years they had found sadly wanting acquired hitherto-unnoticed virtues. As a result, the actions of the new administration during its first months showed far greater evidence of continuity than of change. Like Eisenhower in 1953, George W. Bush in 2001 by and large embraced the policies of his predecessor. As in 1953, Republicans vigorously denied that such was the case, and Democrats found it expedient to minimize the similarities. But those similarities far outweighed the differences. As a result, although the rhetoric changed, the overarching grand strategy—aimed at creating an open and integrated international order dominated by the United States— emerged from the transfer of power intact. This was the case prior to September 11, 2001. And it continued to be the case after that date.

➤ Consider, for example, the Bush administration's approach to the use of force. Throughout eight years during which Democrats controlled the White House, few things raised greater ire among Republicans than Bill Clinton's ineffectual employment of U.S. military power. Attracting particular ridicule was Clinton's penchant for pinprick air attacks that Democrats depicted as demonstrations of toughness and resolve.

Nowhere was this Clinton doctrine more in evidence than in the

U.S. effort to contain Saddam Hussein—the tens of thousands of sorties flown and the hundreds of targets attacked pursuant to enforcing the no-fly zones over northern and southern Iraq. Republicans were correct in asserting that the impact of these efforts on Saddam and his regime had been worse than nil. Indeed, the attacks had emboldened Saddam to mount ever-more-audacious acts of defiance—hence the Republican agitation for a policy aimed at "regime change" in Baghdad.

During the run-up to the 2000 election, Bush and his surrogates let it be known that, if elected, they would jettison the amateurish Clinton doctrine. When it came to using force, George W. Bush would exhibit the prudence and sound judgment that had been a hallmark of his father's administration. By implication, a second Bush presidency would revive some variant of the Powell Doctrine, using U.S. military power only when vital American interests were at stake and then doing so overwhelmingly and decisively. Bush's appointment of General Powell as secretary of state seemingly affirmed this intention.

After January 2001, Iraqi behavior became more defiant still. Iraqi attempts to down patrolling coalition aircraft became more determined. Intrusions of Iraqi combat aircraft into the no-fly zones (and even into Kuwaiti and Saudi airspace) increased in frequency. It was as if, with a Bush reclaiming the White House, Saddam Hussein was eager to renew the contest that he had lost ten years earlier, recovering at the son's expense some of what he had lost at the father's hands. Whatever Saddam's actual intentions, if a new, tougher U.S. policy was in the offing, the Iraqi dictator was providing a convenient pretext to inaugurate it.

But it soon became clear that there would be no new policy, at least not anytime soon. In his confirmation hearings the hawkish Wolfowitz confessed to a Senate committee that if there was any feasible way to remove Saddam from power, "I haven't seen it yet."[12] Overnight, the term *regime change* vanished from the lexicon of the Bush camp.

On February 16, 2001, barely three weeks after Bush's inauguration and a full decade after Operation Desert Storm, the White House announced with much to-do that the new commander-in-chief had sent U.S. forces into action against Iraq: a handful of warplanes had bombed a handful of targets "near" Baghdad. The proximity to Baghdad was crucial to portraying Bush's bombing as somehow different from Clinton's, which had tended to avoid the Iraqi capital. But the effort was unpersuasive: the reality was that under the new administration the policy of tit-for-tat bombing continued. In explaining his decision to bomb Iraq, President Bush took pains to emphasize that doing so had long since become simply "routine."[13] Indeed, the February 16 attack was neither the first nor the last to occur on Bush's watch.[14]

As a practical matter, the Bush administration's feeble assaults on Iraq—like the equally feeble attacks of the Clinton administration that began in December 1998—achieved nothing apart from enabling American pilots to continue their endless patrols. Insisting that those patrols formed "part of a strategy," President Bush vowed that until that strategy changed "we will continue to enforce the no-fly zone." Reporters present for these remarks politely refrained from pressing Bush to explain exactly what that strategy might be.[15]

Within short order the answer to that question became clear: with only the slightest of modifications, Bush adopted the previous administration's policy of containing Iraq. During Secretary Powell's first trip to the Persian Gulf, tough talk about removing Saddam from power was notable by its absence. Instead, Powell touted the administration's plans for "retooling" the sanctions regime established during the presidency of the elder George Bush and adopted by Bill Clinton. Although Saddam over the past decade had shown extraordinary skill in undermining that regime, Powell promised that a new set of unspecified "smart sanctions" would deny Baghdad access to arms and militarily relevant technology, keeping Saddam from causing further mischief while easing the hardships of the long-suffering Iraqi people.[16] Yet stripped of the flourishes intended to convey a sense of novelty, the smart-sanctions policy at its core amounted to little more than a promise to try harder. When smart sanctions met opposition in the UN Security Council, that term, too, disappeared. Nothing remained except more patrols in the no-fly zones, more Iraqi "provocations," and more U.S. and British retaliatory air strikes, with negligible impact.[17] Thus, in the apt judgment of the *Washington Post,* did the Bush administration find itself "adopting the same Iraq policy pursued in recent years by the Clinton administration—a policy President Bush and his top aides repeatedly and vociferously condemned."[18]

On a variety of other issues, the Bush administration spent its first weeks tacking away from the positions taken during the campaign to distinguish Governor Bush from his opponent, back toward the course charted by the Clinton administration. "We really don't need to have the 82nd Airborne escorting kids to kindergarten" in Bosnia and Kosovo, Condoleezza Rice had sniffed during the campaign.[19] Would the new administration act promptly to return U.S. forces to their true vocation as warfighters and leave peacekeeping to others, as Bush and others repeatedly hinted? Not really: soon after his inauguration President Bush announced that he had no immediate plans to withdraw U.S. troops from the Balkans and promised NATO that any changes would occur only after thoroughgoing allied consultation—a signal for nervous Europeans to rest easy. As Secretary Powell assured the allies during his first visit to NATO, "We went in together, we will come out together."[20] Indeed, in August 2001 Bush ordered U.S. troops to take on additional peacekeeping responsibilities, joining other NATO troops for Operation Essential Harvest, an effort to disarm ethnic Albanian guerrillas in Macedonia.[21]

Would the new administration reverse the Clinton policy of showering North Korea with blandishments whenever Pyongyang hinted darkly about acquiring nuclear weapons? Not according to Powell, who announced in early March that the new administration would "pick up where President Clinton and his administration left off."[22] Washington stood ready to resume talks with Pyongyang, without preconditions.

Did Colombia look like another liberal Democratic quagmire in the making, with Clinton's $1.3 billion program of military aid the first step toward plunging the United States into an intractable civil war? Perhaps, but Republicans were not going to take the rap for "losing" Colombia or for conceding defeat in the war on drugs. The Bush administration not only affirmed the existing U.S. commitment to that war but deepened and broadened it. Powell's State Department unveiled a new Andean Regional Initiative promising an additional $882 million in U.S. aid, half of it security assistance. Beneficiaries included not only Colombia but also Bolivia, Brazil, Ecuador, Panama, Peru, and Venezuela—this despite the absence of *any* evidence that ongoing U.S. support for Plan Colombia was producing positive results.[23]

Even when it came to China, the Bush administration's bark

proved to be worse than its bite. When, on April 1, 2001, a Chinese fighter jet collided with a U.S. Navy EP-3 reconnaissance aircraft off China's coast, Bush and his advisers faced their first serious foreign policy crisis. The damaged U.S. spy plane made an emergency landing at a Chinese air base on Hainan Island. The twenty-four American crewmembers ended up in the custody of Chinese officials. And the administration faced its first opportunity, however unsolicited, to show how it intended to deal with China as a "strategic competitor."

Yet after a brief outburst of saber-rattling, the administration went wobbly, opting for conciliation over the risks of confrontation. Dialogue took precedent over noisy public posturing. Beijing demanded an apology. Washington replied that an apology was out of the question, after which U.S. officials spent days offering expressions of "regret" and "sorrow."[24] Secretary of State Powell praised the People's Liberation Army for providing the U.S. detainees with "clean and well-lit" quarters and catered meals and (the former general's ultimate tribute) for treating the Americans regardless of rank as if they were officers.[25] When the widow of the Chinese pilot who lost his life in this incident wrote a letter chiding Bush for not caring, the president immediately penned a mollifying reply. The closest the administration came to dropping the hammer on Beijing was to hint that it might call off the president's upcoming visit or oppose China's bid to host the summer Olympics.

In an immediate sense, conciliation bore fruit. Recognizing that the pronouncements coming out of Washington met almost any definition of an apology, the Chinese released the crew and eventually returned the aircraft. But success came at a cost. Bush provided Beijing with compelling evidence that whatever his administration's professed concerns about human rights, the regional balance of power, or even the security of Taiwan, the United States would go to any lengths to "preserve the relationship." Why? Because Americans had too much at stake economically to permit the relationship to be ruptured—a conclusion that the Clinton administration had reached years earlier and that the Bush administration now tacitly endorsed. As an unnamed U.S. diplomat remarked in explaining why the United States was unable to take a more forceful stance, "we'd be hurting American carmakers and banks and workers as much as we'd be hurting the Chinese."[26] To protect carmakers and banks—and the consumers now accustomed to gorging themselves on cheap Chinese imports—the Bush administration found it expedient to placate its erstwhile "strategic competitor."

Indeed, by the end of July the administration jettisoned that term, too.[27] It turned out that no single label could adequately capture a multifaceted relationship. Opting for more anodyne language, General Powell took to characterizing China as "another nation that has a proud tradition and history and a system that is different from ours. And let's have discussions with that system."[28] Whatever the merits of mollification (not to say appeasement) as a basis of policy, it stood in marked contrast with the pugnacious "get tough" attitude that the Bush team had brought into office. Like Clinton—if even more quickly—Bush had flip-flopped on China.

When it came to transforming U.S. military forces, the new Bush administration found itself foundering on the same shoals on which military reform in the Clinton era had run aground. As promised, shortly after his inauguration President Bush did indeed issue his secretary of defense a broad mandate to undertake such a transformation.[29] Secretary Rumsfeld immediately launched a much-ballyhooed "strategic review"—and promptly encountered a swarm of opposition that all but discredited the initiative even before it reached any conclusions.

Rumsfeld faced two problems: limited fiscal latitude and fierce internal resistance. Once the president secured passage of a $1.35 trillion tax cut (his top domestic priority) and with the administration vowing to make good on its promise to field a ballistic-missile defense system (for the G.O.P., a quasi-theological requirement), little money was left to fund large-scale defense modernization. Transformation would require major investment in research and development and in the procurement of expensive new weapons systems, amounting to tens of billions of dollars per year. But the White House budget office balked at requesting more than a symbolic increase in the overall level of defense spending—$18.5 billion rather than the $90 billion that the top brass insisted the services required.[30] During the 1990s Republicans had frequently lamented that a superpower with global responsibilities was willing to devote only 3 percent of its gross domestic product to defense. Offered the chance in 2001 to make their case for a greater share, they punted. For Republicans and Democrats alike, the economics of national security had seemingly come to rest on an iron rule: worldwide military superiority, yes, but maintained with minimal exertion and sacrifice by the American taxpayer.

Nor was the military itself inclined to sacrifice on behalf of transformation. The alternative to a generous budget increase was to free up resources for modernization by cutting existing (and deeply cherished) forces such as mechanized divisions and carrier battle groups. This option military leaders refused to consider.[31] By the summer of 2001, not only was Rumsfeld's review process in evident disarray; the civil-military fissures so evident during the 1990s—and attributed to the ostensibly antimilitary sensibilities of the Clintonites—reappeared. Senior military officers were miffed with the Bush team on two counts: first, for failing to deliver on the implied promise of a major increase in defense spending; second, for giving short shrift to the military's views during the review process. Voicing a widely held opinion, one recently retired four-star general detected signs of "a strong sense of alienation between the uniformed leadership and the civilians."[32] An officer corps that largely voted Republican had expected better. With the generals publicly hammering away at a "strategy-to-force structure imbalance that has to be corrected," the struggle over control of U.S. national security policy was nakedly displayed.[33] Here, too, the continuity with the Clinton era was striking.

➤ But tallying up evidence of continuity did not sell newspapers. Nor did it offer a useful theme for political adversaries eager to score points at Bush's expense. As a result, the media and Democrats alike labored to make the case that the initial foreign policy moves of the new administration marked an abrupt departure.

Thus, already by the summer of 2001, Bush stood accused, if not convicted, of adopting a policy of high-handed unilateralism. Critics scolded Bush for not listening well. Instead of fixing the "ugly-American problem" the president had professed to worry about, he was exacerbating it, in effect abandoning the timeless principles of liberal internationalism. Others accused Bush of flirting with isolationism. Richard Gephardt, Democrat from Missouri and the House minority leader, reprimanded the administration for pursuing "go-it-alone policies."[34] Tom Daschle, the majority leader of the Senate, worried that as a result of Bush's cavalier treatment of key allies, "instead of asserting our leadership, we are abdicating it." According to Daschle, if the

United States showed a continuing disdain for the concerns of others, "our allies may be tempted to treat us as a dispensable nation."[35] The media were only too happy to amplify this charge.[36]

But the evidence offered to support the charge was largely contrived. To substantiate their indictment, Bush's critics pointed to a half-dozen international agreements or would-be agreements that his administration abandoned during its first months in office. These included the Comprehensive Test Ban Treaty, which the Senate had already rejected during the Clinton presidency; a protocol verifying compliance with a biological weapons convention, which Madeleine Albright had allowed to languish for years without action; and a treaty creating an International Criminal Court, negotiated in 1998 but signed by an unenthusiastic Bill Clinton only on December 31, 2000, when securing ratification would be someone else's problem.[37]

More egregious still, in the eyes of Bush's critics, was the administration's rejection of the Kyoto Protocol, designed to reduce the emission of greenhouse gases. But in this move the Bush administration was guilty of no more than acknowledging openly what had already become evident during the Clinton years: the U.S. Senate would reject any environmental treaty that threatened to affect adversely prospects for U.S. economic growth. By a margin of ninety-five to zero, the Senate had already signaled its opposition to the terms of the Kyoto accord. Unwilling to expend political capital for a lost cause, President Clinton had never even bothered to submit it for ratification. Bush only pulled the plug on an agreement that faced implacable congressional opposition.[38]

➤ In short, the accusations of a new unilateralism were largely fanciful. As one shrewd observer wrote in response to Gephardt's and Daschle's charges: "The music may sound slightly different, but whether the issue has been Iraq, China, defense spending, or trade, the Bush team has answered the fundamental questions of our day in very nearly the same way as its Democratic predecessor. Republicans may prefer to bomb Iraq in the daytime, Democrats in the evening . . . But that's about the sum of their differences in 2001."[39]

How are we to explain the fact that George W. Bush, the professed conservative, chose in most cases to hew to the course set by Bill Clinton, the paladin of liberalism?

Several plausible explanations exist. The first and most obvious is the different perspective that results from assuming the mantle of power. Advocacy when free of responsibility is one thing; action when one will be held to account for the consequences is something quite different. Employed as a basis for actual decisions, campaign rhetoric is as likely to produce disaster as sound policy.

A realistic appraisal of the facts on the ground provides a second possible explanation for similarities between Bush's approach and Clinton's, not only on Iraq but on other issues. The inauguration of a new president left those facts unchanged—facts that when faced head-on became constraints. In the case of Iraq, for example, the facts relevant to the prospects of removing Saddam from power included the strength of the security apparatus sustaining the dictator's grip on power, the apparent haplessness of the Iraqi opposition, the limited appetite of Americans for another large-scale armed conflict in the Persian Gulf, and the cost-benefit calculus that was already persuading other nations that the time had come to cut a deal with Baghdad. None of these suggested that toppling Saddam was going to be easy. Indeed, if regime change had been a simple matter, Bill Clinton would long since have disposed of the noxious Iraqi dictator. Just as Clinton, after berating the elder Bush for coddling China, discovered once in office the merits of "engagement," so, too, the younger Bush, after denouncing Clinton for being soft on Saddam, now found practical alternatives to containment to be few and risky.

But there is a third explanation for continuity between Clinton and Bush, one looking beyond the specifics of policy toward Iraq or China or the Balkans. To an extent that neither partisan supporters nor members of the chattering classes were inclined to concede, when it came to foreign policy George W. Bush and Bill Clinton thought alike. As leading members of the Bush team moved into the White House, the State Department, and the Pentagon, they brought with them a worldview that did not differ significantly from the worldview of the officials they displaced. Bush (and his advisers) and Clinton (and his advisers) conceived of America's proper role in a post–Cold War world in nearly identical terms. They found the same intimate connection between U.S. foreign policy and America's domestic well-being. They shared an identical belief in the importance of U.S. military supremacy. They embraced the same myths about the past. They voiced similar expectations for the future, ascribing the shape of that future to the same set of factors. To a remarkable extent, they agreed on the basic aims that should inform U.S. policy and the principles that should guide its conduct. Even when overlooking or ignoring inconvenient facts, Bush and Clinton shared the same blind spots.

Both Bush and Clinton subscribed to the consensus defining U.S. foreign policy in the global age. Across the entire spectrum of opinion deemed respectable—that consensus by 2001 enjoyed nearly absolute acceptance. It defined the parameters within which the debate about policy took place and provided the language shaping foreign policy discourse. It established priorities and defined options. It focused, disciplined, and excluded. As such, it subsumed labels such as "liberal" and "conservative," at least as those terms had come to be understood. It rendered moot old distinctions between realists and idealists, nationalists and internationalists. To be sure, not every adherent to that consensus agreed on every detail; but on those things that mattered most, agreement was well-nigh unanimous.

➤ This consensus constituted the substructure of post–Cold War U.S. foreign policy, refurbishing the consensus that had prevailed since 1945. So pervasive as to be all but taken for granted, so authoritative as to be virtually immune to challenge, the renewal of this consensus formed the true centerpiece of the foreign policy legacy emerging after 1989.

In addition to the Three Nos—to overt power politics, to war as such, and to limits, each of which conveyed directly into the new century—the consensus consisted of four distinctive but related imperatives. Each had been prefigured during the presidency of the elder George Bush. Each had been ostentatiously displayed in the policies of the Clinton era. Each received explicit affirmation during the initial months of the presidency of George W. Bush.

First was *the imperative of America's mission as the vanguard of history, transforming the global order and, in doing so, perpetuating its own dominance.* The Republicans returning to power were no less adamant than the Democrats they displaced: history has a discernible direction and destination. Furthermore, the United States, alone among all the nations of the world, has discerned and manifests history's purpose. For George W. Bush as for Bill Clinton, it was simply self-evident that the United States defined "the right side of history."[40]

The end toward which history tended under the tutelage of the United States was similarly self-evident. That end was freedom, achieved through the spread of democratic capitalism and embodied in the American Way of Life. (As that way of life mutated, so, too, needless to say, did the meaning of freedom.) The United States, declared Colin Powell, had become "the motive force for freedom and democracy in the world." As such, America's unique responsibility was to assist others toward history's ultimate destination. Of necessity, therefore, America "stands ready to help any country wishing to join the democratic world; any country that puts the [rule of] law in place and begins to live by that rule, any country that seeks peace and prosperity and a place in the sun." Acknowledging the enormity of the task, Powell noted that "there is no country on earth that is not touched by America . . . We are attached by a thousand cords to the world at large, to its teeming cities, to its remotest regions, to its oldest civilizations, to its newest cries for freedom. This means that we have an interest in every place on this earth; that we need to lead, to guide, to help in every country that has a desire to be free, open and prosperous."[41]

The point is not that sentiments such as Powell's qualified as fresh or original. On the contrary, it is precisely to the extent that they expressed a commonplace view regarding America's role in the world that they demand attention. What Powell and others in the Bush administration believed did not differ an iota from anything that Bill Clinton and Madeleine Albright had uttered in their loftiest expressions of Wilsonian exuberance. Republicans and Democrats shared the conviction that providence has summoned America to make the world over again.

Second was *the imperative of openness and integration, given impetus by globalization but guided by the United States.* Well before the 1990s, the United States had committed itself to creating an international order open to free enterprise and above all open to American enterprise. Bill Clinton's genius was to seize upon globalization as the phenomenon that was not only bringing global openness within reach but also endowed it with a sense of inevitability. The new Bush administration concurred, without reservation.

As a retired general serving on the boards of high-tech corporations, Powell had himself come face to face with what Clinton had been preaching. There he discovered that the "information and technology revolutions . . . are reshaping the world as we know it, destroying political boundaries and all kinds of other boundaries as we are able to move information and capital data around the world at the speed of light."[42]

Removing boundaries fostered free trade, to which George W. Bush, like his father before him and like Bill Clinton, evinced a steadfast devotion. With his immediate predecessors, Bush attributed to trade benefits extending beyond mere commercial opportunity. "Free trade brings greater political and personal freedom," he told the Congress shortly after his inauguration. Or, as he put it on another occasion, "the expectation of freedom is fed by free markets and expanded by free trade, and carried across borders by the Internet."[43]

This became a theme that members of the new Bush team repeatedly sounded from the administration's earliest days. According to Powell, "accelerating trade and strengthening democratic institutions go together. They are one and the same." Arguing on behalf of "a new consensus to promote open markets and trade for decades to come," Robert Zoellick reiterated the point: "free trade is about freedom. Economic freedom creates habits of liberty, and habits of liberty create expectations of democracy."[44]

Sweeping aside barriers that had once impeded the movement of goods, capital, ideas, and culture, globalization created boundless new opportunities for the creation of wealth. But Bush and his chief subordinates shared the expectation that globalization also imprinted onto its beneficiaries the expectations and sensibilities of the nation acting as the project's chief sponsor, namely the United States. A world opened up by the forces of globalization would not only be more affluent; it would also be freer, as Americans define freedom. It would be more democratic, as Americans understand democracy. It would be more peaceful, as Americans themselves were a peaceful people.

Not surprisingly, therefore, the administration's very first initiative in economic statecraft focused on building on previous progress toward openness, seeking to extend NAFTA to the entire Western Hemisphere. At the Summit of the Americas in April 2001 George W. Bush vowed to complete the work of integrating the hemisphere eco-

218 \ AMERICAN EMPIRE

nomically by proposing a Free Trade Agreement of the Americas (FTAA).[45]

Similarly, Bush used his first trip across the Atlantic as an opportunity to affirm continuing U.S. support for efforts to "build an open Europe." With that in mind, he declared his support for the further expansion of NATO "eastward and southward." Using a formulation identical with Bill Clinton's, Bush indicated that with regard to bringing additional members into the alliance, "The question of 'when' may still be up for debate . . . The question of 'whether' should not be." As to which nations might qualify for membership, the president was positively buoyant "I believe in NATO membership for all of Europe's democracies" that sought it, he remarked, suggesting that even Ukraine might well find a place in the Western alliance.[46]

But the creation of an open world was not just about encouraging democracy. Thus, according to Secretary Powell, the immediate benefit of the FTAA would be to enable Americans "to sell American goods, technology, and services without obstacles or restrictions within a single market of over 800 million people, with a combined income of $11 trillion."[47] An open global order in which American enterprise enjoyed free rein and in which American values, tastes, and lifestyle enjoyed pride of place was a world that would benefit the United States most of all. As Raymond Aron had observed more than a quarter-century earlier, "A world without frontiers is a situation in which the strongest capitalism prevails."[48] Clinton and his advisers knew this. So did their successors.

Third was *the imperative of American "global leadership" expressed by maintaining U.S. preeminence in each of the world's strategically significant regions.* Only the most devout disciple of Adam Smith would count on the market's "invisible hand" to keep order in a globalized world. If there was one point on which the entire political class—elected and appointed officials, the bureaucracy, the military, policy analysts, and the media—agreed with near unanimity after the Cold War, it was that only the United States could play this role. Clinton, of course, repeatedly affirmed his belief in America's indispensability. For Bush and his team as well this was an article of faith.

What the Clinton administration never could bring itself to acknowledge openly was that *leadership* was really a codeword, one whose use honored the cherished American tradition according to which the United States is not and cannot be an empire, but that obfuscates more than it explains. Leadership had become a euphemism.

In their official pronouncements, members of the new Bush administration like their predecessors adhered to the time-honored practice of describing America's role obliquely—the memory of Wolfowitz's Indiscretion reminding them of the consequences of doing otherwise. But unofficially, they knew the score. In a speech made shortly after the 2000 election, Richard Haass—soon to become director of policy planning in Powell's State Department—went so far as to call on Americans to "re-conceive their global role from one of a traditional nation-state to an imperial power." (Haass hastened to add: "An imperial foreign policy is not to be confused with imperialism.") The imperial foreign policy that Haass advocated was one that sought "to organize the world along certain principles," creating an "informal" empire governed in such a way that "coercion and the use of force would normally be a last resort."[49]

In one sense, leadership meant lighting the way, with America functioning, in the words of Secretary Powell, as the first "universal nation," offering to others a "model of what is possible." In this regard, the United States was called upon to be "a place where people of every background and distinction can live in . . . the kind of peace and harmony that God meant for all His children," thereby showing others how to do likewise.[50]

But as Powell himself acknowledged, this "uplifting concept" was "not always easy to translate into reality, especially far from our shores." For that reason, the U.S. claim to global leadership rested not simply on the appeal of its values, but on its power. In the final analysis, according to George W. Bush, "the advance of freedom depends on American strength."[51] Most of his fellow citizens had long since been conditioned to accept this claim as self-evident.

In other words, leadership required more than setting an example for all God's children. The Pax Americana that Bush inherited from Bill Clinton derived from one very large but indisputable fact: over the previous century, the United States had achieved by force of arms a dominant position in four distinct regions of critical geopolitical and economic importance. Thanks to NATO, the United States remained in 2001 the leading power in Europe, even as the Cold War, the ostensible rationale for that alliance, faded into memory. With its commitment of 100,000 troops in East Asia—a commitment viewed as permanent despite a lapse of three decades since the last significant armed conflict there—the United States was also the leading power in the Pacific. With its various bases and garrisons established in and around the Persian Gulf subsequent to the war with Iraq, it was the guarantor of order and stability in that region as well. And that didn't even count America's sway over the Western Hemisphere, unquestioned for a century.

This breadth of American mastery, greater than that of the British Empire in its heyday, marked the United States after the Cold War as unique in the annals of great powers. But with that level of mastery achieved, there could be no pulling back. To surrender American primacy in any of the four regions might suggest a loss of nerve or an erosion of strength, planting among would-be adversaries the belief that the time was ripe to mount a challenge.

From Washington's perspective, preventing any such challenge from materializing in the first place ranked as the primary measure of strategic effectiveness. One of the top priorities of U.S. policy, according to Condoleezza Rice, was to insure that "no hegemon can rise to threaten stability."[52] A globalized world had room for only a single hegemon, and as far as American elites were concerned that role was already filled.

Fourth was *the imperative of military supremacy, maintained in perpetuity and projected globally.* The image of post–Cold War America—even at the apex of its power and influence—besieged by ominous "new threats" was very much the handiwork of the Clinton years. Yet the Bush administration adopted the idea as its own, the new president affirming his conviction that the United States had entered an era in which challenges to national security were becoming "more widespread and less certain." Among the "new and different threats, sometimes hard to define and defend against" about which the president worried were "terrorism, information warfare, the spread of weapons of mass destruction and the means to deliver them."[53] Borrowing from the Clinton administration, Bush cited the great danger posed by "rogue nations," the "rogue" label obviating any need to evaluate the political motivation or actual capabilities of states placed in this category.[54] For Bush as for Clinton, the utopia implicit in the vision of a globalized world was a precarious one.

Protecting Americans from these "new threats" required coercive power. When Bush remarked amidst the boilerplate of a speech made on the occasion of the commissioning of the aircraft carrier USS *Ronald Reagan* that "we must have a military second to none," the comment raised few if any eyebrows.[55] But it should have: it has been decades since the formulation "second to none" described the yardstick by which officials in Washington measured the adequacy of U.S. military might. More accurately, in the aftermath of the Cold War the officials responsible for national security policy were committed to maintaining military capabilities *in excess of* those possessed by any combination of nations that the United States might plausibly find itself facing.

On this score, too, as Republicans took back control of the White House, the elite consensus remained firm. In mainstream American politics at the beginning of the twenty-first century, there existed nothing even remotely resembling an antimilitary party. Nor did either national party contain a significant antimilitary wing or faction. Indeed, in all of American public life it was difficult to think of a single prominent figure who found fault with the prospect of the United States' remaining the world's sole military superpower until the end of time.[56] Thus, in his attack on Bush's policies, when Senator Daschle noted in passing that U.S. "military expenditures now are larger than those of all other countries combined," he spoke not in a spirit of criticism or amazement or even pride.[57] Rather, he was simply taking note of something that he and most other Americans had come to view as part of the natural order, like Hollywood's worldwide domination of the motion picture industry or the globe-straddling omnipresence of American fast-food franchises.

However fierce the debate over defense policy and defense reform might be, no one in a position of authority—civilian or military, Democrat or Republican—disputed this basic proposition. To the extent that disagreement existed, it concerned how best to secure U.S. military dominance for the long term while satisfying other considerations such as minimizing the burden on a tax-averse and increasingly service-averse electorate.

Furthermore, faced with any threat, the American inclination, by instinct and tradition, was to take the fight to the adversary, whoever and wherever that adversary may be. The American "way of war" had long favored the offensive. As the martial exploits of Clinton era amply demonstrated, this aspect of the American military tradition survived intact into the global era. As a result, the U.S. military establishment entered the twenty-first century designed less to "provide for the common defense" than to project power. It was optimized not to defend the Eastern Seaboard but to crack heads in East Asia, to protect not the breadbasket of the Midwest but the energy resources of the Middle East. If anything, the passing of the Cold War placed an even greater premium on the ability of the United States to move powerful forces quickly and efficiently to any part of the globe. When officials of the new Bush administration discussed the need to create "a future force that is at once more agile, more lethal, and more rapidly deployable," they were signaling their understanding that power projection abroad remained the preferred mode of employing U.S. forces.[58] But they were also reciting the same litany of attributes that the Clinton administration had identified as essential for global interventionism.

Given a military establishment tailored for offensive operations, the most effective way to defend the open order (and to sustain conditions conducive to economic growth) was to expand its perimeter. This project, too, accorded with the preferences of George W. Bush and his team. Aiming "to keep wars as small and as far away as possible," the Bush administration pursued "a policy that tries to protect those zones of peace that we've created in the world, and to try to extend them."[59] Achieving that goal implied an activist posture. It also meant that the United States needed to preserve its capacity to decide when and where to strike. Freedom of action became an imperative.

It was in this context that ballistic-missile defense—advertised in early 2001 as the signature initiative of the Bush-Cheney-Rumsfeld Pentagon—deserved to be understood. The new administration's enthusiasm for national missile defense did not signify an abandonment of Clinton's paradigm regarding the proper role of U.S. forces; if anything, it affirmed that paradigm.

The true purpose of missile defense was not to permit the United States to withdraw behind the ramparts of Fortress America. It was not a step toward isolationism. Rather, in the eyes of its advocates, ballistic-missile defense facilitated the effective projection of U.S. military power abroad. As Condoleezza Rice explained, the United States needed to possess whatever it took to "be certain to prevent blackmail to the United States and our allies, because if the United States is blackmailable, it is not capable of acting with freedom of action."[60] By erecting a missile defense system (assuming that the system actually worked), the United States would be insuring itself against blackmail. By insulating the homeland from reprisal—albeit from only a single type of threat—ballistic missile defenses underwrote the capacity and willingness of the United States to employ its military might to "shape" the environment elsewhere. In short, as Lawrence F. Kaplan, writing in the *New Republic,* correctly discerned, "Missile defense isn't really meant to protect America. It's a tool for global dominance."[61] Credit the Bush administration with having a more realistic appreciation of the military tools that dominance requires. But do not credit it with amending the larger purpose to which Bush's immediate predecessors had already begun to put those tools.

➤ Throughout his career as an eminently successful military professional, and especially during his tenure as chairman of the Joint Chiefs of Staff, Colin Powell acquired a well-earned reputation for being cautious and circumspect. Even as he insisted that he was merely a simple soldier, Powell epitomized the qualities of a surefooted Washington operator, skillfully gauging the prevailing political winds, cultivating influential friends, never overreaching, and always taking care to cover his flanks. But when President-elect Bush introduced Powell in December 2000 as his nominee to be secretary of state, the retired four-star general chose that occasion to reveal a Wilsonian inner self that he had previously repressed. At the dawn of the twenty-first century, he announced, "the world marches to new drummers, drummers of democracy and the free enterprise system." The collapse of communism followed by the collapse of boundaries as a result of globalization was revolutionizing the world. "And at the center of this revolution," Powell declared, "America stands . . ."[62]

Yet if in Washington a new set of drummers had picked up the sticks, the rhythms they would tap out during their first months in power bore more than passing resemblance to those favored by their predecessors. Those rhythms—looking toward the creation of an open and integrated world over which the United States would preside, for its own well-being and that of others—would have been readily familiar to Harry Truman a half-century earlier. From one administration to the next and one era to the next, those tapping out the drumbeat of American statecraft shared much the same vision. In this communion of basic convictions and this consistency of purpose lay much of the genius of U.S. grand strategy.

CHAPTER 9

WAR FOR THE IMPERIUM

These are American principles, American policies. We could stand for no other. And they are also the principles and policies of forward-looking men and women everywhere, of every modern nation, of every enlightened community. They are the principles of mankind and must prevail.

Woodrow Wilson, January 1917

SURVEYING THE WORLD IN MAY 2001, Colin Powell found it "hard to avoid a permanent state of optimism and glee." The secretary of state attributed his outlook to the fact that "the red and blue sides of that old map that I used to worry about so much are gone." Instead of a world divided into opposing camps, "we have this marvelous kaleidoscope of a world trying to find its place."[1] For members of the young Bush administration charged with responsibility for American statecraft, the future looked rosy indeed.

Then came the horrific events of September 11, 2001, when everything, it was said, changed. Much did change. Among other things, Powell himself immediately rang down the curtain on the brief post–Cold War era.[2] In an instant the world was again divided into two opposing and irreconcilable camps.

In one respect at least, public discourse about U.S. policy also changed: with the devastating attack on the World Trade Center and the Pentagon, U.S. officials no longer sought euphemisms for the word *war,* as they had throughout the 1990s. On the contrary, President Bush and senior members of his administration went out of their way to emphasize not only that the United States was indeed at war, but that the conflict was certain to be ugly, costly, and protracted, lasting for years if not decades. Before September 11, the conventional wisdom had been that globalization was fast making war obsolete; after September 11, the conventional wisdom was that globalization was making war an all but permanent and inescapable part of life in the twenty-first century.

Bush administration officials identified the adversary in this war as "terror." But the war against terror was not America's alone. "This is the world's fight," President Bush told Congress and the nation. "This is civilization's fight." As a result, every nation, every movement, every political group had to choose. "Either you are with us or you are with the terrorists," Bush warned.[3] The president who had worried about American arrogance was now issuing ultimatums; thus had September 11 altered the tenor of American diplomacy.

Commentators rushed to compare the surprise attack of September 11, 2001, with the surprise attack of December 7, 1941. But the struggle in which the United States suddenly found itself, according to senior officials, promised to be unlike any that the nation had previously faced. War itself had supposedly changed. Donald Rumsfeld warned that militarily, the United States was sailing into uncharted waters. "What we're engaged in is something that is very, very different from World War II, Korea, Vietnam, the Gulf War, Kosovo, Bosnia, the kinds of things that people think of when they use the word 'war' or 'campaign' or 'conflict.'"[4] Rumsfeld spiked lingering Republican hopes that the Bush administration might revive the Weinberger-Powell doctrine, with its emphasis on clearly defined limited objectives and the use of overwhelming power to achieve crisp, decisive outcomes. The war against terror was not that kind of war. The defense secretary admonished Americans to "forget about 'exit strategies'; we're looking at a sustained engagement that carries no deadlines. We have no fixed rules about how to deploy our troops."[5]

All of that said, some things did *not* change after September 11, chief among them the essentials of U.S. policy. During the 1990s the strategy of openness had encountered sporadic resistance. But that resistance—an earlier attack on the World Trade Center, the bombing of American embassies and barracks abroad, the disabling of the USS *Cole*—had never quite risen above the level of nuisance. Now—as various policymakers had been predicting—the openness that had been the lodestar of U.S. grand strategy had facilitated an act of mass murder on American soil, planned by Osama bin Laden and carried out by his al Qaeda network. Yet rather than prompting members of the Bush administration to reevaluate their commitment to an open world, the disaster of September 11 energized them to press on. There was seemingly no alternative. Once again the reluctant superpower found itself called upon to act.

In short, the war that began on September 11, 2001, was a war to preserve and to advance the strategy of openness. Indeed, if anything, al Qaeda's attack on the American homeland eased constraints that during the previous decade had inhibited U.S. officials in their pursuit of greater openness (and expanded American hegemony).

Out of the wreckage of the World Trade Center and the Pentagon there emerged great strategic opportunity—for those with the wit to seize it. As Rumsfeld was quick to discern, September 11 created "the kind of opportunities that World War II offered, to refashion the world."[6] As had been the case after December 7, 1941, the chance to retaliate carried with it the chance to rectify. Thus, the code name that the Pentagon initially chose for its war against al Qaeda— scrapped only after complaints that it verged on being blasphemous— was Operation Infinite Justice. Woodrow Wilson would have approved.

► On September 14 the Congress handed President Bush a broad mandate to use "all necessary and appropriate force" against the perpetrators of the September 11 attack or anyone who had assisted them.[7] The vote fell just a single vote shy of unanimous.[8] Six days later, in what would easily be the most important speech of his presidency, George W. Bush appeared before a joint session of Congress to explain what he intended to do with that mandate.

Speaking with confidence, conviction, and surprising eloquence, Bush put paid to lingering doubts about the legitimacy of his presidency. His performance was nothing short of masterly, delighting his supporters and silencing, at least for a time, his critics. The moment had seemingly found the man.

Yet however much the atmospherics surrounding such an occasion matter—and they matter a great deal—the words that Bush spoke counted for still more. Not since the end of the Cold War more than a decade earlier had an American leader offered an explanation of foreign policy principles and priorities that enjoyed a half-life longer than a couple of news cycles. Bush's speech outlining his war on terrorism qualified as the first foreign policy statement since the end of the Cold War with a chance of taking its place alongside Washington's Farewell Address, the Monroe Doctrine, Roosevelt's Corollary, and Wilson's Fourteen Points as a sacred text of American statecraft.

Or perhaps a closer analogue lies in Harry S Truman's appearance before a joint session of Congress on March 12, 1947. On that occasion the thirty-third president enunciated what came to be known as the Truman Doctrine, for decades thereafter a cornerstone of U.S. policy. On September 20, 2001, the forty-third president enunciated an equally expansive Bush Doctrine, potentially one of the most influential of the twenty-first century.

Truman's appearance before Congress had been prompted by a faltering British Empire's decision to pull out of southeastern Europe and the Near East. This withdrawal threatened to create a strategic vacuum, requiring immediate U.S. action lest communists turn it to their advantage. Truman came to the Capitol to persuade Congress to assume the burden that Britain had laid down, shoring up the beleaguered governments of Greece and Turkey. But to enlist the support of skeptical and tightfisted legislators the president had been advised that he first needed to "scare hell out of the American people," counsel that he took to heart.

Thus, Truman framed the issue at hand not as a regional problem but as a global challenge. History, he told the Congress, had reached a turning point, one at which "nearly every nation must choose between alternative ways of life." Alas, in too many cases nations were not at liberty to choose of their own volition. Militant minorities, "exploiting human want and misery" and abetted by foreign subversives, were foisting upon such nations the yoke of totalitarianism. Left unchecked, subversion would yield a growing number of regimes relying on "terror and oppression, a controlled press and radio, fixed elections, and the suppression of personal freedoms" to keep themselves in power. The United States alone could stem this tide. Henceforth, Truman declared, "it must be the policy of the United States to support free peoples who are resisting attempted subjugation by armed minorities or by outside pressures."[9]

In the hands of his successors, the Truman Doctrine became a blank check for intervention. Over the next four decades, America's putative obligation to "support free peoples" (some of them in practice not very free) provided political and moral cover for actions overt and covert, wise and foolish, successful and unsuccessful, virtually everywhere.

Substituting "terror" for "armed minorities," George W. Bush's speech on September 20 bore similar earmarks and soon showed signs of giving birth to a comparable legacy. Whether Bush any more than Truman consciously set out to create such a legacy is beside the point. In calling for war not just against al Qaeda but against terror everywhere, Bush succeeded in articulating something that had eluded policymakers since the collapse of the Soviet Union deprived the United States of a readily identifiable enemy: a compelling rationale for a sustained and *proactive* use of American power on a global scale justified as a necessary *protective* measure.

Truman had depicted a planet split into two camps: the free world against totalitarianism. Bush portrayed "the civilized world" as pitted against a terrorist network intent on "remaking the world—and imposing its radical beliefs on people everywhere."[10] Echoing Truman, Bush insisted that history had reached a turning point at which all nations had to choose. Neutrality was not an option.

As in 1947, so, too, in 2001 the stakes were of the highest order. In making the case for the doctrine that would bear his name, Truman alluded to freedom—free peoples, free institutions, liberty, and the like—eighteen times. Bush's presentation contained fourteen such allusions. According to Bush, the events of September 11 showed that "freedom itself is under attack."

Casting the U.S. response to that attack not simply in terms of justifiable retaliation for an act of mass murder but as a necessity to preserve freedom itself imbued Bush's speech with added salience. Although its meaning is both continually shifting and fiercely contested, freedom—not equality, not social justice, not the common good—has long since become the ultimate American value. In political discourse, it functions as the ultimate code word. Defining the war against terror as a war on behalf of freedom served the administration's purposes in three important ways.

First, it enabled Bush to affirm American innocence—not only in the sense that those killed on September 11 were blameless but more broadly, in the sense that the nation's role in the world could not be understood except as benign. "Why do they hate us?" the president asked rhetorically. "They hate our freedoms," he replied, "our freedom of religion, our freedom of speech, our freedom to vote and assemble and disagree with each other." In offering this litany of values as the only explanation for "why they hate us," Bush relieved himself (and his fellow citizens) of any obligation to reassess the global impact of U.S. power, political, economic, or cultural. In doing so the president revalidated a longstanding national preference for discounting the perceptions of others—including allies—who viewed America's influence abroad as occasionally problematic and at times simply wrongheaded.

Second, sounding the theme of freedom enabled Bush to link the first war of the twenty-first century to the great wars of the past. Alluding to the perpetrators of the September 11 attack, the president declared: "We have seen their kind before. They are the heirs of all the murderous ideologies of the twentieth century. . . . they follow the path of fascism, and Nazism, and totalitarianism. And they will follow that path all the way to where it ends: in history's unmarked grave of discarded lies."

The president did not need to remind his listeners that the dangers posed by those murderous ideologies had prompted the reluctant superpower to assert itself in the first place, or that it was the mobilization of American might against the likes of Germany, Japan, and the Soviet Union that had hastened the demise of the ideologies they embodied.

A new war *on behalf of freedom* and *against evil* akin to Nazism relegitimated the exercise of American power both now, in response to the crisis at hand, and until terror had been eradicated and the objectives of American strategy achieved.

Third, engagement in such a war removed the fetters that had hobbled the United States since the demise of its latest ideological competitor. The most important of those constraints related to the use of force. As we have noted, after the Cold War military power emerged as never before as the preferred instrument of American statecraft. But absent an adversary on a par with Nazi Germany or the Soviet Union, neither George H. W. Bush nor Bill Clinton had devised a satisfactory explanation for why the United States was called upon to send its military forces hither and yon with such frequency. Even though American military might dwarfed that of any and all potential adversaries, policymakers during the 1990s had never really enjoyed a free hand in employing that advantage to maximum benefit, especially in places far from home.

The Clinton administration justified its penchant for intervention by claiming that it acted in response to claims of conscience. But ordinary citizens evinced precious little willingness to succor the afflicted in faraway lands if doing so posed the slightest risk to U.S. troops. As a result, during the 1990s the greatest military power in history found itself constrained by self-imposed shackles, chief among them an obsession with avoiding casualties. That the experiments in peace-making and peacekeeping dotting the 1990s so often resulted in semi-permanent commitments of questionable efficacy only increased popular skepticism.

Bush's declaration of war on terror made it possible for policy-makers to reclaim the freedom of action provided by the Truman Doctrine. The calculations defining tolerable risk changed consider-ably. Anyone qualifying for the label "terrorist" now became a bona fide target (although the United States intended to reserve for itself the final say on which terrorists were *really* terrorists).[11] As one astute commentator noted, the advantage of defining the war as one against such an amorphous adversary was that "if things go well it creates an opportunity to take care of other items on the agenda."[12]

Furthermore, defining the adversary as "terror" made it easier to deflect public attention from evidence suggesting that it was Amer-ica's quasi-imperial role that was provoking resistance—and would continue to do so. In truth, as Daniel Pipes has correctly noted, terror is a tactic, not an enemy.[13] But by insisting that its quarrel was with terror—rather than, for example, with radical Islam—the United States obscured the political roots of the confrontation. U.S. officials dismissed as irrelevant the fact that Osama bin Laden's actions (how-ever contemptible) represented an expression of strongly held con-victions: a deep-seated resentment of the U.S. military presence in the Persian Gulf and a determination to remove that presence by whatever means necessary.[14]

In the weeks following the terrorist attack on New York and Wash-ington, a rift about how best to proceed appeared at the highest levels of the Bush administration. Should the United States embark upon what the president in an unscripted moment referred to as a "cru-sade" against evildoers everywhere? Or should it confine itself to eliminating those directly responsible for launching a vicious attack on American soil? In the near term, the advocates of the narrow ap-proach prevailed. When Operation Enduring Freedom began on Oc-tober 7, 2001, the United States explicitly singled out al Qaeda for destruction along with the Taliban regime that had offered bin Laden sanctuary in Afghanistan. Yet U.S. officials also hinted that the offensive in Afghanistan was only the initial phase of a broader, multipart campaign—carefully refraining from specifying what phase two or phase three might entail. It turned out that the president had not rejected the idea of a crusade; he had merely deferred it while keeping all options open.[15]

Whenever it did become opportune to move on to the next phase, proponents of action could be counted on to cite the Bush Doctrine to bolster their case. But the doctrine promulgated on September 20 was likely to prove useful to advocates of intervention even after Bush had left office. As White House spokesman Ari Fleischer put it, the United States now asserted as a matter of policy that it had "the right to defend itself wherever it is necessary."[16] The campaign in Afghanistan marked the first shot in America's war on terror, but it was unlikely to be the last. The Bush Doctrine, like the Truman Doctrine that it superseded, offered policymakers a sheaf of promissory notes to be redeemed at their convenience.[17]

➤ Bush's war against terror and for freedom was at its core a war on behalf of the American project of creating an open and integrated world.[18] The president and others in his administration understood that the events of September 11 posed large questions about the project's cost and feasibility and about the capacity of American power to sustain it. In the aftermath they wasted no time in putting those questions to rest, affirming the administration's steadfast support for greater openness. "Terrorists want to turn the openness of the global economy against itself," Bush told Asian leaders gathered in Shanghai in October 2001. "We must not let them." Bush rejected any thought of compromising openness as a way to enhance security. There could be no trade-off; both were essential.[19] In the wake of September 11, administration officials restated their belief in the dogma of openness—that in the long run removing barriers promised not vulnerability but utopia. A prerequisite for prosperity at home, an open economic order, wrote Secretary of State Powell, "reinforces democracy, growth, and the free flow of ideas" in the world at large.[20] Openness remained "America's trump card," proclaimed Robert Zoellick, thirteen days after al Qaeda's attack. "Openness to goods, to services, to capital, to people, to ideas" enabled the United States to "draw on the best that the world has to offer." Neither Zoellick nor the administration he represented would agree to "erecting new barriers and closing old borders."[21] In the war against terror, trade itself was a weapon. "We will defeat them," Bush told a gathering of business executives, "by expanding and encouraging world trade."[22] From offstage, former President Bill Clinton, sounding nearly identical themes, chimed in.[23]

Just as September 11 did not change America's strategic purpose, neither did it change the Pentagon's methods for employing force to advance that purpose. Granted, whereas Bill Clinton had used force to spank and scold, George Bush sought to achieve decisive results. Yet in the war against terror, the Clinton-era reliance on gunboats and Gurkhas survived intact.

Although the war that Bush declared was global in scope—involving a host of actions to round up al Qaeda members and to cut off their sources of financial support—the war that Americans could actually see in phase one was confined to Afghanistan, al Qaeda's main operating base. Although Secretary Rumsfeld pronounced the war one in which "fixed rules" did not apply, in practice the military bureaucracies that conduct wars cannot function without rules. If political leaders do not provide the rules, the generals find them elsewhere, typically by adverting to the familiar. In short, they tend to fight the war at hand—whatever its character—by adhering to routines that seemed to work the last time out.

This was certainly true in the Afghan War of 2001. As it unfolded, Operation Enduring Freedom resembled Bill Clinton's Operation Allied Force far more than it did George H. W. Bush's Operation Desert Storm. The centerpiece of the U.S. effort was a measured air campaign, with operational objectives that were in tension if not simply incompatible. As the bombing commenced, Rumsfeld announced: "The effect we hope to achieve through the raids . . . is to create conditions for sustained anti-terrorist and humanitarian relief operations in Afghanistan," as if dealing death and destruction and doing good works were on a par.[24] Along with bombs, the U.S. Air Force dropped rations and other relief supplies (with mixed results), hoping to counter perceptions that the United States was venting its wrath on the much-abused Afghan people.[25]

But even as Pentagon briefers characterized the air campaign as "sustained" and "intensifying," the initial level of effort fell well short even of that against the Serbs in 1999, averaging fewer than a hundred combat sorties per day.[26] Further complicating the problem was the fact that such a backward, war-ravaged country offered a dearth of meaningful targets. President Bush scoffed at using "$2 million dollar missiles to hit a $10 dollar tent that's empty."[27] Yet a reliance on high-tech air power meant on occasion doing just that.

To prosecute its war in Afghanistan, the Pentagon showed little enthusiasm for going beyond the use of air power.[28] Although the Bush team did not explicitly forswear the use of ground troops as Clinton had done regarding Kosovo, it made no preparations to take the fight directly to the Taliban except with small contingents of special operations forces. Through the first month of the campaign, overt action by U.S. forces in (as opposed to above) Afghanistan was confined to a single raid by about a hundred Army Rangers, as inconsequential as it was brief.[29] Even the grievous wounds that the nation sustained on September 11 seemingly did not outweigh a now-pronounced reluctance to close with the enemy, even one as primitive and ill equipped as the Taliban.

By the time the bombing was entering its third week, U.S. forces had gained air supremacy against all-but-nonexistent Afghan air defenses, but not much else. Signs of real progress were few. At the Pentagon's daily press briefing, the chief spokesman for the Joint Staff was paying tribute to the Taliban as "tough warriors" and admitting that he was "a bit surprised at how doggedly they're hanging on." Defeating the Taliban was going to require a "long, long campaign," he predicted.[30]

At this juncture, to avert a stalemate, the United States turned again to Gurkhas. As had been the case in Kosovo, those actually available to play the role of proxies were an unsavory lot. The main internal opposition, known as the Northern Alliance, had itself ruled Afghanistan until forcibly driven from power by the Taliban in 1996. During its years in power the Alliance's philosophy of governance had more closely resembled Al Capone's than Thomas Jefferson's. The Alliance made Afghanistan the world leader in the production of opium and heroin.[31] Since being driven from Kabul, fractious Alliance warlords had fought ineffectually among themselves and against the Taliban to no particular end. Now, under U.S. auspices, they were about to become "freedom fighters."[32]

Cozying up to the Northern Alliance had another downside as well: doing so might well strain U.S. relations with Pakistan. Before September 11, that newly rediscovered ally had been the Taliban's chief benefactor and adamantly opposed returning the Northern Alliance to power. For public consumption, therefore, the United States made a show of keeping the Alliance at arm's length. As late as November 4, General Tommy Franks, the commander-in-chief of U.S. Central Command, was still insisting that "we have not sought to—to prompt or to direct their activities."[33]

In fact, by that date small teams of American and British commandos and CIA operatives were already in Afghanistan offering their services to anti-Taliban resistance leaders in a variety of roles—adviser, coach, quartermaster, paymaster, intelligence liaison, and, above all, facilitator of American firepower.[34] The operative concept, as one CENTCOM officer acknowledged, now became one of "getting Afghan to fight Afghan," with U.S. air power helping one side.[35]

At first Northern Alliance commanders professed to be unimpressed with U.S. air strikes.[36] By early November, with heavy B-52 bombers now unloading on frontline Taliban forces, they revised that assessment.[37] Hitherto reluctant units of the Northern Alliance finally began to march.[38] When they did so, the "tough warriors" crumbled. On November 9 the key Taliban stronghold of Mazar-e Sharif fell. Four days later Northern Alliance forces entered the capital of Kabul, all but unopposed. After a brief siege, other U.S.-supported anti-Taliban factions seized Kandahar, headquarters of Taliban leader Mullah Mohammed Omar.[39] "We've got a first-world air force connected to a fourth-world army—B-1 bombers and guys on horses," Secretary Powell exulted, in explaining the sudden turn of events, "and what we have done in the last five weeks is sort of connect these two."[40]

Two months after Enduring Freedom began, with a new Afghan coalition government installed in Kabul, little was seemingly left but mopping up. Pentagon officials toyed with—and then rejected—the idea of sending U.S. ground troops in for the kill. Instead, they left that task to anti-Taliban fighters backed by U.S. air power to root bin Laden's main army out of its mountain redoubts, killing, capturing, or dispersing al Qaeda fighters—and perhaps assisting in their escape.[41] General Franks observed at one point that at the end of the day it was "the people on the ground [who] make the determination of who wins and who loses."[42] As Operation Enduring Freedom wound down, the people on the ground were mostly Afghans whose interests, now that the Taliban had been deposed, did not necessarily coincide with those of the United States. At year's end, the whereabouts of Mullah Mohammed Omar and Osama bin Laden remained unknown, casting a shadow over what otherwise appeared to be an impressive victory.

In gaining that victory, the United States lost a bare handful of American soldiers in enemy action.[43] Sympathetic observers were quick to credit the Bush administration with devising an innovative formula for using U.S. military power.[44] More accurately, as one skeptic noted, Operation Enduring Freedom was "Kosovo Redux." As in Kosovo, the idea was to have "American pilots bombing from 15,000 feet, while our local allies . . . do the fighting on the ground"—albeit with U.S. special forces as invaluable intermediaries. It was a war won "not with American blood and guts" but with "the blood and guts of the Northern Alliance, helped by copious quantities of American ordnance and a handful of American advisers."[45]

The task allotted to America's own warriors, explained one U.S. Navy carrier pilot just returned from the war, was "to club 'em like baby seals . . . and then come home."[46] Inevitably some of those clubbed were noncombatants; unofficial estimates of Afghan civilian deaths resulting from Enduring Freedom ranged between 1,000 and 4,000. The Pentagon saw little to be gained from tallying the number of Afghan civilians killed or maimed by American bombs.[47] In truth, the question was not one that interested Americans generally. In this regard, too, the war in Afghanistan bore the imprint of U.S. military practice as it had evolved during the previous decade.

Wars—even successful wars—leave loose ends. Almost inevitably, Operation Enduring Freedom saddled the United States with new commitments and obligations. Having as a candidate derided his predecessor's experiments in "nation-building," President Bush after September 11 declared that Americans had an abiding interest in the well-being of the long-suffering Afghan people.[48] By the end of December he was telling reporters that he expected U.S. troops to be staying in Afghanistan for "quite a long period of time."[49]

At the war's outset, Washington sought and gained access to operating bases in Pakistan, Uzbekistan, and Turkmenistan, vital for conducting the air campaign. But foreign support for U.S. military operations came with strings attached. American officials found themselves obliged to pay court to the strongmen governing Afghanistan's neighbors.[50] Washington also embraced Pakistan's military regime, lifting sanctions imposed when the generals had seized power (overthrowing a democratically elected government) and offering a handsome package of economic aid and security assistance.[51] Uzbekistan reportedly got promises that the United States would come to its defense if it was attacked.[52] Having secured a foothold in Central Asia during Operation Enduring Freedom, the Pentagon showed little inclination to surrender it once the fighting stopped. As had so frequently been the case after earlier conflicts, direct U.S. military involvement in the region was unlikely to end anytime soon.[53] In effect, Central Asia was now joining Europe, East Asia, the Persian Gulf, and the Western Hemisphere as a region in which the United States assumed the privileges—and shouldered the burdens—of primacy.

➤ Back home, meanwhile, the attack of September 11 evoked an enormous surge of patriotism. Overnight, homes, businesses, college dormitories, automobiles, and pickup trucks sprouted flags. The Stars and Stripes became the season's number-one fashion accessory, appearing on T-shirts, sweaters, tattoos, buttons, rhinestone-encrusted stickpins, and various other gewgaws. For the moment, at least, overtly expressing love of country was back in style. The relative merits of "America the Beautiful" and "God Bless America" as anthems became a subject of considerable discussion—"The Star-Spangled Banner" being oft sung but as ever not much loved.[54]

But it was a curious patriotism—doubtless heartfelt, but arguably wider than it was deep. As the United States embarked upon its global war against terror, political leaders carefully refrained from demanding much of individual Americans. Apart from expressions of national unity (boosting this president's popularity as the Gulf War had boosted his father's), not very much was offered. The president ordered modest numbers of national guardsmen to active duty—far fewer than in 1990—but most citizen-soldiers called to the colors were assigned duties no more hazardous than providing backup security inside airport terminals.[55] The primary responsibility of the average citizen for the duration of the emergency remained what it had been in more peaceful times: to be an engine of consumption. The

Bush administration called on Americans to get out and spend, energetically, for the sake of the nation's economic well-being.[56] "Get on board," urged the president. "Fly and enjoy America's great destination spots. Get down to Disney World in Florida. Take your families and enjoy life."[57] (Perhaps tellingly, among traditional patriotic songs, "The Battle Hymn of the Republic" with its explicit summons to sacrifice—"as He died to make men holy, let us die to make men free"— did not enjoy a post–September 11 popular revival.)

Meanwhile, those serving in uniform were lionized. Cops, firefighters, and soldiers momentarily eclipsed Hollywood celebrities and professional athletes as American heroes. Whether any of this signified a permanent change in the prevailing culture remained to be seen. Certainly, the war on terror did not send youngsters stampeding to their local armed forces recruiting stations.[58] Indeed, less than a month after the September 11 attack, the *New York Times* declared that pop culture was already back in the saddle.[59]

Without question, September 11 reinforced the post–Cold War consensus for maintaining unquestioned military superiority. As events in Afghanistan unfolded, the Congress voted by huge margins the largest increase in defense spending in a decade.[60] The war on terror also lent further impetus to the militarization of American policy. In the State Department, retired general Colin Powell designated retired general Anthony Zinni, former proconsul, as his envoy to restart the Israeli-Palestinian peace process.[61] President Bush chose another retired general as his national coordinator on counterterrorism.[62] Not to be outdone, former governor Tom Ridge, the first chief of homeland security, appointed a retired four-star admiral to serve as his deputy.[63] Still another retired general became the State Department's ambassador at large for counterterrorism.[64] Meanwhile the four regional CINCs made the case for adding Treasury and FBI agents to their staffs. Viewing this as a bid to give each proconsul his own "miniature Washington-style bureaucracy," some observers in the nation's capital worried that further expanding the power of the CINCs would "ultimately undercut the defense secretary's authority."[65] But public interest in the issue was close to nil.

➤ Speaking in December 2001, three months after September 11 and ten years after the final collapse of the Soviet Union, President Bush vowed that "America will lead the world to peace."[66] Given the events of the preceding decade, given in particular the events of Bush's first year in office, it was a brave prediction.

By even the most optimistic calculation, world peace was likely to be a long time coming. September 11 and its aftermath brought Bush face to face with disconcerting realities that during the 1990s his two predecessors had either missed or wished away. The assault on two great symbols of American economic and military power demolished expectations that in an increasingly open world the American home-land might remain a safe haven. In doing so it also swept aside illu-sions that the United States could enjoy the benefits deriving from the exercise of what it called global leadership without cost and without sacrifice. In pursuit of its strategy of openness the United States faced the prospect of opposition greater in scope, intensity, and duration than any national leader had been willing to acknowledge, despite the absence of any great-power adversary comparable to the Soviet Union. Although Bush and his lieutenants might continue to reiter-ate their conviction that greater openness married to American power would lead unerringly to the ultimate triumph of democratic capitalism, evidence that the way ahead was strewn with landmines had now become incontrovertible.

Indeed, apart from the death and devastation wreaked at the World Trade Center and the Pentagon, the most disturbing aspect of the entire episode was the reaction that September 11 evoked abroad. In some quarters—notably across much of the vast Islamic world—the terrorist attack became cause for wild celebration.[67] In the eyes of many millions, Osama bin Laden's act affirmed his status as an illus-trious hero. Elsewhere, despite official expressions of sympathy and support, there was evidence of quiet satisfaction that Americans were at long last getting their comeuppance.[68]

Through an impressive demonstration of military might, George Bush (helped by the strong-arm tactics of allies who suppressed anti-U.S. sentiment) for the moment at least quelled those who took de-light in America's anguish. But coercion does not win hearts and minds; at best, it temporarily stays the hand. Only the foolhardy would imagine that the Afghan War of 2001 had made an end to ha-tred, envy, fear, and resentment directed at the United States.

Terror posed a particular threat to openness—essential for Ameri-can economic expansion and, for that reason, the principle according to which the United States intended to organize the international order. But even a decisive victory over global terror, however that victory might be defined, was unlikely to fulfill the president's expectations of world peace. Terror, after all, was not the source of opposition to the United States, but only one especially malignant expression of that opposition. Given the record of the previous decade (not to mention the previous century), the pursuit of ever-greater openness was likely to encounter further resistance, if not from Islamic radicals, then from other states or movements or individuals persuaded (not without reason) that globalization was "just a shorthand for a new world dominated by Americans" and unhappy with that prospect.[69]

Some of that resistance was likely to come from groups opposed not to globalization as such but intent simply on grabbing a bigger share of the loot. Although Americans take it as a given that the United States should benefit disproportionately from the spoils that economic openness throws up in such profusion, to others the logic of this arrangement is not self-evident. They scheme to uncover shortcuts for transferring wealth from American pockets to their own. They flout the rules, trafficking in drugs, organizing sophisticated international criminal cartels, and pirating American products and technologies.

Others resist because they are unpersuaded by the hypothesis that openness renders power politics obsolete, that henceforth nations can best fulfill their aspirations not through old-fashioned competition, but through collaborative engagement in a globalized (and American-dominated) economy. This prospect is not without appeal to nations physically and morally depleted by the cataclysms of the twentieth century and now content with their lot—notably, the once-great powers of Europe. But others, less satisfied with the hand that history has dealt them—China, Russia, and India, for example—beg to differ.

A third category of opposition—displayed daily in places like the West Bank—includes those who reject universalism of any stripe and cling ferociously to their own particularistic vision. Not for these groups the tolerant pluralism and easygoing multiculturalism that is the ultimate promise of an open world. Refusing to condone any blurring of distinctions between "us" and "them," they persist in believing that identity is sacred, indelible, and rooted in place, that ownership of a particular plot of land remains as in ancient times a cause worth fighting and even dying for.

Constituting one final category of opposition are those who advance a distinctive view of history's purpose and their own distinctive claims to truth. Critics speaking on behalf of such groups assert that American values have less to do with authentic freedom than with a culture that they depict as vulgar and meretricious, where not simply debased and dehumanizing—more Miramax, Madonna, and Eminem than Martin Luther King.[70] They are determined to prevent that culture from overwhelming their own.

This was part of Osama bin Laden's professed agenda, in attempting to purge the land of the Prophet of occupying soldiers from the West. Yet the refusal to endorse the universality of reigning American values finds favor in more reputable quarters as well. Highly regarded individuals, with impeccable credentials as proponents of democracy and human rights, question whether moral relativism, radical individualism, and conspicuous consumption constitute a formula guaranteeing the fulfillment of mankind's deepest aspirations. "If there is no ultimate truth to guide and direct political activity," John Paul II has pointedly observed, "then ideas and convictions can easily be manipulated for reasons of power." Uncoupled from truth, the pursuit of liberty as the ultimate value points toward a self-absorbed "culture of death." "As history demonstrates," the pope warned, "a democracy without values easily turns into open or thinly disguised totalitarianism."[71] Even if expressed peacefully, the resistance that such a culture incites is likely to be fierce and unrelenting, thereby encouraging, even if inadvertently, those willing to employ violence in what they see as a similar cause.

To cope with this resistance—expressed either as instability or as a refusal to abide by the norms governing an open world—American policymakers, even as they proclaim their peaceful intentions, will resort to force. That at least is the conclusion suggested by the record of U.S. actions throughout the 1990s. During that decade, whether by choice or by default, but with increasing frequency, in an ever-widening array of circumstances, and across an ever-greater expanse, America's reliance on military power to set things right reached new heights. During his first year in office, George W. Bush affirmed this reliance on military action and promised if anything to widen its scope. The nation's defensive perimeter now encompasses the globe.

This penchant for projecting military power, with policymakers counting on technology and willing surrogates to insulate Americans as much as possible from the direct effects of fighting, implies new obligations, expanded requirements to police and protect, and fresh opportunities to "shape the environment." Those charged with satisfying America's burgeoning security requirements will take little comfort from mere military superiority, even at an unprecedented level. As of September 11, 2001, finding a satisfactory answer to the old question "How much is enough?" became more elusive. As long as memories of that date remain fresh, anyone judging existing military capabilities to be "not enough" will receive a sympathetic hearing. The result is less likely to be a world genuinely at peace than a Pax Americana, periodically challenged in ways large and small and maintained by force of American arms.

➤ "America is not to be Rome or Britain," insisted a testy Charles Beard, writing on the eve of war in 1939. "It is to be America."[72] Beard was certain that a second world war, like its predecessor two decades earlier, would be at root a contest for empire. If the United States allowed itself to be drawn into such a conflict, it would surely succumb to the imperial temptation, forfeiting, perhaps forever, its true vocation as the Great Republic.

A half-century later, in 1989, any American recalling the now all-but-forgotten historian's fears probably considered them to have been overwrought and misplaced. After all, World War II turned out to be the paradigmatic "good war" in which the United States played a leading role in vanquishing monstrous evil. If doing so had obliged it to collaborate with another comparably evil regime, then by the end of the 1980s, with the Soviet empire disintegrating and the Soviet Union facing imminent collapse, the United States had atoned for its error by prevailing over *that* monster as well.

By the early 1990s America had swept the field. From nearly a century of struggle it emerged victorious, becoming unarguably the greatest power in all recorded history. At the very zenith of American strength and influence most citizens still comforted themselves with the belief that as the sole superpower the United States was *nothing* like Rome or Britain. In its relations with the world at large, as in so many other respects, theirs remained a different, exceptional, indeed, unique nation.

During the Cold War itself, a few dissenters following in Beard's footsteps had dared to question this proposition. They suggested that the exercise of American power throughout the twentieth century could not be fully understood except as a deliberate project aimed at accruing wealth and influence and military might. To persist in pretending otherwise was to indulge in what William Appleman Williams termed a "grand illusion," "the charming belief that the United States could reap the rewards of empire without paying the costs of empire and without admitting that it was an empire."[73]

As long as the Soviet-American rivalry persisted, critics like Williams never got very far. Whatever the scholarly merits of the argument they advanced, the grand illusion survived, if only because throughout the long decades of the Cold War it served a useful purpose. The conviction that America was not Rome imparted to U.S. policy a compelling moral resonance. That the United States was leading (not imposing itself upon) the free world for the sole purpose of defending democracy, liberty, and world peace (rather than out of any sordid, self-aggrandizing motives) helped to affirm the legitimacy of what was an arduous and interminable struggle.

Events in the very first decade following the Cold War—beginning with armed intervention to secure the energy-rich Persian Gulf in 1990 and ending with the horrific events of September 11, 2001— made the grand illusion increasingly difficult to sustain. Indeed, as the Cold War has receded into the past, the conceit that America is by its very nature innocent of imperial pretensions has become not only untenable but also counterproductive: it impedes efforts to gauge realistically the challenges facing the United States as a liberal democracy intent on presiding over a global order in which American values and American power enjoy pride of place.

That effort is unlikely to succeed except through protracted and strenuous exertions, if at all. In short, although the United States has not created an empire in any formal sense—what would be the point of doing so?—it has most definitely acquired an imperial problem. This is the dirty little secret to which the elder George Bush, Bill Clinton, and George W. Bush each in turn refused to own up.

Holding sway in not one but several regions of pivotal geopolitical importance, disdaining the legitimacy of political economic principles other than its own, declaring the existing order to be sacrosanct, asserting unquestioned military supremacy with a globally deployed force configured not for self-defense but for coercion: these are the actions of a nation engaged in the governance of empire. Continuing to pretend otherwise—in the words of Reinhold Niebuhr, "frantically avoiding recognition of the imperialism which we in fact exercise"— won't make America's imperial problem any easier to manage and certainly won't make it go away.[74]

The reality that Beard feared has come to pass: like it or not, America today *is* Rome, committed irreversibly to the maintenance and, where feasible, expansion of an empire that differs from every other empire in history. This is hardly a matter for celebration; but neither is there any purpose served by denying the facts.

Governing any empire is a political, economic, and military undertaking; but it is a moral one as well. Along with principles, it demands foresight, consistency, and self-awareness. Scaling imperial ambitions to fit imperial assets; balancing means and ends; distinguishing between minor annoyances and large threats and between the genuinely essential and the merely desirable, coordinating near-term goals with long-term interests, fostering military strength without forfeiting political responsibility, navigating between the rocks of timidity and the shoals of hubris, reconciling what is necessary with what is right: all pose daunting challenges for any great power. But for a postmodern, postindustrial, postheroic democracy bent on remaking the world in its own image they pose greater challenges still.

The question that urgently demands attention—the question that Americans can no longer afford to dodge—is not whether the United States has become an imperial power. The question is what sort of empire they intend theirs to be. For policymakers to persist in pretending otherwise—to indulge in myths of American innocence or fantasies about unlocking the secrets of history—is to increase the likelihood that the answers they come up with will be wrong. That way lies not just the demise of the American empire but great danger for what used to be known as the American republic.

NOTES

INTRODUCTION

1. Bill Clinton, "Remarks at the World Trade Organization in Geneva, Switzerland," May 18, 1998. The phrase derives from St. Paul's letter to the Galatians 4:4. In the King James Version of the Bible, the text reads: "When the fulness of the time was come, God sent forth his Son, made of a woman, made under the law."

    Absent any reference to a specific printed source, all quotations from statements and documents of the Clinton administration were taken from the White House Web site (www.whitehouse.gov). Since January 20, 2001, the Clinton White House Web site has been electronically archived at the Web site of the National Archives and Records Administration (www.clinton.nara.gov).

2. Bill Clinton, "American Security in a Changing World," George Washington University, August 5, 1996.

3. Quoted in John F. Harris, "Despite 'Lessons,' Clinton Still Seen Lacking Strategy," *Washington Post,* March 27, 1999, p. A15. A scholarly assessment of Clinton's diplomatic legacy, published even before he had left office, skewered the president for being "indecisive, incoherent, contradictory, confused, lacking in vision and purpose"; Emily O. Goldman and Larry Berman, "Engaging the World: First Impressions of the Clinton Foreign Policy Legacy," in *The Clinton Legacy,* ed. Colin Campbell and Bert A. Rockman (New York, 2000), p. 226.

4. Bill Clinton, "Remarks Prepared for Delivery, Foreign Policy Association," April 1, 1992; copy in the author's possession.

5. Quoted in Jane Perlez, "For 8 Years, a Strained Relationship with the Military," *New York Times,* December 28, 2000, p. A13.

6. Richard N. Haass, "The Squandered Presidency," *Foreign Affairs* 79 (May/June 2000): 139.

7. Quoted in Elaine Sciolino, "A Gore Adviser Who Basks in the Shadows," *New York Times,* April 25, 2000, p. A1.

8. "Independence Day Address Delivered at the Home of Thomas Jefferson," in *Public Papers of the Presidents of the United States: Harry S. Truman, January 1 to December 31, 1947* (Washington, D.C.: Government Printing Office, 1963), pp. 323–326.

1. THE MYTH OF THE RELUCTANT SUPERPOWER

1. Ernest R. May, *Imperial Democracy: The Emergence of America as a Great Power* (New York, 1961), p. 270. May's epigram derives from Shakespeare's

Twelfth Night, act II, scene 5: "Some are born great, some achieve greatness, and some have greatness thrust upon them."

2. Arthur Schlesinger Jr., "Origins of the Cold War," *Foreign Affairs* 46 (October 1967): 23.

3. Bill Clinton, "A New Covenant for America," Georgetown University, December 12, 1991; copy in the author's possession.

4. Peter Novick, *That Noble Dream* (Cambridge, 1988), p. 453.

5. The literature examining Beard's life and work is extensive. The most recent account is Clyde W. Barrow, *More than a Historian: The Political and Economic Thought of Charles A. Beard* (New Brunswick, N.J., 2000). Other important sources include Bernard C. Borning, *The Political and Social Thought of Charles A. Beard* (Seattle, 1962); H. W. Brands, *What America Owes the World* (New York, 1998), pp. 109–143; Thomas C. Kennedy, *Charles A. Beard and American Foreign Policy* (Gainesville, Fla., 1975); Richard Hofstadter, *The Progressive Historians* (New York, 1968), pp. 167–346; and Ronald Radosh, *Prophets on the Right* (New York, 1975), pp. 17–65.

6. Eric F. Goldman, *Rendezvous with Destiny* (New York, 1953), p. 153.

7. The lack of a faculty appointment did not reduce his standing within the academy. During the interwar period he served as president of the American Historical Association and later of the American Political Science Association.

8. Barrow, *More than a Historian,* pp. 1, 7.

9. Hofstadter, *The Progressive Historians,* p. 344.

10. Mumford's comment appeared in a letter to the editor of the *Saturday Review of Literature;* quoted in Novick, *That Noble Dream,* p. 292. See also Radosh, *Prophets on the Right,* p. 39.

11. Charles A. Beard, *President Roosevelt and the Coming of the War 1941* (New Haven, 1948), pp. 3, 8.

12. David M. Kennedy, *Freedom from Fear: The American People in Depression and War, 1929–1945* (New York, 1999), pp. 448–449, 480–481, 491, 497–498. Kennedy's prize-winning and resolutely mainstream history provides a positive overall assessment of FDR's achievements as national leader and world statesman. But even he finds that Roosevelt's conduct leading up to U.S. entry into war was characterized by "dissembling," "deviousness," and repeated efforts to mislead and manipulate the American people.

13. Barrow, *More than a Historian,* pp. 4–6.

14. Charles A. Beard, *An Economic Interpretation of the Constitution of the United States* (New York, 1913), p. 324.

15. Charles A. Beard and Mary R. Beard, *The Rise of American Civilization,* vol. 2 (New York, 1930), pp. 4, 6–7.

16. Charles A. Beard, *American Government and Politics,* rev. ed. (New York, 1914), p. 331.

17. George T. Blakey, *Historians on the Homefront* (Lexington, Ky., 1970), pp. 12–13, 16, 52.

18. For a general account of World War I revisionism that describes the evolution of Beard's views on the subject, see Warren I. Cohen, *The American Revisionists* (Chicago, 1967), esp. pp. 123–141.

19. Beard and Beard, *The Rise of American Civilization*, 2: 344–345.

20. Quoted in Barrow, *More than a Historian*, p. 20.

21. Charles A. Beard and William Beard, *The American Leviathan* (New York, 1930), p. 701.

22. Charles A. Beard, *The Nature of the Social Sciences in Relation to Objectives of Instruction* (New York, 1934), p. 153.

23. Charles A. Beard and Mary R. Beard, *America in Midpassage*, vol. 1 (New York, 1939), p. 381; Charles A. Beard, *The Open Door at Home* (New York, 1935), p. 301.

24. Beard, *The Open Door at Home*, p. 37.

25. Ibid., p. 38.

26. Ibid., pp. 36, 38.

27. Ibid., p. vii.

28. Ibid., p. 66.

29. Ibid., pp. 125–126.

30. Ibid., p. 241. Beard surveyed war's adverse impact on civil liberties in "Preparedness: An American Issue," *Current History* 42 (May 1935): 179–186.

31. Beard, *The Open Door at Home*, p. 202.

32. Ibid., p. 210.

33. Ibid., pp. 47, 55–56.

34. Ibid., p. vii.

35. Radosh, *Prophets on the Right*, p. 24.

36. The prospect of U.S. involvement in another foreign war made it all the more important to trim the chief executive's prerogatives. With Europe by the mid-1930s already edging toward crisis, Beard endorsed the several neutrality acts passed between 1935 and 1937 to prevent any recurrence of the events of 1914–1917 that found the United States professing neutrality while actually supporting the Allies. Erecting these legislative barriers would, he hoped, "keep the power to make war in Congress, where it belongs under the Constitution, and of right"; Charles A. Beard, "Heat and Light on Neutrality," *New Republic* 86 (February 12, 1936): 9.

37. Charles A. Beard, "In Time of Peace Prepare for War," *New Republic* 86 (March 18, 1936): 158.

38. Charles A. Beard, *The Devil Theory of War* (1936; reprint, New York, 1963), p. 29. This book reprints in revised form the essays that appeared in the *New Republic* that same year.

39. Charles A. Beard, "'Going Ahead' with Roosevelt," *Events* 1 (January 1937): 12.

40. Charles A. Beard, "Dr. Beard's Rejoinder," *Events* 2 (September 1937): 164.

41. Charles A. Beard, "Collective Security: A Reply to Mr. Browder," *New Republic* 93 (February 2, 1938): 357–359.

42. Charles A. Beard, "We're Blundering into War," *American Mercury* 46 (April 1939): 398.

43. Charles A. Beard, *A Foreign Policy for America* (New York, 1940), p. 11.

44. Charles A. Beard, "War with Japan," *Events* 8 (November 1940): 323.

45. The standard biography is Paul M. Buhle and Edward Rice-Maxim, *William Appleman Williams: The Tragedy of Empire* (New York, 1995). In summarizing the details of Williams' life I have drawn largely on their account.

46. "An Interview with William Appleman Williams," *Radical History Review* 22 (Winter 1979–80): 65–66.

47. Buhle and Rice-Maxim, *William Appleman Williams*, p. 36.

48. William Appleman Williams, "Charles Austin Beard: The Intellectual as Tory-Radical," in *American Radicals: Some Problems and Personalities*, ed. Harvey Goldberg (New York, 1957), p. 305. See also William Appleman Williams, *The Contours of American History* (1961; reprint, New York, 1966), pp. 454, 463–464.

49. John Patrick Diggins, *The Rise and Fall of the American Left* (New York, 1992), p. 223.

50. William A. Williams, "A Proposal to Put the American Back into American Socialism," *New Politics* 1 (Spring 1962): 41.

51. William Appleman Williams, "On the Restoration of Brooks Adams," *Science and Society* 20 (Summer 1956): 248; idem, *Empire as a Way of Life* (New York, 1980), p. 113; idem, *Contours of American History*, p. 355.

52. Williams, *The Great Evasion*, p. 42.

53. William Appleman Williams, *The Tragedy of American Diplomacy*, rev. ed. (New York, 1972), pp. 50, 52.

54. William A. Williams, *America Confronts a Revolutionary World, 1776–1976* (New York, 1976), p. 43.

55. William A. Williams, "The President and His Critics," *The Nation* 196 (March 16, 1963): 227. Elsewhere Williams wrote that "the American empire has not been the result of evil intentions or irrational behavior. It was created by men who knew precisely what they were doing because they considered it necessary for their own welfare and desirable for the well-being of others"; "A Natural History of the American Empire," *Canadian Dimension* 4 (March–April 1967): 12.

56. Williams, *Empire as a Way of Life*, p. 128.

57. Williams, *Contours of American History*, p. 17.

58. Williams, "A Proposal," p. 44.

59. William Appleman Williams, "What This Country Needs . . . ," *New York Review of Books,* November 5, 1970, pp. 8–10.

60. William Appleman Williams, "The Frontier Thesis and American Foreign Policy," *Pacific Historical Review* 24 (November 1955): 395.

61. Arthur Schlesinger Jr., letter to the editor, *New York Review of Books,* October 20, 1966, p. 37.

62. Williams, *Contours of American History,* pp. 487–488.

63. "An Interview with William Appleman Williams," *Radical History Review* 22 (Winter 1979–80): 72.

64. William A. Williams, "How Can the Left Be Relevant?" *Current* 109 (August 1969): 22, a reprint of an essay published in *Liberation* in June 1969. Williams was never quite the wild-eyed radical he pretended to be. His writing, observes Eugene Genovese, "breathes a spirit of Puritanism—of discipline, civic responsibility, self-restraint and a respect for order—and it breathes a profound respect for those traditions and sensibilities which have sustained men for centuries and which cannot on mere prejudice and without evidence be dismissed as obstacles to freedom"; Eugene D. Genovese, "William Appleman Williams on Marx and America," *Studies on the Left* 6 (January–February 1966): 85. In another era, Williams might have declared himself a principled conservative, defending the social fabric against the assault of unbridled individualism, disdaining crass materialism, and wary of overweening institutional power and the dangers of militarism. Living in an era when conservatism had fallen into disrepute, he remained only a fellow traveler, so far in the closet that few on the right saw Williams for the potential ally that he was.

65. On the nostalgic and implicitly conservative strain in Williams' thought, see Ronald Radosh, "Remembering William Appleman Williams," *Heterodoxy* 4 (May/June 1996): 17; Richard A. Melanson, "The Social and Political Thought of William Appleman Williams," *Western Political Quarterly* 31 (September 1978): 400; and Clifford Solway, "Turning History Upside Down," *Saturday Review,* June 20, 1970, p. 62.

66. As early as 1956 Williams had already concluded that "the expansionist philosophy of history has carried the United States to the last round-up where a nation confronts itself. America's moment of truth is here and now"; William Appleman Williams, "Challenge to American Radicalism," *Frontier* 7 (June 1956): 6.

67. William Appleman Williams, "America II," *Partisan Review* 38 (January 1971): 77.

68. Arthur M. Schlesinger Jr., *The Cycles of American History* (Boston, 1986), p. 141.

69. William Appleman Williams, "Conclusion," in *From Colony to Empire,* ed. Williams (New York, 1972), p. 476.

70. Williams, *Empire as a Way of Life,* p. 213.

2. GLOBALIZATION AND ITS CONCEITS

1. Bill Clinton, "Press Conference by President Clinton and President Jiang Zemin," Washington, D.C., October 29, 1997.

2. "We Can Build a Good Positive Partnership" (excerpts from President Clinton's news conference in Hong Kong), *Washington Post,* July 4, 1998, p. A21. By way of comparison, recall the words Nikita Khrushchev flung at the capitalist world in 1956: "Whether you like it or not, history is on our side. We will bury you."

3. "Interview of the President with Radio Free Asia," June 24, 1998.

4. Madeleine K. Albright, "Commencement Address," Harvard University, June 5, 1997. Unless specified otherwise, all quotations from State Department officials come from the department's Web site at www.state.gov.

5. Condoleezza Rice, "American Foreign Policy in the 21st Century," Los Angeles World Affairs Council, January 15, 1999, www.lawac.org/speech/rice.html.

6. Condoleezza Rice, "Promoting the National Interest," *Foreign Affairs* 79 (January/February 2000): 45–46.

7. Richard Lugar, "World Leadership in the New Millennium," Commonwealth Club of San Francisco, January 20, 2000, www.senate.gov/~lugar/000120.htm. Also reflecting the conventional wisdom was Lugar's belief that the end of the Cold War had left the United States "unchallenged in its primacy" and had endowed it with "enormous opportunities . . . to shape the world in ways that enhance U.S. security and prosperity."

8. Madeleine K. Albright, "The United States and the United Nations: Confrontation or Consensus," Council on Foreign Relations, New York, January 26, 1995.

9. Madeleine K. Albright, "The Testing of American Foreign Policy," *Foreign Affairs* 77 (November–December 1998): 50. The allusion is to Dean Acheson's deservedly famous memoir, *Present at the Creation* (New York, 1969).

10. Warren Christopher, *In the Stream of History* (Stanford, Calif., 1998), p. 42. The quotation is from a presentation to the Chicago Council on Foreign Relations on March 22, 1993.

11. General Henry H. Shelton, "Remarks at the U.S. Naval Academy Graduation, Class of 2000," Annapolis, May 24, 2000. Unless otherwise noted, all quotations of senior military officers and defense officials come from the Defense Department's Web site at www.defenselink.mil.

12. Madeleine K. Albright, "Remarks and Q & A Session at Howard University," April 14, 1998.

13. Anthony Lake, "From Containment to Enlargement," Paul H. Nitze School of Advanced International Studies, Washington, D.C., September 21, 1993.

14. William S. Cohen, "Remarks to International Institute for Strategic Studies," San Diego, September 9, 1999.

15. Bill Clinton, "A Foreign Policy for the Global Age," University of Nebraska at Kearney, December 8, 2000; Madeleine K. Albright, "Address to the Milwaukee Business Community," October 2, 1998; William S. Cohen, "U.S. Must Remain Active in Post–Cold War Foreign Affairs," Foreign Policy Association, New York City, April 2, 1998.

16. Samuel R. Berger, "Challenges Approaching the 21st Century," Woodrow Wilson Center for Scholars, Washington, D.C., June 18, 1996.

17. Thomas L. Friedman, "A Manifesto for the Fast World," *New York Times Magazine,* March 28, 1999, p. 42.

18. Bill Clinton, "The State of the Union," *New York Times* (Internet edition), January 28, 2000. Berger has likewise identified globalization as "the central phenomenon of our time"; Samuel Berger, "Remarks to the National Press Club," Washington, D.C., January 7, 2000.

19. William Jefferson Clinton, "American Security in a Changing World," George Washington University, August 5, 1996. See also idem, "Remarks by the President at World Economic Forum," Davos, Switzerland, January 29, 2000. At Davos Clinton told his well-heeled listeners that globalization is "tearing down doors and building up networks between nations and individuals, between economics and cultures."

20. Sandy Berger, "Press Briefing," Rio de Janeiro, October 15, 1997.

21. Clinton, "Foreign Policy for the Global Age," December 8, 2000; idem, "Remarks on Foreign Policy," February 26, 1999.

22. Brent Scowcroft, "Who Can Harness History? Only the U.S.," *New York Times,* July 2, 1993, p. A15.

23. Clinton, "Foreign Policy for the Global Age," December 8, 2000.

24. As James W. Ceasar has remarked, the usefulness of *globalization* as a term employed in political discourse derives in some measure from its capacity "to soften or obscure the reality of power relationships"; "The Great Divide: American Interventionism and Its Opponents," in *Present Danger: Crisis and Opportunity in American Foreign and Defense Policy,* ed. Robert Kagan and William Kristol (San Francisco, 2000), p. 41.

25. Newt Gingrich, *To Renew America* (New York, 1995), pp. 7–8.

26. Clinton, "Remarks at World Economic Forum," January 29, 2000.

27. Bill Clinton, "Remarks on China," Paul H. Nitze School for Advanced International Studies, March 8, 2000.

28. Friedman, "Manifesto for the Fast World," p. 42.

29. Joseph S. Nye Jr. and William A. Owens, "America's Information Edge," *Foreign Affairs* 75 (March/April 1996): 20. Nye served as an assistant secretary of defense in the Clinton administration. Owens was a career naval officer whose final assignment was vice-chairman of the Joint Chiefs of Staff.

30. Samuel R. Berger, "A Foreign Policy for the Global Age," Georgetown University, October 19, 2000.

31. Theodore Levitt, "The Globalization of Markets," *Harvard Business Review* 61 (May–June 1983): 93, 96.

32. Friedman, "Manifesto for the Fast World," p. 43.

33. Benjamin R. Barber, *Jihad vs. McWorld* (New York, 1995), p. 4; Bill Gates with Nathan Myhrvold and Peter Rinearson, *The Road Ahead,* rev. ed. (New York, 1996), p. 266; Bill Clinton, "Remarks by the President to the Council on Foreign Relations," New York City, September 14, 1998.

34. Bill Clinton, "Remarks by the President to Opening Ceremony of the 1998 International Monetary Fund/World Bank Annual Meeting," Washington, D.C., October 6, 1998.

35. W. Bowman Cutter, Joan Spero, and Laura D'Andrea Tyson, "New World, New Deal," *Foreign Affairs* 79 (March/April 2000): 82. The authors served in the Clinton administration as, respectively, deputy assistant to the president for economic policy; undersecretary of state for economic, business, and agricultural affairs; and chair of the Council of Economic Advisers.

36. Christopher, *In the Stream of History,* pp. 24, 29. The text reprints Christopher's testimony before the Senate Foreign Relations Committee on January 13, 1993.

37. Rubin and Kantor quoted in Steven Erlanger and David E. Sanger, "On Global Stage, Clinton's Pragmatic Turn," *New York Times,* July 29, 1996, p. A16.

38. According to Alfred E. Eckes Jr., "From colonial times the 'Spirit of Commerce' has inspired and shaped America's relations with the world"; *Opening America's Market: U.S. Foreign Trade Policy since 1776* (Chapel Hill, N.C., 1995), p. 1.

39. Madeleine K. Albright, "Confirmation Hearing," Senate Foreign Relations Committee, January 8, 1997; Strobe Talbott, "Democracy and the National Interest," *Foreign Affairs* 75 (November/December 1996): 49.

40. William S. Cohen, "Presentation to the Annual Bernard Brodie Lecture," University of California at Los Angeles, October 28, 1998.

41. Herman Melville, *White Jacket* (New York, 1850), chap. 36.

42. Patrick E. Tyler, "U.S. Strategy Plan Calls for Insuring No Rivals Develop," *New York Times,* March 8, 1992, p. 1.

43. Barton Gellman, "Aim of Defense Plan Supported by Bush," *Washington Post,* March 12, 1992, p. A18.

44. Dick Cheney, "Defense Strategy for the 1990s: The Regional Defense Strategy," Washington, D.C., January 1993, p. 1.

45. Not so incidentally, Powell in 1984 had served as Weinberger's military assistant.

46. Richard Halloran, "The U.S. Will Not Drift into a Latin War, Weinberger Says," *New York Times,* November 29, 1984, p. A1.

47. George Bush and Brent Scowcroft, *A World Transformed* (New York, 1998), p. 354.

48. Colin L. Powell, *My American Journey* (New York, 1995), p. 576.

49. Eliot A. Cohen, "The Mystique of U.S. Air Power," *Foreign Affairs* 73 (January/February 1994): 110.

50. Martin Fletcher, "White House Denies U.S. Will Withdraw from Leadership Role," *New York Times*, May 27, 1993.

51. Christopher, *In the Stream of History*, p. 40.

52. Scowcroft, "Who Can Harness History?" p. A15; Jack Kemp, "Why America Must Lead," Los Angeles World Affairs Council, February 23, 1998; Gingrich, *To Renew America*, p. 66; Bush and Scowcroft, *A World Transformed*, p. 566.

53. Clinton, "Remarks to Council on Foreign Relations," September 14, 1998.

54. Strobe Talbott, "American Eagle or Ostrich," Milwaukee Town Hall Meeting, September 12, 1995; Al Gore, "Vice President's Remarks at West Point, U.S. Military Academy," October 17, 1995; William Jefferson Clinton, "American Security in a Changing World," George Washington University, August 5, 1996.

55. Gingrich, *To Renew America*, p. 187.

56. Kemp, "Why America Must Lead," February 23, 1998.

57. Albright, "Testing of American Foreign Policy," p. 50.

58. Samuel R. Berger, "NSC 50th Anniversary Symposium," Washington, D.C., October 31, 1997.

59. X [George F. Kennan], "The Sources of Soviet Conduct," reprinted in *The American Encounter: The United States and the Making of the Modern World*, ed. James F. Hoge Jr. and Fareed Zakaria (New York, 1997), p. 169. The essay originally appeared in the July 1947 issue of *Foreign Affairs*.

60. Clinton, "Foreign Policy for a Global Age," December 8, 2000.

61. Charles A. Beard and Mary R. Beard, *America in Midpassage*, vol. 1 (New York, 1939), p. 395.

62. Reinhold Niebuhr, *The Irony of American History* (New York, 1952), p. 71.

3. POLICY BY DEFAULT

1. George Bush and Brent Scowcroft, *A World Transformed* (New York, 1998), pp. 16–17; David Allan Mayers, *Wars and Peace: The Future Americans Envisioned, 1861–1991* (New York, 1998), p. 119.

2. James A. Baker III, *The Politics of Diplomacy* (New York, 1995), pp. xiii, 18.

3. Ibid., p. 40.

4. George Bush, National Security Review 12: "Review of National Defense Strategy," March 3, 1989. The George Bush Presidential Library and Museum at Texas A & M University has posted all of George H. W. Bush's public papers on its Web site at http://bushlibrary.tamu.edu.

5. Bush and Scowcroft, *A World Transformed*, p. 544.

6. On German unification, the authoritative account is Philip Zelikow and Condoleezza Rice, *Germany Unified and Europe Transformed* (Cambridge, Mass., 1995).

7. Bush and Scowcroft, *A World Transformed*, p. 400.

8. See, for example, Paul Kennedy, *The Rise and Fall of the Great Powers* (New York, 1987), chap. 8.

9. Japan and Germany had a role to play, but it was the unglamorous one of picking up the tab. Along with Saudi Arabia and Kuwait, they paid billions of dollars to reimburse the members of the coalition—chiefly the United States—for costs incurred in fighting the war.

10. George Bush, "Address before a Joint Session of the Congress on the Cessation of the Persian Gulf Conflict," March 6, 1991.

11. Mayers, *Wars and Peace*, p. 36.

12. George Bush, "The President's News Conference on the Persian Gulf Conflict," March 1, 1991.

13. Paul Lewis, "Raid on Iraq; U.S. Is Broadening Enforcement Role," *New York Times*, January 17, 1993, p. A8.

14. Bush and Scowcroft, *A World Transformed*, p. 487. The ellipsis appears in the original.

15. William J. Crowe Jr., "Give Sanctions a Chance," testimony before the Senate Armed Services Committee, November 28, 1990, reprinted in *The Gulf War Reader*, ed. Micah L. Sifry and Christopher Cerf (New York, 1991), pp. 234–237.

16. Zbigniew Brzezinski, "The Drift to War," testimony before the Senate Foreign Relations Committee, December 5, 1990, reprinted in Sifrey and Cerf, *The Gulf War Reader*, pp. 251–254.

17. Bob Woodward, *The Commanders* (New York, 1991), p. 325.

18. Baker, *The Politics of Diplomacy*, p. 336. The quotation is from a press conference that Baker gave on November 13, 1990.

19. The administration's policy toward Iraq following the Persian Gulf War reinforced this impression. Having declared Saddam Hussein to be a latter-day Hitler, Bush suppressed any inclination to haul the Iraqi dictator into the dock or even to remove him from power. When Saddam's domestic opponents attempted to overthrow him, Bush did nothing. The United States stood by while Saddam brutally crushed the Iraqi opposition. On this point see, for example, Charles Krauthammer, "Tiananmen II," *Washington Post*, April 5, 1991, p. A19.

20. For an excellent summary of the events at Tiananmen and their aftermath, see James Mann, *About Face* (New York, 1999), pp. 175–209.

21. Bush and Scowcroft, *A World Transformed*, p. 102.

22. As if distancing himself from the modest sanctions that his own government had imposed on China after Tiananmen, Bush assured Deng that "the

actions that I took as President of the United States could not be avoided. As you know, the clamor for stronger action remains intense. I have resisted that clamor, making clear that I did not want to see destroyed this relationship that you and I have worked hard to build. I explained to the American people that I did not want to unfairly burden the Chinese people through economic sanctions." The text of Bush's letter to Deng is reprinted in ibid., pp. 100–102.

23. Mann, *About Face,* p. 206.

24. Bush and Scowcroft, *A World Transformed,* p. 108.

25. See, for example, Ann Devroy and David Hoffman, "White House Reveals Earlier China Mission," *Washington Post,* December 19, 1989, p. A1; Stephen Kurkjian and John Mashek, "Bush Advisers Visited Beijing after Massacre," *Boston Globe,* December 19, 1989, p. 3; and Thomas Oliphant, "Bush's China Card," *Boston Globe,* December 15, 1989, p. 27.

26. George Bush, "Remarks to the Supreme Soviet of the Republic of the Ukraine in Kiev, Soviet Union," August 1, 1991.

27. Linda Diebel, "Bush Taps into Symbolism of Ukrainian Freedom," *Toronto Star,* August 4, 1991, p. H1.

28. Brent Scowcroft insists that the speech was misinterpreted, that Bush's actual intent was to plead on behalf of reform, democracy, and tolerance; Bush and Scowcroft, *A World Transformed,* pp. 515–516.

29. William Safire, "Soviet Disunion, Baltic Courage Led to Yeltsin's Moscow Stand," *Detroit Free Press,* August 30, 1991, p. 9A.

30. For a dispassionate and comprehensive account of the Bosnian civil war see Steven L. Burg and Paul S. Shoup, *The War in Bosnia-Herzegovina* (Armonk, N.Y., 1999). On the dissolution of Yugoslavia and the origins of the Bosnian civil war, see especially pp. 62–120.

31. For a recent account that captures the moral significance attributed to the Spanish Civil War—"the only political cause which, even in retrospect, appears as pure and compelling as it did in 1936"—see Eric Hobsbawm, *The Age of Extremes* (New York, 1994), pp. 156–161.

32. Laura Silber and Allan Little, *Yugoslavia: Death of a Nation,* rev. ed. (London, 1996), p. 201.

33. The Spanish Civil War broke out in July 1936. Although existing U.S. neutrality legislation did not apply to civil wars, Roosevelt called for Americans to observe a "moral embargo" and to refrain from providing assistance to either side. When that proved insufficient, Roosevelt asked Congress for additional legislation that would prohibit munitions shipments to any party involved in the Spanish war. Congress passed that legislation with only a single dissenting vote in January 1937. For a brief account, see James MacGregor Burns, *Roosevelt: The Lion and the Fox* (New York, 1956), pp. 355–356.

34. The standard account of the U.S. invasion of Panama is Thomas Donnelly, Margaret Roth, and Caleb Baker, *Operation Just Cause* (New York, 1991).

35. Woodward, *The Commanders,* p. 32.

36. An electronic search of Bush's public papers yielded a single reference to globalization on three occasions: April 23 and September 13 and 14, 1992.

37. George Bush, "Address to the 46th Session of the United Nations General Assembly," New York City, September 23, 1991.

38. George Bush, "Remarks and a Question-and-Answer Session with the Economic Club of Detroit in Michigan," September 10, 1992.

39. George Bush, "Address before the 45th Session of the United Nations General Assembly," New York City, October 1, 1990.

40. George Bush, "Remarks at the Greek-American Chamber of Commerce," Athens, Greece, July 19, 1991.

41. George Bush, "Remarks at the Opening of the AmeriFlora '92 Exposition in Columbus, Ohio," April 20, 1992.

42. Bush, "Remarks and Question-and-Answer Session with Economic Club of Detroit," September 10, 1992.

43. Bush and Scowcroft, *A World Transformed,* p. 491.

44. George Bush, "Remarks at a Luncheon Hosted by Prime Minister Ruud Lubbers in The Hague," November 9, 1991.

45. George Bush, "Remarks and a Question-and-Answer Session at a Luncheon Hosted by the Commonwealth Club in San Francisco, California," February 7, 1990.

46. George Bush, "Remarks at the Bush-Quayle Fundraising Dinner," Houston, October 31, 1991; idem, "Remarks to the American Enterprise Institute," Washington, D.C., December 4, 1991; idem, "Remarks to World War II Veterans and Families," Honolulu, December 7, 1991.

47. Bush, "Remarks to World War II Veterans and Families," December 7, 1991.

48. On the latter point see Walter A. MacDougall, *Promised Land, Crusader State* (Boston, 1997), pp. 39–40.

49. Bush and Scowcroft, *A World Transformed,* p. 566.

50. Quoted in Ann Devroy, "Bush Defends Sending Secret Mission to China," *Washington Post,* December 22, 1989, p. A27.

4. STRATEGY OF OPENNESS

1. Robert D. Putnam, *Bowling Alone* (New York, 2000), pp. 247–276.

2. Christopher Lasch, *The Revolt of the Elites and the Betrayal of Democracy* (New York, 1995), pp. 3–22.

3. In 1996, 49 percent of the voting-age population cast a ballot for president. From the beginning of World War II through the 1960s, the average turnout in presidential elections had been 59.1 percent; in the 1970s and 1980s it had averaged 53; U.S. Census Bureau, "Participation in Elections for Presi-

dent and U.S. House of Representatives: 1932–1998," in *Statistical Abstract of the United States: 1999* (Washington, D.C., 1999), p. 301.

4. A nation of over 270 million today finds itself increasingly hard pressed to recruit the 200,000 qualified volunteers needed annually to sustain its military forces. For further discussion of this point, see Andrew J. Bacevich, "Losing Private Ryan," *National Review* 51 (August 9, 1999): 32–34.

5. David Brooks, *Bobos in Paradise: The New Upper Class and How They Got There* (New York, 2000).

6. Lasch, *Revolt of the Elites*, pp. 22, 82.

7. Michael Lind, *The Next American Nation* (New York, 1995), pp. 6–7.

8. For a comprehensive survey, see Michael Kammen, *Mystic Chords of Memory* (New York, 1991), pp. 299–527.

9. Eugene D. Genovese, *The Southern Tradition* (Cambridge, Mass., 1994), p. 38; Gertrude Himmelfarb, *One Nation, Two Cultures* (New York, 1999), p. 118.

10. Lind, *Next American Nation*, p. 97.

11. Bill Clinton, "A Foreign Policy for the Global Age," University of Nebraska at Kearney, December 8, 2000.

12. Al Gore, "Remarks by the Vice President in Foreign Policy Speech," Milwaukee, January 6, 1994.

13. Paul Richard, "Scrawling in the Margins: New York's Whitney Biennial Spits in the Face of Convention," *Washington Post*, March 4, 1993, p. C1. For another incisive critique of the 1993 Whitney Biennial, see Christopher Knight, "Crushed by Its Good Intentions," *Los Angeles Times*, March 10, 1993, p. F1.

14. The "works" on display at the Whitney Biennial included performance artists who would do a "native dance" or display their genitals, depending upon the amount of money offered, to make a political statement about the marginalization of Native Americans; large gnawed blocks of chocolate and lard intended to make a political statement about bulimia; numerous photographs of the nude male backside to make a political statement about homosexuality; an array of gilded gym shoes to make a political statement about the plight of young African-American men; and red telephones with instructions to dial 1-900-DESIRES providing the listener (for a fee) the opportunity to hear a woman discuss biracial sex.

15. The term *skeptical relativism* is that of Pope John Paul II, from his 1991 encyclical *Centesimus Annus*.

16. See, for example, the analysis of the United States Commission on National Security/21st Century, *New World Coming: American Security in the 21st Century* (Washington, D.C., 1999), p. 127, arguing that "multicultural fragmentation, . . . shifts in generational attitudes, [and] the decline in overt manifestations of national identification" are contributing to "a serious undermining of American identity and national will."

17. Michael Ledeen, *Freedom Betrayed: How America Led a Global Democratic Revolution, Won the Cold War, and Walked Away* (Washington, D.C., 1996), p. 147. In a similar vein, see Joshua Muravchik, *The Imperative of American Leadership: A Challenge to Neo-Isolationism* (Washington, D.C., 1996), pp. 1, 35, 173, 181.

18. Steven Erlanger and David E. Sanger, "On Global Stage, Clinton's Pragmatic Turn," *New York Times,* July 29, 1996, p. A16. Economists agreed. Jeffrey Garten, undersecretary of commerce for international trade from 1993 to 1995 before returning to academe as dean of the Yale School of Management, wrote in 1997 that absent increasing access to foreign markets, "The country can no longer generate enough growth, jobs, profits, and savings from domestic sources." Enough for what? Garten does not say. Jeffrey E. Garten, "Business and Foreign Policy," *Foreign Affairs* 76 (May/June 1997): 69.

19. Sandy Berger, "Press Briefing," Rio de Janeiro, October 15, 1997; Madeleine K. Albright, "Confirmation Hearing," Senate Foreign Relations Committee, January 8, 1997; Bill Clinton, "Remarks by the President to the Council on Foreign Relations," New York, September 14, 1998. This putative correlation between trade and economic growth was not merely the stuff of speeches. It was integral to official U.S. national security strategy. By 1998 published strategy would state categorically that "we must expand our international trade to sustain economic growth at home"; William J. Clinton, *A National Security Strategy for a New Century* (Washington, D.C., 1998), p. 29.

20. Lawrence H. Summers, "Globalization That Works for People," Democratic Leadership Annual Conference, Washington, D.C., October 14, 1999, www.ustreas.gov/press/releases/ps154.htm.

21. John Lukács, *The Passing of the Modern Age* (New York, 1970), p. 22.

22. For a superb essay describing the essential continuity of U.S. grand strategy in the twentieth century and the economic considerations shaping that strategy, see Benjamin C. Schwarz, "The Arcana of Empire and the Dilemma of American National Security," *Salmagundi* 101–102 (Winter–Spring 1994): 182–211.

23. Ronald Steel, *Temptations of a Superpower* (Cambridge, Mass., 1995), p. 22. For a similar argument that containment alone did not describe U.S. strategy during the Cold War, see William Kristol and Robert Kagan, "Introduction: National Interest and Global Responsibility," in *Present Dangers: Crisis and Opportunity in American Foreign and Defense Policy,* ed. Robert Kagan and William Kristol (San Francisco, 2000), p. 12.

24. Bill Clinton, "Remarks Prepared for Delivery," Foreign Policy Association, New York, April 1, 1992.

25. Clinton had explained his strategy in a letter to Colonel Eugene Holmes, director of the Reserve Officer Training Corps (ROTC) program at the University of Arkansas, in 1969. The complete text of the letter is available in "The

1992 Campaign: A Letter by Clinton on his Draft Deferment," *New York Times,* February 13, 1992, p. A25.

26. R. Jeffrey Smith and Julia Preston, "U.S. Plans Wider Role in U.N. Peace-keeping," *Washington Post,* June 18, 1993, p. A1. Largely the handiwork of Madeleine Albright, then serving as U.S. ambassador to the United Nations, "assertive multilateralism" envisioned expanded American support to peacemaking missions with the United States working through international organizations, especially a reformed and strengthened UN, rather than unilaterally. The concept emerged during the summer of 1993 and did not survive the collapse of peacemaking efforts in Somalia that fall. For a detailed explanation of the concept see Madeleine Albright, Testimony before the Terrorism, Narcotics, and Operations Subcommittee of the Senate Foreign Relations Committee, June 9, 1993, Federal News Service, accessed through LEXIS-NEXIS, August 28, 2000.

27. William G. Hyland, *Clinton's World: Remaking American Foreign Policy* (Westport, Conn., 1999), p. 67.

28. Bill Clinton, "A New Covenant for American Security," Georgetown University, December 12, 1991; Clinton quoted in Steven Erlanger and David E. Sanger, "On Global Stage, Clinton's Pragmatic Turn," *New York Times,* July 29, 1996, p. A16.

29. Charles A. Beard, *The Open Door at Home* (New York, 1935), p. 301.

30. William Appleman Williams, "The Nature of Peace," *Monthly Review* 9 (July–August 1957): 112.

31. Thomas L. Friedman, "The Transition: Plans and Policies," *New York Times,* November 6, 1992, p. A1.

32. Warren Christopher, "Statement before the Senate Foreign Relations Committee," November 3, 1993.

33. There existed a handful of exceptions to this generalization, Russia and Israel being the foremost.

34. Richard C. Holbrooke, *To End a War* (New York, 1999), pp. 41–42.

35. CBS News Transcripts, "Campaign '92: Presidential Debate," October 11, 1992.

36. Christopher, *In the Stream of History,* p. 346.

37. Ibid., p. 347.

38. James Mann, *About Face* (New York, 1999), pp. 281–284.

39. Christopher, *In the Stream of History,* p. 154.

40. Mann, *About Face,* pp. 285–288, 294–297.

41. Christopher, *In the Stream of History,* p. 153.

42. Ibid., p. 160.

43. David Holley, "In China, Brown Cites Success on Trade, Rights," *Los Angeles Times,* August 31, 1994, p. A1.

44. Christopher, "Statement before Senate Foreign Relations Committee," November 3, 1993.

45. Bill Clinton, "President Clinton's Speech at American University," February 26, 1993.

46. Henry Kissinger, "NAFTA Will Fuel Latin Revolution in Government, Commerce," *Houston Chronicle*, July 25, 1993, p. 5.

47. Bill Clinton, "Remarks by the President to the People of Detroit," October 22, 1996.

48. Bill Clinton, "Remarks by the President at Democratic Leadership Council Retreat," Franklin Delano Roosevelt Presidential Library, Hyde Park, N.Y., May 21, 2000.

49. Garten, "Business and Foreign Policy," p. 70. From 1993 through 1995, Garten served as undersecretary of commerce for international trade.

50. Bill Clinton, "Remarks by President Clinton, Sen. Dole, Sen. Moynihan, Sen. Packwood, and Ambassador Kantor," Washington, D.C., November 23, 1994; idem, "Remarks to the People of Detroit," October 22, 1996.

51. John E. Rielly, ed., *American Public Opinion and U.S. Foreign Policy 1999* (Chicago, 1999), p. 35.

52. Office of Management and Budget, http://w3access.gpo.gov/usbudget/fy2001, accessed August 22, 2000.

53. United States Trade Representative, "The WTO and U.S. Economic Growth," March 2, 2000, http://www.ustr.gov/new/wtofact2.html. Through 1999, U.S. exports in goods and services had jumped by over 50 percent during the Clinton era, from $617 billion to $956 billion. Imports had almost doubled, from $652 billion to $1.2 trillion. Data are from the International Trade Administration of the Department of Commerce, www. ita. doc.gov, accessed on August 22, 2000. Labor and wage statistics are from the Bureau of Labor Statistics, Department of Labor, http://stats.bls.gov/blshome.htm, accessed August 22, 2000.

54. Anthony Lake, "From Containment to Enlargement," Johns Hopkins University, September 21, 1993.

55. In a contemporaneous interview, Lake described his approach as "pragmatic neo-Wilsonianism"—in his mind, evidently, an important distinction; Thomas L. Friedman, "Clinton's Foreign Policy: Top Adviser Speaks Up," *New York Times*, October 31, 1993, p. 8.

56. "Clinton's Three Big Objectives Include Peace through Trade," *New York Times*, July 29, 1996, p. A17.

57. Warren Christopher, "Leadership for the Next American Century," John F. Kennedy School of Government, January 18, 1996.

58. Madeleine K. Albright, "International Economic Leadership: Keeping America on the Right Track for the 21st Century," Institute for International Economics, Washington, D.C., September 18, 1998; idem, "Address to the 10th Annual George C. Marshall Lecture," Vancouver, Wash., October 30, 1998; idem, "Address to the Milwaukee Business Community," October 2, 1998.

59. Berger, "Press Briefing," October 15, 1997; "A Pied Piper in Hanoi," *Boston Globe*, November 18, 2000, p. A16. The *Globe* editorial was written on the occasion of Clinton's end-of-term visit to Vietnam. It described the president's "bravura address" at Hanoi's National University as "irresistible" and concluded that if Vietnam's leaders would take his advice "to open the country to foreign capital and globalization," then Clinton, who had "already done his part for prosperity in America," would be remembered "as the president who did the most to undo communism in Vietnam."

60. Lake, "From Containment to Enlargement," September 21, 1993.

61. Bill Clinton, "Statement by the President on NATO Expansion," Washington, D.C., May 14, 1997.

62. Bill Clinton, "Remarks by the President at Intervention for the North Atlantic Council Summit," Brussels, January 10, 1994.

63. Office of the Press Secretary, The White House, "NATO Summit: The New Strategic Concept," April 24, 1999.

64. Steven L. Burg and Paul S. Shoup, *The War in Bosnia-Herzegovina* (Armonk, N.Y., 1999), pp. 384, 412.

65. Robert Fisk, "Was It Rescue or Revenge?" *The Independent* (London), June 21, 1999, p. 5.

66. Ivo H. Daalder and Michael E. O'Hanlon, *Winning Ugly: NATO's War to Save Kosovo* (Washington, D.C., 2000), p. 85.

67. Bill Clinton, "Remarks by the President to AFSCME Biennial Convention," Washington, D.C., March 23, 1999.

68. "Press Briefing by National Security Adviser Samuel Berger and National Economic Adviser Gene Sperling," Washington, D.C., May 25, 2000.

69. Bill Clinton, "Remarks by the President at the U.S. Coast Guard Academy's 119th Commencement," New London, Conn., May 17, 2000.

70. In the Maghreb, preliminary efforts to open the Arab world were already under way. In April 1999 the Clinton administration launched its "U.S.–North Africa Economic Partnership." According to Stuart Eizenstat, a senior Treasury Department official and point man for this policy, the aim was to prod Algeria, Tunisia, and Morocco "to open up their economies." The Eizenstat initiative sought "to provide the kind of investment climate through deregulation, through privatization, through transparent procurement rules, [and] through protecting intellectual property, that will enable us to encourage successfully U.S. companies to invest"; Stuart Eizenstat interview with Doris McMillon on Worldnet's "Dialogue," June 14, 1999.

71. As noted earlier, the strategy of openness cannot explain every facet of post–Cold War U.S. foreign policy. American support for Israel and the obsession of U.S. policymakers with the Middle East peace process provide two striking examples of commitments at best tangentially related to openness. The very genuine (but not necessarily irreversible) U.S. commitment to Israel is a reminder of the extent to which domestic politics, history, religious conviction, and a sense of moral obligation also affect policy. The

never-ending maneuverings related to the peace process offer a reminder of how bureaucratic habit and the vanity of politicians yearning to win a Nobel Peace Prize can warp policy. That said, the assumptions underlying the peace process—that national identity is atavistic, that Arabs and Jews are basically alike, that the road to peace lies not through partition and separation but through reconciliation and integration—are all consistent with the American vision of an open world.

72. Bill Clinton, "Remarks by the President to the Community of Kisowera School," Mukono, Uganda, March 24, 1998; idem, "Remarks by the President to the People of Ghana," Accra, March 23, 1998.

73. Susan E. Rice, "Address before the Morehouse College Andrew Young Center for International Relations," Atlanta, March 25, 1999. See also idem, "U.S. and Africa in the 21st Century," World Affairs Council, Seattle, November 9, 1999.

74. Bill Clinton, "Remarks by the President at Bill Signing of Trade and Development Act of 2000," Washington, D.C., May 18, 2000.

75. In some respects, the level of U.S. engagement in Africa decreased in the 1990s. For example, the amount of aid provided to South Africa decreased from $210 million in 1994 to $47 million in 1999. Among the twenty-four most industrialized nations, by the end of the 1990s the United States ranked last in its economic aid to Africa; Kurt Shillinger, "Carter, Others say U.S. has Faltered in Africa," *Boston Globe*, December 8, 1999, p. A2.

76. For a concise account of Sudan and its recent history, see Ann Mosely Lesch, *The Sudan—Contested National Identities* (Bloomington, Ind., 1998).

77. U.S. Department of State, Bureau of Democracy, Human Rights, and Labor, *1999 Country Reports on Human Rights Practices: Sudan* (Washington, D.C., February 25, 2000).

78. The figure on U.S. aid comes from Madeleine K. Albright, "Message from Secretary Albright to the Sudan Summit," Washington, D.C., November 9, 1999. A cynic might suggest that the chief objective of this aid effort is to purchase the acquiescence of humanitarian relief organizations in a policy otherwise characterized by inaction.

79. William J. Clinton, Executive Order pursuant to section 204(b) of the International Emergency Economic Powers Act, 50 U.S.C. 1703 (b), November 4, 1997.

80. Statement by the Press Secretary, The White House, "Sudan: Declaration of Emergency and Imposition of Sanctions," November 4, 1997.

81. Susan E. Rice, "Statement before the Subcommittees on Africa and on International Operations and Human Rights of the House International Relations Committee," Washington, D.C., July 29, 1998. See also Albright, "Message to the Sudan Summit," November 9, 1999.

82. Bill Clinton, "Address to the Nation by the President," Washington, D.C., August 20, 1998.

83. Kenneth R. McKune, "Sudan and Terrorism," Testimony before the Sub-committee on Africa, Senate Foreign Relations Committee, Washington, D.C., May 15, 1997. McKune was the State Department's acting coordinator for counterterrorism.

84. William S. Cohen, "We Are Ready to Act Again," *Washington Post,* August 23, 1998, p. C1.

85. James Risen and David Johnston, "Experts Find No Arms Chemicals at Bombed Sudan Plant," *New York Times,* February 9, 1999, p. A5.

86. Richard C. Holbrooke, "Statement during the Open Meeting on the Month of Africa," New York City, January 31, 2000.

87. William J. Clinton, "Opening Remarks at the National Summit on Africa," Washington Convention Center, Washington, D.C., February 17, 2000.

88. Andrew England, "U.S. Pledges to Ease Suffering in Sudan," *Boston Globe,* November 21, 2000, p. A8.

89. Explaining why the United States had limited itself to a largely consultative role in addressing the conflicts raging in Sudan, the Congo, Sierra Leone, Angola, and elsewhere, Samuel R. Berger explained that it was U.S. policy "to help Africans find African solutions to African conflicts." Such diffidence and self-restraint does not inhibit the U.S. from acting in regions such as Europe and the Persian Gulf, which command real strategic importance. Samuel R. Berger, "Remarks by Samuel R. Berger," Africare Dinner, Washington, D.C., September 27, 1999.

90. Madeleine K. Albright, "Remarks and Q & A Session," Howard University, April 14, 1998.

91. Albright, "Confirmation Hearing," Senate Foreign Relations Committee, January 8, 1997.

92. Bill Clinton, "Remarks by the President to Opening Ceremony of the 1998 International Monetary Fund/World Bank Annual Meeting," Washington, D.C., October 6, 1998.

93. Ibid.

94. Bill Clinton, "Remarks by the President to the Next Generation of Russian Leaders, Moscow University of International Relations," September 1, 1998.

95. Ibid.

96. Madeleine K. Albright, "Statement before the Senate Foreign Relations Committee," Washington, D.C., February 10, 1998.

97. Ibid.; Albright, "Confirmation Hearing," Senate Foreign Relations Committee, January 8, 1997.

98. Bill Clinton, "The State of the Union," *New York Times* (Internet edition), January 28, 2000; "Clinton's Three Big Objectives Include Peace through Trade," *New York Times,* July 29, 1996, p. A17. This article consists of excerpts from an interview with President Clinton conducted on July 8, 1996.

99. Albright, "Remarks and Q & A Session," Howard University, April 14, 1998.

100. Summers, "Globalization That Works for People"; Al Gore, "Remarks Prepared for Delivery by Vice President Al Gore, Kennan Institute/U.S.-Russia Business Council," Washington, D.C., October 19, 1995.

101. Thomas L. Friedman, "A Manifesto for the Fast World," *New York Times Magazine*, March 28, 1999, p. 43.

102. Woodrow Wilson, "An Address to the Senate," January 22, 1917, in *The Papers of Woodrow Wilson*, ed. Arthur S. Link et al., vol. 40 (Princeton, 1982), p. 539.

103. For a concise account of Wilson and Mexico, see Mark T. Gilderhus, *Diplomacy and Revolution: U.S.-Mexican Relations under Wilson and Carranza* (Tucson, 1977).

5. FULL SPECTRUM DOMINANCE

1. Bill Clinton, "Remarks by the President at the U.S. Coast Guard Academy's 119th Commencement," New London, Conn., May 17, 2000. See also idem, "Helping Write 21st Century International Rules," National Defense University, January 29, 1998, www.defenselink.mil/speeches/1998/di1305.html.

2. Madeleine K. Albright, "Remarks and Q & A Session," Howard University, April 14, 1998.

3. Madeleine K. Albright, "Address to the Milwaukee Business Community," Milwaukee, October 2, 1998.

4. Clinton, "Remarks at U.S. Coast Guard Academy Commencement," May 17, 2000.

5. Bill Clinton, "Remarks by the President on Keeping America Secure for the 21st Century," National Academy of Sciences, Washington, D.C., January 22, 1999.

6. An average of 537 per year for 1981–1990; an average of 381 per year for 1991–2000; U.S. Department of State, *Patterns of Global Terrorism, 2000* (April 2001), http://www.state.gov/s/ct/rls/pgtrpt/2000.

7. Ibid.

8. Ambassador Philip Wilcox, "Special Briefing on the Release of *Patterns of Global Terrorism, 1996*," April 30, 1997.

9. William S. Cohen, "Preparing for a Grave New World," *Washington Post*, July 26, 1999, p. A19.

10. Judith Miller and William J. Broad, "Clinton Describes Terrorism Threat for 21st Century," *New York Times*, January 22, 1999, p. A1; William J. Broad and Judith Miller, "Germ Defense Plan in Peril as Its Flaws Are Revealed," *New York Times*, August 7, 1998, p. A1.

11. Jessica Stern, *The Ultimate Terrorist* (Cambridge, Mass., 1999), pp. 1–2.

12. Tim Weiner, "The Man Who Protects America from Terrorism," *New York Times,* February 1, 1999, p. A3.

13. Bill Clinton, "Remarks by the President of the United States at the United States Naval Academy Commencement," Annapolis, May 22, 1998.

14. John Deutch, "Off-Line: At War with Info-Terrorists," *The Observer* (London), July 7, 1996, p. 7. The article reprints Deutch's testimony before the U.S. Senate Government Affairs Committee on June 25, 1996.

15. Al Gore, "Remarks as Prepared for Delivery by Vice President Al Gore, United Nations Security Council Opening Session," January 10, 2000, New York; Bill Clinton, "A Foreign Policy for a Global Age," University of Nebraska at Kearney, December 8, 2000. Samuel Berger, national security adviser during Clinton's second term, went even further, declaring that the administration had "made the fight against deadly infectious diseases a national security priority," not limiting that fight to any particular group of diseases or region; Samuel R. Berger, "A Foreign Policy for the Global Age," *Foreign Affairs* 79 (November/December 2000): 32.

16. One wonders if even the policymakers believed. Although the Clinton administration warned of an anthrax attack at home, its policy focused almost entirely on protecting U.S. soldiers deploying abroad. Even on that count, the administration's efforts were problematic. See Andrew J. Bacevich, "Bad Medicine for Biological Terror," *Orbis* 44 (Spring 2000): 221–236.

17. Joshua Muravchik, *The Imperative of American Leadership: A Challenge to Neo-Isolationism* (Washington, D.C., 1996), p. 135.

18. George F. Kennan, *American Diplomacy, 1900–1950* (Chicago, 1951), p. 17.

19. For polling data supporting this assertion, see Gallup Organization, "Being Number One Militarily Is Important to Americans, but Defense Not among Most Important Issues in Election," September 27, 2000, www.gallup.com/poll/releases/pr000927.asp.

20. Walter Millis, *Arms and Men: A Study in American Military History* (New York, 1956), pp. 13–53. Though dated, Millis' account remains a classic narrative of the evolution of U.S. military policy and practice. Millis begins his book by quoting Emerson's "Hymn Sung at the Completion of the Battle Monument, Concord," written in 1837.

21. Through 1993 U.S. forces deployed abroad other than for war or for normal peacetime activities a total of 234 times, a number that excludes most of the militarily active Clinton administration. See Congressional Research Service, "Instances of Use of United States Forces Abroad, 1798–1993," October 7, 1993, http://www.history.navy.mil/wars/foabroad.htm.

22. The standard history of the U.S. Army is Russell F. Weigley, *A History of the United States Army,* rev. ed. (Bloomington, Ind., 1984). Narrative accounts of the U.S. Navy are far more numerous. Among the most recent is Nathan Miller, *The U.S. Navy: A History,* 3d ed. (Annapolis, 1997).

23. U.S. Department of Defense, *DoD Selected Manpower Statistics, FY91* (Washington, D.C., 1991), pp. 55–56, 59.

24. For a bracing defense of traditional U.S. military policy, making the case for the superior effectiveness of citizen armies, see Victor Davis Hanson, *The Soul of Battle* (New York, 1999), pts. II and III.

25. Michael S. Sherry, *In the Shadow of War* (New Haven, 1995), pp. 188–205, 233–236.

26. Samuel R. Berger, "American Leadership in the 21st Century," National Press Club, Washington, D.C., January 6, 2000.

27. Buchanan makes his case for reducing U.S. military commitments in *A Republic, Not an Empire* (Washington, D.C., 1999).

28. Samuel R. Berger, "American Power: Hegemony, Isolationism, or Engagement," Council on Foreign Relations, New York, October 21, 1999.

29. In 1998, for example, the U.S. defense budget stood at $266 billion. The combined defense spending of the United Kingdom, France, Germany, Italy, Israel, Japan, Russia, and China was $269 billion; International Institute for Strategic Studies, *The Military Balance* (London, 1999), pp. 300–305.

30. *Report of the Quadrennial Defense Review* (Washington, D.C., May 1997), sec. X.

31. William J. Clinton, *A National Strategy for a New Century* (Washington, D.C., 1998), p. 8.

32. William S. Cohen, "U.S. Must Remain Active in Post–Cold War Foreign Affairs," Foreign Policy Association, New York, April 2, 1998.

33. Bill Clinton, "Remarks by the President to the Economic Club of Detroit," Cobo Conference Center, January 8, 1999.

34. William J. Perry, "Defense in an Age of Hope," *Foreign Affairs* 75 (November/December 1996): 69. See also news release, Office of the Assistant Secretary of Defense (Public Affairs), "U.S. Forces Travel to Croatia for Amphibious Exercise," September 12, 2000; C. J. Chivers, "Long before War, Green Berets Built Military Ties to Uzbekistan," *New York Times*, October 25, 2001, p. A1. In its edition of September 11, 2000, the *New York Times* featured a photograph of American paratroopers from the 82d Airborne Division, dropping from a C-17 transport into Kazakhstan. No article accompanied the photograph, the rationale for a U.S. military presence in Central Asia apparently being self-explanatory.

35. The dominant position to which the United States ascended in the international arms trade offers another striking example of how wielding American military clout became noncontroversial. Following the end of the Cold War, the U.S. share of the global arms trade roughly doubled, so that, measured by value, the United States now sells half of all the weapons sold worldwide. In 1999, for example, that amounted to $26.2 billion in weapons sold abroad. Trailing the United States, which controlled 49.1 percent of the market in 1999, were the United Kingdom with 18.7 percent, France

with 12.4 percent, and Russia with 6.6 percent. Whether the effects of this flourishing trade in arms on international security were good, bad, or indifferent was an issue in which neither political elites nor the national media showed much interest. Like U.S. military dominance in general, American dominance of the international arms market was simply accepted as a fact of life. For details, see International Institute for Strategic Studies, *The Military Balance, 2000–2001* (London, 2000), pp. 288–289. For an update including data from 2000, see Thom Shanker, "Global Arms Sales Rise Again, and the U.S. Leads the Pack," *New York Times,* August 20, 2001, p. A3.

36. William S. Cohen, "Security in a Grave New World," Council on Foreign Relations, New York, September 14, 1998; idem, "Economic Strategy Institute Global Forum," Washington, D.C., May 15, 2000; idem, "International Community Still Relies on U.S. Leadership," Wehrkunde Conference, Germany, February 8, 1998; idem, "World Economic Forum," Washington, D.C., May 24, 2000. For further discussion of this theme, see Cohen, "Economic Strategy Institute Global Forum," May 15, 2000.

37. Cohen, "U.S. Must Remain Active in Post–Cold War Foreign Affairs," April 2, 1998.

38. Chalmers Johnson, *Blowback: The Costs and Consequences of American Empire* (New York, 2000), p. 11.

39. Ibid., pp. 34–64.

40. The cited text appears in ads for the F-22—dubbed "the anti-war plane"—placed in major newspapers by the consortium of Lockheed Martin, Boeing, and Pratt & Whitney. See *Washington Post,* March 18, 1997, p. A14, and April 22, 1997, p. A4.

41. William S. Cohen, "Remarks to International Institute for Strategic Studies," San Diego, September 9, 1999; idem, "Economic Strategy Institute Global Forum," May 15, 2000.

42. General John M. Shalikashvili, *Joint Vision 2010* (Washington, D.C., 1996), p. 2.

43. Ibid., pp. 13, 18, 27, 29.

44. Ibid., passim; see also Jim Garamone, "Joint Forces Command to Test Revolutionary Combat Concept," Armed Forces Information Service, May 8, 2000, http://www.defenselink.mil/cgi-bin/dlprint.

45. General Henry M. Shelton, *Joint Vision 2020* (Washington, D.C., 2000), p. 8. Included among the missions in this category are peacekeeping, peace enforcement, humanitarian relief operations, and "support to domestic authorities."

46. Cohen, "Security in a Grave New World," September 14, 1998.

47. Shalikashvili, *Joint Vision 2010,* p. 2.

48. William S. Cohen, "New Defense Strategy: Shape, Respond, and Repair," testimony before the Senate Armed Services Committee, February 3, 1998.

"Our vision can be characterized in one word: transformation," Cohen told the senators.

49. Colin L. Powell, *My American Journey* (New York, 1995), p. 437.

50. Bill Clinton, "A New Covenant for American Security," Georgetown University, December 12, 1991.

51. Secretary of Defense Les Aspin, "New Force for a New Era: How the Clinton Administration Is Reshaping American Defense," Georgetown University, September 2, 1993, Federal News Service.

52. Secretary of Defense Les Aspin, "FY94 Budget for the Department of Defense," testimony before the Senate Appropriations Committee, September 14, 1993, Federal Document Clearing House.

53. Donald Kagan and Frederick W. Kagan, *While America Sleeps: Self-Delusion, Military Weakness, and the Threat to Peace Today* (New York, 2000), p. 303.

54. General Colin Powell, "Department of Defense News Conference," The Pentagon, Washington, D.C., September 1, 1993.

55. For several cases in point, see Thomas E. Ricks and Anne Marie Squeo, "The Price of Power: Why the Pentagon Is Often Slow to Pursue Promising New Weapons," *Wall Street Journal,* October 19, 1999, p. A1.

56. On this point, for the views of one frustrated RMA advocate, a four-star admiral, see Bill Owens with Ed Offley, *Lifting the Fog of War* (New York, 2000), pp. 150–177.

57. For an insightful account of how traditional service identity creates barriers to innovation, see Ricks and Squeo, "The Price of Power."

58. Eliot A. Cohen, "Defending America in the Twenty-first Century," *Foreign Affairs* 79 (November/December 2000): 40–42. For a more extended treatment of this theme, see William Greider, *Fortress America: The American Military and the Consequences of Peace* (New York, 1998).

59. In 2000 the U.S. Army's inventory of aircraft numbered over 5,300, a number that included 292 fixed-wing aircraft and 1,502 attack helicopters. The Navy and Marine Corps had another 1,456 combat aircraft and 543 armed helicopters. The entire Royal Air Force mustered a total of 429 aircraft; International Institute for Strategic Studies, *The Military Balance, 2000–2001,* pp. 26, 28, 82.

60. In 2000 the total strength of the British army was 114,000, the French army 169,300, and the Italian army 153,000; ibid., pp. 29, 58, 67, 80.

61. Cohen, "Defending America in the Twenty-first Century," p. 40. Nor did the component parts change much despite all the talk of revolution. The U.S. Army's "Division XXI" became almost a parody of institutional inertia. Beginning with an organization of approximately 15,000 soldiers organized into three maneuver brigades along with one brigade of helicopters and one of field artillery, the Army invested years of effort to come up with a new design that consisted of approximately 15,000 soldiers organized into three maneuver brigades along with one brigade of helicopters and one of field artillery. Both the old and the new divisions relied chiefly on M1 Abrams

tanks and M2 Bradley Fighting Vehicles. For an effort to depict this as a radical breakthrough see *Military Review* 78 (May–June 1998).

62. Kagan and Kagan, *While America Sleeps.*

63. General Henry H. Shelton, "Remarks at the Fletcher Conference 2000," Arlington, Va., November 16, 2000.

64. Steven Lee Myers, "Military Chief Seeks Money, Saying Forces Are Strapped," *New York Times,* December 15, 2000, p. A22.

65. Gallup Organization, "Gallup Poll Topics: A–Z (Military and National Defense)," www.gallup.com/poll/indicators/indmilitary.asp. Gallup also found that the percentage of Americans believing that the United States spent "too much" on defense had steadily declined, from 50 percent in 1990 to 20 percent in 2000. This Gallup Report included polling completed during August 24–27, 2000.

66. Frank Bruni, "Bush Vows Money and Support for Military," *New York Times,* September 24, 1999, p. A22; Eric Schmitt and Steven Lee Myers, "Bush Courts Key Lawmakers for Support on Defense Goals," *New York Times,* January 9, 2001, p. A1.

6. GUNBOATS AND GURKHAS

1. Thomas L. Friedman, "A Manifesto for the Fast World," *New York Times Magazine,* March 28, 1999, p. 40. The credit for the cover photo describes it as "Freedom's Fist."

2. Madeleine Albright, "Remarks at Town Hall Meeting," Ohio State University, February 18, 1998.

3. U.S. Commission on National Security/21st Century, *New World Coming: The United States Commission on National Security/21st Century* (Washington, D.C., 1999), p. 128.

4. For a useful participant's account of the entire Somalia episode, see John L. Hirsch and Robert B. Oakley, *Somalia and Operation Restore Hope: Reflections on Peacemaking and Peacekeeping* (Washington, D.C., 1995).

5. Bush emphasized the limits of the mission in remarks directed to the Somali people: "We do not plan to dictate political outcomes. We respect your sovereignty and independence. . . . We come to your country for one reason only, to enable the starving to be fed"; "President Bush's Speech to the Nation, December 4, 1992," *Foreign Policy Bulletin,* January–April 1993, p. 22.

6. The uniformed military shared the view that Operation Restore Hope had gone swimmingly well. Testifying before a Senate committee, Rear Admiral Mike W. Cramer, director of Current Intelligence (J-2) in the Office of the Joint Chiefs of Staff, assured senators that "there has been none—no—zero—organized resistance to either U.S. forces or the coalition forces by any of the major factions"; U.S. Senate, Committee on Armed Forces, *Joint Chiefs of Staff Briefing on Current Military Operations in Somalia, Iraq, and Yugo-*

slavia, January 29, 1993 (Washington, D.C.: Government Printing Office, 1993).

7. Quoted in Julia Preston, "U.N. Establishes Force for Somalia; All but 9,000 U.S. Troops to Leave by May," *Washington Post,* March 26, 1993, p. A13.

8. An after-action report by a U.S. Army aviation unit touted the utility of the "20mm gun in flex mode [as a] great crowd breaker"; Task Force Raven, "Operation Continue Hope, 27 Aug 93—9 Jan 94, Lessons Learned," filed with Oral History Interview RHIT-C-347, August 20, 1994, U.S. Army Center for Military History, Washington, D.C. See also Captain Charles P. Ferry, "Mogadishu, October 1993," *Infantry* 84 (November–December 1994): 37.

9. Total Somali casualties during the insurgency remain unknown. One senior U.S. officer estimated that between 6,000 and 10,000 Somalis—two-thirds of them women and children—were killed in clashes with peacekeepers; Eric Schmitt, "Somali War Casualties May Be 10,000," *New York Times,* December 8, 1993, p. A14.

10. According to one journalist who reported on Somalia, "The American command believed the Somalis to be intellectually primitive, culturally shallow, and militarily craven"; Jonathan Stevenson, *Losing Mogadishu* (Annapolis, 1995), p. 115.

11. Ibid., p. 94.

12. For the Pentagon's account of the action on October 3, see the testimony by Lieutenant General John Sheehan and Rear Admiral Mike Cramer, *Hearings before the Committee on Armed Services, United States Senate,* October 4, 1993 (Washington, D.C.: Government Printing Office, 1994), pp. 37–64. For a bestselling narrative, see Mark Bowden, *Black Hawk Down: A Story of Modern War* (New York, 1999).

13. The best analysis of the operation, the so-called Warner-Levin Report, debunks the notion that armor would have made any difference. The report "Review of the Circumstances Surrounding the Ranger Raid on October 3–4, 1993 in Mogadishu, Somalia," dated September 29, 1995, was prepared by Senators John Warner and Carl Levin.

14. The Pentagon's response to the genocide in Rwanda the following year emphasized its willingness to obstruct or undermine policies not to its liking. When the killing began in Rwanda in May 1994, an administration badly burned by Mogadishu had no intention of risking a major involvement of U.S. troops. But to make at least a show of concern, President Clinton offered to provide out of U.S. stocks in Europe several dozen armored personnel carriers to outfit an intervention force being assembled under UN auspices. The UN requested the vehicles on May 16. On May 27 the Clinton administration agreed to fulfill that request. Nearly two months elapsed before U.S. aircraft actually delivered them to Africa. The Pentagon had spent the ensuing weeks haggling with UN officials over the terms of the lease. Among other things, the Pentagon was insistent that the vehicles be flown (not shipped) to the United States once they were no longer required.

When the vehicles did finally arrive—without the machine guns and radios and therefore unusable—the genocide had run its course. There is no question that if the Pentagon had wanted this operation to move forward, it would have been completed in a matter of days. See Donatella Lorch, "Bodies from Rwanda Cast a Pall on Lakeside Villages in Uganda," *New York Times*, May 28, 1994, p. 1; Julia Preston, "U.N. Rwanda Force Beset by Shortages, Disputes," *Washington Post*, June 8, 1994, p. A27; Michael R. Gordon, "U.N.'s Rwanda Deployment Slowed by Lack of Vehicles," *New York Times*, June 9, 1994, p. A10; Michael R. Gordon, "U.S. to Supply 60 Vehicles for U.N. Troops in Rwanda," *New York Times*, June 16, 1994, p. A12; Richard Dowden, "U.S. Tardiness 'Made Genocide Easier,'" *The Independent* (London), August 4, 1994, p. 14.

15. Some analysts questioned whether the public's sensitivity to casualties was real or only apparent. For example, see Peter D. Feaver and Christopher Gelpi, "A Look at . . . Casualty Aversion," *Washington Post*, November 7, 1999, p. B3. No one disputed that policymakers *believed* it to be real and acted accordingly. As did the officer corps itself: the traditional responsibility of leaders to care for their soldiers mutated into a new imperative in which mission accomplishment took a back seat to casualty avoidance. "I tell my men every day there is nothing there worth one of them dying for" was the not atypical comment offered by one young officer regarding his service in Bosnia. "Because minimizing—really prohibiting—casualties is the top-priority mission I have been given by my battalion commander"; Tom Bowman, "Debating a No-Casualty Order," *Boston Globe*, April 9, 2000, p. A21.

16. William Appleman Williams, *Empire as a Way of Life* (New York, 1980), p. 127.

17. The June 1993 cruise missile attack was by no means the first post–Desert Storm punitive strike against Iraq. The Bush administration had also launched small-scale attacks, the most recent just days before George H. W. Bush left office. On January 17, 1993, forty-five Tomahawk cruise missiles attacked a nuclear fabrication plant in Zaafaraniyah, south of Baghdad. The following day coalition aircraft attacked components of the Iraqi air defense system in the southern no-fly zone. See Paul Lewis, "Raid on Iraq; U.S. Is Broadening Enforcement Role," *New York Times*, January 18, 1993, p. A8; Paul K. White, *Crises after the Storm* (Washington, D.C., 1999), pp. 23–24.

18. Bill Clinton, "Remarks by the President in Address to Nation," Washington, D.C., June 26, 1993.

19. For criticism of the operation from opposite ends of the political spectrum, see Charles Krauthammer, "Baghdad Bungle," *Washington Post*, July 9, 1993, p. A21; and Alexander Cockburn, "An Attack as American as Apple Pie," *Los Angeles Times*, June 29, 1993, p. B7.

20. American devotion to Kurdish well-being was less than absolute. Though committed to protecting the Kurds from Saddam, the United States turned a blind eye to periodic Turkish incursions into northern Iraq intended to prevent the revival of a Kurdish insurrection that had previously threatened

Turkey. Only by allowing the Turks free rein against the Kurds could the United States secure continued use of the Turkish air base from which U.S. forces operated to protect the Kurds from Iraq; Jonathan S. Landay, "Turkey's Leader Poses Hard Test for Clinton," *Christian Science Monitor*, April 18, 1995, p. 3.

21. Bill Clinton, "Statement by the President," September 3, 1996.

22. One enthusiastic commentator observed that "the president's limber trigger finger is making it hard for the yahoo right to keep portraying him, as it loves to do, as 'President Sissy'"; Tom Teepen, "No 'President Sissy' for U.S.," *Cleveland Plain Dealer*, September 18, 1996, p. 2C.

23. International Committee of the Red Cross, *Iraq: A Decade of Sanctions* (December, 14, 1999), www.icrc.org. This report describes the sharp rise in infant mortality and malnourishment, the collapse of the public health system, and the limited availability of drinkable water, sewage treatment, and electric power in Iraq during the decade since sanctions were imposed in 1990.

24. Jack Keller, "Iraqis' Wrath Intensifies with Their Suffering," *USA Today*, January 18, 1999, p. 12A.

25. William S. Cohen, "DoD News Briefing," Washington, D.C., December 16, 1998.

26. White, *Crises after the Storm*, pp. 58–60.

27. For a critical assessment of press coverage, see Seth Ackerman, "Bombs Away!" *In These Times* 23 (February 7, 1999): 8.

28. Cohen, "DoD News Briefing," December 19, 1998; Linda D. Kozaryn, "Zinni Says Saddam's 'Shaken, Desperate,'" Armed Forces Information Service, January 21, 1999.

29. The northern no-fly zone encompassed Iraqi territory north of the 36th parallel. Initially, the southern no-fly zone encompassed all of Iraq south of the 32d parallel. In September 1996, at the time of the Irbil incursion, the zone was extended northward to the 33d parallel. When first implemented, British and French combat aircraft joined U.S. aircraft in enforcing the zones. On December 15, 1998, French forces suspended their participation.

30. White, *Crises after the Storm*, pp. 61–65.

31. Brigadier General David A. Deptula, quoted in John T. Correll, "Northern Watch," *Air Force Magazine*, February 2000, p. 32. Deptula commanded U.S. forces policing the northern no-fly zone. Needless to say, U.S. officials argued that hostilities with Iraq did not constitute war as such. "We are not at war with Iraq," remarked Under Secretary of State Thomas Pickering seven months into the campaign, preferring the phrase "state of animosity"; Lisa Hoffman, "Chess Game Continues above Iraq," *Chicago Sun-Times*, July 13, 1999, p. 23.

32. For details on Operation Northern Watch see the excellent Web site of the Federation of American Scientists, www.fas.org/man/dod-101/ops/north-

ern_watch.htm. On Operation Southern Watch, see http://www.fas.org/
man/dod-101/ops/southern_watch.htm.

33. "Six Killed in Air Raid, Baghdad Says," *Boston Sunday Globe,* January 21,
2001, p. A4; International Institute for Strategic Studies, *Strategic Survey
2000–2001* (London, 2000), "Strategic Geography 2000/2001," p. v.

34. To reduce the prospect of public attention even further, the United States
went to extraordinary lengths to keep the number of Iraqi noncombatant
casualties low, even using inert warheads on very expensive precision
guided munitions; Steven Lee Myers, "Defter Weapon against Iraqis: Concrete Warhead," *New York Times,* October 7, 1999, p. A1.

35. In a maritime equivalent of the no-fly zones, U.S. Navy surface ships also
enforced an embargo on Iraq intended to prevent Saddam Hussein from il-
legally exporting oil and from importing prohibited goods. This effort, too,
was largely meaningless, since Saddam found other ways to circumvent the
economic sanctions—for example, through illicit trading with neighbors
such as Turkey and Jordan.

36. Bill Clinton, "Address to the Nation by the President," August 20, 1998;
William S. Cohen, "We Are Ready to Act Again," *Washington Post,* August
23, 1998, p. C1.

37. According to South Korean sources, in what would have been an even
more spectacular demonstration of gunboat diplomacy, the Clinton administration also came very close to bombing North Korea. In June 1994
a U.S. carrier task force off Korea's east coast was reportedly poised to
launch strikes aimed at destroying North Korea's suspected nuclear weapons development facility at Yongbyon. In an urgent last-minute appeal to
the White House, South Korean President Kim Young-Sam reportedly
talked Bill Clinton into calling off the attack; Agence France Press, "South
Korea Stopped U.S. Strike on North Korea: Former President," May 24,
2000.

38. Major General Charles Wald, "Dueling Doctrines: The New American Way
of War," Center for Strategic and International Studies, Washington, D.C.,
June 25, 1998, quoted in White, *Crises after the Storm,* p. 83. Wald was director of strategic plans for the U.S. Air Force.

39. U.S. Census Bureau, *Statistical Abstract of the United States: 2000,* table 565,
www.census.gov/prod/www/statistical-abstract-us.html.

40. *Budget of the United States Government, Fiscal Year 2000,* http:\\w3.access.gpo.
gov/usbudget/fy2000/maindown.html.

41. U.S. Department of Labor, Bureau of Labor Statistics, *Consumer Expenditures
in 1999* (May 2001), table A, http:\\stats.bls.gov/csxhome.htm.

42. Census Bureau, *Statistical Abstract, 2000,* tables 1 and 577; Allan R. Millett
and Peter Maslowski, *For the Common Defense,* rev. ed. (New York, 1994),
app. B, p. 655.

43. Only the 1980s came close. But the death toll resulting from the Beirut
bombing of 1983 alone almost equaled the losses incurred as a result of hos-

tile acts during all of the 1990s. See "The Toll: Losing Troops," *New York Times,* June 4, 1999, p. A17. During the 1990s the number of American soldiers committing suicide (2,058) exceeded the number killed in action by a factor of eight; Census Bureau, *Statistical Abstract, 2000,* table 582.

44. Quoted in Mark Sullivan, *"Our Times": The United States, 1900–1925,* vol. 1 (New York, 1926), p. 48.

45. Of all the post-Mogadishu occasions on which the Clinton administration employed force, only the intervention in Haiti in 1994 conformed to neither the gunboat nor the Gurkha paradigm. As planned, Operation Uphold Democracy would have involved sending large numbers of U.S. ground troops into combat. Although the invading forces would undoubtedly have made quick work of Haiti's feeble security forces, the campaign could well have involved real fighting and real casualties. Only the fact that the ruling junta in Port-au-Prince at the eleventh hour capitulated in the face of direct U.S. threats averted that prospect. U.S. forces arrived, to great fanfare restored Jean Bertrand Aristide to the presidency, made a brief stab at solving some of Haiti's underlying problems, and then left, having achieved next to nothing. For a vividly written and highly critical account, see Bob Shacochis, *The Immaculate Invasion* (New York, 1999). Uphold Democracy merits attention less as an illustration of any "new" strategy than as testimony to the continuing vitality of a centurylong tradition of U.S. armed intervention in the Caribbean. By dispatching U.S. troops to occupy Haiti, Bill Clinton added his name to the long list of predecessors—Republicans and Democrats, conservatives and liberals, "isolationists" and internationalists—stretching back to William McKinley, who found disorder or defiance in or near the Caribbean Basin intolerable. A tabulation of overt and covert U.S. armed intervention in the Caribbean over the past one hundred years would include William McKinley (Cuba and Puerto Rico); Theodore Roosevelt (Panama, the Dominican Republic, and Cuba); William Howard Taft (Nicaragua); Woodrow Wilson (Mexico, Haiti, the Dominican Republic); Calvin Coolidge (Nicaragua); Dwight D. Eisenhower (Guatemala); John F. Kennedy (Cuba); Lyndon B. Johnson (the Dominican Republic); Ronald Reagan (Grenada, Nicaragua, El Salvador); George Bush (Panama); and Bill Clinton (Haiti). The strategy of openness does not oblige the United States to surrender its long-standing prerogative to police the "American Lake." Clinton's intervention in Haiti indicated that the lake remained closed to outsiders.

46. Bill Clinton, "Remarks by the President upon Departing from Auckland, New Zealand," September 14, 1999.

47. Australia provided 4,500 troops out of 7,500 deployed; International Institute for Strategic Studies, "The East Timor Crisis," *Strategic Comments* 5 (October 1999): 1.

48. Jan Wesner Childs, "U.S. Forces in East Timor Change Command," *Pacific Stars and Stripes,* February 1, 2000, http://www.fas.org/man/dod-101/ops/2000/000201-timor-edtu.htm.

49. David Watts, "Howard's 'Sheriff' Role Angers Asians," *The Times* (London), September 27, 1999.

50. For a concise account of Sierra Leone's history and recent travails, see John L. Hirsch, *Sierra Leone: Diamonds and the Struggle for Democracy* (Boulder, 2001). Hirsch served from 1995 to 1998 as U.S. ambassador in Freetown.

51. Ryan Lizza, "Where Angels Fear to Tread," *New Republic* 223 (July 24, 2000): 22–27; William Reno, "The Failure of Peacekeeping in Sierra Leone," *Current History* 100 (May 2001): 219–225.

52. Jane Perlez, "U.S. to Send G.I.'s to Train Africans for Sierra Leone," *New York Times,* August 9, 2000, p. A1.

53. Ivan Watson, "Green Berets Train Nigerian Troops to Quell Rebel Violence in Sierra Leone," *San Francisco Chronicle,* January 26, 2001, p. A12.

54. Madeleine K. Albright, "Press Briefing: International Narcotics Control Strategy Report, 1996," Washington, D.C., February 28, 1997.

55. According to a 1997 State Department report, the United States "made solid gains against the drug trade in 1996." The solid gains were an 18 percent reduction in coca production in Peru and a 12 percent reduction in Bolivia, which the report went on to acknowledge "was more than offset by a 32 percent increase in both coca cultivation and potential coca leaf production in Colombia"; U.S. Department of State, "International Narcotics Control Strategy Report, 1996," Washington, D.C., March 1997.

56. The U.S. role in drafting Plan Colombia is suggested by the fact that when the plan first appeared in September 1999, it was written in English; a Spanish-language version appeared only months later; Tina Rosenberg, "The Great Cocaine Quagmire," *Rolling Stone,* April 12, 2001, p. 52.

57. In 1995 Colombia had received $30 million in security assistance from the United States. By 2000 only Israel and Egypt surpassed Colombia in the amount of U.S. military aid; John Donnelly and Richard Chacon, "Worlds Apart," *Boston Globe,* February 22, 2000, p. A6.

58. For a detailed description of U.S. security assistance in support of Plan Colombia, see Center for International Policy, "Colombia," http://www.ciponline.org/facts/co.htm, June 22, 2001. The Colombian military has a notoriously poor human rights record. U.S. officials vowed that human rights considerations would be central to U.S. support for Plan Colombia. In fact, in August 2000 President Clinton issued a waiver indicating that assistance to the Colombian security forces would *not* be contingent on their respect for human rights; William J. Clinton, memorandum for the Secretary of State, "Presidential Determination on Waiver of Certification under Section 3201 'Conditions on Assistance for Colombia,' in Title III, Chapter 2 of the Emergency Supplemental Act, FY 2000, as Enacted in Public Law 106–246, August 23, 2000."

59. Training of the first battalion, which began more than a year before Congress approved the $1.3 billion package in July 2000, was paid for out of Pentagon discretionary funds. The United States trained three battalions in

all, the last completing the program in May 2001; Center for International Policy, "Colombia."

60. John Donnelly and Richard Chacon, "Worlds Apart," *Boston Globe,* February 22, 2000, p. A6. The brackets are in the original text. The Clinton administration adamantly insisted that Colombia would not be another Vietnam. It said that the United States was supporting the Colombian army's attacks on drug trafficking, not its war on rebel groups such as the Revolutionary Armed Forces of Colombia (FARC) and the National Liberation Army (ELN). Yet with the United States freely admitting that rebel groups were in the drug business and at least one senior official acknowledging that "if the guerrillas are armed and protecting the drug trafficking, they are part of a counter-narcotics operation," the distinction between the two was a fine one. Under Secretary of State Thomas R. Pickering, "Under Secretary Pickering on His Trip to Colombia," Washington, D.C., November 27, 2000.

61. Julian Borger and Martin Hodgson, "A Plane Is Shot Down and the U.S. Proxy War on Drug Barons Unravels," *The Guardian* (London), June 2, 2001, http://www.guardian.co.uk/Archive/Article/0,4273,4197028,00. html.

62. In 1992 three DynCorp employees were killed flying counternarcotics missions in Peru. In 1998 two more died when their crop-duster crashed in Colombia. In neither case did the incident provoke more than a passing ripple of interest. Sam Dillon, "Peru Rebels Say They Downed U.S. Chopper," *Miami Herald,* January 20, 1992, p. A11; "U.S. Pilots Die in Colombia," *New York Times,* July 29, 1998, p. A2.

63. Ken Silverstein, "Privatizing War," *The Nation* 265 (July 28–August 4, 1997): 12.

64. MPRI also numbered among the private-sector security firms that played a part in protecting the diamond mines of war-wracked Sierra Leone; Hirsch, *Sierra Leone,* p. 66.

65. Silverstein, "Privatizing War," pp. 15–16.

66. David Shearer, *Private Armies and Military Intervention,* Adelphi Paper 316 (London: Oxford University Press, 1998), p. 62.

67. As late as June 1995 the president clung to this position. See Bill Clinton, "Remarks by the President in Town Hall Meeting," Billings, Mont., June 1, 1995: "All that [military intervention] would do is get a lot of Americans killed and not achieve the objective."

68. Quoted in Richard Holbrooke, *To End a War* (New York, 1999), p. 21.

69. Steven L. Burg and Paul L. Shoup, *The War in Bosnia-Herzegovina* (Armonk, N.Y., 1999), pp. 324–325.

70. Robert C. Owen, "The Balkans Air Campaign Study: Part 2," *Airpower Journal* 11 (Fall 1997), www.airpower.maxwell.af.mil/airchronicles/apj/apj97/ fal97/fal97.html. Colonel Owen, a senior faculty member of the Air War College, was the principal coordinator of the U.S. Air Force official report on Operation Deliberate Force. This article, along with Part 1, appearing in the

summer 1997 issue of *Airpower Journal,* provides an unclassified summary of that report.

71. Benjamin S. Lambeth, *The Transformation of American Air Power* (Ithaca, N.Y., 2000), pp. 174–178, titled "Operation Deliberate Force Scores a Win."

72. Burg and Shoup, *The War in Bosnia-Herzegovina,* p. 327.

73. Holbrooke, *To End a War,* p. 73.

74. Thomas K. Adams, "The New Mercenaries and the Privatization of Conflict," *Parameters* 29 (Summer 1999) 109–110; Shearer, *Private Armies and Military Intervention,* pp. 58–61.

75. Holbrooke, *To End a War,* p. 160.

76. Only at this juncture did the administration evince willingness to commit U.S. ground troops. In December 1995 a robust contingent of 20,000 G.I.s led a large NATO force into Bosnia to supervise the peace, with an explicit presidential promise to terminate the mission in one year. Even then, a risk-averse administration and a military leadership suspicious of anything that even smacked of "nation-building" ordered the Americans to operate under the narrowest conceivable terms of reference. Bosnia would not become another Somalia. Bill Clinton, "Statement by the President," Washington, D.C., November 27, 1995.

77. Shearer, *Private Armies and Military Intervention,* p. 62.

78. For more on this theme, see Eliot A. Cohen, "Kosovo and the New American Way of War," in *War over Kosovo: Politics and Strategy in a Global Age,* ed. Andrew J. Bacevich and Eliot A. Cohen (New York, 2001), pp. 38–62.

7. RISE OF THE PROCONSULS

1. Frank Rich, "The Age of the Mediathon," *New York Times Magazine,* October 29, 2000, p. 58. For an evaluation of the Persian Gulf War's large if problematic legacy, see Andrew J. Bacevich, "A Less than Splendid Little War," *Wilson Quarterly* 25 (Winter 2001): 83–94.

2. For an interpretive overview of U.S. civil-military relations, see Andrew J. Bacevich, "Neglected Trinity: Kosovo and the Transformation of U.S. Civil-Military Relations," in *War over Kosovo: Politics and Strategy in a Global Age,* ed. Andrew J. Bacevich and Eliot A. Cohen (New York, 2001), pp. 155–188.

3. Colin Powell, *My American Journey* (New York, 1995), p. 532.

4. Some officers found these expressions of regard less than persuasive. General Wesley K. Clark's view was that after Desert Storm "Americans *tried* to make up with their armed forces"; Clark, *Waging Modern War* (New York, 2001), p. 18 (emphasis added).

5. For a detailed account of Tailhook, see Office of the Inspector General, Department of Defense, *The Tailhook Report* (New York, 1993), especially pp. 37–74.

6. David Singband, "Hazing Persists at Military Academies, Report Says," *Cleveland Plain Dealer,* November 22, 1992, p. 8A.

7. The marines would experience similar problems with training units at Fort Leonard Wood, Missouri; James Dao, "A Sexual Harassment Scandal Confronts the Marines," *New York Times*, April 25, 2001, p. A13.

8. See Kelly Flinn, *Proud to Be: My Life, the Air Force, the Controversy* (New York, 1997).

9. For a book-length assessment of the military and gender by a journalist critical of what she perceives as a feminized force, see Stephanie Gutmann, *The Kinder, Gentler Military: Can America's Gender-Neutral Fighting Force Still Win Wars?* (New York, 2000).

10. Laurence M. Cruz, "General Fined for Having Affairs," *Boston Globe*, March 18, 1999, p. A17. Two admirals were also disciplined and reduced in rank for charges relating to adulterous relationships; Frank Bruni, "Adultery Alone Often Fails to Prompt a Military Prosecution," *New York Times*, December 18, 1998, p. 29.

11. Christopher Marquis, "General Seeks to Retire as Charges Are Supported," *New York Times*, July 8, 2000, p. A9.

12. In remarks to the press, the admiral had wondered aloud why some U.S. marines accused of raping a young Okinawan girl had not availed themselves of the services of a prostitute instead; John Diamond, "Admiral's Relationship with Officer Assailed," *Chicago Sun-Times*, October 16, 1996, p. 28.

13. Dana Priest, "Controversy Erupts over General Ralston," *Washington Post*, June 6, 1997, p. A1.

14. For an example of the latter, see the savage attack on the Navy's senior leaders by Naval Academy graduate, highly decorated marine combat veteran, and former secretary of the navy James H. Webb, "The Navy Adrift," *Washington Post*, April 28, 1996, p. C7. Webb accused members of the Navy's leadership of being "guilty of the ultimate disloyalty: To save or advance their careers, they [have] abandoned the very ideals of their profession to curry favor with politicians."

15. Peter Boyer, "Admiral Boorda's War," *New Yorker*, September 16, 1996, pp. 68–86.

16. The characterization is that of Major General Harold Campbell speaking at a U.S. Air Force banquet in the Netherlands on May 24, 1993; Michael R. Gordon, "General Ousted for Derisive Remarks about President," *New York Times*, June 19, 1993, p. 9.

17. The press coverage generated by this controversy was massive. But see, for example, John H. Cushman Jr., "Top Military Officers Object to Lifting Homosexual Ban," *New York Times*, November 14, 1992, p. 9.

18. David S. Jonas and Hagen W. Frank, "Basic Military Leadership," *Washington Post*, April 4, 1993, p. C7.

19. Thomas E. Ricks, "Military Is Becoming More Conservative, Study Says," *Wall Street Journal*, November 11, 1997, p. A20; Adam Clymer, "Sharp Divergence Found in Views of Military and Civilians, *New York Times*, Septem-

ber 9, 1999, p. A15. The authoritative study is Peter D. Feaver and Richard H. Kohn, eds., *Soldiers and Civilians: The Civil-Military Gap and American National Security* (Cambridge, Mass., 2001).

20. At its national convention in 1996 the Republican party went to great lengths to cement its identity as the "military party." See Andrew J. Bacevich and Richard H. Kohn, "The Grand Army of the Republicans," *New Republic* 217 (December 8, 1997): 22–25. In addition, the party directed advertising campaigns at military voters that accused the commander-in-chief and the vice president of having "damaged our military's readiness and hurt troop morale," after which "they even bragged about it." See the ad "Keeping the Commitment: Republicans Reverse Years of Military Neglect," paid for by the Republican National Committee, appearing in the *Air Force Times,* December 13, 1999, p. 57.

21. For something of a milestone in this regard, see Charles G. Boyd, "America Prolongs the War in Bosnia," *New York Times,* August 9, 1995, p. A19. Boyd was an Air Force four-star general who had just stepped down from his position as deputy commander-in-chief of United States European Command. His *Times* op-ed—published in longer form as an essay in *Foreign Affairs*—offered an extended critique of the Clinton administration's Balkan policy and made the case for the military's preferred policy of noninvolvement.

22. See, for example, Bill Gertz, *Betrayal: How the Clinton Administration Undermined American Security* (Washington, D.C., 1999), a bestseller written by a journalist who is a favored recipient of classified documents leaked by the Pentagon.

23. Richard H. Kohn, "Out of Control: The Crisis in Civil-Military Relations," *National Interest* 35 (Spring 1994): 3–17; Charles J. Dunlap Jr., "The Origins of the American Military Coup of 2012," *Parameters* 22 (Winter 1992–93): 2–20. But see also idem, "Welcome to the Junta: The Erosion of Civilian Control of the U.S. Military," *Wake Forest Law Review* 29 (1994): 341–392; A. J. Bacevich, "Clinton's Military Problem—and Ours," *National Review* 45 (December 13, 1993): 36–40; idem, "Civilian Control: A Useful Fiction?" *JFQ: Joint Force Quarterly* 6 (Autumn/Winter 1994–95): 80–83.

24. Andrew J. Bacevich, "Losing Private Ryan," *National Review* 51 (August 9, 1999): 32–34.

25. By 1999, for example, the U.S. Army was spending $11,000 to enlist a single recruit—costs per capita far greater than in the private sector—and yet still came up 6,300 soldiers short for the year; Andrea Stone, "Paying High Price for Preparedness," *USA Today,* October 22, 1999, p. 18A. The other services also encountered recruiting challenges to varying degrees, the marines less so than the Navy and Air Force. All made major increases in the resources devoted to recruiting, in terms of advertising dollars, enlistment bonuses, and personnel devoted to recruiting. See Greg Jaffe, "The Military Wages Uphill Battle to Find the Willing and Able," *Wall Street Journal,* September 23, 1999, p. A1.

26. Among Clinton's top advisers, only Vice President Al Gore had served on active duty.

27. For an essay that attributes civil-military friction to the interplay of institutional stress induced by change in three dimensions—culture, technology, and strategy—see Andrew J. Bacevich, "Tradition Abandoned: America's Military in a New Era," *National Interest* 48 (Summer 1997): 16–25.

28. Jane Perlez, "For 8 Years, a Strained Relationship with the Military," *New York Times,* December 28, 2000, p. A13.

29. For a concise discussion of the legislation and the controversies surrounding its creation, see John Whiteclay Chambers II, ed., *The Oxford Companion to American Military History* (New York, 1999), p. 300.

30. Powell, *My American Journey,* pp. 437, 558–559.

31. In this regard, Goldwater-Nichols proved to be a boon, however inadvertently. Formerly, a president hell-bent on using the military to implement some new initiative had felt obliged to solicit the support of all the chiefs; now he had to persuade only a single officer. As for the chiefs of the individual services, having been cut out of the decisionmaking loop they found themselves able to do little other than to leak their dissatisfaction to the press. See David Fulgham, "Military Chiefs Miffed by Lack of Oversight," *Aviation Week and Space Technology,* October 12, 1998, pp. 22–23.

32. Anthony Zinni, remarks at "The Commanders," conference sponsored by the United States Naval Institute, Cantigny, Ill., March 9, 2000.

33. Dana Priest, "A Four Star Foreign Policy? U.S. Commanders Wield Rising Clout, Autonomy," *Washington Post,* September 28, 2000, p. A1. This is part one of an insightful three-part series published under the heading "The Proconsuls." Parts two and three appeared on the following two days.

34. For example, Admiral Raymond Spruance, the victor at Midway, became U.S. ambassador to the Philippines. Lieutenant General Walter Bedell Smith, Eisenhower's chief of staff in the European theater of operations, subsequently served as U.S. ambassador to Moscow and as undersecretary of state.

35. The most complete account of Wood's life is Hermann Hagedorn's uncritical two-volume *Leonard Wood: A Biography* (New York, 1931).

36. On the relationship between Wood and one such protégé, see A. J. Bacevich, *Diplomat in Khaki: Major General Frank Ross McCoy and U.S. Foreign Policy, 1898–1949* (Lawrence, Kans., 1989).

37. On the adventures of the U.S. Marine Corps as "State Department troops" policing the Caribbean, see Allan R. Millett, *Semper Fidelis: The History of the United States Marine Corps* (New York, 1980), pp. 147–211. On Butler, who at the end of his career declared, "I was a racketeer, a gangster for capitalism," see "Smedley Butler on Interventionism," http://www.fas.org/man/smedley.htm.

38. Anthony Zinni, "A Commander's Reflections," U.S. Naval Institute, March 9, 2000, www.proceedings.org/proceedings/articles00/prozinni.htm.

39. Typical are the comments of Admiral Dennis C. Blair, commander-in-chief of United States Pacific Command: "foreign officers who attend American military colleges develop an understanding of the value of professional armed forces, removed from politics and subordinate to civilian government authority. They come to appreciate that reliance on force to resolve internal disputes rather than political accommodation and economic development, stokes the fires of rebellion and drives away investments needed for national growth. They also acquire a deeper appreciation of America's interest in maintaining international security so all may prosper." "Statement of Admiral Dennis C. Blair, U.S. Navy, Commander in Chief, United States Pacific Command, before the Senate Armed Services Committee on Fiscal Year 2002 Posture Statement, 27 March 2001," www.pacom.mil/speeches/sst2001/010327blairtestimonySASC.pdf, accessed July 9, 2001.

40. The staffs of U.S. European Command, Central Command, and Pacific Command each exceed in size the Executive Office of the President. At Southern Command, the smallest of the four, the staff consists of approximately 1,100; Priest, "A Four Star Foreign Policy?"

41. Between 1990 and 2000 the combined budgets of the four regional CINCs rose from $190 million to $381 million, with figures adjusted for inflation; ibid.

42. Peter Pace, "Testimony of Gen. Peter Pace, commander-in-chief, U.S. Southern Command," Senate Armed Services Committee, March 27, 2001, www. ciponline.org/colombia/032701.htm, accessed July 8, 2001; www. pacom. mil/about/pacom.htm, accessed July 9, 2001; www.eucom.mil/strategy/summary.htm, accessed July 9, 2001.

43. www.centcom.mil/theater_strat/theater_strat.htm, accessed July 9, 2001.

44. Dennis C. Blair, "Remarks by Admiral Dennis C. Blair at the World Affairs Council," Anchorage, Alaska, June 25, 2000, www.pacom.mil/speeches/sst2000/WORLD.htm, accessed July 9, 2001.

45. U.S. European Command and U.S. Pacific Command each had their own campuses for instructing foreign officers and defense officials: the George C. Marshall Center for Security Studies in Garmisch, Germany, and the Asia-Pacific Center for Security Studies in Hawaii. The Department of Defense operated three more of these "regional security centers" in the United States: the Center for Hemispheric Studies (focused on the Western Hemisphere), the Africa Center for Strategic Studies, and the NESA Center for Strategic Studies (focused on the Near East and South Asia).

46. www.pacom.mil/speeches/speeches.htm, accessed July 9, 2001.

47. Priest, "A Four Star Foreign Policy?"

48. Dana Priest, "Tension and Teamwork in Indonesia," Washington Post, September 30, 2000, p. A1.

49. Priest, "A Four Star Foreign Policy?" Clark's approach echoed that of General Powell, who recorded that early in his career he had embraced the pre-

cept "you don't know what you can get away with until you try"; Powell, *My American Journey,* p. 167.

50. What do you call the soldiers who do a proconsul's bidding? Terms traditionally favored by Americans, such as Minutemen, doughboys, G.I.'s, or even "the troops," no longer quite capture their essence. In a moment of candor, General Henry Shelton may have supplied the answer when he referred to the members of the post–Cold War armed services as "new centurions"; General Henry Shelton, "Military Priorities and Challenges," Defense Orientation Conference Association Annual Meeting," October 4, 2000.

51. Dana Priest, "With Military, U.S. Makes an Overture to Algeria," *Washington Post,* November 12, 1998, p. 1.

52. At the actual time of the attack on the *Cole,* Zinni was no longer commander-in-chief of U.S. Central Command, having just retired.

53. There were exceptions, among them the journalist William Pfaff. See, for example, his "The Praetorian Guard," *National Interest* 62 (Winter 2000–01): 57–64, which objects to the distortion of U.S. foreign policy through excessive military influence.

54. Clark, *Waging Modern War,* p. xxxi.

55. Clark credits himself with devising the key principles that would form the basis of the Weinberger (and subsequently Weinberger-Powell) doctrine. He quotes himself as a young lieutenant colonel working in the Pentagon telling then–Brigadier General Colin Powell, "Isn't the most important thing never to commit U.S. troops again unless we're going to win? No more gradualism and holding back like in Vietnam, but go in with overwhelming force?"; ibid., p. 7.

56. Ibid., pp. 55, 60, 65–66, 68.

57. Ibid., pp. 68, 111, 129.

58. Ibid., pp. 117, 128.

59. Ibid., p. 119.

60. Ibid., p. 170.

61. Ibid., p. 171.

62. Bill Clinton, "Address by the President to the Nation," Washington, D.C., March 24, 1999.

63. "I don't see this as a long-term operation," Secretary Albright remarked in a televised interview on the first evening of the war; Madeleine Albright, "Interview on PBS Newshour with Jim Lehrer," Washington, D.C., March 24, 1999. The prevailing assumption was that the air campaign would last a handful of days at most.

64. Though considerably embroidered, Clark's promise echoed—no doubt intentionally—General Powell's famous statement at the beginning of Operation Desert Storm about the fate awaiting the Iraqi army: "First, we're going

to cut it off, and then we're going to *kill* it"; Powell, *My American Journey,* p. 509.

65. Clark, *Waging Modern War,* p. 183. At least one subordinate heard them differently. According to Lieutenant General Michael C. Short, Clark's senior air commander, SACEUR's three measures of merit were (1) protect NATO ground forces in the region, (2) maintain alliance unity, and (3) avoid the loss of aircraft or pilots; John A. Tirpak, "Short's View of the Air Campaign," *Air Force* 82 (September 1999), www.afa.org/magazine/watch/0999watch. html.

66. Ivo H. Daalder and Michael E. O'Hanlon, *Winning Ugly: NATO's War to Save Kosovo* (Washington, D.C., 2000), pp. 91–96.

67. Clark, *Waging Modern War,* p. 148.

68. Daalder and O'Hanlon, *Winning Ugly,* pp. 108–115. In all there would be some 850,000 refugees.

69. Francis X. Clines, "NATO Hunting for Serb Forces; U.S. Reports Signs of 'Genocide,'" *New York Times,* March 30, 1999, p. A1.

70. Tirpak, "Short's View of the Air Campaign." "Tank plinking" referred to the use of combat aircraft to destroy individual combat vehicles on the ground.

71. Bill Clinton, "Address by the President to the Nation," Washington, D.C., March 24, 1999; Clark quoted in William M. Arkin, "Operation Allied Force: 'The Most Precise Application of Air Power in History'," in Bacevich and Cohen, *War over Kosovo,* p. 9. By his own account, Clark continued throughout the war to prod his air commanders to do a better job of protecting the Kosovars. It is not clear that their efforts on that score were ever more than halfhearted. See Clark, *Waging Modern War,* pp. 210, 216, 237, 241–242, 245; Michael C. Short, "Testimony before the Armed Services Committee," U.S. Senate, October 21, 1999, www.senate.gov/armed_services/hearings/1999/c991021.htm.

72. On the KLA's background, see Gary T. Dempsey and Roger W. Fontaine, *Fool's Errands* (Washington, D.C., 2001), pp. 138–139.

73. Defense Department spokesman Kenneth Bacon acknowledged on March 30, 1999, that "right now, it is difficult to say that we have prevented one act of brutality at this stage"; quoted in Eric Schmitt, "Bad Weather Hampers Bombers' Effectiveness, U.S. Says," *New York Times,* March 31, 1999, p. A11.

74. Clark, *Waging Modern War,* p. 220.

75. By the end of the campaign NATO had committed 829 aircraft to Operation Allied Force; Arkin, "Operation Allied Force," p. 21.

76. On the unhappy saga of Task Force Hawk, see Michael G. Vickers, "Revolution Deferred: Kosovo and the Transformation of War," in Bacevich and Cohen, *War over Kosovo,* pp. 197–198.

77. Clark, *Waging Modern War,* pp. 278–279.

78. Ibid., pp. 240, 273. The dashes appear in the original text.

79. Ibid., pp. 262–263.

80. Ibid., pp. 245, 424; Arkin, "Operation Allied Force," pp. 11, 28–29.

81. Dana Priest, "United NATO Front Was Divided Within," *Washington Post*, September 21, 1999, p. A1.

82. Arkin, "Operation Allied Force," p. 18.

83. Daalder and O'Hanlon, *Winning Ugly*, p. 171.

84. For example, at Rambouillet the draft agreement had given NATO peace-keepers unlimited access to all of Yugoslavia. Now NATO indicated that it would be satisfied to confine its forces to Kosovo.

85. Clark, *Waging Modern War*, pp. 327–329, 332–337; Daalder and O'Hanlon, *Winning Ugly*, pp. 151–153; Tom Walker and Aidan Laverty, "CIA Aided Kosovo Guerrilla Army," *Sunday Times* (London), March 12, 2000.

86. Steven Erlanger, "NATO Was Closer to Ground War in Kosovo than Is Widely Realized," *New York Times*, November 7, 1999, p. 6.

87. Jane Perlez, "Clinton and the Joint Chiefs to Discuss Ground Invasion," *New York Times*, June 2, 1999, p. A12.

88. For the text of the agreement, see Daalder and O'Hanlon, *Winning Ugly*, pp. 267–272.

89. Arkin, "Operation Allied Force," p. 21. The United States provided the majority of the aircraft participating in Operation Allied Force, including virtually all of those that could effectively deliver precision munitions. Overall, U.S. combat aircraft delivered 83 percent of all munitions dropped on Kosovo and Serbia.

90. The *New York Times* reported that "as the Serbs pulled out over 11 days, NATO commanders counted 220 tanks, 300 armored personnel carriers and 308 artillery batteries along with hundreds of other vehicles and all manner of military equipment loaded on trucks"; Steven Lee Myers, "Damage to Serb Military Less than Expected," *New York Times*, June 28, 1999, p. A8. That Yugoslav forces departed in such apparently good shape triggered an ongoing controversy about the effectiveness of NATO bombing. Clark insisted that Serb forces had suffered grievously. Others challenged that view. See, for example, William Drozdiak, "NATO's Clark Rebuts Critics of Yugoslavia Air War," *Boston Globe*, September 18, 1999, p. A11; John Barry and Evan Thomas, "The Kosovo Cover-Up," *Newsweek*, May 15, 2000, p. 22.

91. Robert G. Kaiser and David Hoffman, "Russia Had Bigger Plan in Kosovo," *Washington Post*, June 25, 1999, p. A1.

92. Clark, *Waging Modern War*, p. 385.

93. Bradley Graham, "NATO Insubordination in Kosovo Is Recalled; General's Orders Disregarded, Shelton Says," *Washington Post*, September 10, 1999, p. A33.

94. Clark, *Waging Modern War*, pp. 394–399.

95. Bill Clinton, "Address to the Nation," June 10, 1999, Federal Document Clearing House.

96. In addition to fifteen pilotless aircraft, NATO did lose two jet fighters, both belonging to the U.S. Air Force, to hostile fire. In both cases the pilot was successfully recovered; International Institute for Strategic Studies, *The Military Balance, 1999–2000* (London, 1999), pp. 20, 102.

97. John M. Broder, "Laurels Elude President as Public Judges a War," *New York Times,* June 22, 1999, p. A22.

98. For a thoughtful exploration of moral issues raised by the war, see Alberto R. Coll, "Kosovo and the Moral Burdens of Power," in Bacevich and Cohen, *War over Kosovo,* pp. 124–154.

99. In 2001 Russia and China signed a "treaty of friendship and cooperation," widely viewed as a strategic partnership directed against the United States. The treaty specified that both sides would "uphold recognized principles and norms of international law against any actions aimed at exerting pressure or interfering, under pretext, with the internal affairs of the sovereign states." This was a clear allusion to the sort of interference that both parties had viewed as so objectionable in Kosovo; "In the Treaty's Words: 'International Stability,'" *New York Times,* July 16, 2001, p. A8.

100. William M. Arkin, "How 'Smart' Was This War Really," June 13, 1999, www.msnbc.com/news/279214.asp. According to Human Rights Watch, NATO's bombing campaign killed at least 500 civilians; Human Rights Watch, "Civilian Deaths in the NATO Air Campaign," February 2000, www.hrw.org/reports/2000/nato/.

101. Interview with Margot Adler, "All Things Considered," National Public Radio, June 29, 1999.

102. Clark, *Waging Modern War,* p. 371.

103. Scott Glover, "Revenge Attacks Fill Police Blotter in Postwar Kosovo," *Los Angeles Times,* July 28, 1999, p. A1; Robert Fisk, "Serbs Murdered by the Hundred since 'Liberation,'" *The Independent* (London), November 24, 1999, p. 15.

104. Dempsey and Fontaine, *Fool's Errands,* pp. 144–148.

105. R. Jeffrey Smith, "A GI's Home Is His Fortress," *Washington Post,* October 5, 1999, p. A11.

106. Don M. Snider, John A. Nagl, and Tony Pfaff, *Army Professionalism, the Military Ethic, and Officership in the 21st Century* (Carlisle Barracks, Pa., 1999); Don M. Snider and Gayle L. Watkins, "The Future of Army Professionalism: A Need for Renewal and Redefinition," *Parameters* 30 (Autumn 2000): 9.

107. Erlanger, "NATO Was Closer to Ground War."

8. DIFFERENT DRUMMERS, SAME DRUM

1. The language, from the 1952 Republican party platform, is quoted in John Lewis Gaddis, *Strategies of Containment* (New York, 1982), p. 128.

2. Herbert S. Parmet, *Eisenhower and the American Crusades* (New York, 1972), pp. 123–125.

3. Robert R. Bowie and Richard H. Immerman, *Waging Peace: How Eisenhower Shaped an Enduring Cold War Strategy* (New York, 1998), pp. 186, 191.

4. "Vice President Gore and Governor Bush Participate in Second Presidential Debate Sponsored by the Presidential Debate Commission," October 11, 2000, Federal Document Clearing House Political Transcripts, accessed on LEXIS-NEXIS, August 6, 2001.

5. See, for example, James Traub, "W's World," *New York Times Magazine*, January 14, 2001.

6. "Excerpted remarks of Bush, Powell," *Boston Sunday Globe*, December 17, 2000, p. A53.

7. This quotation and those that follow are extracted from George W. Bush, "A Distinctly American Internationalism," November 19, 1999, Simi Valley, Calif., www.georgebush.com/speeches/foreignpolicy/foreignpolicy.asp, accessed December 11, 1999.

8. This quotation and those that follow are extracted from George W. Bush, "A Period of Consequences," September 23, 1999, Charleston, S.C., www.georgebush.com/speeches/defense/citadel.asp, accessed February 9, 2000.

9. The Bush campaign promised to increase defense spending by $45 billion over ten years—an increase of 1.5 percent. The Gore campaign promised an increase of $100 billion over the same period; Robert Suro, "Gore, Bush Defense Plans Short of Military Demands," *Washington Post*, October 28, 2000, p. A11.

10. To find the semblance of debate about U.S. foreign policy it was necessary to look beyond the two parties holding a monopoly on political power in America. In the 2000 presidential campaign, the candidate of the Green party, Ralph Nader, and especially the candidate of the Reform party, Patrick J. Buchanan, advanced critiques of what they perceived—accurately—to be a deeply rooted consensus pervading the political establishment. Of the two, Buchanan's views were the more comprehensive. To lay the basis for his latest run for the presidency, Buchanan had written two books on U.S. foreign policy. In *The Great Betrayal* (Boston, 1998), he unleashed a furious broadside against free trade and the prevailing nostrums of U.S. international economic policy. In the sequel, *A Republic, Not an Empire*, he offered a critique of liberal internationalism more generally. Buchanan's preferred approach to policy, which he styled "enlightened nationalism," contained large elements of populism laced with more than a tincture of nativism. Yet Buchanan was almost alone in posing critical questions about U.S. military adventurism in the 1990s, in calling attention to the plight of Americans penalized by the process of globalization, and in acknowledging the quasi-imperial basis of U.S. grand strategy. For his views, he was pilloried by the press and roundly denounced by mainstream Republicans and Democrats alike. See Patrick J. Buchanan, *A Republic, Not an Empire: Reclaiming America's Destiny* (Washington, D.C., 1999), especially pp. 3–42 and 325–356.

11. Quoted in "Forging a New Iraq Policy," *Washington Post*, March 4, 2001.

Wolfowitz independently made the case for a policy of overthrowing Saddam. See Paul Wolfowitz, "Bring Saddam Down," *Ottawa Citizen*, November 25, 1998, p. A19.

12. Testimony of Paul Wolfowitz, "Nomination of Paul Wolfowitz to Be Deputy Secretary of Defense," Senate Armed Services Committee, February 27, 2001, accessed on LEXIS-NEXIS, March 2, 2001.

13. James Dao and Steven Lee Myers, "U.S. and British Jets Strike Air-Defense Centers in Iraq," *New York Times*, February 17, 2001, p. A1.

14. See, for example, Jane Perlez, "Allies Bomb Iraqi Air Defenses in Biggest Attack in 6 Months," *New York Times*, August 11, 2001, p. A6.

15. "In the President's Words on the Bombing: 'It's a Routine Mission,'" *New York Times*, February 17, 2001, p. A4.

16. Jane Perlez, "Powell Goes on the Road and Scores Some Points," *New York Times*, March 2, 2001, p. A6.

17. Craig R. Quigley, "DoD News Briefing," July 31, 2001, http://www.defenselink.mil/news/Jul2001/t07312001_t731dasd.html; Thomas E. Ricks and Vernon Loeb, "Rumsfeld: Iraq Has Rebuilt Defenses," *Washington Post*, August 4, 2001, p. A7; Robert Burns, "U.S. Fighters Bomb Iraq Site in Retaliatory Site," *Boston Globe*, August 8, 2001, p. A8.

18. "Forging a New Iraq Policy," *Washington Post*, March 4, 2001.

19. Quoted in Michael R. Gordon, "Bush Would Stop U.S. Peacekeeping in Balkan Fights," *New York Times*, October 21, 2000, p. A1.

20. Quoted in Alan Sipress, "Powell Vows to Consult Allies on Key Issues," *Washington Post*, February 28, 2001, p. A22.

21. Donald G. McNeil Jr., "NATO Conditionally Approves Troops for Macedonia," *New York Times*, August 22, 2001, p. A3.

22. Quoted in David R. Sands, "Mixed Signals Sent on Evolving Bush Foreign Policy," *Washington Times*, March 9, 2001, p. A1. See also Colin L. Powell, "Remarks with Minister of Foreign Affairs and Trade Han Seung Soo," Seoul, Korea, July 27, 2001 Unless otherwise noted, all quotations by Colin Powell as secretary of state can by found at www.state.gov.

23. R. Rand Beers et al., "On the Record Briefing: Andean Regional Initiative," Department of State, Washington, D.C., May 16, 2001, http://www.state.gov/g/inl/narc/prsrl/index.cfm?docid=2925, accessed August 9, 2001. On the progress achieved as a result of the Clinton administration's efforts, see Christopher Marquis, "America Gets Candid about What Colombia Needs," *New York Times*, February 25, 2001, p. wk1; and Juan Forero, "Foundations for Disaster," ibid., p. wk5; see also Christopher Marquis, "U.S. Finds That Coca Cultivation Is Shifting to Colombia," *New York Times*, March 2, 2001, Internet edition, accessed March 2, 2001.

24. "Letter from Ambassador Prueher to Chinese Foreign Minister of Foreign Affairs Tang," April 11, 2001, http://www.whitehouse.gov/news/releases/2001/04/20010411–1.html.

25. Colin L. Powell, "On the Record Press Briefing (China)," April 6, 2001.

26. David E. Sanger, "Collision with China: The Overview," *New York Times,* April 10, 2001, p. A1.

27. Colin L. Powell, "Press Briefing Enroute to Canberra, Australia," July 29, 2001.

28. Colin L. Powell, "Interview by Judy Woodruff of CNN," August 1, 2001.

29. Thomas E. Ricks, "Pentagon Study May Bring Big Shake-Up," *Washington Post,* February 9, 2001, p. A1.

30. Steven Lee Myers and James Dao, "Bush Plans Modest Increase for the Pentagon," *New York Times,* February 1, 2001, Internet edition, accessed February 1, 2001.

31. James Dao and Thom Shanker, "Military Agenda Appears at Risk," *New York Times,* June 3, 2001, p. A1; Thom Shanker, "Rumsfeld Says Plans for Military Transformation Are Limited," *New York Times,* August 18, 2001, p. A8.

32. Thomas E. Ricks, "Review Fractures Pentagon," *Washington Post,* July 14, 2001, p. A1; Thomas E. Ricks, "For Rumsfeld, Many Roadblocks," *Washington Post,* August 7, 2001, p. A1. The quotation is from General Anthony Zinni.

33. Thom Shanker, "Rumsfeld Is Facing a Deadline in Effort to Reshape the Military," *New York Times,* August 9, 2001, p. A1. The quotation is from General Richard B. Myers, vice chairman of the Joint Chiefs of Staff.

34. Richard A. Gephardt, "The Future of Trans-Atlantic Relations: Collaboration or Confrontation?" Carnegie Endowment for International Peace, Washington, D.C., August 2, 2001, www.ceip.org/files/events/gephardt_transcript.asp.

35. Tom Daschle, "A New Century of American Leadership," Woodrow Wilson International Center for Scholars, Washington, D.C., August 9, 2001, www.senate.gov/daschle/pressroom/speeches/2001AO9615.html.

36. In August 2001, for example, the *New York Times* and the *Washington Post* devoted major same-day coverage to an opinion poll purporting to show public dissatisfaction in Great Britain, France, Italy, and Germany with Bush's foreign policies. By implication, U.S. policies that failed to meet with the approval of public opinion abroad were, by definition, defective; Adam Clymer, "Surveys Find European Public Critical of Bush Policies," *New York Times,* August 16, 2001, p. A6; Keith B. Richburg, "Europeans Object to Bush Approach on Foreign Policy," *Washington Post,* August 16, 2001, p. A17.

37. Barbara Hatch Rosenberg, "Allergic Reaction: Washington's Response to the BWC Protocol," *Arms Control Today,* July/August 2001, http://www.arms control.org/act/2001_07–08/rosenbergjul_aug01.asp; Thomas E. Ricks, "U.S. Signs Treaty on War Crimes Tribunal," *Washington Post,* January 1, 2001 , p. A1. If Somalia had been a "gift" that the elder Bush bequeathed to Clinton, then the International Criminal Court was among the gifts that Clinton handed to Bush's son.

38. Eric Schmitt, "Global Warming: Congress, the Kibbitzer at the Climate Table, Waits for Its Turn," *New York Times*, December 1, 1997, p. F6; James Bennet, "Warm Globe, Hot Politics," *New York Times*, December 11, 1997, p. A1; John M. Broder, "Clinton Adamant on 3d World Role in Climate Accord," *New York Times*, December 12, 1997, p. A1.

39. Lawrence F. Kaplan, "On Foreign Policy, Democrats Court European Voters," *Wall Street Journal*, August 16, 2001, p. A14.

40. Condoleezza Rice, "Condoleezza Rice Delivers Remarks on Foreign Policy Issues," Federal Document Clearing House Political Transcripts, November 16, 2000, accessed on LEXIS-NEXIS, March 14, 2001.

41. Colin L. Powell, "Remarks at Confirmation Hearing," Senate Foreign Relations Committee, Washington, D.C., January 17, 2001.

42. "Excerpted Remarks of Bush, Powell," *Boston Sunday Globe*, December 17, 2000, p. A53.

43. George W. Bush, "Address of the President to the Joint Session of Congress," Washington, D.C., February 27, 2001; idem, "Remarks by the President at Christening Ceremony for the USS *Ronald Reagan*," Newport News, Va., March 4, 2001. Unless otherwise noted, all statements by President George W. Bush can be found at www.whitehouse.gov.

44. Colin L. Powell, "Remarks at Council of the Americas' 31st Washington Conference, Washington, D.C., May 7, 2001; Robert Zoellick, "President Bush's Trade Agenda," testimony before the House Ways and Means Committee, March 7, 2001, Federal News Service.

45. David E. Sanger, "Bush Links Trade with Democracy at Quebec Talks," *New York Times*, April 21, 2001, p. 1.

46. "Bush's Vision: 'We Will Not Trade Away the Fate of Free European Peoples,'" *New York Times*, June 16, 2001, p. A8.

47. Colin L. Powell, "The Work of a Hemisphere," *New York Times*, April 19, 2001, p. A25.

48. Raymond Aron, *The Imperial Republic: The United States and the World, 1945–1973* (Englewood Cliffs, N.J., 1974), p. 176.

49. Richard N. Haass, "Imperial America," paper presented at the Atlanta Conference, November 11, 2000, www.brook.edu/views/articles/haass/2000 imperial.htm, accessed October 22, 2001.

50. Colin L. Powell, "Third Annual Kahlil Gibran Spirit of Humanity Awards Gala," Arab American Institute Foundation, Washington, D.C., May 5, 2001.

51. Bush, "Remarks at Christening Ceremony for USS *Ronald Reagan*," March 4, 2001.

52. Interview by Haim Zaltzman, "The Future of Foreign Policy," *Hoover Digest*, no. 4 (1999), Hoover Institution, hoover/stanford.edu/publications/digest/994/rice.html.

53. George W. Bush, "Remarks by the President to Central Intelligence Employees," CIA Headquarters, Langley, Va., March 20, 2001.

54. George W. Bush, "Address of the President to the Joint Session of Congress," February 27, 2001.

55. Bush, "Remarks at Christening Ceremony for USS *Ronald Reagan*," March 4, 2001.

56. Some might cite Patrick Buchanan as an exception. But Buchanan received less than 1 percent of the vote in the 2000 presidential election.

57. Daschle, "New Century of American Leadership," August 9, 2001.

58. Wolfowitz, "Nomination to Be Deputy Secretary of Defense," February 27, 2001.

59. Ibid.

60. Rice, "Remarks on Foreign Policy Issues," November 16, 2000.

61. Cover text, *New Republic* 224 (March 12, 2001).

62. "Excerpted Remarks of Bush, Powell."

9. WAR FOR THE IMPERIUM

1. Colin L. Powell, "Remarks at Council of the Americas' 31st Washington Conference," Washington, D.C., May 7, 2001.

2. Patrick E. Tyler, "Russia and U.S. Optimistic on Defense Issues," *New York Times*, October 19, 2001, p. A1.

3. George W. Bush, "President Bush's Address to a Joint Session of Congress and the American People," September 20, 2001.

4. Donald H. Rumsfeld, "DoD News Briefing—Secretary Rumsfeld," September 20, 2001. Unless otherwise noted, all quotations from Donald H. Rumsfeld and other senior defense officials or military officers can be found at www.defenselink.mil.

5. Donald H. Rumsfeld, "A New Kind of War," *New York Times*, September 27, 2001. Even defining victory in such a war posed a daunting challenge. One of Rumsfeld's first efforts to do so produced the following: "I say that victory is persuading the American people and the rest of the world that this is not a quick matter that is going to be over in a month or a year or even five years"; quoted in Thomas E. Ricks and Steven Mufson, "In War on Terrorism, Unseen Fronts May Be Crucial," *Washington Post*, September 23, 2001, p. A3.

6. "Secretary Rumsfeld Interview with the New York Times," October 12, 2001.

7. "Text of Joint Resolution Allowing Military Action," *New York Times*, September 15, 2001, p. A16.

8. In the Senate the vote was 98–0. In the House of Representatives, it was 420–1, with California Democrat Barbara J. Lee casting the sole dissenting vote.

9. "President Harry S. Truman's Address before a Joint Session of Congress, March 12, 1947," The Avalon Project at the Yale Law School, www.yale. edu/lawweb/avalon/trudoc.htm, accessed October 3, 2001.

10. Bush, "Address to Joint Session of Congress and American People," September 20, 2001.

11. On this point see Nicholas D. Kristof, "Our Friends the Terrorists," *New York Times,* December 21, 2001, p. A39.

12. Michael Kinsley, "Defining Terrorism," *Washington Post,* October 5, 2001, p. A37.

13. Daniel Pipes, "What Bush Got Right—and Wrong," *Jerusalem Post,* September 26, 2001.

14. In a videotape released on October 7, 2001, Osama bin Laden vowed to continue his war against the United States until "all the army of infidels depart the land of Muhammad," referring to the U.S. military presence in Saudi Arabia; "Bin Laden's Statement: 'The Sword Fell,'" *New York Times,* October 8, 2001, p. B7.

15. As early as October 8, 2001, the United States notified the UN Security Council that "we may find that our self-defense requires further actions with respect to other organizations and other states"—seen as hinting at a wider war; Irwin Arieff, "U.S. Warns It May Target Others," *Boston Globe,* October 9, 2001, p. A7.

16. Quoted in ibid.

17. Even before the outcome of the Afghanistan campaign had become clear, influential leaders were calling for the United States to turn next on Iraq and to overthrow Saddam Hussein. Such a decision would mark a watershed. From a U.S. perspective, the situation in Iraq after the Persian Gulf War had been unsatisfactory. But it had not been intolerable. After September 11, the United States flirted for the first time since 1898 with a "war of choice"—undertaking a war not because war had been thrust upon it but simply because it chose to do so. See Elaine Sciolino and Patrick E. Tyler, "Some Pentagon Officials and Advisers Seek to Oust Iraq's Leader in War's Next Phase," *New York Times,* October 12, 2001, p. B6. See also Joe Lieberman, "After bin Laden, We Must Target Saddam," *Wall Street Journal,* October 29, 2001, p. A22. A Democratic senator from Connecticut, Lieberman was Al Gore's running mate in 2000.

18. Robert B. Zoellick, "Countering Terror with Trade," *Washington Post,* September 20, 2001, p. A35.

19. Quoted in David E. Sanger, "Bush Calls World Economy Goal of Attacks on U.S.," *New York Times,* October 21, 2001, p. A8.

20. Colin Powell, "Put Trade on the Fast Track," *Wall Street Journal,* October 16, 2001, p. A26.

21. Robert B. Zoellick, "American Trade Leadership: What Is at Stake," Institute for International Economics, Washington, D.C., September 24, 2001, www. iie.com/papers/zoellick1001.pdf.

22. George W. Bush, "Remarks by the President at the California Business Association Breakfast," Sacramento, October 17, 2001.

23. In a speech delivered on November 7, 2001, Clinton reiterated his view that "the lines between foreign and domestic policy are becoming meaningless, distinctions without a difference." Because of the impact of globalization and the information revolution, "the barriers of nation[al] borders don't count for much anymore." But opening up the world had a "dark side." "You cannot collapse walls, collapse differences and spread information without making yourself more vulnerable to forces of destruction. You cannot claim the benefits of this new world without becoming more vulnerable at home." Still, there was no turning back: "there's no way for us to put the Genie back in the bottle . . . It's not like we can reverse the world we live in." Therefore, "We've got to win the fight we're in"—a fight that in Clinton's view required also making an end to global poverty, spreading democracy, ending the AIDs epidemic, solving the problem of global warming, and getting "rid of our arrogant self-righteousness." "Remarks as delivered by President William Jefferson Clinton," Georgetown University, November 7, 2001, www.georgetown.edu/admin/publicaffairs/protocol_events/events/clinton_glf110701.htm, accessed November 14, 2001.

24. Donald H. Rumsfeld, "Statement of the Secretary of Defense," October 7, 2001.

25. Amy Waldman, "Food Drops Go Awry, Damaging Several Homes," New York Times, November 21, 2001, p. B2; between October 7 and December 13, 2001, when the operation ended, U.S. Air Force C-17 cargo aircraft flying from Germany dropped 2,423,700 Humanitarian Daily Rations into Afghanistan; "Humanitarian Situation in Afghanistan," www.whitehouse. gov/afac/, accessed December 31, 2001.

26. William M. Arkin, "A Week of Air War," washingtonpost.com, October 14, 2001, accessed October 15, 2001.

27. Quoted in Michael R. Gordon, Eric Schmitt, and Thom Shanker, "Scarcity of Afghanistan Targets Prompts U.S. to Change Strategy," New York Times, September 19, 2001, p. A1.

28. A month into the war, the total number of U.S. troops committed to Operation Enduring Freedom was approximately 50,000, or less than 4 percent of the total active force; Michael Gordon, "A Month in a Difficult Battlefield: Assessing U.S. War Strategy," New York Times, November 8, 2001, p. B4.

29. Eric Schmitt and Steven Lee Myers, "More Than 100 G.I.'s in Afghan Ground Raid," New York Times, October 20, 2001, p. A1.

30. Rear Admiral John D. Stufflebeem, "DoD News Briefing—Rear Adm. Stufflebeem," October 24, 2001.

31. Department of State, Bureau of International Narcotics and Law Enforcement Affairs, "Narcotics Control Report" (2000), http://www.state.gov/g/inl/rls/nrcrpt/2000/index; Human Rights Watch, "Afghanistan: Crisis of Impunity" (July 2001), sec. II, http://www.hrw.org/reports/2001/afghan2/.

32. At a secret meeting in Uzbekistan on October 30, 2001, General Tommy Franks, CENTCOM commander-in-chief, reportedly promised General Mohammed Fahim, the Northern Alliance defense minister, that the U.S. would put American air power at the service of Alliance troops; Michael Kranish, "Turning the Tide in Afghanistan," *Boston Globe*, December 31, 2001, p. A1.

33. George Stephanopoulos, interview with General Tommy Franks, "This Week with Sam Donaldson and Cokie Roberts," ABC News, November 4, 2001.

34. Bob Woodward, "Secret CIA Units Play a Central Combat Role," *Washington Post*, November 18, 2001, p. A1.

35. Quoted in William A. Arkin, "Dropping 15,000 Pounds of Frustration," *Los Angeles Times*, December 15, 2001, www.latimes.com/news/nationwide/nation/la-121501arkin.story, accessed December 15, 2001.

36. See, for example, Allan Cullison and Robert S. Greenberger, "Head of Afghanistan's Northern Alliance Voices Complaint about U.S. Airstrikes," *Wall Street Journal*, October 15, 2001, p. A26.

37. Steve Mufson and William Branigin, "U.S. Sets Stage for Offensive," *Washington Post*, November 2, 2001, p. A1.

38. Keith B. Richburg and William Branigin, "Attacks from Out of the Blue," *Washington Post*, November 18, 2001, p. A24.

39. Kandahar fell not to the Northern Alliance but to an ethnically distinctive group of anti-Taliban fighters whom U.S. officials styled the Southern Alliance.

40. Quoted in Patrick E. Tyler, "Powell Says Muslim Nations Should Be Peacekeepers in Kabul; 3 Offer Troops," *New York Times*, November 13, 2001, p. B4.

41. Michael R. Gordon, "Gains and Limits in New Low-Risk War," *New York Times*, December 29, 2001, p. A1; Patrick Healy, "Ex-Taliban Hide Their Histories to Rejoin Society," *Boston Sunday Globe*, December 30, 2001, p. A1.

42. Stephanopoulos, interview with General Franks.

43. Through the end of 2001, only one American was lost as a result of hostile action—a CIA operative; during that period there were three U.S. military combat deaths. All were the result of friendly fire—U.S. troops killed by stray American bombs.

44. James Webb, "A New Doctrine for New Wars," *Wall Street Journal*, November 30, 2001, p. A14.

45. Max Boot, "This Victory May Haunt Us," *Wall Street Journal*, November 14, 2001, p. A22. In late November the first substantial contingent of U.S. ground troops arrived in Afghanistan, a Marine Expeditionary Unit. But the mission assigned to the marines was not to attack the Taliban or al Qaeda, but to establish a camp in which to secure prisoners handed over by anti-Taliban commanders.

46. Quoted in Robert Schlesinger, "As Darkness Fell, Fighter Pilots Took Off," *Boston Globe,* December 24, 2001, p. A6.

47. Michael Evans, "'Precision Weapons' Fail to Prevent Civilian Mass Casualties," *The Times* (London), January 2, 2002, Web edition, http://www.thetimes.co.uk/article/0,,3–2002000258,00.html. The Pentagon refused to make any estimate of the number of noncombatants killed; Kevin Canfield, "No Winners in Battle to Gauge Cost of War," *Hartford Courant,* December 26, 2001, p. A1.

48. George W. Bush, "Remarks by the President to State Department Employees," Washington, D.C., October 4, 2001.

49. Quoted in Vernon Loeb, "U.S. Forces to Stay in Afghanistan for a While, Bush Says," *Washington Post,* December 29, 2001, p. A8.

50. C. J. Chivers, "General Gives Uzbek Leader Warm Words and Spotlight," *New York Times,* October 31, 2001, p. B3.

51. The United States arranged for Pakistan to receive $600 million in cash from the International Monetary Fund along with a $300 million line of credit. Efforts to reschedule Pakistan's external debt were also initiated; Michael Kranish, "Turning the Tide in Afghanistan," *Boston Globe,* December 31, 2001, p. A1.

52. Guy Chazan and Steve LeVine, "U.S. Indicates New Military Partnership with Uzbekistan," *Wall Street Journal,* October 15, 2001, p. A16. Uzbek president Islam Karimov agreed to the stationing of 1,000 U.S. troops at a military base in Khanabad.

53. Kamran Khan and John Pomfret, "Pakistan Extends U.S. Access," *Boston Globe,* December 4, 2001, p. A41. This article reported that the government of Pakistan had turned over to the U.S. military a large air base in Jacobabad, 300 miles north of Karachi. American plans for upgrading the base, for example the construction of air-conditioned barracks for U.S. troops, suggested something other than a brief stay.

54. Ellen Goodman, "We Need a New Anthem," *Boston Globe,* October 18, 2001, p. A11; Clifford Pugh and Charles Ward, "Comfort in Times of Tragedy," *Houston Chronicle,* December 9, 2001, p. 8.

55. Between September 11 and the end of the year, fewer than 62,000 reservists were federalized; DoD news release, "National Guard and Reserve Mobilized as of Jan. 2," January 2, 2002, http://www.defenselink.mil/news/Jan2002/b01022002_bt002–02.html.

56. Robert B. Reich, "How Did Spending Become Our Patriotic Duty?" *Washington Post,* September 23, 2001, p. B1.

57. George W. Bush, "Remarks by the President to Airline Employees, O'Hare International Airport," Chicago, September 27, 2001.

58. Tony Perry, "Lots of Interest, Little Action at Recruiting Office," *Los Angeles Times,* October 26, 2001, p. A17. According to this, the four military services reported no increase in enlistments in the wake of September 11.

59. Rick Lyman and Bill Carter, "In Little Time, Pop Culture Is Almost Back to Normal," *New York Times*, October 4, 2001, p. A1.

60. Helen Dewar, "Defense Bill Passes; Base Closings Delayed," *Washington Post*, December 14, 2001, p. A43. The 2002 defense budget, which passed the House of Representatives by a vote of 382–40 and the Senate by 96–2, increased defense spending by $33 billion to a total of $343.3 billion. President Bush signed the legislation into law. Meanwhile, the services signaled their implacable determination to resist external pressures to "transform" themselves. Thomas E. Ricks, "Bull's-Eye War: Pinpoint Bombing Shifts Role of G.I. Joe," *Washington Post*, December 2, 2001, p. A1.

61. Eric Schmitt, "Envoy Forges Bonds and Reaps Benefits," *New York Times*, November 28, 2001, p. A10. Schmitt described Zinni as a commander who had "pushed the bounds of convention in redefining the U.S. military's role in the post–cold war world and in understanding the global context in which it had to operate."

62. Elizabeth Becker, "Bush Chooses Retired General as His National Counterterrorism Coordinator," *New York Times*, October 1, 2001, p. B6. The individual was General Wayne Downing, U.S. Army (retired).

63. "Admiral Is New Domestic Security Aide," *New York Times*, October 22, 2001, p. B7. The individual was Admiral Charles Stevenson Abbot, U.S. Navy (retired).

64. Erik Eckholm, "U.S. Official Praises China for Its Cooperation in Rooting Out bin Laden's Terror Network," *New York Times*, December 7, 2001, p. B5. The individual was Frank Taylor.

65. Eric Schmitt, "4 Commanders Seek Staff Role for F.B.I.," *New York Times*, November 20, 2001, p. A1.

66. George W. Bush, "Remarks by the President at the Citadel," December 11, 2001, Charleston, S.C.

67. Peter Ford, "Why Do They Hate Us?" *Christian Science Monitor*, September 27, 2001, p. 1.

68. See, for example, Charlotte Raven, "A Bully with a Bloody Nose Is Still a Bully," *The Guardian* (London), September 18, 2001, p. 18

69. Michael Wines, "A World Seeking Security Is Told There's Just One Shield," *New York Times*, July 22, 2001, sec. 4, p. 1.

70. The view is not entirely without merit. See A. J. Bacevich, "Exporting the Culture Wars," *Crisis* 15 (March 1997): 23–26.

71. John Paul II, "Centesimus Annus: On the Hundredth Anniversary of 'Rerum Novarum,'" 1991, available on the Vatican Web site (www.vatican.va).

72. Charles A. Beard, *Giddy Minds and Foreign Quarrels* (New York, 1939), p. 87.

73. William Appleman Williams, *Empire as a Way of Life* (New York, 1980), p. 170.

74. Reinhold Niebuhr, *Reinhold Niebuhr on Politics* (New York, 1960), p. 294.

ACKNOWLEDGMENTS

Writers accrue debts, and mine are many. My first is to Eliot A. Cohen. When I most needed it, Eliot extended his hand in friendship. He gave me a start. He opened the doors that led to opportunities large and small. What I owe him cannot be repaid.

For taking on a chance on a rookie academic, a retread from another line of work, and for believing that the dilemmas of American global hegemony might offer a fruitful field of inquiry, I am grateful to Nadia Schadlow and Marin Strmecki and to the Smith Richardson Foundation.

At Boston University, my colleagues in the Colloquium on U.S. Foreign Policy challenged and stimulated my thinking about America's role in the post–Cold War world. I have shamelessly borrowed their insights and continue to profit from our ongoing conversation.

John Silber, Jon Westling, and Dennis Berkey, leaders of a great university, honored me by giving me the opportunity to be part of an exciting enterprise. I thank my friend and department chairman Erik Goldstein for creating an environment that encourages both high professional standards and a spirit of collegiality. And I thank Claudine Husainy, our departmental administrator, for keeping the trains running on time—and making it look easy. Within the Center for International Relations, Jain Yu and Emily Thompson assisted in myriad ways large and small, always cheerfully and always competently. They run the show and make me look good.

I have benefited greatly from the students who have enrolled in the Seminar on Post–Cold War U.S. Foreign Policy, which served as a testing ground for my own ideas. In particular, I want to thank Greg Metzger, who served in exemplary fashion as my research assistant and whose own work on American isolationism informed my thinking about that much-abused and much-misunderstood subject. In the final stages, Adam Ratner pitched in ably and enthusiastically.

I am also grateful to my fellow "civ-mil paranoids"—especially Eliot Cohen, Tom Donnelly, Peter Feaver, Tom Keaney, Dick Kohn, Tom Ricks, and Mike Vickers—for allowing me to participate in their continuing dialogue about civil-military relations in this country. We may yet succeed in persuading others that the topic is a sadly—perhaps dangerously—neglected one.

Friends who generously reviewed earlier drafts and in doing so saved me from innumerable gaffes include David Mayers, Richard H. Kohn, Chris Gray, and Nick Rizopoulos. Responsibility for any errors that remain is mine alone.

At Harvard University Press, Jeff Kehoe phoned one day out of the blue and asked if I had thought about writing a book. To my amazement and delight, a contract materialized. When Jeff moved on, Kathleen McDermott picked up the project and saw it seamlessly through to completion. Ann Hawthorne edited the entire manuscript with immense sensitivity and skill. Editors don't come any better.

I thank Kate, who, like her older sisters and older brother, has with great generosity of spirit put up with a father distracted by matters of far less importance than being her dad.

Finally—and above all—I thank Nancy, who in the fourth decade of our marriage remains as always the apple of my eye.

Walpole, Massachusetts
July 2002

INDEX

Afghanistan, U.S. intervention (Operation Enduring Freedom), 231, 233–236
Africa Crisis Response Initiative, 158
Africa Growth and Opportunity Act, 108
AirScan, 161
Albright, Madeleine, 1, 51, 83, 197, 213, 216; quoted, 33, 35, 36, 42, 48, 52, 86, 101–102, 112, 113, 118, 142, 143, 159; Albright's Rule, 46–49, 225; and Kosovo, 104–105, 181–182, 184; on America's global role, 113; on Somalia, 143
Andean Regional Initiative, 209
Armitage, Richard, 205, 206
Aron, Raymond, 218
Asia Pacific Economic Cooperation (APEC) forum, 73
Aspen, Les, 134, 146
Aviation Development Corporation, 161

Baker, James, 56; on Persian Gulf crisis, 64; on crisis in Bosnia, 68
ballistic missile defense, 203, 222–223
Barber, Benjamin R., 40
Base Force, 134
Beard, Charles A., 11–23, 24, 30–31, 54, 71, 81, 85, 88, 90, 242, 243, 244; early life and career, 11–12; major writings, 12–16, 20, 22; critique of U.S. foreign policy, 17–20
Beard, Mary R., 11, 81
Berger, Samuel R., 37, 38, 40, 53, 85, 102, 125, 126, 180, 197
Beveridge, Albert, 79, 95, 156
Blair, Dennis C., 175, 179, 180
Boorda, Mike, 170
Booz-Allen & Hamilton, 162
Bosnia, 67–68; U.S. intervention (Operation Deliberate Force), 104, 164–165, 209
Bottom-Up Review, 134–135
Brooks, David, 80
Brown, Ronald H., 94

Brzezinski, Zbigniew, 64
Buchanan, Patrick J., 125
Bush, George H. W., 1, 142, 143, 149, 163, 233, 243; quoted, 51, 57, 58, 59, 60, 66, 73, 74, 75–76, 77–78; as Cold War president, 55–57; and Persian Gulf War, 58–61; use of force, 62, 154; and China, 64–66; "Chicken Kiev" speech, 66; and Bosnia, 67–68; and Panama, 69–71; anticipating policies of Bill Clinton, 72–77; on globalization, 72–73; on openness, 73–74; on NATO expansion, 74–75; on isolationism, 75–76; and Africa, 109–110
Bush, George W., 1, 199, 213, 243; quoted, 139–140, 200, 202, 203, 204, 208, 217, 218, 221, 226, 229–230, 232, 233, 234, 236, 238; on defense reform, 139–140, 203–204; as presidential candidate, 200–204; on ballistic missile defense, 203, 222–223; selection of senior foreign policy advisers, 205–206; use of force, 207–208, 233–235; and Iraq, 207–208; and China, 209–211; and North Korea, 209; use of U.S. troops for peacekeeping, 209; foreign policy principles, 214–223; post–September 11 address to Congress, 228–230; war on terror, 233–237; and Central Asia, 236–237
Butler, Smedley, 177

Carville, James, 79
Cheney, Richard, 56, 205
Christopher, Warren, 36, 41, 50, 85, 91, 92, 93–94, 101
civil-military relations, U.S., 168–172, 203, 212
Clark, Wesley K., 104, 180; and Operation Allied Force, 182–195
Clarke, Richard A., 120
Clinton, Bill, 1, 2, 102, 139, 197, 199, 213, 214, 216, 218, 219, 233, 243;